**The John Wesley
Christian Perfection Library**

Volume Two

JOHN WESLEY'S THEOLOGY OF CHRISTIAN PERFECTION

Developments in Doctrine
& Theological System

Revised

By
Mark K. Olson

Truth In Heart
Fenwick, Michigan

2007

Olson, Mark K., 1957-

John Wesley's Theology of Christian Perfection: Developments in Doctrine & Theological System
(The John Wesley Christian Perfection Library. Volume II.)

ISBN: 10:1-932370-88-9
       13: 978-1-932370-88-1

Library of Congress Control Number: 2007930874

Copyright © 2007, 2009
Revised 2009
Mark K. Olson
All Rights Reserved

Unless otherwise noted
all scripture quotations are from:
The Holy Bible, The King James Version

To order more copies of this book:
Truth In Heart
TruthInHeart.com
8071 Main St.
Fenwick, MI 48834
(989) 637-4179

John Wesley's Theology of Christian Perfection

Developments in Doctrine & Theological System

Revised

By
Mark K. Olson

Volume Two
of
The John Wesley
Christian Perfection Library

The John Wesley
Christian Perfection Library
in
Five Volumes

VOLUME ONE
JOHN WESLEY'S 'A PLAIN ACCOUNT OF CHRISTIAN PERFECTION'
THE ANNOTATED EDITION
(Released 2005)

VOLUME TWO
JOHN WESLEY'S THEOLOGY OF CHRISTIAN PERFECTION
DEVELOPMENTS IN DOCTRINE & THEOLOGICAL SYSTEM
(Revised 2009)

VOLUME THREE
THE JOHN WESLEY READER ON CHRISTIAN PERFECTION
1725 – 1791
(Released 2008)

VOLUME FOUR
JOHN WESLEY'S DOCTRINE OF CHRISTIAN PERFECTION
SYSTEMATIC FORMULATION FOR CONTEMPORARY RELEVANCE

VOLUME FIVE
JOHN WESLEY'S PREACHING ON CHRISTIAN PERFECTION
FOR THE 21ST CENTURY

John Wesley Booklets also available:

Thoughts on Christian Perfection
Farther Thoughts on Christian Perfection
(Fully Annotated)

BY
MARK K. OLSON

TRUTHINHEART.COM

Table of Contents

	PAGE
Abbreviations	vi
Introduction	ix

Section One: Early Developments
1. The Gospel of Holiness — 2
2. The Gospel of Faith Alone — 81
3. The Gospel of Two Works of Grace — 119

Section Two: Mature Enlargements
4. Aldersgate II — 178
5. Sin in the Ordo Salutis — 216
6. Spiritual Father — 244
7. The Gospel of Universal Holiness — 275

Section Three: Making Sense
8. A Plain Account of Christian Perfection — 308
9. The Faith Journey — 326
10. Evolving Contours — 342
11. The Achilles Heel — 367

Appendices:
A. Timeline on Wesley's Doctrinal Development — 382
B. John Wesley's Confessions — 390
C. Early Testimonies of Perfect Love — 412
D. The Evolution of the New Birth — 429
E. The Roots of Wesley's Servant Theology — 437
F. Clement of Alexandria: A Second Century Wesleyan? — 449
G. Doctrinal Resource Lists — 458

Bibliography — 475
Index A: John Wesley's Writings — 486
Index B: Scripture References — 493
Index C: Subject — 496

List of Abbreviations

cf.	see
ch(s)	chapter, chapters
l._	line(s) + number (for Bicentennial Edition)
n, nn	note, notes
e.n.	end note
sec	section
v, vv	verse, verses
vol(s)	volume, volumes
§, §§	paragraph, paragraphs

The John Wesley Christian Perfection Library:
Plain Account (PA)   'A Plain Account of Christian Perfection': The Annotated Edition

John Wesley

Wesley	John Wesley
JW	John Wesley
Works J	Jackson Edition of Wesley's Works
Works B	Bicentennial Edition of Wesley's Works
StSer	Standard Sermons, Sugden Edition
JWJ	Journal (date)
JWJ MS	Manuscript Journal (date)
JWD	Diary (date)
JWL	Letter(s) (date)
JWL B	Letter(s) Bicentennial Edition
JWL T	Letter(s) Telford Edition
JWL J	Letter(s) Jackson Edition
JWS	Sermon(s) (# or title)
NT Notes	Explanatory Notes Upon the New Testament
PA	Plain Account of Christian Perfection

Charles Wesley

CW	Charles Wesley
CWJ	Journal
CWS	Sermon(s)
CWL	Letter(s) (date)

John Wesley's Gospels
GosH	Gospel of Holiness
GosFA	Gospel of Faith Alone
GosTW	Gospel of Two Works of Grace
GosUH	Gospel of Universal Holiness

Latin Terms
Sola gratia	grace alone
Sola fide	faith alone
Sola scriptura	scripture alone
Sola Christus	Christ alone
via salutis	way of salvation
via media	middle way
ordo salutis	order of salvation
fide	faith, assent
fiducia	faith, trust
imago Dei	image of God
opus operatum	mode of operation
homo unius libri	man of one book

Old Testament:
Genesis	Gen	Ecclesiastes	Ecc
Exodus	Ex	Song of Songs	SS
Leviticus	Lev	Isaiah	Is
Numbers	Num	Jeremiah	Jer
Deuteronomy	Deut	Lamentations	Lam
Joshua	Josh	Ezekiel	Eze
Judges	Jdg	Daniel	Dan
Ruth	Ruth	Hosea	Hos
1 Samuel	1 Sam	Joel	Joel
2 Samuel	2 Sam	Amos	Am
1 Kings	1 Kgs	Obediah	Ob
2 Kings	2 Kgs	Jonah	Jon
1 Chronicles	1 Ch	Micah	Mic
2 Chronicles	2 Ch	Nahum	Nah
Ezra	Ezra	Habakkuk	Hab
Nehemiah	Neh	Zephaniah	Zep
Esther	Es	Haggai	Hag
Job	Job	Zechariah	Zec
Psalms	Ps	Malachi	Mal
Proverbs	Pr		

New Testament:

Matthew	Matt
Mark	Mk
Luke	Lk
John	Jn
Acts	Acts
Romans	Rom
1 Corinthians	1 Cor
2 Corinthians	2 Cor
Galatians	Gal
Ephesians	Eph
Philippians	Php
Colossians	Col
1 Thessalonians	1 Th
2 Thessalonians	2 Th
1 Timothy	1 Tim
2 Timothy	2 Tim
Titus	Tit
Philemon	Phm
Hebrews	Heb
James	Ja
1 Peter	1 Pet
2 Peter	2 Pet
1 John	1 Jn
2 John	2 Jn
3 John	3 Jn
Jude	Jude
Revelation	Rev

Introduction

When John Wesley published his *A Plain Account of Christian Perfection* in 1766, his aim was primarily twofold.[1] In the wake of the great revival in the early sixties multitudes were professing the experience of perfect love and Wesley wanted to counsel them further regarding the path of inward holiness. But besides this pastoral concern there was a more immediate one. Many charged Wesley with being inconsistent in his message of full salvation. Thomas Maxfield (Wesley's "son in the gospel"), and a young recruit, George Bell, spearheaded a version of attainable perfection that proved to be in sharp contrast to John Wesley's message of perfect love.[2] Besides being accused of inconsistency, Wesley was charged with changing his message.[3] Critics outside of Methodism seized upon Maxfield and Bell's enthusiasm to attack Wesley over his beloved doctrine of Christian perfection.[4]

In response, Wesley felt compelled to clarify his thoughts and to present a definitive apology of his perfection doctrine. So in 1764 he took the time to comprise an eleven-point summary of his perfection beliefs and in 1765 he put those beliefs into writing in his definitive work on the subject, *A Plain Account of Christian Perfection*. As John Peters so aptly states, the *Plain Account* represents the "most comprehensive exposition" of John Wesley's doctrine of full salvation.[5] Though the book went through several editions in Wesley's lifetime and was recommended by him to earnest seekers of the experience, the question of Wesley's consistency has remained an open one. It is this latter question that engages this present study. To answer this question

---

[1] See Volume One: *John Wesley's 'A Plain Account of Christian Perfection: The Annotated Edition*, 11-16; hereafter *Plain Account* or PA.
[2] Works J 3:126; PA chs 20-22, 25:105-167.
[3] PA 27:3 n.
[4] See JW's letter to John Newton (JWJ 5/14/65); PA chs 27-28 and notes.
[5] *Christian Perfection and American Methodism*, 32.

John Wesley's Theology of Christian Perfection

we must examine carefully what holiness meant to Wesley at different periods of his career and track his theological journey.

John Wesley enjoyed a very lengthy career.[6] Beginning at Oxford and his hometown surroundings, he later ministered in America, throughout England, and became a founding leader of the burgeoning evangelical awakening of the eighteenth century. While it is commonly reported that he preached over 40,000 sermons and traveled around 250,000 miles during his lifetime, Wesley was also embroiled in controversy much of his career. At times this controversy centered on his perfection theology. All these factors played a role in shaping his convictions and thoughts regarding salvation from all sin. But to fully grasp *how* Wesley's doctrine took shape over time, and *why* it took the path it did, we must return to his Oxford period and map out the theology that first informed his perfection beliefs. This is where this study begins. We can then proceed to demarcate the theological path Wesley traveled as his perfection doctrine evolved into a complete, mature theological system. Only in this way can we hope to answer the question whether Wesley was consistent in his message of holiness, and if so, to what degree.

This volume moves beyond volume one of the series. That volume focuses on Wesley's doctrine of perfection as articulated in the *Plain Account*. The purpose is to clarify what Wesley's mature doctrine looked like, and to empower students of Wesley to dig deeper into the nuances of his perfection theology. This study compliments volume one by capturing the development within Wesley's theological journey over the course of his long career, thereby empowering a firmer grasp of the subtle nuances that informed his theology of perfection at different periods of his career. Hopefully, the reader will receive the blessing of not only learning to appreciate the faith journey John Wesley traveled, but will be stirred to reflect more deeply on the subject of Christian discipleship as well.

---

[6] In terms of this study 66 years (from 1725 to 1791).

Introduction

Methodology

Something should be said about my approach and guiding principles. As was just noted, Wesley's career was long. Accordingly, historians have found it helpful to divide his career into three periods: early, middle, and late.[7] Early Wesley covers his time at Oxford and in America, until he set foot again on English soil in early 1738. Middle Wesley picks up the story leading to his Aldersgate "heart-warming" conversion and his involvement in the evangelical revival, and ends in the mid-sixties when his theology and message coalesced into its mature articulation. Late Wesley continues from this point until his death on March 2, 1791. The three-epoch scheme has been helpful to understand the broad contours of his lengthy career. The reader should note that in this present study I often use these labels to identify Wesley's thought at specific eras of his career.

But in the attempt to present an in-depth study explaining *how* Wesley's theology of perfection developed over time, and to probe into the reasons *why* it took the path it did, I found the three-period scheme cumbersome and less than helpful. My research led me to look for a different framework to explain the *why's* and *how's* of Wesley's doctrinal evolution. For starters, this a doctrinal study, not a biographical one. While history plays a large part, it is not the central focus of the book. So I searched for a framework more suited to my purpose. Also, Wesley's perfection theology experiences major shifts within each era of the three-period model. As we will learn in section one, Wesley moves from one theology of perfection to another in a matter of approximately two-plus years following his Aldersgate conversion. A framework was needed that would highlight these doctrinal transitions. So a four-gospel scheme was chosen to structure the evolution of Wesley's thought. Each gospel is labeled to help the reader remember the essential idea and related concepts of that particular perfection theology. It is hoped this will make

---

[7] Chapter 10 explores this subject in greater depth. Cf. PA 1:3 n.

John Wesley's Theology of Christian Perfection

the development of Wesley's perfection theology easier to remember and to recall. In the chapter *Evolving Contours*[8] this subject is addressed more fully. A five-period approach is used to historically review the main contours of Wesley's theological development over his long career.

While the locus of this study is the development of Wesley's perfection theology, a secondary theme emerges as the study progresses. Like a subplot, the story of how Wesley's doctrine of perfect love matured also parallels the formation of his theological system. I am referring specifically to the order of salvation (*ordo salutis*). A related term used heavily in this book is the "faith journey," which refers to the believer's spiritual journey toward full renewal in God's image. The reader will soon learn that Wesley's doctrinal development is inextricably bound to his own faith journey. In many ways, Wesley's theology serves as a mirror to his own faith journey to find God and his fullness. So this study shows how Wesley's perfection beliefs profoundly shaped his theological system (hence the longer subtitle: *Developments in Doctrine & Theological System*). This broader interest led me to refer often to Wesley's "theology of perfection" (or its shorter version "perfection theology"). This means the purpose of this study is more comprehensive in scope than volume one of the series. This study seeks to look at how Wesley's doctrine of Christian perfection informed his theological system (*ordo salutis*) and visa versa. Hence the book's main title: *John Wesley's Theology of Christian Perfection*.

Connected to this purpose is the need to identify Wesley's views at each period within his ministry. To do this I have relied on Wesley's own literary corpus, not on secondary literature about him. I deliberately chose to place the footnotes at the bottom of the page to make them easier for the reader to check the

---

[8] Chapter 10. In this study the terminology of evolution is used to convey the process of development and maturation within JW's perfection theology. While some may feel uncomfortable with this term, the reader should remember its general and broader use and not confuse it with the question of origins in the natural sciences.

Introduction

sources as they move through the book. Along with identifying Wesley's views at specific periods is the purpose to highlight those factors which shaped and changed his views. We want to understand the reasons behind the development of his thought, not just the thought themselves. This entails probing into Wesley's letters and other writings for important clues.

A similar purpose is to recognize those trends which influenced his doctrinal development. Again, this requires close attention to the details embedded in Wesley's many writings. For by doing so we will recognize subtle shifts emerging within his perfection theology. In this area I do open myself up to potential criticism. Some, no doubt, will want to chastise me for overstating my positions at times. For example, in chapter four I speak of works being reintroduced into Wesley's gospel system. It would be easy to point to a number of Wesley's earlier writings to rebut my point. But after much thought on the subject I still hold to my guns: what we see in the latter sixties is an emerging trend in Wesley's thought regarding works in the salvation process that culminates in the controversial 1770 Conference Minutes. I believe such language is warranted to emphasize the point being made. No doubt some will see it differently than I do. Another issue might be my use of terminology, like the use of "states" to identify specific stages in the *ordo salutis*.[9] But Wesley did use such terminology himself, and it accurately conveys his expectations of specific attainments at each stage in the discipleship process. So the use of such language is defendable and warranted, but must not be pushed beyond its proper limits.

One more point. While this is not an historical study, nor a biographical one, it does pay close attention to chronology when quoting Wesley or referring to his views. This methodological principle is essential if we are to accurately grasp any shifts within his perfection theology. Utmost care must be maintained at this point. Yet, Wesley himself was not always helpful in this

---

[9] Many prefer to speak of *via salutis*, the way of salvation. Compare Kenneth Collins' perspective (*The Scripture Way of Salvation*, 70) to that of Randy Maddox (*Responsible Grace*, 157).

regard. Since he was not interested in systematics, he seldom worried about being comprehensive whenever he addressed a subject. Though this is to be expected in his letters (which are situational by nature), it is also true of his sermons and other writings. Wesley often expresses only the points he needs to make at a given time. So we must remain sensitive as to how Wesley quotes and publishes himself. Now that I have covered the methodological principles guiding this study, we can turn to an overview of the book's organization and design.

Organization & Overview

The book is divided into three major sections, followed by an extensive appendix. Section I addresses the early developments within Wesley's theology of perfection, from 1725 to the early 1740's when his two-works gospel became a staple feature of his theological system. Section II picks up the story in the early sixties and traces further developments within his mature perfection theology over the next three decades. After this, Section III addresses how to best make sense of Wesley's holiness views and the evolution of his thought. Let's now look at each section in turn.

In Section I the reader is introduced to the three gospel systems that will inform Wesley's perfection theology: Holiness, Faith Alone, and Two Works of Grace. Chapter one presents a thorough survey of the theology that informed Wesley's early perfection beliefs. Though this chapter is long, it is crucial since it lays the foundation for the rest of the book. In Wesley's Oxford period lie the seeds that will later blossom into his mature theology of perfection. So a careful reading of this chapter is indispensable to the rest of the book. Those less familiar with Wesley's early sermons and letters will find an ample amount of quotations in the text and footnotes, offering strong support for the points made. Some of the conclusions might surprise the reader, like Wesley's early evangelical leanings, his belief in a present for-

Introduction

giveness of sins (though he did not equate this with justification), and a robust doctrine of salvation assurance.

We next trace the steps which led Wesley to embrace the Moravian message of salvation by faith alone, in Christ alone, through the Spirit alone, in an instant alone. Even though Aldersgate is the best known event in the life of John Wesley, the theology which informed that event is less known and often misunderstood. Possibly, even less understood is the degree of influence which Moravian stillness theology played in Wesley's expectations at Aldersgate. We will learn how stillness served to fuel his struggles over assurance in the months following his Aldersgate conversion. Yet, it was through the fires of personal struggle, combined with the continuing controversies between the revival's key players, which led Wesley to embrace a gospel of two works. This story is covered in chapter three, and sets the stage for later developments within his mature theological system.

Section II picks up the story when Wesley's Gospel of Two Works enters a new phase of major development. The sixties opened with a powerful revival that emphasized the instantaneous gift of full salvation. But as volume one in this series so poignantly reminds us, the revival soon sank into open schism. It was the revival and schism that finally compelled Wesley to reevaluate his perfection beliefs. As a consequence, Wesley began to alter the emphasis within his holiness message; and, most significantly, led him to rethink his own faith journey following his Aldersgate conversion. This personal crisis I call "Aldersgate II." So powerful was this spiritual upheaval within Wesley's self-understanding that it propelled his perfection theology and *ordo salutis* into new directions. But I leave it to the reader to take the journey in chapter four and discover for themselves what I believe is one of the most significant insights of this study.

As Wesley's two-works gospel matured, so did his doctrine of sin. To understand this process, chapter five examines the structural organization of Wesley's mature doctrine of sin. In addition, this chapter explores how Wesley related the Christian doctrine of original sin to his theology of perfection. Few studies offer a better survey of the subject, and none offers a better visual explanation through a series of connected charts. We next turn to Wesley's letters to pick up significant insights into the maturation of his thought. Chapter six looks at his later correspondence to gain a better appreciation of what perfection meant to the early Methodists. Interesting bits of insight are gleaned about their struggles and the obstacles they faced as they sought to attain and retain the experience of perfect love.

Next, we close Section II by examining how Wesley's robust doctrines of prevenient grace and the *faith of a servant* broaden his *ordo salutis*. This opened the door for a much stronger inclusivist understanding of salvation within his theology. At the other end of the faith journey spectrum, the hope of a fully restored new creation inspired Wesley to envision the process of perfection beyond the article of death. As redeemed humanity will rise one day to the level of the angels, so at the resurrection the animal kingdom will be loosed from its servitude to "irregular passions," rising to the level of the human race in present intelligence and knowledge of God. Accordingly, in chapter seven we see John Wesley's theology of perfection attain full maturity in its articulation and development.

In Section III we shift directions and take a more panoramic view of Wesley's long theological journey. We begin by returning to *A Plain Account of Christian Perfection*. The purpose is to isolate the essential themes of his mature doctrine of heart holiness. The *Plain Account* serves as Wesley's most comprehensive statement from his own pen on his doctrine of perfect love. After this, in chapter nine, we reflect on Wesley's mature understanding of the faith journey, or as we theologically refer to as the *ordo salutis*. Through the help of several charts, the major stages of spiritual development are identified along with their chief characteristics. In this way, our study adds an additional blessing by leading the reader to ponder the nature of discipleship itself. If God's redemptive goal is to conform his children into the image of Christ, how is this accomplished? And, what marks each stage in the life transformation process? What we learn is that Wesley's

Introduction

lifelong passion to articulate a cogent doctrine of perfect love provides a lens by which we can tackle these questions.

The next chapter takes another historical review of Wesley's career to clarify those factors which shaped his perfection theology through the decades. Several factors of a historical and doctrinal nature are identified as profoundly shaping his thought. In this way the reader gains additional insights into what influenced the development of Wesley's doctrine of perfect love. Finally, the last chapter probes into the question of an Achilles heel in Wesley's message of full salvation. I will leave it for the reader to agree or disagree with my conclusions. But the question of whether Wesley was consistent demands that we ask the question.

We can now turn to the Appendices. These are a series of specialized studies of a smaller nature and cover a variety of topics (this is one reason for their placement in the appendix section). Their purpose is to enrich more fully the reader's understanding of Wesley's doctrine of holiness. There are seven in number:

Timeline on Wesley's Doctrinal Development: Covers the entire period under study in this book (1725-1791).

John Wesley's Confessions: This appendix examines his four January 1738 journal confessions to show that the last one (the post-script to journal extract one) was not written in January 1738 as is often assumed. Therefore, the theology contained in the last confession does not reflect his early theological system, but his Gospel of Faith Alone.

Early Testimonies of Perfect Love: These early testimonies are ordered according to Wesley's three gospels. They add support to the conclusions in this study. This collection can also be compared to those in volume one so the reader can compare how Wesley's message of holiness possibly changed over a period of twenty-plus years.[10]

The Evolution of the New Birth: This appendix shows that Wesley's understanding of the new birth was interwoven with his doctrine of perfect love up until the late fifties. When reading many of Wesley's earlier sermons and writings this study reminds the reader to be cognizant of this fact.

The Roots to Wesley's Servant Theology: The servant state profoundly shaped Wesley's later doctrinal development, and empowered a robust doctrine of prevenient grace within his mature theological system.

Clement of Alexandria: A Second Century Wesleyan?: This small study compares Wesley's views to that of Clement on the subject of perfection and holiness. In this way the reader can appreciate how Wesley was inspired by this church father.

Doctrinal Resource Lists: Included here are all the significant references in the entire Wesley corpus (sermons, letters, journal, and other writings) to empower personal study of the shifts and growth in Wesley's perfection theology. The references are grouped according to the four gospel framework used in this study. Also included are the references for Wesley's servant state and doctrine of sin.

All together this book represents one of the most exhaustive and penetrating studies available to the public on the development of John Wesley's theology of perfection. It is my hope the reader will come to appreciate the faith journey Wesley traveled, and how this path led to his mature understanding of perfect love— love which conquerors all sin, both inward and outward; while at

---

[10] *Plain Account* ch 24 end note.

Introduction

the same time acknowledging the sober reality of this present age that awaits full redemption in the new creation.

Revised Edition

In this revised edition no change has been made to any fundamental argument concerning the development of Wesley's perfection theology. After further study and reflection this author feels even stronger about the interpretation presented in this study. There is no other work available to the public that explores the issues addressed in this work with such thoroughness and depth. In this revised edition many sections were rewritten to sharpen the arguments for better clarity. A number of the footnotes were rewritten that reflect further research. Smaller errors were corrected and some formatting issues resolved.

The John Wesley Christian Perfection Series

With the release of this second volume the series is one more step toward completion. A few words about the series are in order. The original idea of doing a series came from the publisher while the first volume was being prepared for release. At the time three volumes were envisioned. The first would be on Wesley's *Plain Account* followed by a second and third volume dealing with historical and systematic issues. Volume two is now released. But during the process of writing this present work I realized the need for a companion reader that would reflect Wesley's doctrinal journey. So a fourth volume was conceived (now volume three in the series): *The John Wesley Reader on Christian Perfection*. The *Reader* will (1) organize Wesley's writings according to their chronological order, and (2) compliment volume one by including sermons, letters and writings not included in the *Plain Account*. My purpose is to provide a comprehensive three-

John Wesley's Theology of Christian Perfection

volume corpus suitable for study and learning.[11] Together, the first three volumes of the series will offer the most comprehensive foundation available to build a solid understanding of John Wesley's doctrine of Christian perfection.

The last two projected volumes will attempt to bring Wesley's doctrine of perfection into dialogue with our contemporary context. Wesley was not fond of systematics. His most comprehensive work on the subject, the *Plain Account*, includes only a select number of writings from his early and middle periods. Volume four will draw upon the text of the *Plain Account* to present Wesley's perfection doctrine in a systematic format. This volume will be titled: *John Wesley's Doctrine of Christian Perfection: Systematic Formulation for Contemporary Relevance*. The *Doctrine* will compare Wesley's views to that of the Holiness Movement of the nineteenth and twentieth centuries to bring out further clarification of his unique contribution to subject of Christian holiness. Moreover, each chapter will offer the reader a study guide by which he or she can develop their own views. In this way, volume four will empower the reader to build their own biblical and systematic theology of holiness.

During the process of writing this present volume a fifth volume was conceived. It requires no insight to say that the world has changed dramatically since Wesley's day. The need to communicate the scripture truth of heart holiness is arguably greater now than ever before. Yet many holiness organizations are stymied in their ability to present a cogent message of holiness today.[12] While I don't pretend to think I can solve the issues that confront us, I do believe a study into how Wesley promoted his message could be helpful to his descendants today. Thus, *John Wesley's Preaching of Christian Perfection for the 21st Century*

---

[11] Besides JW's text the *Reader* will include brief introductions showing how the particular texts fit into his doctrinal development.

[12] By saying this I cast no aspersions. The reasons are many and complex. The statement just reflects current reality. My own denomination (The Church of the Nazarene) is currently wrestling with the issue (Quanstrom, Mark R. *A Century of Holiness*. Beacon Hill: Kansas City. 2004).

Introduction

will explore the variety of means Wesley used to communicate holiness to his generation. We can then explore the applicability of those methods to spread Scriptural holiness among the nations in our present context.

To conclude, John Wesley believed the essence of Christian perfection to be that God can so transform the believer's dispositional nature that his love, even his perfect love, can become the natural and habitual characteristic of the Christian's life. Yet, the holy life continues to be characterized by ignorance, mistake, temptation and trial—all the human frailties that are inescapable in this life. To this end John Wesley gave himself completely and without reserve:

> Almighty God, unto whom all hearts be open, all desires known, and from whom all secrets are hid; cleanse the thoughts of our hearts by the inspiration of thy Holy Spirit, that we may perfectly love thee, and worthily magnify thy holy Name, through Christ our Lord. Amen.[13]

---

[13] White, Jame F. *John Wesley's Prayer Book: The Sunday Service of the Methodists in North America.* OSL Publications: Akron, 1991; 125.

Section One

Early Developments in John Wesley's Theology of Christian Perfection

By holiness I mean a complex habit of lowliness, meekness, purity, faith, hope, and love to God and man

Letter to Samuel Wesley
December 10, 1734

ONE
The Gospel of Holiness

Toward the end of January 1738, as John Wesley approached his return to England, what most concerned him was the question of personal salvation. Being aboard ship offered him time to reflect on his two-plus years in America, and to write several summary statements of what was transpiring within his soul. One such statement is a memorandum dated January 25. In it Wesley acknowledges his concern over the question of salvation according to the scriptures, and his wrestling with the issue of correct interpretation. He shares how he was warned early in life to steer clear of Catholicism because of its over-reliance on outward works. He states his dissatisfaction with some Lutheran and Calvinist authors because they went to the opposite extreme, magnifying faith to unwarranted degrees. He finds deficient his past reliance upon certain English writers because they failed to reconcile various scripture passages. He criticizes his past trust in certain writings of the ancient church, since they placed the church on equal footing with Holy Scripture. Finally, Wesley repudiates his earlier fascination with the mystics because their magnification of love over faith and good works. While these reflections are interesting to the historian, what should catch our attention is Wesley's answer as to what scripture teaches about salvation. When he asks the question "What must I do to be saved?" his response is straightforward:

> Keep the commandments. Believe, hope, love; follow after these tempers till thou hast fully attained, that is, till death, by all those outward works and means which God hath appointed, by walking as Christ walked.[1]

---
[1] Works B 18:212, n 95. See JW's 1737 sermon *On Love* P.4 for a similar response. This summary reflects the impact that William Law's book *A Practical Treatise on Christian Perfection* had on JW, which the latter read in 1732.

The Gospel of Holiness

In this succinct response we have the heart of John Wesley's early understanding of the gospel. At its hub is the notion that sanctification is the foundation for justification before God. If one wants to be saved they must faithfully practice those means appointed by Christ, and which appropriate God's grace, until the tempers of faith, hope and love are fully realized in the article of death. We will call this system the Gospel of Holiness. This system had one central goal: to prepare the Christian to dwell in God's eternal kingdom, where his holy presence fills everything. Thus, inward holiness became the "one thing needful." Perfection became the engine that drove his program of holy living. To understand *how* Wesley's doctrine of perfect love developed as it did, and *why* it did so, we must return to this early period[2] when the Gospel of Holiness was his message, and take a fresh look at the theology that undergird it, and provided the rationale for his program of holy living.

For many readers this study will offer several surprises. Among them are Wesley's already present leanings toward an evangelical understanding of the new birth, his affinity with contemporary notions of assurance, and, last, what really led this Oxford don to radically change his understanding of salvation in 1738 and thereafter. What this chapter offers, in bold and in subtle ways, is an extensive survey of Wesley's early soteriology, leading to a reinterpretation of what led him toward Aldersgate and its aftermath.[3] But first we begin with a sketch of his life during this period to give context to his early perfection theology.

---

[2] JW's career is often divided into three periods: early 1725-1738, middle 1738-1765, and late or mature 1765-1791. This chapter focuses solely on his early period. Cf. ch 10.

[3] Many studies on early JW focus almost exclusively on his letters, diary, and journal. Since this study aims at clarifying his theological system the sermons play a central role in our evaluation.

John Wesley's Theology of Christian Perfection

A Sketch of 1725 to 1738

We begin in January 1725 when the young John Wesley (age 22) expressed to his parents his desire to pursue a ministerial career. In his extant letters, we see Wesley's father Samuel encouraging his son to prepare for such a career through critical learning. But John was more prone to listen to his mother, who advised him to pursue "practical divinity."[4] During Lent of that year Wesley began perusing Thomas `a Kempis' *The Imitation of Christ* and Bishop Taylor's *Rule and Exercises of Holy Living and Dying*. He would later record the impact these books made on him.[5] It was from Taylor's book that Wesley began the habit of keeping a diary to measure his progress in attaining inward holiness. After being ordained deacon on September 19, 1725, Wesley was accepted into Lincoln College on March 17 the following year. During the fall of 1725 Wesley wrote his first two sermons that offer important insights into the broad contours of his soteriology at the time.[6] After receiving his M.A. in February 1727, John returned home that summer to serve as curate under his father in Epworth and Wroot. The next major event was his ordination as priest in the Anglican Church on September 22, 1728. Wesley records many years later of the spiritual awakening he experienced during this period.[7] Over the next couple years he penned several more sermons, of which four remain.[8] These ser-

---

[4] JWL 2/23/25. Does this explain why JW became what Albert Outler calls a "folk theologian"?

[5] *Plain Account* chs 2, 3.

[6] *Death and Deliverance* (9/19/25); *Seek First the Kingdom* (11/21/25) Works B 4:215. The basic contours are: 1. Perfection is only attained in death. 2. The goal is the eternal kingdom. 3. Attaining righteousness (inward holiness) is the prerequisite for entering the kingdom. These contours do not change throughout the early period under study.

[7] PA chs 3-4; but compare with JW's earlier reflection in #5 of his Aldersgate memorandum (Works J 1:99).

[8] *Guardian Angels* (9/29/26); *On Mourning for the Dead* (1/11/27); *On Corrupting the Word of God* (10/6/27); *On Dissimulation* (1/17/28); see Works B vol. 4. Some insights are: 1. Angels guard God's people against sin. 2. No

mons add further insight into his developing theological system and his early doctrine of perfection. Among his many letters that survive, the ones most important to our study are the exchange between his mother and himself from late May through mid-November in 1725.[9]

John's younger brother Charles began meeting with other students at Oxford during the summer of 1729. In November John moved back to Oxford and soon became the group's leader. Wesley records in his *Plain Account* it was during that winter he became a person of one book, the Holy Scripture.[10] The group became scandalously known by several names, including the "Holy Club." Richard Heitzenrater informs us the group studied classics and divinity, and faithfully attended university sermons and the sacrament.[11] By late summer of 1730 the Holy Club began doing works of mercy by ministering to inmates at Castle Prison, teaching orphan children, and caring for the old and poor. Throughout 1731 these works of mercy expanded to other prisons and to more children in and around Oxford.[12] It was during this same period Wesley began to read William Law's *Christian Perfection* and *Serious Call to a Devout and Holy Life*.[13] Wesley would later remember the impression Law's writings left on him, "The light flowed in so mightily upon my soul, that everything appeared in a new view."[14] During this time his perfection theol-

---

complete perfection in this life. 3. The importance of rightly dividing the Word. 4. The importance of sincerity in religion.
[9] Cf. Works B 25:162-185.
[10] *Plain Account* 5:1; 10:29.
[11] *Wesley and the People Called Methodists*, 39. These disciplines identify with 'works of piety', one of the groups identified by JW as a means of grace. On means of grace, see JW's sermon by the same title.
[12] Works of mercy is the second major group of the means of grace essential in attaining inward holiness. The first group is works of piety.
[13] *Plain Account* ch 4.
[14] JWJ 5/24/38 §5.

ogy blossomed into a coherent theological system. This is evidenced by several sermons, including two university homilies.[15]

Often not realized by many students of Wesley is the popularity he enjoyed as a preacher, even though he was considered by many to be an enthusiast. In 1732 the Holy Club began reading the church fathers, which led to the practice of keeping specific fasts. In the following year Wesley was introduced to various mystic writers, which emphasized perfection as spiritual (mystical) union with God. Under this influence Wesley's perfection theology gravitated toward an emphasis on love. While he would later regret his involvement with the mystics,[16] their influence did leave an indelible imprint on his doctrine of Christian perfection. Beginning in January 1734, Wesley became even more exact in his discipline by keeping a detailed daily record measuring his spiritual tempers. From his Holy Club era several sermons survive, most notably *The Circumcision of the Heart*. This apology for the Methodist program of holy living highlights several doctrinal principles within the little movement.[17] In 1732 Wesley transcribed several sermons from other authors.[18] While these sermons are not original in the sense that Wesley authored them, the fact he transcribed, edited, and preached them reveals their usefulness to discern aspects of his doctrinal system. They add interesting bits of insight into his theology of perfection at the time. Another noteworthy event was Wesley's publication of Kempis' *The Imitation of Christ* (1735). The preface to this tract

---

[15] *On the Sabbath* (7/4/30); *The Promise of Understanding* (10/13/30); *The Image of God* (11/1/30); *The Wisdom of Winning Souls* (7/12/31); *The Circumcision of the Heart* (1/1/33); *The Love of God* (9/15/33); *One Thing Needful* (5/34); *The Trouble and Rest of Good Men* (9/21/35).
[16] Cf. JWL 11/23/36 to his older brother Samuel.
[17] Some of these are: 1. A dynamic, even evangelical, understanding of the Holy Spirit's role in salvation. 2. The progressive stages in attaining perfection. 3. Perfection is love. 4. Faith begins to emerge in importance. 5. Inward holiness as a requirement for entering heaven.
[18] *The Duty of Constant Communion* (2/19/32); *On the Resurrection of the Dead* (6/7/32); *On Grieving the Holy Spirit* (10/28/32). See Outler's remarks, Works B Vol. 4 Appendix C.

The Gospel of Holiness

offers the reader a good taste of Wesley's present understanding of the gospel, especially concerning the means of attainment and the stages of the faith journey toward perfection. Stepping back a couple years, we note his first publication with *A Collection of Forms of Prayers for Every Day in the Week* (1733). The collection went through several editions during Wesley's lifetime, with the preface spelling out five stages in the path toward perfection. During his Oxford era over forty people were actively involved at one time or another in the Holy Club program. The group gained notoriety in and around Oxford for its rigorous disciplines and methodical practice of the means of grace.

During the summer of 1735 Wesley decided to go to Georgia as a missionary. He acknowledged to a friend that his primary motive was to save his own soul.[19] Along with his friends, he left England on October 15 and landed in Georgia on February 6, 1736. During his missionary phase Wesley produced two more sermons that brought his Gospel of Holiness to full maturity.[20] While he expected to come to the American wilderness to get away from worldly English society, and thereby focus on perfecting his own soul, God had other sovereign plans. Wesley's journal tracks the events which led him through a personal and theological crisis. On the voyage to America several large storms so struck terror in his soul that he became acutely aware of his spiritual deficiencies:

> At night I was awaked by the tossing of the ship and roaring of the wind, and plainly showed I was unfit, for I was

---

[19] JWL 10/10/35. This comment has been mistaken as a confession by JW of his lack of assurance in regard to salvation. We will soon see that we must be very careful when drawing conclusions about JW's statement's regarding assurance or his lack there of.

[20] *Single Intention* (2/3/36); *On Love* (2/20/37). Specifically, these are: (1) The single intention begins in a new birth, the process of which is completed in glory. (2) Perfection is love. (3) Attaining higher degrees of perfection prepares one to face death with assurance and confidence. (4) JW offers two testimonies of persons attaining perfection just before the article of death. In this sense, perfection can be attained in this life.

unwilling, to die...O how pure in heart must he be, who would rejoice to appear before God at a moment's warning![21]

To Wesley's utter amazement, aboard ship was a group of Moravian Christians who sang quietly during the storms. When he asked if they had any fear of dying, one of them responded, "I thank God, no." This kind of assurance punched holes in Wesley's spiritual armor and began a process that would lead him to a whole new experience of grace. It was during this same period he began to lose confidence in the teachings of the mystics.[22] From all outward appearances, Wesley's ministry in America was a near complete failure. While late in life he would say that the small groups he formed in Georgia was the second rise of Methodism, in reality he returned to England filled with dejection and defeat. He would spend much time aboard ship musing over his spiritual state and asking himself some tough questions. Facing more storms on his return trip only confirmed the bankruptcy he felt inside, exposing the underbelly of his present understanding of the gospel. Wesley was forced to acknowledge he had only a "fair summer religion."[23] The spiritual crisis prepared him for something new, something fresh. At the time, though, only God knew what was in store for this seeker of inward holiness.

Spiritual Awakening

Wesley informs us in *A Plain Account of Christian Perfection* that he came to embrace the doctrine of Christian perfection in 1725 when he experienced a powerful spiritual awakening to the necessity of inward holiness:

---

[21] JWJ 11/23/35, 1/17/36.
[22] Cf. footnote 10.
[23] JWJ 1/24/38.

The Gospel of Holiness

> Instantly I resolved to dedicate all my life to God, all my thoughts, and words, and actions; being thoroughly convinced, there is no medium; but that every part of my life (not some only) must either be a sacrifice to God, or myself, that is, in effect, to the devil.
>
> I saw, that giving even all my life to God would profit me nothing, unless I gave my heart, yea, all my heart, to him.
>
> I determined, through his grace, to be all-devoted to God, to give him all my soul, my body, and my substance.[24]

These statements are revealing: Wesley's faith journey was grounded on a powerful work of divine grace within his heart. Note how he describes his experience in the above quotations. He speaks of making a definite decision, of changing his heart, of having his life immediately altered and heading in a new direction. This is the language of conversion. In 1765, when Wesley wrote the *Plain Account*, he used the language of conversion to describe what transpired within his soul forty years earlier. This choice in terminology could be interpreted as the reflections of the post-Aldersgate Wesley, who now proclaimed an evangelical gospel of new birth by faith alone in Christ alone. If all we had was Wesley's comments in the *Plain Account* we could entertain such a conclusion. But with several of his early manuscript sermons available for study, we have sources by which to test this hypothesis.

---

[24] *Plain Account* 2:2, 3:2, 4:2. JW's remarks in the PA imply that he experienced a series of awakenings over several years. See Susanna's letter to John on Feb.23, 1725. In this letter she comments on John's "alteration" in his spiritual tempers, and trusts this change has been produced by the "operations of God's Holy Spirit." She then encourages her son to "resolve to make religion the business of your life." This is the "one thing" that is necessary, says Susanna. She then exhorts John to examine himself to see if he has a "reasonable hope of salvation." These themes play an important role in the development of JW's theology during the early period.

John Wesley's Theology of Christian Perfection

When we turn to these early sermons startling facts begin to emerge. First, Wesley was much more evangelical during his early period than is often assumed. Even Albert Outler acknowledges there was "more evangelical teaching in Oxford than one would surmise from Wesley's later descriptions of the place."[25] For example, in Wesley's sermon *The Wisdom of Winning Souls*, a program of winning converts is proposed that reflects evangelical priorities. The program involved three steps. Outler summarizes them well:

> The first step in 'winning souls' is bringing the seeker both to a conscious desire for the purification of his heart from 'its darling lusts' and to the deliberate 'regulating of the affections'. This must then be followed by a positive commitment to holy living as a gift and a task. The final step in the transaction is a 'fixing' of the convert in his new-found 'generous resolutions'. None of this is possible, of course, by human resolution alone; it is all the work of grace.[26]

The progression of awakening, decision and establishment emphasizes the evangelical call to a moment of decision. It also expresses the evangelical priority to intentionally win converts. We must be reminded at this time Wesley did lack an understanding of faith commitment to Christ for present justification. Instead, what Wesley stressed was the convert's commitment to God for the attainment of inward holiness (perfection), in the certain hope that God will justify his servant on the final day. In other words, Wesley's message was a gospel of *holiness*, not the *cross*. This gospel, in several ways, called for a faith centered more on God than on Christ. Hence, Wesley made sanctification the means for justification before God. In this sense we can say Wesley was not yet evangelical; but, we must add, he was evangelical in the sense

---

[25] Works B 1: 400.
[26] Works B 4:305.

of winning adherents through a definite moment of decision. For this was how he personally experienced renewal in his own life.

Wesley's evangelical propensities become even more evident through his use of evangelical terminology to describe this moment of decision. In *The Single Intention* Wesley exhorts his fellow Georgians to make a firm decision:

> Consider that no man can serve two masters; ye cannot serve God and mammon. Either therefore ye must give God your whole heart, or none at all; he cannot, will not, be served by halves. Either wholly lay aside the thoughts of pleasing him, and choose you another master, or let the pleasing him be your one view in all your thoughts, all your words, and all your actions. Believe our Lord, you can find no middle way.[27]

When Wesley spoke of giving God one's heart he was using popular evangelical phraseology to describe the moment of decision. Again, note the classic evangelical terminology, "Behold, all things about you are become new! Be ye likewise new creatures! From this hour at least let your eye be single: whatever ye speak, or think, or do, let God be your aim, and God only! Let your one end be to please and love God!"[28]

Other examples can be found. In *One Thing Needful* Wesley told his audience what they need is a spiritual resurrection, "'Awake, thou that sleepest, and arise from the dead!' Hath not Christ given thee light? Why then sittest thou still in the shadow of death?"[29] Again, in *The Wisdom of Winning Souls* this transformation is said to be an "entirely new turn" in which the convert "undergoes such a change as is that from death to life."[30] How does one arise from spiritual death? Wesley's answer is

---

[27] *Single Intention* P.1.
[28] *Single Intention* II.9.
[29] *One Thing Needful* III.1; Eph. 5:14.
[30] Works B 4:315.

straightforward: "fix" the heart, have one "pure unmixed intention."[31]

So Wesley did believe and teach the necessity of an evangelical-like spiritual awakening prior to his Aldersgate conversion in 1738. After all, this is what he personally experienced within his own heart in 1725. In the instant of heart-felt resolution, Wesley was spiritually awakened to the call for complete renewal in God's image. In simple terms, Wesley experienced a new birth, the beginning of a new life.[32] He felt within the "operations of God's Holy Spirit"[33] and found his "whole body" to be "full of light."[34] Christ had given him light; the Spirit indwelt his spirit; God had poured forth his grace into his heart. John Wesley was on the path to Christian perfection.

Wesley's early evangelical orientation is further seen in his doctrine of the Holy Spirit. In the early thirties he began to develop a more coherent understanding of the work of the Spirit in the process of salvation.[35] In October 1732 he transcribed the sermon of William Tilly, titled *On Grieving the Holy Spirit*, which is based on Ephesians 4:30.[36] In this homily the Holy Spirit is called the believer's "best Friend" and God's "immediate presence," which is "so closely united to the Spirit that we are said to be 'one spirit with him.'" The Spirit is the source of the Christian's "regeneration" and "new nature," which is already at work in the seeker of inward holiness. These fruits come from the Spirit producing "holy motions" within the heart. Wesley closes the sermon by elaborating on the meaning of the Spirit's sealing. First, the Spirit seals by healing our "disordered souls" and making us "partakers of the divine nature."[37] Second, the Spirit seals

---

[31] *One Thing Needful* III.2.
[32] Cf. note 20 above.
[33] Cf. note 16 above.
[34] Matt. 6:22; *One Thing Needful* III.2.
[35] A designation for the Christian. See *Death and Deliverance* §1; *Seek First the Kingdom* §§1, 4; *A Single Intention* §1; *Trouble and Rest of Good Men* II.7.
[36] Sermon #138 in Works J 7:485. See Outler's comments, Works B 4:531.
[37] 2 Peter 1:4; *On Grieving the Holy Spirit* III.1.

the believer by being the "sign of God's property within us, becoming a mark that we belong to Christ." Finally, the Spirit is the "security of our salvation" by serving as a deposit and thereby becoming the "title to eternal happiness." We will see below how the Gospel of Holiness did offer a clear doctrine of assurance based upon the gift of the Spirit, a present pardon of sin, and the integrity of the single intention. But John Wesley's early doctrine of assurance must be carefully nuanced if we are to grasp his theological evolution, and understand what exactly changed in his theology at Aldersgate.

We find similar evangelical descriptions of the Spirit's work in the benchmark sermon *The Circumcision of the Heart*. The message of this homily is straightforward: circumcision of the heart is the "distinguishing mark of the true follower of Christ" (P.3). The following excerpts reflect an evangelical understanding of the Spirit's role:

> He (true Christian) feels what is 'the exceeding greatness of his power' who, as he raised up Christ from the dead, so is able to quicken us—'dead in sin'—'by his Spirit which dwelleth in us'. (I.7)

> This is the next thing which the 'circumcision of the heart' implies—even the testimony of their own spirit with the Spirit which witnesses in their hearts, that they are the children of God. Indeed it is the same Spirit who works in them that clear and cheerful confidence that their heart is upright toward God. (I.9)

> It is his daily care, by the grace of God in Christ, and through the blood of the covenant…that he whose very 'body is the temple of God' ought to admit into it nothing common or unclean; and that 'holiness becometh' that 'house for ever' where the Spirit of holiness vouchsafes to dwell (I.10).

> He continually feels in his inmost soul that without the Spirit of God resting upon him he can neither think, nor desire, nor speak, nor act, anything good or well-pleasing in his sight. (II.1)

The salvific work of the Holy Spirit is to quicken and to indwell, to empower and to rest upon, to circumcise inwardly and to bear witness. All these expressions are evangelical and reflect a robust pneumatology. They emphasize life transformation grounded upon the inward work of the Spirit, conditioned upon faith:

> Our gospel, as it knows no other foundation of good works than faith, or of faith than Christ, so it clearly informs us we are not his disciples while we either deny him to be the author or his Spirit to be the inspirer and perfecter both of our faith and works. 'If any man have not the Spirit of Christ, he is none of his.' He alone can quicken those who are dead unto God, can breathe into them the breath of Christian life, and so prevent, accompany, and follow them with his grace as to bring their good desires to good effect. And 'as many as are thus led by the Spirit of God, they are the sons of God.' This is God's short and plain account of true religion and virtue; and 'other foundation can no man lay'. (II.4)

These quotations express a dynamic understanding of the Holy Spirit's work in redemption. Wesley's early pneumatology incorporates an evangelical flair, a soteriological focus, and a God-moment emphasis. According to John Wesley, when the decision of the single intention is made, the Spirit of Christ begins to indwell and produce holy designs and desires within the heart. This *new nature* then grows in holiness and in the image of God until perfection is attained in the article of death.

Wesley describes this moment of decision in evangelical terms and categories. The moment of wholehearted devotion is a new birth, a regeneration, a resurrection from the dead. These are not idle descriptions of a person's own efforts. Instead, Wesley understands the sinner to be completely incapable of producing such transformation in their own strength. Only God's Spirit can produce this profound change, this renewal of the fallen nature. Later in life Wesley will draw the same conclusion: the lowest degree of Christian perfection is to have a single intention—"one desire and one design."[38] In light of Wesley's progressive understanding on attaining perfection,[39] we can see where the root of this idea came from. Drawing upon his own experience, the light of Scripture, and from the books he was reading, Wesley learned that the path to perfection begins with a single intention. This explains his zeal to make powerful appeals to his audiences:

> 'Give me thy heart,' for it was I that made it, it was I that gave it thee! It was I that bestowed its vital motion, and that for no other end but to direct and incline it toward me. I only am thy true good: in me alone canst thou find rest for thy soul; all the springs of thy happiness are in me. Therefore, my son, give me thy heart. I only merit, and 'tis I alone that can reward, thy love! Let none have any share therein but me; and let me have it all!'[40]

Imago Dei

If we are looking to find the bedrock doctrine that undergirds his Gospel of Holiness, we need to look no further than his teaching on the restored image of God. In *One Thing Needful* Wesley makes this clear:

---

[38] JWL J CCLII; Works J 12:283. Only then the single intention will be located in a second work following regeneration.
[39] Cf. *Plain Account* ch 3 e.n.; 12:9, 29; 25:59-60, 62-63. In the sermons *One Thing Needful* and *Single Intention* the new birth is said to begin at the moment of decision but completed in glory.
[40] *The Love of God* III.8.

> Now this great work, this one thing needful, is the renewal of our fallen nature. In the image of God was man made, but a little lower than the angels. His nature was perfect, angelical, divine. He was an incorruptible picture of the God of glory. He bore his stamp on every part of his soul; the brightness of his Creator shone mightily upon him. But sin hath now effaced the image of God. He is no longer nearly allied to angels. He is sunk lower than the very beasts of the field. His soul is not only earthly and sensual, but devilish. Thus is the mighty fallen! The glory is departed from him! His brightness is swallowed up in utter darkness![41]

The theme of Adam, created in God's image and likeness, became the meta-narrative, the over-arching paradigm of Wesley's theological system throughout his life.[42] In his first written sermon we see the imprint of this Adamic paradigm when he refers to the sin which our "first father entailed on his whole race of mankind."[43] Wesley's most thorough treatment of this motif during his Oxford days is found in his first university sermon *The Image of God*. Outler summarizes, "The argument is ordered into three stages: first, the original perfections of the *imago Dei* in Adam and Eve; second, the fall and defacement of that image; and third, the mystery of grace and the promise of the image's restoration. It is, therefore, an important statement of Wesley's

---

[41] *One Thing Needful* § 2.

[42] E.g. see *Justification by Faith* I.1-4; *Original Sin* III.5. JW's basic view of religion never changed, "I take religion to be...a constant ruling habit of the soul; a renewal of our minds in the image of God; a recovery of the divine likeness; a still-increasing conformity of heart and life to the pattern of our most holy Redeemer" (JWL 1/15/34). "I entirely agree with you that religion is love and peace and joy in the Holy Ghost" (JWL 3/28/37). "I am convinced, as true religion or holiness cannot be without cheerfulness, so steady cheerfulness, on the other hand, cannot be without holiness or true religion" (JWL 3/29/37).

[43] *Death and Deliverance* § 1.

early basic understanding of the *ordo salutis* (order of salvation)."[44]

Wesley defines the pristine image of God as "unerring understanding, an uncorrupted will, and perfect freedom." He then adds one more quality, the crowning of happiness (I.4). These exalted views of humanity's original perfection are in sharp contrast to the depths of depravity that characterized Adam's fall. Adam's understanding mistook "falsehood for truth," with error and ignorance increasing (II.2). Besides the darkness that captured the mind, the human will was "seized by legions of vile affections" (II.3), resulting in a loss of freedom and slavery to vanity and vice (II.4). The consequence was death, misery, and the loss of happiness (II.5), with the human race becoming a slave to the devil. Wesley uses graphic language to describe humanity's bondage to sin. The entire race is now in the "basest" of bondage, bound by Satan to a "thousand chains" of "vile affections." Human affections are described as "diabolical" and human nature as "full of diseases and wounds and putrifying sores."[45] Every child of Adam is "so loaded that he cannot lift up an eye, a thought to heaven." So weighted down is the sinful human heart that the "whole soul cleaveth unto the dust!"[46]

Turning to another sermon, we see just how devastating the loss of pure love was in the fall:

> But when he (Adam) had wilfully degraded himself from that state of happiness and perfection, by transgressing the single prohibition which was appointed for the test of his love, a more particular law became needful for him, for a

---

[44] Works B 4:290.

[45] *One Thing Needful* I.4.

[46] *One Thing Needful* I.2-3. "It convinces us that in our best estate we are of ourselves all sin and vanity; that confusion, and ignorance, and error, reign over our understanding; that unreasonable, earthly, sensual, devilish passions usurp authority over our will: in a word, that there is no whole part in our soul, that all the foundations of our nature are out of course" (*The Circumcision of the Heart* I.2).

remedy of those many inventions he had found out, whereby, being alienated from the love of God, he was enslaved to the love of his creatures, and consequently to error and vice, to shame and misery.[47]

In *The Image of God* an interesting interpretation is offered to explain how the forbidden fruit infected the first human pair. The tree of the knowledge of good and evil contained a juice, which had particles that adhered to the artery and blood vessel walls, and brought about all the illnesses that now lead to death (II.1). So the forbidden fruit affected the blood from which life comes. As human blood is now infected and diseased, in the same way vile affections enslave the soul. Only through Christ's pure blood, as the second Adam, are these afflictions healed. Therefore, the goal of redemption is the "one thing needful"—the restoration of the *imago Dei*. Wesley asks his university audience:

> Who indeed shall recover us from the body of this death? Who shall restore our native immortality? We answer with the Apostle, 'I thank God, Jesus Christ our Lord!' 'As in Adam all died, so in Christ shall all be made alive'—all who accept of the means which he hath prepared, who walk by the rules which he hath given them. All these shall by dying conquer the first death, and shall never taste the second. The seeds of spiritual death they shall gradually expel, before this earthly tabernacle is dissolved, that this too, when it has been taken down and thoroughly purged, may be rebuilt 'eternal in the heavens'.[48]

This passage is quoted at length because it informs us, not only how the Gospel of Holiness answers the human dilemma, but lays out the rationale for Wesley's program of pursuing inward

---

[47] *The Love of God* P.2.
[48] *The Image of God* III.P.

holiness. In good Pauline fashion Wesley proclaims that Jesus Christ now redeems us from the pit of sin and death. But note the switch! No mention is made of Christ's atoning death for our justification—present or final. What Christ offers are the *means* and *rules* by which those who walk accordingly find life through the gradual expelling of the "seeds" of spiritual death. The goal is that after being fully purged in the article of death, when our "earthly tabernacle is dissolved," the believer is prepared to enter eternal glory. This is the Gospel of Holiness.

One of the curiosities of Wesley's early theological system was his identification of Adamic perfection to the nature of angels. In 1726 he wrote the sermon *On Guardian Angels*. Drawing upon Psalm 91:11—*He shall give his angels charge over thee, to keep thee in all thy ways*—Wesley enunciates several blessings these angels offer the heirs of salvation. Most notably for our purposes, guardian angels assist the believer when facing bodily pain or "violent passions." Their ministry is to "ward off the approaching evil" (I.2). In this way the angels aid God's servants in the pursuit of holiness and perfection. In other places Wesley defines the *imago* in terms of angelic nature. In the fragment sermon *In Earth as in Heaven,* the perfection of God's will in heaven is identified with the perfect obedience of holy angels (Matt 6:10). The angels always do God's will in heaven and thereby serve as an example for believers on earth.

A month later, Wesley again links our perfection to the nature of angels. In the sermon *One Thing Needful*, our pristine perfection is described as "angelical." But "sin hath now effaced the image of God." Consequentially, mankind is "no longer nearly allied to angels" (I.2). According to Wesley's theology of perfection, Adam was originally made a little lower than the angels (Ps 8:5); in the end the redeemed child of Adam will be restored to the nature of angels.

One further point should be made. Wesley's doctrine of the *imago Dei* links the concepts of perfection and salvation within his theological system. Several summary descriptions of the Christian faith highlight this connection. In a letter written to his

John Wesley's Theology of Christian Perfection

older brother Samuel upon the eve of his departure to America, Wesley defines Christianity, not as a "negation, or an external thing, but a new heart, a mind conformed to that of Christ, faith working by love."[49] In a letter to Richard Morgan, he describes religion as a "constant ruling habit of the soul; a renewal of our minds in the image of God; a recovery of the divine likeness; a still-increasing conformity of heart and life to the pattern of our most holy Redeemer."[50] The doctrine of *imago Dei* became the paradigm by which Wesley understood and explained God's plan of redemption. As his mother exhorted him in February 1725, Wesley saw true religion, real Christianity, as the recovery of our first estate: "to re-exchange the image of Satan for the image of God, bondage for freedom, sickness for health. Our one great business is to rase out of our souls the likeness of our destroyer, and to be born again, to be formed anew after the likeness of our Creator."[51] The one thing needful is to "shake off this servile yoke and to regain our native freedom." The linking of perfection and holiness with salvation will have very significant ramifications for Wesley personally, for his theology as a whole, and for his holiness gospel in particular. This will become evident as we proceed in our study.

The Goal of Perfection

One of the unique features in Wesley's holiness gospel was the dual role that holiness serves within the system. In one sense Kenneth Collins is certainly correct when he writes, "Wesley came to understand quite clearly the end or goal of religion, which is sanctification or holiness, that is, loving God and neighbor in all sincerity and devotion and with suitable affections."[52] Yet, in another sense, this statement falls short. For in

---

[49] JWL 10/15/35.
[50] JWL 1/15/34.
[51] *One Thing Needful* I.5.
[52] *John Wesley: A Theological Journey,* 42.

relation to the *final goal* Wesley's own writings reveal that holiness also serves as the *means* of religion. This can be confusing unless we keep in mind his early soteriological system.

True religion was identified with the pursuit of holy living. In a letter to his father Wesley shares his desire to have a "'clean heart', a single eye, a soul full of God."[53] In another letter to Mary Pendarves he confesses, "I was made to be happy; to be happy I must love God…To love God I must be like him, holy as he is holy."[54] For early Wesley, the "one thing needful" is the restoration of our fallen nature. In Adam we all die; in Christ, the second Adam, we are made alive—through the renewal of our nature after its original perfection. So it is fair to say that according to Wesley holiness is the *goal* of faith. Yet, this is only a part of the story.

Holiness also serves as the *means* by which the true follower of Jesus attains the ultimate goal—heaven itself. We noted before that Wesley's first two sermons lay out in broad contours the heart of his perfection theology.[55] Outler refers to the first sermon as preoccupied with the "art of dying."[56] According to the *ars moriendi* motif the supreme purpose of life is to prepare oneself for death and life thereafter. Life's ultimate purpose is to fit one for eternity when they are "delivered from all those cares, afflictions, and dangers…in this transitory life."[57] This same theme permeates his second sermon, in which he expounds upon the following words of Jesus, "Seek ye first the kingdom of God, and

---

[53] JWL 6/13/33. See also his letter to his mother, dated 1/28/34: "'I come to do thy will, O God.' 'I seek not myself, but Christ crucified.' This is that perception of the presence of God which I desire (Alas, how faintly!) to attain to! This is that recollection which I study to advance in day by day; this seems to me one stair of 'the ladder to heaven', one degree of Christian simplicity" (Works B 25:373).
[54] JWL 7/19/31.
[55] Note 4 above.
[56] Works B 4:205.
[57] *Death and Deliverance* §13. JW also describes the temporality of life by calling it a "tedious dream life" (*On Mourning for the Dead* §4, 19). As dreams are short-lived, so is this earthly existence. See note 58.

his righteousness, and all these things shall be added unto you."[58] Wesley proceeds to define the kingdom as heaven, the eternal realm,[59] and God's righteousness as one's duty to neighbor and as the "sum of the Christian religion." He then places the kingdom and righteousness in their proper order: attaining heaven is the reason why we seek God's righteousness, "But lest we should imagine any to have a claim to these eternal mansions beside those that do the will of their heavenly Father, we are expressly commanded to seek his righteousness as well as his kingdom."[60]

Several years later in *The Circumcision of the Heart* Wesley warns his lukewarm audience that it is a "vain hope to attain the crown of incorruption, whose heart is not circumcised by love" (II.9). Several months after this he puts it in clear terms, "The chief sense of the words is doubtless this: that whatsoever we do, and whatsoever we suffer, if we are not renewed in the spirit of our mind by the love of God shed abroad in our hearts by the Holy Ghost given unto us, we cannot enter into life eternal."[61]

If entering heaven is the goal, then attaining holiness is the means:

> Let us then labour to be made perfectly whole, to burst every bond in sunder; to attain the fullest conquest over this body of death, the most entire renovation of our nature; knowing this, that when the Son of man shall send forth his angels to cast the double-minded into outer darkness, then shall the single of heart receive the one thing they sought, and shine forth as the sun in the kingdom of their Father![62]

---

[58] Matt 6:33; quoted from JW's sermon.
[59] "The kingdom which our blessed Lord here requires us to seek is that which he himself assures us is not of this world. All things here are subject to corruption or decay. But the crown which God has prepared for those who diligently seek it is incorruptible and fadeth not away" (*Seek First the Kingdom* §6).
[60] *Seek First the Kingdom* §6.
[61] *The Love of God* III.2.
[62] *One Thing Needful* III.3.

The Gospel of Holiness

The theme of heaven as perfection's goal was pervasive in Wesley's thought. In 1727 he preached at the funeral service for his close friend Robin Griffiths. Today, the sermon reads more like an exhortation than words of comfort. But even in this situation he did not fail to remind Griffiths' mourners that in a "few years, perhaps hours, which will soon be over, and not only this but all our other desires will be satisfied; when we shall exchange the gaudy shadow of pleasure we have enjoyed for sincere, substantial, untransitory happiness."[63] Then in a letter to his mother Wesley opens up, "I am to renounce the world as well as you. That is the very thing I want to do; to draw off my affections from this world, and to fix them upon a better world."[64]

The core message of the Gospel of Holiness is to call people to seek wholeheartedly the perfecting of holiness in preparation for death and eternity. God is absolutely holy; nothing impure will enter the eternal city (Rev 21:27). Only those renewed in the spirit of their minds will be fit to enjoy the beatific vision of the Lofty and Holy One. This demand for perfect holiness requires that the corruption of human nature be purged and corrected. This point cannot be over-emphasized: the fundamental goal of the gospel is to prepare the Christian for death and eternity. This basic truth gives needed insight into the rationale for Wesley's steadfast devotion to attain inward holiness at all costs. He wanted to be ready to face death. His entire program was designed to prepare him for the inevitable—death itself. This explains why in his early soteriology sanctification became the foundation for salvation, including justification itself. And it clarifies why Wesley was concerned from the time of his spiritual awakening with the "art of dying." We will see in the next chapter how this single insight sheds much light into why he made the mega-shift in his soteriology, profoundly shaping his perfection theology.

---

[63] *On Mourning for the Dead* § 17.
[64] JWL 2/28/32.

John Wesley's Theology of Christian Perfection

One more aspect on this theme needs to be noted. As was mentioned, in 1732, Wesley transcribed a number of sermons from other authors. One of these homilies was by Benjamin Calamy, which addressed the nature of the future resurrection.[65] Since Wesley preached this sermon at Castle prison in 1732 and 1734, it does represent his thought at the time. For a starter, this homily, once again, makes the argument that holiness is necessary if one is to enter heaven (III.1). But interestingly, the main argument is that God will raise up on that final day the exact same body which died. He argues his case upon the premise of God's omnipotence to restore the human (resurrection) body from the exact same decomposed participles of the dead body.

Concerning the nature of the resurrection body three points are drawn from 1 Corinthians 15. First, the body will be raised incorruptible and immortal, no longer subject to death and decay. Second, the body will be raised in glory. By glory Wesley understood the resurrected body will shine with brilliant light, like the stars (angels?), thus reflecting God's absolute holiness. Finally, the body will be raised in power and will be a spiritual body, no longer bound by earthly, carnal limitations. In regard to the body being raised in glory, Wesley offers insights into a further necessity for holiness as the condition to entering heaven:

> For although all the children of God shall have glorious bodies, yet the glory of them all shall not be equal. "As one star differeth from another star in glory, so also is the resurrection of the dead." They shall all shine as stars; but those who, by a constant diligence in well doing, have attained to a higher measure of purity than others, shall shine more bright than others.[66]

In the resurrection some believers will shine brighter due to their attainment of higher degrees of inward holiness in this life. This

---

[65] The sermon is #137 in Works J. For Outler's remarks see Works B 4:528.
[66] *On The Resurrection of the Dead* III.3.

The Gospel of Holiness

places even more weight upon having a single intention. As perfection is required to enter heaven, the believer's eternal reward also depends on the degree of holiness attained in this life. The question arises: how much holiness must be attained for one to enter heaven? While this question brings up the subject of assurance, which will be dealt with in detail below, it is necessary we give a brief answer to the question at hand.

Since Wesley believed there is going to be degrees of reward based upon differing levels of holiness attained in this life, it was only logical for him to conclude that one did not have to attain an absolute standard of holiness in this life to enter eternal glory. Nor did he believe the Christian must live in insecurity concerning their eternal wellbeing. In one letter he assures his dear friend Ann Granville: "our hope is sincerity, not perfection, not to do well, but to do our best. If God were to mark all that is done amiss, who could abide?"[67]

The example of the Apostle Paul is next mentioned to bring further encouragement. When Paul had finished his course in this life and was "ripe for paradise" (note the emphasis on being fit for death) he still was not "perfect" (Php 2:12). Wesley here asserts that Paul was perfect in terms of a "voluntary breach of a known law," by which he meant "habits of such sin," but in regard to single acts Paul had confidence that Christ promised to forgive these, even to "seventy times seven."[68] In response, Wesley quips with confidence that God will forgive a "thousand times a thousand" if the Christian sincerely desires it. The real Christian need not fret over their eternal salvation. God looks for a single intention to love him wholeheartedly, not absolute perfection or flawless performance.

---

[67] JWL 10/3/31. See JWL 12/12/30 where he acknowledges his failings and falling short. The God in whom he trusts does not "always require wisdom and prudence, yet *some degree* of purity" is required from the Christian (Works B 25:260, italics mine).

[68] Matthew 18:22. JW is quoting the KJV here. The NIV has "seventy-seven times."

John Wesley's Theology of Christian Perfection

The Nature of Perfection

It would be good to pause at this point and clarify more specifically how Wesley conceptually understood perfection. In volume one of this series there are listed dozens of synonyms from *A Plain Account of Christian Perfection* and the *Journal* (1961-1766). Wesley's doctrine of perfection was multi-faceted and he incorporated several conceptual models[69] to communicate the doctrine. Words are 'tricky' things. We depend upon them to communicate our ideas and thoughts, but we have all experienced how easily prone they are to misinterpretation. Wesley's doctrine of perfection suffered the same fate. In response, he used a number of concepts to communicate his idea of perfection. We have already come across several of them. We saw above that the cornerstone doctrine of his early theological system was the *imago Dei*. In the transcribed sermon *On Grieving the Holy Spirit* he conceptualizes perfection as our "likeness to God," which he defines as the "conformity of our will and affections to his will." This is "properly speaking, holiness" (III.1). One of the most succinct definitions of perfection he ever penned is found in *The Circumcision of the Heart*:

> In general we may observe it is that habitual disposition of soul which in the Sacred Writings is termed 'holiness', and which directly implies the being cleansed from sin, 'from all filthiness both of flesh and spirit', and by consequence the being endued with those virtues which were also in Christ Jesus, the being so 'renewed in the image of our mind' as to be 'perfect, as our Father in heaven is perfect' (I.1).

Habitual disposition served as a core conceptual model when defining holiness to his father, "By holiness I mean, not fasting, or

---

[69] A *conceptual model* is a title or phrase JW uses to explain and communicate the *idea* behind his doctrine of Christian perfection.

bodily austerity, or any other external means of improvement, but that inward temper to which these are subservient, a renewal of soul in the image of God. I mean a complex habit of lowliness, meekness, purity, faith, hope, and love of god and man."[70] As *imago Dei* points to the larger picture of what perfection means in terms of redemption's goal, habitual disposition conveys the core idea Wesley sought to communicate: God inwardly transforms the dispositional nature by rooting out the corruptions of Adamic nature, replacing them with the virtues of Christ's holy nature. Thus, the Christian is being restored to the pristine perfection Adam originally enjoyed.

The most common conceptual model Wesley employs throughout his career is that of love perfected and thereby made pure. In volume one of this series we noted the foundational role this term conveys in his enunciation of the doctrine.[71] In a letter to a friend Wesley once remarked that our "ultimate end is the love of God."[72] In his first university sermon Wesley defines Adam's pristine nature as possessing a single primary affection: "Love filled the whole expansion" of Adam's soul; it "possessed him without a rival." Wesley intertwines the motifs of habitual affection with perfect love to describe Adam's nature as love having "every movement of his heart."

Love was Adam's "vital heat;" it "animated his whole frame."[73] Wesley was drawn to the Great Commandments and saw the commands to love God and neighbor as the "royal law of heaven and earth."[74] In the 1730's he wrote two sermons on the theme of love as the end or goal of holiness, with both inspired by Paul's description in 1 Corinthians 13. One of his best early portrayals on love are found in a rhetorical question he asked his audience:

---

[70] JWL 12/10/34.
[71] *Plain Account* 6:3-5 n; 26:6b-7 n.
[72] JWL 12/12/30.
[73] *The Image of God* I.2.
[74] *The Circumcision of the Heart* I.11.

John Wesley's Theology of Christian Perfection

> The charity which our Lord requires in all his followers is the love of God and man: of God, for his own, and of man, for God's sake. Now, what is it to love God but to delight in him, to rejoice in his will, to desire continually to please him, to seek and find our happiness in him, and to thirst day and night for a fuller enjoyment of him?[75]

Perfect love is a heart full and overflowing with joy and satisfaction in God. Note the emotionally rich terms he uses to communicate his meaning: "delight...rejoice...desire...happiness and fuller enjoyment". No wonder he saw such love as the "first principle of all religion."[76] Wesley then explains why this love is perfection itself:

> You cannot wrong one you love: therefore, if you love God with all your heart, you cannot so wrong him as to rob him of his glory, to take to yourself what is due to him only. You will own that all you are, all you have, is his; that without him you can do no good thing; that he is your light and your life, your strength and your all, and that you are nothing, yea, less than nothing, before him. And if you love your neighbour as yourself, you will not be able to prefer yourself before him. You will not be able to despise, any more than to hate him. Nay, you will think every man better than yourself.[77]

Since perfect love is God's love filling and ruling the heart, such love roots out the contrary dispositions of pride and selfishness, thereby eliminating competing rivals within the affections. Perfect love is complete dependency and reliance upon God's grace, so that without him "you can do no good thing." This love further eliminates all contrary attitudes and dispositions that keep the Christian from loving their neighbor. Hence, perfect love neces-

---

[75] *On Love* II.2.
[76] *On Love* II.4.
[77] *On Love* II.8.

sarily implies a love made pure, a heart freed from contrary or sinful tempers.

One final insight into how early Wesley understood perfect love. In 1735 he published *The Christian's Pattern* (or *The Imitation of Christ*) by Thomas `a Kempis. The preface offers an overview of the book's contents and goals, defining perfection in terms of spiritual union. Wesley draws upon 1 Corinthians 6:17 and 2 Peter 1:4 to define perfect love as the "union of our will with the divine as makes the Christian one spirit with God...whereby he that loves God is made a partaker of the divine nature" (II.4).

Another conceptual model was Christ-likeness. In 1765 Wesley recalls that it was in the winter of 1729-30 he became a person of one book, the Holy Scriptures.[78] At the same time he remembers seeing in clearer light the necessity of following Christ as the "grand Exemplar," the "most perfect Pattern of all holiness."[79] Christ perfectly modeled the humility, self-renunciation, consecration, and love required of every believer to be perfect. Those who would follow Jesus must take up their cross daily (Lk 9:23) and be planted in the likeness of his death (Rom 6:5) if they are to live as Christ did. Wesley saw Christ as the most perfect pattern to imitate because Jesus is the radiance of God's glory (Heb 1:3), thereby becoming for his followers a sure path toward full renewal in God's likeness.[80]

In the same year *The Christian's Pattern* was published, he wrote a couple letters to his mother outlining his views on perfection through the lens of freedom. Wesley says he has had a "great deal of conversation lately on the subject of Christian liberty" and

---

[78] *Plain Account* 5:1; 10:29.
[79] *Plain Account* 5:4; *Preface to the Christian's Pattern* III.1.
[80] In this passage of the preface to *The Christian's Pattern* JW chastises the person who so loves oneself and the world that they will not walk as Christ walked, "crucifying the flesh and all its affection, and nailing all its desires to the cross of Christ" (III.1). This is "the mind (set) of Christ" that JW sought to emulate and to impress on his followers.

John Wesley's Theology of Christian Perfection

desires her input on the subject.[81] Accordingly, Christians enjoy (1) liberty from willful sin, which the spiritually unconcerned lack; (2) freedom from "slavish fears," which the "awakened sinner" suffers from; and (3) liberty from "things of an indifferent nature," which the conscience of the "advanced" and "confirmed" Christian allows, but not those who are still "weak."[82] "Infant Christians" lack this latter kind of freedom since they still hold to many indulgences and lack the inner strength to overcome. Those who are "stronger" have renounced these worldly carnalities, like "superfluous clothes" and furniture.[83] This is the first explicit reference in Wesley's writings to differing spiritual states or stages within the Christian's faith journey. What is distinguished here between mature and immature will later become a critical distinction within his perfection theology.[84]

In a similar vein Wesley proclaimed an attainable perfection for the overcoming of willful sin. In the fall of 1731 he wrote to Ann Granville offering spiritual counsel for a mutual friend. As was noted earlier, in this letter the Apostle Paul is said to be perfect only in the sense of overcoming deliberate habits of sin,[85] but remained imperfect because he continually needed forgiveness for "single acts," even if they numbered into the thousands.

He further warned his friend that there is no total freedom in this life from "wandering thoughts in prayer, or perhaps from such as would be wicked were they chosen or voluntarily indulged, but which when they are not voluntary are no more voluntary than the panting of the heart or the beating of the arteries."[86] Wesley then acknowledged that "the common lot of humanity seems to be, to be various and fluctuating in all things,

---

[81] JWL 1/13/35.
[82] All these categories will play are future role in the development of his perfection theology. See ch 3.
[83] JWL 2/14/35.
[84] *Christian Perfection* II.1, 21; *Plain Account* 12:9, 29; 19:86; 25:59-66.
[85] JW's exact words are "sin, strictly speaking, which is a voluntary breach of a known law, at least from habits of such sin."
[86] JWL 10/3/31.

more particularly in the things that pertain to God, from whom we are so far estranged by nature."

The above quotations demonstrate that Wesley already discriminated between different kinds of sin: deliberate, willful, habits, and single acts. These distinctions, while still undeveloped, play a critical role in the later formulation of his perfection doctrine as salvation from all voluntary sin.[87]

Another conceptual model was the motif of health, wellness, and wholeness. This theme is found in his writings throughout his career. In *One Thing Needful* Wesley teaches that the influences of the Spirit are given to "restore us to health, to liberty, to holiness." Whether God gives us joy or sorrow, dryness or vigor, his one design is to "heal those inbred diseases of our nature, self-love, and the love of the world." In Adam our nature became ill and sickly, so that the one thing needful is for our soul to have "proper nourishment" for the recovery of God's love to the "health of our souls." Therefore, the Christian needs to "press towards this mark of the prize of our high calling; to emerge out of chains, diseases, death, into liberty, health, and life immortal!"[88]

Sin

On the flip side was Wesley's doctrine of sin. When he usually approached this subject he did so from the angle of his core doctrine *imago Dei*. We saw above that Adam was created perfect in his understanding, will, liberty and happiness.[89] But when sin was introduced, human nature became infected, like a disease which spreads through the whole body. We now find our understanding clouded with ignorance and error, leading our dispositions to be "seized by legions of vile affections."[90] The result is

---

[87] *Plain Account* 19:23-25; *On Perfection* III.9. Cf. ch 5.
[88] *One Thing Needful* II.5; III.1.
[89] *Image of God* I.1-4.
[90] *Image of God* II.3.

loss of freedom and happiness. Misery now attends our earthly sojourn[91] and the human race groans under the weight of the mortal body.[92] As a result, there is no perfect holiness on earth and no perfect happiness either; for "some remains of our disease will ever be felt, and some physic be necessary to heal it."[93] Therefore, when early Wesley spoke of sin he nearly always did so in context of that corruption of nature we inherit from Adam.

Our corrupt nature is at times referred to as the sinful nature, because of its proneness to evil.[94] Human nature now tends to follow the path of Lucifer in his arrogant attacks on God's goodness. Wesley's early doctrine of theodicy maintained that God sought to guard us against such pride by keeping us in ignorance of his ways:

> Here then is one wise and merciful reason for the present weakness of our understanding, that God, by hiding himself from man, might teach him humility, and so bring man to himself more surely. Another reason why he now hides himself from us is to fulfill his eternal purpose, that man, as long as he continued upon earth, should walk by faith, not by sight.[95]

Such pride leads to the sin of idolatry. Human sinfulness is demonstrated by the fact that love towards God is exchanged for love toward the creature.[96] Corrupt nature[97] makes human reason imperfect[98] as it distorts the reasonableness of loving God supremely. When referring to the Great Commandments Wesley wrote, "As to the measure of love prescribed in these words, all

---

[91] *Death and Deliverance* § 1.
[92] *The Trouble and Rest of Good Men,* Preamble.
[93] *The Trouble and Rest of Good Men,* Preamble.
[94] *On Mourning for the Dead* § 4.
[95] *The Promise of Understanding* III.2.
[96] *The Love of God* P.2.
[97] *Preface to The Christian's Pattern* II.14.
[98] *On Mourning for the Dead* § 6.

commentators agree that they mean at least thus much: we must not love anything more than God, we may not love the creature above the Creator."[99] Such is the "inbred pollution" of the human heart.[100] So deep is this perverseness that while sin can be defined as a "voluntary breach of a known law," only God can know "how far this breach of his law is voluntary in each particular person."[101] Consequently, only God knows who shall perish and who shall be saved. In the end, Wesley held strong views of human sinfulness rooted in Adamic corruption. He agreed with the Apostle John that human nature is now filled with the "lusts of the flesh, the lusts of the eye, and the pride of life."[102]

The Fruit of Perfection

A pervading theme in Wesley's early theology was holiness as the condition to finding real happiness in life:

"I was made to be happy; to be happy I must love God; in proportion to my love of whom my happiness must increase. To love God I must be like him, holy as he is holy; which implies both the being pure from vicious and foolish passions and the being confirmed in those virtues and rational affections which God comprises in the word charity."[103]

If this life is filled with misery due to Adamic corruption, then the opposite is also true: happiness is dependent upon our renewal in holiness. When he wrote to Mary Chapman from Savannah in 1737, he attempted to correct her false notions on religion, "As true religion or holiness cannot be without cheerfulness,

---

[99] *The Love of God* I.4.
[100] *The Circumcision of the Heart* I.11.
[101] JWL 6/19/31.
[102] 1 John 2:16; JWL 10/15/35.
[103] JWL 7/19/31.

so steady cheerfulness, on the other hand, cannot be without holiness or religion." Real religion has nothing "sour, austere, unsociable," or "unfriendly" in it, but is filled with the "most winning sweetness, the most amiable softness and gentleness."[104]

In the homily *On Love* he elaborates even further, "By happiness I mean, not a slight, trifling pleasure, that perhaps begins and ends in the same hour; but such a state of well-being as contents the soul, and gives it a steady, lasting satisfaction" (III.4).

When Wesley stood before his university audience in the fall of 1733, he declared with all his might the happiness which the good news of holiness offers:

> So far from it that love, entire love, is the point wherein all the lines of our holy religion centre. This is the very happiness which the great Author of it lived and died to establish among us. And a happiness it is, worthy of God! Worthy of infinite goodness and infinite wisdom to bestow! A happiness not built on imagination, but real and rational; a happiness that does not play before our eyes at a distance, and vanish when we attempt to grasp it, but such as will bear the closest inspection, and the more it is tried will delight the more. In the happiness of love there is no vanity, neither any vexation of spirit. No delusion, no disappointment is here; peace and joy ever dwell with love.[105]

A second fruit of perfection is the fullness of God's presence. One of his favorite passages was Matthew 6:22-23, "The light of the body is the eye: if therefore thine eye be single, thy whole body shall be full of light. But if thine eye be evil, thy whole body shall be full of darkness. If therefore the light that is in thee

---

[104] JWL 3/29/37.
[105] *On Love to God* III.6. On degrees of happiness JW further affirms that the happiness of those in eternal glory would be greater than those who have crossed the threshold of death (*Death and Deliverance* § 16).

be darkness, how great *is* that darkness!"[106] Wesley understood Jesus to mean by the "single eye," a single intention to please God in the "deliberate movement of the understanding and affections."[107] He then revels in the blessings promised to such devotion:

> Be your eyes fixed on this one point, and your whole bodies shall be full of light. God shall continually lift up, and that more and more, the light of his countenance upon you. His Holy Spirit shall dwell in you, and shine more and more upon your souls unto the perfect day. He shall purify your hearts by faith from every earthly thought, every unholy affection…He shall fill you with peace, and joy, and love! Love, the brightness of his glory, the express image of his person! Love which never rests, never faileth, but still spreads its flame, still goeth on conquering and to conquer, till what was but now a weak, foolish, wavering, sinful creature, be filled with all the fullness of God![108]

While happiness and God's fullness crown the believer who wholeheartedly sets their intent on pleasing him, the chief fruit of holiness is peace and comfort when facing death. In 1732 Wesley comforted the men at Castle prison, "We are now but on our journey towards home, and so must expect to struggle with many difficulties; but it will not be long ere we come to our journey's end, and that will make amends for all." He then exhorts them to fortify themselves against the "fear of death: It is now disarmed, and can do us no hurt."[109]

We saw above that holiness was a necessary means to enter heaven and eternal glory. Wesley believed with great confidence

---

[106] See *The Love of God* II.3; *The One Thing Needful* III.2; *The Single Intention* (Text). For Matt 6:23 see *The Promise of Understanding* III.1.
[107] *The Single Intention* I.1.
[108] *Single Intention* II.9.
[109] *On The Resurrection of the Dead* III.3.

that the pursuit of inward holiness would bring comfort and peace when facing death; that the more one loves God with a pure heart, the more one would be ready, and willing, to leave this mortal world for the riches of eternity. In America he explains the kind of comfort promised in his Gospel of Holiness, "By comfortable I do not mean stupid, or senseless. I would not say he died comfortably who died by an apoplexy, or by the shot of a cannon…But by a comfortable death I mean a calm passage out of life, full of even, rational peace and joy."[110] Such comfort perfect love offers to the dying soul.

What might surprise readers less familiar with Wesley's early writings is the inclusion of two testimonies of believers attaining a significant degree of perfection in the article of death. The first person was his father who passed away at Epworth on April 25, 1734, after several months suffering from an ulcer. Both John and Charles were at their father's bedside when he finally expired. Wesley recalled his father exclaiming, "God doth chasten me with strong pain; but I thank him for all, I bless him for all, I love him for all!" When the family asked Samuel if God's consolations were small to him, he responded "No, no, no!" John then recalled how his father called the family members by name and gathered them around his bed. He then exhorted them, "Think of heaven, talk of heaven! All the time is lost when we are not thinking of heaven!"

For his audience in America Wesley drove the point home that only perfect love can bring comfort to the dying soul:

> Now, this was the voice of charity; and so far as that prevailed, all was comfort and peace and joy. But as his love was not perfect so neither was his comfort. He had intervals of anger or fretfulness, and therein of misery, giving by both an incontestable proof that as love can sweeten both life and death, so when that is either absent from, or

---

[110] *On Love* III.5.

obscured in, the soul, there is no peace or comfort there.[111]

After this he shares another testimony. But this time the person attains an even greater degree of perfection, and thereby possesses a greater degree of comfort in the face of death. Henry Lascelles traveled to America at the same time that Wesley did, but on a different ship. He became very ill that following spring, and on May 31 he had Wesley draw up his will. Wesley comments on Henry's physical weakness and notes that his spirit revived when the two of them talked of death and eternity. Mr. Lascelles passed away on June 20, 1736.[112] Wesley's recollection of Henry's testimony is worth quoting in full:

> It was in this place that I saw the other good soldier of Christ grappling with his last enemy, death. And it was indeed a spectacle worthy to be seen, of God and men and angels. Some of his last breath was spent in a psalm of praise to him who was then giving him the victory; in assurance whereof be began the triumph even in the heat of the battle. When asked, 'Hast thou love?' he lifted up his eyes and hands, and answered, 'Yes, yes!' with the whole strength he had left. To one that inquired if he was afraid of the devil, whom he had just mentioned as making his last attack upon him, he replied: 'No, no: our loving Saviour hath conquered every enemy. He is with me. I fear nothing.' Soon after he said, 'The way to our loving Saviour is sharp—but it is short.' Nor was it long before he fell into a sort of slumber, wherein his soul sweetly returned to God that gave it. Here, we may observe, was no mixture of any passion or temper contrary to charity.

---

[111] *On Love* III.7. See also JW comments regarding his father's passing in his letter to John Smith on Mar. 22, 1748 (§ 6), and in the sermon *On Temptation* III.5. In both places he speaks more favorably of his father final testimony before he passed away.
[112] Cf. JWJ 5/31/36 - 6/19/36.

Therefore was there no misery, perfect love casting out whatever might have occasioned torment. And whosoever thou art who hast the like measure of love, thy last end shall be like his![113]

The fruit of holiness is wonderful and sweet. It brings happiness to the heart. It fills the soul with God's presence and love. And, most importantly, perfect love prepares the faithful servant for eternity by imparting peace and comfort when facing death. Oh, how important it is that our hearts are transformed by God's love! This life might be filled with trouble and misery,[114] but the gospel makes the single-minded believer fit to enter eternity with strong assurance and comfort. Thus, we return once again to the "art of dying" motif in Wesley's perfection theology. As we will soon see, this insight into Wesley's thought holds the key to understanding why he radically changed his theology leading up to Aldersgate.

The Timing of Perfection

We have learned so far that Wesley's early understanding of the gospel centered on the theme of inward holiness as the recovery of the image of God. Grounded upon a spiritual awakening, the *real* Christian pursues the mind of Christ with the sincerity of the single intention. The goal of Wesley's program was to attain perfect happiness, the fullness of God, and a readiness to meet death with confidence and peace. Therefore, inward holiness must be attained. Perfection is the heart of Wesley's gospel and the central aim of his program of holy living.

Since perfection, in some degree, must be attained to enter heaven, when could the believer hope to attain it? As we will soon see, Wesley held to a progressive understanding. One passes

---
[113] *On Love* III.8.
[114] The opening premise of JW's twin sermons on Job 3:17, *On Death and Deliverance* and *The Trouble and Rest of Good Men*.

through several stages in the process of renewal. But when were significant stages attained? What was the nature of these attainments? And, how were these stages attained on a personal level?

To recap, the process of renewal begins decisively in the moment of the single intention. From this point the "altogether" Christian grows in holiness and true righteousness. The next major stage is when perfect love is attained. When Wesley stood before his university audience on January 1, 1733 and proclaimed the rationale for the Holy Club's existence, he told his listeners that if they wanted to be perfect they needed to develop humility, faith, hope and the crowning jewel of love: "'Love is the fulfilling of the law,' 'the end of the commandment.' Very excellent things are spoken of love; it is the essence, the spirit, the life of all virtue. It is not only the first and great command, but it is all the commandments in one."[115] This is the kind of love his father partially tasted, and of which Henry Lascelles more fully experienced.

In an earlier sermon Wesley sought to remind his grieving audience that "this tedious dream, life, will be soon at an end, and then even with these eyes shall I gaze upon him; then shall I behold him again, and behold him with that perfect love, that sincere and elevated softness, to which even the heart of a parent is here a stranger!"[116] But before we experience the fullness of perfection in the glories of heaven, the believer must be freed from the stain of Adamic sin when the body is laid aside in death. In his first written sermon Wesley articulates himself very clearly as to when all sin is removed:

> Add to this that they are freed from the tyranny of sin, a yoke they could never hope to cast off entirely as long as they carried about them those mortal bodies in which the seeds of corruption were so deeply implanted. The law of our members is now continually warring against the law

---

[115] *The Circumcision of the Heart* I.11.
[116] *On Mourning for the Dead* § 3.

> of our mind, and even when we would do good, evil is present with us. But we lay down these infirmities with this veil of flesh, and the spirit will then be able as well as willing to perform its duty; and the more sensible we are of our present weakness, the more shall we rejoice at our deliverance from it.[117]

In this life there is no perfection that removes all sin from the heart. Wesley affirms the flesh is always with us, warring against the law of God revealed in the mind. Only in death is this tyranny "cast off entirely." Exactly ten years later he preached another sermon on the same text (Job 3:17), and drew the same conclusion:

> But as perfect holiness is not found on earth, so neither is perfect happiness: some remains of our disease will ever be felt, and some physic be necessary to heal it… Death will deliver us. Death shall set those free in one moment who were 'all their lifetime subject to bondage'. Death shall destroy at once the whole body of sin, and therewith of its companion, pain. And therefore, 'there the wicked cease from troubling, and there the weary be at rest.'[118]

This is a foundational truth in the Gospel of Holiness: Adam's stain is never fully removed in this life. As long as the Christian dwells in this mortal body, "some remains of our disease will ever be felt." These two sermons, one written at the beginning and the other at the end, serve as bookends to Wesley's early period. Only in death are the sins which pollute our love to God and neighbor finally destroyed. Wesley did believe in the destruction of original sin in the impartation of perfect love, yet he maintains that such purging only takes place in the article of death.

---

[117] *Death and Deliverance* §14.
[118] *The Trouble and Rest of Good Men* §P.

The Gospel of Holiness

Understanding Wesley's early position on the destruction of the carnal nature gives insight into the later antagonism he received from his co-workers in the revival. When Wesley began in 1739-40 to proclaim an attainable perfection in this life, both his Moravian and Calvinist colleagues were taken back by the thought. They reacted strongly to this message because they believed him to be teaching "sinless perfection." George Whitefield summarized what many felt when he told Wesley, "You have set a mark you will never arrive at, till you come to glory...O dear sir, many of God's children are grieved at your principles."[119] This response is understandable since Wesley had not taught up to this time the attainability of perfection in this life.

The Journey to Perfection

We now turn to his program of holy living. But before we do let's review what we have covered so far. Wesley began proclaiming his gospel of holiness in 1725, the year of his spiritual awakening. This profound experience forever shaped his character so that holiness became the DNA of his spiritual temperament.[120] Wesley's message centered on the biblical metanarrative of humanity's renewal in God's image through the transformation of the tempers. This goes to the core of his gospel message: the human heart, depraved and fallen, is now being restored to its pristine perfection through the redemptive work of Christ, the Second Adam. The goal of perfection is to prepare the believer for eternity in the presence of an absolutely holy, yet loving God. The demand of perfection, viewed as inward holiness, requires that the servant of God have a single intention to attain this perfection as the sole purpose of life. It is the single intention that Wesley, in his early period, normally emphasized as the beginning point of the faith journey. But there was an even

---

[119] JWL 11/9/40.
[120] Throughout this study DNA is used as shorthand for the core convictions that form JW's character, faith, and deep-seated beliefs.

earlier starting point within his *ordo salutis*. To understand the full orb of his early doctrine of perfection this is where we must begin.

When Wesley began his Aldersgate memoranda on May 24, 1735, he noted it was not until he was about ten years old that he had "sinned away" the washing of regeneration given to him in baptism. In a similar manner, his later *Treatise On Baptism* identified as one of the benefits baptism proffers, when duly administrated, is the grace of regeneration.[121] Wesley maintained a lifelong belief in baptism as the *ordinary* means[122] by which saving grace is initially received. This is seen in his firm support for infant baptism.[123] As the infant is christened in the name of the Holy Trinity, God graciously removes the guilt of Adam's sin and receives the child into his family. Baptism imparts present salvation and is the *ordinary* starting point of the faith journey toward perfection. Harold Lindstrom summarizes Wesley's perspective succinctly, "Following the orthodox view Wesley's places the commencement of the Christian life in man at baptism."[124]

---

[121] Works J 10:192. This tract was originally written by JW's father, Samuel. Though published by JW in 1756, many years after the period under study, the theology contained in this tract reflects JW's long-held beliefs on the subject.

[122] This is a key word in JW's doctrine of baptism. JW's baptismal doctrine is complex but consistent. In the *Treatise On Baptism* JW explains himself, "It is true, the Second Adam has found a remedy for the disease which came upon all by the offence of the first. But the benefit of this is to be received through the means which he hath appointed; through baptism in particular, which is the ordinary means he hath appointed for that purpose; and to which God has tied us, though he may not have tied himself" (Works J 10:193). Ole Borgan explains Wesley's main point, "The basis for such a statement (*as Wesley just made*) is that God may save through any of the means (such as the Word), or without any means at all. Thus, Baptism is not necessary for salvation in the absolute sense. None of the means are. If they were, then God would be tied to the ordinances and unable to save without such means, a limitation of God's freedom and omnipotence which Wesley would not allow" (*John Wesley on the Sacraments*, 123; italics mine).

[123] *A Treatise On Baptism* IV; Works J 10:193ff.

[124] *Wesley and Sanctification*, 106.

The Gospel of Holiness

But in good Arminian fashion Wesley maintained that grace can be lost through the commission of willful sin.[125] This opened the door for the need of the renewal process to begin again in the decision of the single intention. The single intention was further defined and explained through the use of evangelical terminology: resurrection to life,[126] giving the heart to God,[127] making a decision for God,[128] being born of God,[129] becoming a new creature,[130] having a new nature,[131] and possessing the indwelling presence of the Holy Spirit.[132] This means that only those who embrace such a resolution were considered "whole" Christians.[133]

By now it must be obvious that the Gospel of Holiness highlights the attainment of perfection through a process of degrees. This was hinted at above when we looked at the testimonies of his father Samuel and Mr. Lascelles.[134] The difference in degrees of attainment between these two men illustrates the processal nature of his early *ordo salutis*. The idea of stages or degrees comes early in Wesley's doctrinal development. This is apparent in his early correspondence with his mother.[135] In two of Susanna's let-

---

[125] *On Grieving the Holy Spirit* I.3. JW held strongly to the possibility of losing saving grace. See below on the discussion of Wesley's views on present forgiveness and assurance.

[126] *The Wisdom of Winning Souls* II "death to life." *One Thing Needful* III.1 "Awake, thou that sleepest, and arise from the dead."

[127] *The Love of God* III.8; *A Single Intention* P.1; II.9.

[128] *The Circumcision of the Heart* II.10; *A Single Intention* P.1.

[129] *The Circumcision of the Heart* I.9.

[130] *A Single Intention* II.9.

[131] *On Grieving the Holy* II.

[132] *On Grieving the Holy Spirit* I.1; The *Circumcision of the Heart* I.7, 10; *On Love* III.2.

[133] JWL 1/24/27. In *The Wisdom of Winning Souls* II JW refers to those who "use God and enjoy the world" as "half Christians." The whole Christian "use the world, but enjoys God."

[134] Cf. section: *The Timing of Perfection*.

[135] One of the examples of her pervading influence on her son is found in her letter to JW on February 23, 1725, (Works B 25:160). She exhorts him to make religion the "business" of his life, to ascertain the spiritual state of his

ters to her son in the summer of 1725 she refers to "greater degrees of Christian perfection."[136] By the early thirties Wesley began to articulate the specific stages a devoted follower passes through while on the faith journey toward full renewal. One way he did this was to make lists of inward virtues and then elaborate on their meaning. Here are three lists he published:

Preface to A Collection of Prayers (1732)	*The Circumcision of the Heart* (1733)	*Preface to Christian's Pattern* (1735)
Renouncing self	Humility	Humility
Devotion to God	Faith	Self-renunciation
Self-denial	Hope	Resignation
Mortification	Love	Union of will
Christ living within		Love

A comparison between the three lists is instructive. The first list is said by Wesley to comprise the "whole system of Christian duty." Renouncing self is a "thorough conviction that we are not our own," and includes the resolution to live accordingly. This "naturally leads to the devoting of ourselves to God." Repentance leads to the one thing needful: a single intention to live wholly unto God. This stage leads to the next level: denying self and taking up the cross daily. Sinful desires must be denied for the sake of God's will. By the "constant exercise of self-denial," the devoted Christian "continually advances in mortification," which is deadness to this world, until he or she can say "I am crucified unto the world; I am dead with Christ; I live not, but Christ liveth

---

soul, and whether he had a confident assurance of salvation. These became JW's major concerns as he pursued inward holiness.

[136] JWL 6/8/25; JWL 7/21/25. One thing to note is that Susanna never speaks of attaining Christian perfection in its fullness. All we can hope to attain is a "great degree."

The Gospel of Holiness

in me."[137] Since Wesley identifies the single intention with conversion, and here lists renouncing self before the single intention, the implication is that some understanding of prevenient grace already existed within his theology, yet undeveloped.

The Circumcision of the Heart parallels the same process but begins with the virtue of humility. The cultivation of humility produces inward contrition over sin that awakens a realization of spiritual need. Spiritual poverty roots out pride and vanity from the heart. Grace-inspired humility leads to further transformation through faith. Such faith is energized by the power of God to dispel carnal reasoning that feed evil habits. Saving faith inwardly sees that our calling is to glorify God, thereby leading the Christian to devote oneself completely to God. Having been born of God, the Holy Spirit gives the believer an assurance of being a child of God. The result of this confidence is an empowerment to engage in spiritual warfare and perseverance in troublesome times. Even though humility, faith, and hope have in "good measure cleansed (the) heart from its inbred pollution" (I.11), the crowning jewel of perfection is love. Love fulfils the Great Commandments. Love lets the human spirit return to God that gave it, with the "whole train of its affections." If the heart is filled with love, then nothing will be loved except for "his sake."

By comparing the two lists we see a relationship exists between the parallel virtues: renouncing self—humility; devotion—faith; self-denial/mortification—hope; Christ living within—love. To be noted is how faith serves as the foundation for full devotion to God. Wesley's understanding of saving faith will be further explored below.

The preface to the *Christian's Pattern* follows in a similar manner, "In order to attain this perfect love, there are several stages to be passed through: For it is necessary, not only that the soul be fully purged from all willful, habitual sin; but likewise

---

[137] *A Collection of Forms of Prayer for every Day of the Week. Sixth Edition 1775;* Works J 14:270-72.

that it be enlightened by the knowledge and practice of all virtue, before it can be united to God."[138]

Again, humility heads the list with self-renunciation moderating the "appetite" for "earthly and sensible things." This cleanses the soul from impurities so that heavenly things are desired. This leads to full unreserved resignation and consecration to God. Through these stages the sinful passions are purged. While it is through the "constant practice of all the virtues" that the soul is enlightened to further knowledge of God, the crowning jewel, once again, is perfect love: "such a union of our will with the divine as makes the Christian one spirit with God." So the journey to perfection begins with the single intention grounded in humility, the renunciation of the corrupted self, and moves through the stages of devotion, mortification, hope, and further consecration until perfect love is fully attained in death and eternal glory. What we see is a dual emphasis. Negatively, perfection removes all sin; positively, perfect love fills the heart. These are the twin motifs that will guide Wesley over time in developing his doctrine of Christian perfection.[139]

While his early program of holy living is often viewed as little more than a system of works, in reality early Wesley shunned all reliance upon oneself. Again, the homily *The Circumcision of the Heart* corrects this misunderstanding:

> At the same time we are convinced that we are not sufficient of ourselves to help ourselves; that without the Spirit of God we can do nothing but add sin to sin; that it is he alone 'who worketh in us' by his almighty power, either 'to will or do' that which is good—it being as impossible for us even to think a good thought without the supernatural assistance of his Spirit as to create ourselves, or to renew our whole souls in righteousness and true holiness.[140]

---

[138] *Preface to The Christian's Pattern* II.9; Works J 14:204.
[139] *Plain Account* ch 3 e.n.; 26:6b-7.
[140] *The Circumcision of the Heart* I.3.

The Gospel of Holiness

In the same sermon Wesley drives the point home:

> Our gospel, as it knows no other foundation of good works than faith, or of faith than Christ, so it clearly informs us we are not his disciples while we either deny him to be the author or his Spirit to be the inspirer and perfecter both of our faith and works. 'If any man have not the Spirit of Christ, he is none of his.' He alone can quicken those who are dead unto God, can breathe into them the breath of Christian life, and so prevent, accompany, and follow them with his grace as to bring their good desires to good effect. And 'as many as are thus led by the Spirit of God, they are the sons of God.' This is God's short and plain account of true religion and virtue; and 'other foundation can no man lay.'[141]

The Christian is to wholeheartedly pursue inward holiness through the appointed means of grace, but never to depend upon these efforts to merit heaven. With his interest in attaining inward holiness, it is no surprise that Wesley's program focused on cultivating the inward virtues. These virtues now require a closer look.

The foundation virtue is *humility*. Wesley's interest in humility began upon the heels of his spiritual awakening in 1725. His exchange of letters with his mother continually brings up the sub-

---

[141] *The Circumcision of the Heart* II.4. JW shares the same thought in a letter to William Wogan, "I entirely agree with you that religion is love and peace and joy in the Holy Ghost...So soon as God shall adorn my soul with them, and without any other than these, with the power of the Holy Ghost preventing, accompanying, and following me, I know that I (that is, the grace of God which is in me) shall save both myself and those who hear me!" (JWL 3/28/37). Again, this same truth is stated in the sermon *On Love*, "The chief sense of the words is doubtless this: that whatsoever we do, and whatsoever we suffer, if we are not renewed in the spirit of our mind by the love of God shed abroad in our hearts by the Holy Ghost given unto us, we cannot enter into life eternal" (III.2).

ject.[142] In one of these letters, Wesley's passing statement—"Humility is undoubtedly necessary to salvation"—reveals just how critical a role this virtue played in his *via salutis*. Several years later Wesley made the same point to a couple friends: humility is the "root of Christian virtue" and the "sole inlet to all virtue." [143] Humility is a "right judgment of ourselves" and cleanses our "minds from those high conceits" which our fallen nature deceitfully inspires. God uses humility to root out that primary sinful temper, pride, and "convinces us that in our best estate we are of ourselves all sin and vanity." Hence, humility is the beginning of the path toward perfection because it exposes our insufficiency and reveals our need for God's Spirit to "renew our whole souls in righteousness and true holiness."[144]

Wesley's understanding of humility is closely related to his concept of self-renunciation and informs his doctrine of prevenient grace. We saw above that such renunciation involves a "thorough conviction" that we do not belong to ourselves, the essence of pride, by pursuing our own desires and living for ourselves.[145] Through this knowledge of our "disease" we are prepared for the next stage in attaining perfection: saving faith.

Wesley's correspondence throughout the early period shows an intense interest in the nature of *faith*. Wesley scholars have often noted his struggles to understand faith as trust. They are quick to point out his tendency to define faith in terms of intellectual assent.[146] Kenneth Collins highlights Wesley's deficiency in

---

[142] Letters from Wesley 5/28/25, 6/18/25; letters from Susanna: 7/21/25, 8/18/25, 11/10/25.
[143] JWL 4/14/31; 10/3/31.
[144] *The Circumcision of the Heart* I.2; cf. *The Image of God* III.1 where humility is said to be the "first step" in the transformation process.
[145] Cf. note 130.
[146] "I call faith an assent upon rational grounds because I hold divine testimony to be the most reasonable of all evidence whatever. Faith must necessarily at length be resolved into reason. God is true, therefore what he says is true" (JWL 7/29/25). Susanna's response, "All faith is an assent, but all assent is not faith" (*Letter 8/18/25*). Susanna then pointed her son to see faith as an "assent to whatever God has revealed to us, because he has revealed it." In

grasping the correct nature of saving faith, and adds, that in spite of Susanna's correction and Wesley's agreement with her, he continued to define faith only as assent.[147]

However, a close reading of his early sermons does reveal he did see faith as trust. For example, in *Seeking First the Kingdom* Wesley calls upon his audience to trust God to provide all their needs:

> Wherefore, if God so clothe the grass, the common product of the field, 'which today is', appears beautiful and glorious…'shall he not much more clothe you, O ye of little faith?' —ye who after so many promises, and so many daily instances of his goodness, dare not trust so indulgent, so careful a father? (§3)

The same sermon speaks of the "certainty" of the promise ("all these things shall be added unto you" Matt 6:33) grounded upon the immutable character of God. Again, Wesley calls upon his audience to decisively exercise trust, "Here, therefore, we fix our belief" (§10). He appeals to his listeners to come to Christ to find "rest" (Matt 11:28): To those desiring happiness or relief from some misfortune, Christ imparts "quiet" to their souls; to those struggling with "extreme want" or a wounded spirit, Christ will meet their need. Wesley then gently appeals for a response of trust:

> Cast ye all your care on me, and I will exalt you in due time. Be ye firmly persuaded that the things you so much desire either are not for your real advantage, however they may appear to you who see through a glass darkly; or that if they are they shall most certainly be added to those that

---

other words, faith is not rooted in reason but in God's immutable nature and revelation. Wesley later included assent in his definition of faith, but was careful to point out that faith involves much more than mere intellectual assent. See *The Circumcision of the Heart* I.7; *Salvation By Faith* I.4.

[147] *John Wesley: A Theological Journey*, 37.

learn of me when I, the most proper judge, see a convenient season. (§13)

Faith as trust is implicitly present in many of his early sermons. Simply stated, early Wesley has been somewhat misread on the subject of faith: *Aldersgate did not introduce faith as trust into Wesley's soteriology.* He did hold to an evangelical understanding on the nature of saving faith *before* his return to England in 1738. We must postpone for now why Wesley's early concept of saving faith was deficient, but it was not because he believed faith to be only assent and not trust. [148]

Finally, there are the inward virtues of *mortification, resignation, hope* and *love*. The reader, by now, should have a clear sense of what Wesley understood regarding the necessity of mortification (dying to sin) and resignation (submissive, yielded heart). We will suspend our treatment of hope until our study on his doctrine of assurance, since the two are closely related. As for the inward virtue of love we can briefly recap what has been covered above. We saw that the goal of perfection is the renewal of the human race in the image and likeness of God. Specifically, this means that a transformation of the dispositional nature is required: replacing Adamic corruption with Christ's holy nature.

This process of renewal was early seen as a recovery of that perfect love, which Adam lost and Christ enjoined in the two Great Commandments. We saw that Wesley's interest in perfect love increased in the early 1730's as he came into contact with the writings of several mystics. From this influence he began to extol perfection as the fullness of love.[149] In the fall of 1733 he preached to his university audience that love could be understood in two senses. First, there is the love of delight. Every reasonable

---

[148] In a letter to Richard Morgan Wesley confirms that faith is a temper of the heart, "…those tempers which alone are acceptable to God, and procure acceptance for which our Redeemer lived and died, are, (i), Faith, without which it is still impossible either to please him or to overcome the world…" (3/15/34; Works B 25:382).

[149] *The Circumcision of the Heart* I.11-13.

creature is to love God for his power, wisdom, goodness, and other perfections. Then there is love of benevolence. According to the latter sense, "'We love Him', says the Apostle, 'because he first loved us.'"[150] Love became the central and primary conceptual model Wesley used to teach, proclaim, expound, and defend his doctrine of perfection. As a means to attaining inward holiness, love became the inner drive that fueled the other virtues.[151]

So love became both the means and the goal of perfection. Wesley definitely saw love to be the spirit behind his program of holy living. Since some degree of Adamic corruption always remains in this life, full and complete perfection in love will only be realized in the article of death and in the resurrection. Only then will the redeemed see and delight in God as he truly is, in all his infinite perfections.

The Means of Grace

Wesley's holy living program relied heavily on the means of grace. When Wesley wrote to Mary Granville in December 1730, he spelled out the role which the means play in attaining holiness, "If our ultimate end is to love God, to which the several particular Christian virtues lead us, so the means leading to these are to communicate every possible time…(and) to pray without ceasing."[152] Their role is clear: The means of grace serve as the normal channels through which God graciously infuses holy dispositions within the heart. Through the means of grace we attain the inward virtues, and by the acquisition of these virtues we attain perfect love. Accordingly, Wesley saw the faithful practice of the means of grace as essential to the renewal process.

Wesley always held definite views on the efficacy of *Holy Communion*. He believed that when the believer communicated

---

[150] *On Love* I.3; quoting 1 John 4:19. JW quotes this text often throughout his ministerial career.
[151] *The Christian Pattern* II.4, Works J 14:203.
[152] JWL 12/12/30.

in a worthy manner, with "faith, humility, and thankfulness," their prior sins were *"ipso facto* forgiven."[153] This benefit alone motivated Wesley and his Holy Club colleagues to communicate whenever possible. In 1732 he transcribed an extract of Nonjuror Robert Nelson's *Companion for the Festivals and Fasts of the Church of England (1704)* for his students at Lincoln College. This extract was later rewritten by Wesley and published as a sermon in 1787, demonstrating continuity in his sacramental theology over his lifetime. The sermon lists several blessings for partaking, including forgiveness of past sins and the enablement to exercise faith, love, obedience, and repentance. In this way communicating serves as a powerful means in the faith journey toward perfection. Following the counsel of the Apostle Paul in 1 Corinthians 11, Wesley exhorted his readers to prepare themselves by self-examination and prayer. The Lord's Table serves as an outward sign of inward grace, offering the sincere believer the merits of Christ's death and resurrection.[154]

The next means to be mentioned often is *prayer*. In the letter just quoted above, Wesley gave further exhortations to Mary Granville to be not content with set times of prayer, whether public or private, but to at "all times and in all places" offer up spontaneous "ejaculations" of intercourse to God. The holy life is a prayer-filled, prayer-saturated life. So important was prayer that Wesley published a collection of prayers in 1732, titled *A Collection of Forms of Prayer for Every Day in the Week*.[155]

---

[153] JWL 6/18/25 (italics his).
[154] *The Duty of Constant Communion* I.2-6. An excellent study on JW's sacramental theology is Ole Borgen's *John Wesley On The Sacraments: A Definitive Study of John Wesley's Theology of Worship*. Borgen writes, "The Lord's Supper does not only function as a memorial which *shows* Christ's death and suffering; in it, by the power of the Holy Spirit and through the enabling means of faith, time and space are transcended. Christ does not only invite men *to* his sacrifice; he actually offers to make his sacrifice theirs: as he offers himself to God, so he offers himself to man" (183, italics his). Therefore, Holy Communion serves as a powerful means for attaining perfection.
[155] The preface is found in Works J 14:270.

The Gospel of Holiness

Another means is *Holy Scripture*.[156] In the *Plain Account* Wesley notes that it was upon his return to Oxford that he became *homo unius libri*.[157] While his early sermons do not have the same biblical orientation and grounding as his later ones, they still contain numerous scripture references and expositions. The sermon *On Corrupting the Word of God* stands as a model expressing the seriousness by which young John Wesley took the Bible as God's word. This homily condemns those who corrupt the scriptures by introducing heresy, false interpretations, or who subtract from the message by prophesying "smooth things" that satisfy the "taste of their hearers" (I.3). Ten years later Wesley told Mary Chapman:

> I feed my brethren in Christ, as he giveth me power, with the pure unmixed milk of his Word. And those who are as little children receive it, not as the word of man, but as the Word of God. Some grow thereby, and advance apace in peace and holiness.[158]

The "pure unmixed milk" of Holy Scripture advances the believer in holiness by imparting knowledge of God, which the "natural man" cannot discern. Later, he defined such knowledge as "inward, practical, experimental, (and) feeling knowledge." Wesley believed salvific knowledge is not derived from "com-

---

[156] In *The Preface to the Christian's Pattern* II.4 scripture is listed as a "chief instrument" in attaining perfection.

[157] Meaning: a man of one book. *Plain Account* 5:1 & 10:29. 5:1 locates the year as 1729 while 10:29 says it was in 1730. This difference is easily reconciled when we remember JW returned to Oxford in the middle of November 1729. It was soon after that he recalls experiencing a further spiritual awakening that focused his attention on scripture as the "only standard of truth, and the only model of pure religion" (5:1).

[158] JWL 3/29/37. On a side note, this letter contains the earliest reference this author has found of JW quoting 1 Thessalonians 5:16-18 in relation to perfection. This text plays an important role in the later development of JW's doctrine of perfect love (See PA 26:7). Two earlier letters, JWL 12/12/30 and 11/17/31, refer to vv 16 and 17 individually, but not to all three verses.

mentaries" but by those "readers who have read the same things in their own souls;" that is, experientially.[159] The scriptures serve as a powerful means for the life transformation process.

As God's word serves as a means to instill godly character, so the practice of *fasting* serves to regulate the appetites and affections. In 1732 the Holy Club began to faithfully keep the stationary fasts of the early church on Wednesdays and Fridays. Nothing was supposed to be eaten before 3 p.m. on those days. The practice of fasting was later applied to other areas of diet. On his trip to America in 1735, Wesley records that "believing the denying of ourselves, even in the smallest instances, might by the blessing of God be helpful to us, we wholly left off the use of flesh and wine, and confined ourselves to vegetable food, chiefly rice and biscuit."[160] Closely allied to fasting was the practice of *early rising*. Holy Club members were expected to rise at four in the morning for prayer and other devotions. These disciplines were designed to regiment self-denial and the mortification of the affections.

Another important means of grace was the forming of *resolutions* for the purpose of self-evaluation. Wesley specifically lists this practice in his preface to *The Christian's Pattern* (II.13) along with prayer, scripture, and communicating. The writing out of resolutions for self-examination was a fairly popular activity at the time.[161] Heitzenrater offers good clarification of Wesley's purpose, "Contrary to the impression carried by many of his contemporaries and perpetuated by subsequent analysts, Wesley's lifestyle (and that of the Oxford Methodists) was neither circumscribed by negative injunctions nor impelled primarily by a set of rules. Their actions were guided by lists of questions for self-examination that were arranged according to the virtues for each

---

[159] *The Preface to the Christian's Pattern* III.6.

[160] JWJ 10/20/35.

[161] For example, across the Atlantic the young Jonathan Edwards composed seventy resolutions to guide his spiritual development (*The Works of Jonathan Edwards* Vol. I, Edinburgh UK: The Banner of Truth Trust, 1834, reprint 1979; page xx)

day of the week: love for God, love for neighbor, humility, mortification and self-denial, resignation and meekness, and thanksgiving."[162] The practice of self-evaluation through the asking of questions was later incorporated in the *Rules of the Band Societies*[163] and in Wesley's many letters to seekers of perfection.[164] To Mary Pendarves, Wesley offered counsel concerning those means that "seldom" fail:

> Are you attentive in prayer? Pray oftener. Do you address God twice a day already? Then do so three times. Do you find yourself very uneasy before sacrament, though you receive it every month? Your next resolution, with God's leave, should be to receive it every week. [165]

Sometimes, instead of asking pertinent questions, Wesley offered succinct exhortations that serve the same purpose. To Mary Chapman he followed up several questions in the first part of a letter with a series of biblical injunctions: "Be fervent in spirit! Rejoice evermore! Pray without ceasing! In everything give thanks! Do everything in the name of the Lord Jesus. Abound more and more in all holiness, and in zeal for every good word and work!"[166]

Wesley does not specifically mention *fellowship* as a means of grace, but his practice of cultivating groups, first at Oxford (the first rise of Methodism), and then in America (the second rise of Methodism), for the sole purpose of pursuing holiness reveals just how important a role fellowship played in his program. The same conclusion can be drawn from his correspondence.

---

[162] *Wesley and the People Called Methodists*, 47.
[163] Works B 9:77
[164] In later correspondence JWL 1/27/58; 2/10/58; 4/23/71; 1/22/72. See ch 6.
[165] JWL 8/12/31.
[166] JWL 3/29/37. Scripture references JW quotes are Rom 12:11; 1 Th 5:16-18; Col 3:17; 1 Th 4:1; 2 Th 2:17. See JW's Journal for his apologetic letter to Richard Morgan wherein are listed a series of questions to critics of the Holy Club (Works B 18:128).

John Wesley's Theology of Christian Perfection

Wesley was an avid letter writer and his interest in promoting holiness in other people is a characteristic of his early letters.[167] Wesley would later say, "The gospel of Christ knows no religion, but social; no holiness but social holiness."[168] This was one of the reasons he gave to his father for not accepting the curate position at Epworth in 1734. Wesley felt that staying at Oxford offered a better environment for the promotion of personal holiness and of salvation. One of those advantages was fellowship:

> The first of these is daily converse with my friends...To have such a number of such friends constantly watching over my soul...administrating reproof, advice, or exhortation, with all plainness and all gentleness, is a blessing I have not yet found any Christian to enjoy in any part of the kingdom. And such a blessing it is, so conducive, if faithfully used, to the increase of all holiness, as I defy anyone to know the full value of till he receives his full measure of glory.[169]

After a few years of drinking in the mystic authors, by 1736 Wesley began to turn away from their vision on how to attain perfection. His main argument was their diminution of the means of grace, including their tendency to view religion as a solitary enterprise. According to mystic theology, everything is love and only love; therefore, "choose such means as lead you most to love; those alone are necessary."[170] As a good Anglican, Wesley could not stomach such theology for very long. Fellowship would always play a powerful role in his program of holy living and became one of his most significant legacies to the Christian church: holiness is always social in nature.

Another means of grace is *Sabbath-keeping*. So important was this to the young Oxford don that he wrote an entire sermon

---

[167] Cf. chapter 6.
[168] *Preface to Hymns and Sacred Poems I* §5; Works J 14:321.
[169] JWL 12/10/34.
[170] JWL 11/23/36.

on the subject. Albert Outler informs us in his introduction that a Sabbath controversy ensued between the Puritans and Anglicans for well over a century leading up to Wesley's day. Wesley, an Anglican priest, surprisingly sided with the Puritans.

Foundationally, Wesley believed the Sabbath to be still in force since God never officially repealed it (I.1). Of course, he believed the Christian Sabbath to be on Sunday and not Saturday. He then offers three overlapping reasons for continued Sabbath observance. First, the "great end" of Sabbath observance is the imitation of God. Just as God worked six days and rested the seventh, so man, by working six days and resting on the seventh, learns to "remember who it was that created" him (I.2).

This leads to the Sabbath's second purpose: to lead to a fuller knowledge of God. The various Jewish holidays and Sabbaths taught the Israelites that God was the source of their virtue and happiness (I.3). As the believer keeps God's Sabbath, one learns God is their source for holiness and his departure leads to a lapse into "sin and misery."

These two purposes lead to the final reason for Sabbath keeping: to make the Christian "holy as God is holy" (I.4). God's purpose is that "having finished his six days," God's servant "might on the seventh retire from this world, and ascend in heart and mind into the heaven of heavens" in worship of God with prayer and praise (I.2; III.1). God thereby restores "lost man to pardon and peace," and gives him a "second, better life of holiness," which is the "noblest gift" (III.1). Wesley then gets to the heart of the matter:

> We must now especially work together with him; we must labour to conform ourselves to his likeness, to be holy as he is holy. We must make it our peculiar business to perfect his image in our souls, to bind mercy and truth about our neck, to write them deep on the tablet of our heart. (III.1)

John Wesley's Theology of Christian Perfection

Since the Gospel of Holiness centered on the *imago Dei*, it empowered a vision that calls the Christian to make it their "peculiar business" to become perfect as their heavenly Father is perfect (Matt 5:48). Yet, this gospel message did not rest here. In accordance with his Arminian convictions, Wesley firmly maintained that this vision involves a synergism of God and believer working together for the latter's dispositional transformation. This basic soteriological orientation will never change throughout Wesley's career.

Finally, we need to look at Wesley's attitude toward *persecution*. Though persecution is not listed formally as a means, Wesley's letters reveal that he did see such suffering as a quasi-means for the promotion of inward holiness.[171] In the fall of 1732 rumors began to spread around Oxford and beyond that William Morgan's death had been caused by the rigorous disciplines of the Holy Club. In October Wesley penned an apologetic letter to William's father, Richard, explaining the Club's program and goals. As pubic criticism and notoriety of the group began to spread, Wesley's ability to be unflinching in the face of persecution begins to emerge. In response to Richard Morgan, Wesley dismisses his critics' name-calling as a "compliment." He than adds, "We have not so learned Christ as to renounce any part of his service, though men should say all manner of evil against us."[172]

This ability to become "stubborn" when facing opposition is a trait that will remain with John Wesley throughout his life. When the Sophy Williamson incident exploded in Georgia during the

---

[171] In a letter to his father (12/10/34) JW identifies persecution with a state of salvation, "Till he be thus contemned, no man is in a state of salvation…contempt is a part of the cross…the badge of discipleship, the stamp of his profession, the constant seal of his calling, insomuch that though a man may be despised without being saved, yet he cannot be saved without being despised" (Works B 25:406-07).

[172] JWL 10/19/32. See also Richard Heitzenrater, *The Elusive Mr. Wesley: John Wesley His Own Biographer*, 63.

The Gospel of Holiness

summer of 1737,[173] Wesley's attitude toward persecution becomes quite revealing.

In the sermon *On Love*, an allusion to Jesus' parable of the sower is made in passing when persecution is said to arise because of the Word,[174] implying that all true followers of Christ will face persecution. As the Word imparts grace to the heart, so it is by facing persecution that the powers of darkness are defeated. When we remember that the Gospel of Holiness was designed to prepare one for death and eternity, it should not surprise us that Wesley saw martyrdom (literally and figuratively) as a means of grace. When Wesley read David Humphreys' account that nine out of ten missionaries in America were suffering martyrdom, he wrote to Mr. Humphreys:

> When God shall put it into the hearts of some of his servants, whom he hath already delivered from earthly hopes and fears, to join hand in hand in this labor of love; when out of these he shall have chosen one or more to magnify him in the sight of the heathen by dying, not in stoical or Indian indifference, but blessing and praying for their murderers, and praising God in the midst of the flame, with joy unspeakable and full of glory; then the rest, 'waxing bold by their sufferings', shall go forth in the name of the Lord god, and by the power of his might cast down every high thing that exalteth itself against the faith of Christ.[175]

As Wesley's situation in the Williamson affair soured, Sophy's uncle charged him with several indictments. Of course, Wesley saw himself as innocent in the entire ordeal. This led him to see himself as persecuted for doing what he thought were the pre-

---

[173] It is not our purpose to go into the history of such incidences. Our focus is on the evolution of JW's theology of perfection. The reader will find ample coverage of this incident in the standard JW biographies.
[174] Matthew 13:21. *On Love* P.1.
[175] JWL 7/22/37. See also JWL 6/16/37.

rogatives of his office. Though we don't have the letter John wrote to his brother Charles (who was now back in England), we do have Charles' response. In his letter to John, Charles echoes his brother's "martyr" theology by glorifying the persecution John was facing in Georgia. Charles felt nothing but "joy" and believed that *now* John had become a "disciple of Christ." He then quotes the New Testament, which promises that all of Jesus' followers will suffer persecution.[176] Charles reminds his brother, "You *know* the absolute impossibility of being inwardly conformed to Christ without this outward conformity, this badge of discipleship, these marks of Christ."[177] The Gospel of Holiness demands that we surrender our all if we are to possess fully the nature of Christ, even if the price is our life.

But the tendency of Wesley's program was to focus heavily on outward disciplines to transform inward dispositions. This implicitly led to reliance upon one's works, even if such trust was officially repudiated. Wesley later made the same point in 1739 when he acknowledged that for ten years he had been "fundamentally a Papist, and knew it not."[178] Yet, when we look at the chosen means in light of his overall theology, this conclusion must be tempered. For we saw above that Wesley's message contained a strong emphasis on the Holy Spirit dynamically living within the true Christian. Wesley would later come to the same conclusion when he reevaluated his Aldersgate conversion in the 1770's.[179]

These insights will need to be remembered when we look into what really happened at Aldersgate and why his perfection theology evolved as it did. The rigor of Wesley's punctuality in maintaining his program of holy living offers insight into why he chose to go to America. This brings us to one of the most important subjects in Wesley's early period: his doctrine of assurance.

---

[176] Quoted is John 15:20; 2 Timothy 3:12
[177] JWL 1/2/38 (emphasis his).
[178] JWJ 8/27/39.
[179] This subject will be explored in chapter 4.

The Gospel of Holiness

Assurance

On the eve of his departure Wesley acknowledged that his chief motive for going to America was to save his own soul, "I hope to learn the true sense of the gospel of Christ by preaching it to the heathens." Wesley wanted to find the "right faith" that would "open the way for a right practice…toward mortifying the lust of the flesh, (and) the desire of sensual pleasures."[180] Wesley then explains his meaning. In America he will have only simple food to live on, no women to arouse his lusts, no pomp or show to awaken any pride, and he hopes no situations will arise that will cause him to lose his tongue.[181] So, what he really sought was an uncorrupted environment in which to pursue with utmost singularity the perfecting of his own salvation.

Heitzenrater mistakenly concludes from this letter that Wesley went to America out of anxiety due to a lack of assurance over his salvation.[182] But Wesley's explanation requires a more nuanced reading in light of the letter's contents and his overall soteriology. Many have assumed that throughout his early period Wesley suffered from an almost chronic plague of anxiety over his eternal state. This author confesses that he too had subscribed to this interpretation. However, a careful reading of Wesley's letters, diary, journal and sermons reveal a different story.

For example, when the subject of assurance is raised today, we naturally think of a person's eternal destiny. When we ask a seeker "If you died tonight, are you sure you would go to heaven?" we are addressing their level of confidence or assurance in relation to their eternal destiny. So it is often assumed that when Wesley raised the subject of assurance he was questioning his eternal salvation. *This assumption is wrong and leads to a mistaken reading of Wesley's intention.* Why is early Wesley misread regarding his spiritual state? One probable reason is an

---

[180] JWL 10/1/35.
[181] JW confesses he has a problem controlling his tongue.
[182] Essay: *Great Expectations: Aldersgate and the Evidences of Genuine Christianity*; in Maddox, Randy Ed. *Aldersgate Reconsidered*, 61-62.

over-reliance on his Aldersgate memorandum in which he strongly scrutinizes his prior faith journey.[183] Since this is the subject of the next chapter we need not focus on that evaluation at this time.

What is important to note is *why* Wesley says he is going to America. Yes, he is going to learn the "true sense of the gospel." Yes, he is going to learn a "right faith." But it is the rest of the letter that conveys his meaning. Wesley is confident he already *knows* the gospel message; what he wants to *learn* is the true spirit of the gospel: a greater impartation of inward holiness within his life.

In other words, Wesley did not go to America because he lacked assurance over his eternal salvation. Instead, he chose to go because he believed America to be an environment better suited for him to learn experientially the nature of God's holiness.[184] Thus, he hoped to receive a greater degree of assurance when he attained a higher degree of holiness, thereby preparing himself to face death and eternity with even greater confidence. This distinction is crucial if we are to grasp his meaning in his later journal remarks upon his return to England.[185] The simple truth is John Wesley did not agonize over his eternal state as deeply as is often assumed.

---

[183] JWJ 5/24/38.

[184] It is important to add here that when William Morgan died there is not the slightest hint that his eternal destiny was ever in jeopardy. See the eulogy written by JW's brother Samuel, Works B 18:133-135.

[185] JW's words need to be read very carefully and in context. An illustration is found many years later in the 1746 Conference Minutes. The question is asked, "Wherein does our doctrine now differ from that we preached when at Oxford? Answer. Chiefly in these two points: 1. We then knew nothing of the righteousness of faith in justification; nor 2. Of the nature of faith itself as implying consciousness of pardon" (Outler, *John Wesley*, 160). We have already noted above that early JW did not have any concept of present justification, and he did not grasp faith as he did later at Aldersgate. But to understand #2 to say that JW had no concept of present assurance or pardon while at Oxford is not true, as we will see shortly. The key is to note that he speaks here of pardon grounded solely upon faith. In this sense it is true. But JW did have an understanding of present forgiveness in his GosH.

The Gospel of Holiness

Like a three-legged stool, Wesley's early doctrine of assurance was grounded on a three-prong approach, involving God, the believer, and the appointed means of grace. Let's look at each in turn.

We have already seen that early Wesley's doctrine of assurance was based on the presence of the Spirit within the Christian's heart. On January 1, 1733, Wesley boldly proclaimed before the university that the distinguishing mark of a genuine Christian is the circumcision of the heart. This "mark," says Wesley, belongs to every person, "who *is* in a state of acceptance with God."[186] Note the present tense of the word "is". The inward circumcision of the Spirit begins with the spiritual awakening of the single intention. The true Christian is on the path of regeneration—possessing a new nature and becoming a new creature in Christ—and to that degree is in a state of acceptance with God.[187] Even though the process of regeneration is never fully complete until the eschatological resurrection, Wesley was explicit that the Christian does have a radiant hope. For God's Spirit witnesses to the believer their eternal salvation.[188]

A second ground for assurance involves the present forgiveness of sins. In the section on the means of grace we saw that his sacramental theology understood Holy Communion to provide a present pardon for sin. When Wesley transcribed Robert Nelson's sermon in 1732, he plainly declared that one of the benefits of communicating was the "forgiveness of our past sins." Soon after his spiritual awakening in 1725 Wesley expressed the same point to his mother:

---

[186] *The Circumcision of the Heart* P.3 (emphasis mine).
[187] See the section above, *Spiritual Awakening*.
[188] Many quotes have already been provided to demonstrate this point. See *The Circumcision of the Heart* I.9, II.5; *The Trouble and Rest of Good Men* II.5-6; *Single Intention* II.9; *On Love* III.5-8. The Christian's eternal salvation is *never* questioned in any of JW's sermons. Instead, JW constantly affirms, explicitly and implicitly, the "whole" Christian has no need to fear facing death.

> If his (Taylor) opinion be true, I must own I have always been in a great error; for I imagined that when I communicated worthily, i.e. with faith, humility, and thankfulness, my preceding sins were *ipso facto* forgiven me – I mean, so forgiven that unless I fell into them again I might be secure of their ever rising in judgment against me, at least in the other world.[189]

In a sermon he transcribed and preached to the prisoners at the Castle in the early 1730's, Wesley refers to those who have "known his pardoning love."[190] Yet, he also held that our final forgiveness would not be fully realized until we pass to that happy shore, "I hear a voice from heaven saying, Come away, and rest from thy labors; 'thy warfare is accomplished, thy sin is pardoned,' 'and the days of thy mourning are ended.'"[191] This dual emphasis on present and future forgiveness laid the ground for an understanding of forgiveness within the process of sanctification. In other words, just as inward holiness is attained by degrees, so our forgiveness is attained by degrees. In a letter to his mother Susanna, Wesley appears to confuse forgiveness with sanctification:

> What I so much like is his (Taylor's) account of the pardon of sins, which is the clearest I ever met with:
>
>> Pardon of sins in the Gospel is sanctification: 'Christ came to take away our sin by turning every one of us from our iniquities.' (Acts 3:26)...As we hate sin, and grow in grace, and arrive at the state of holiness...in the same degree we are to judge concerning the forgiveness of sins. For indeed that is the evangelical forgiveness, and it signifies our pardon, because it affects it; or rather, it is in the

---

[189] JWL 6/18/25.
[190] *On Grieving the Holy Spirit* I.2, Works J 7:488.
[191] *The Trouble and Rest of Good Men* II.6.

The Gospel of Holiness

> nature of the thing, so that we are to inquire into no hidden records. Forgiveness of sins is not a secret sentence, a word, or a record. But it is a state of change, and effected upon us; and upon ourselves we are to look for it, to read it and understand it.
>
> In all this he (Taylor) appears to steer in the middle road exactly: to give assurance of pardon to the penitent, but to no one else.[192]

Wesley's attention was so focused on the attainment of inward holiness that it colored his understanding of all other doctrines. While avoiding the Calvinist interpretation of some secret divine decree or counsel, he swings the pendulum to the other extreme and absorbs forgiveness within the sanctification process. This failure to properly discriminate between the two led to the error of not connecting present pardon to a present justification.

Throughout his early period Wesley consistently held that justification takes place only at the last judgment. Aldersgate will radically alter this aspect of his doctrinal system. Wesley will later learn to distinguish between what God does *for* us from what he does *in* us. The former refers to our legal standing before God, while the latter involves our renewal in God's image.[193] Even so, Wesley continued to believe in double justification throughout his life.[194]

But present assurance was not limited to the Holy Spirit's purifying presence or to present forgiveness of sins. Wesley also

---

[192] JWL 2/28/30. JW's concluding statement seems to say that he did not fully link forgiveness to sanctification. After all, the present penitent enjoys an assurance of pardon even though the sanctification process remains unfinished. The quotation does demonstrate that sanctification was the controlling motif in his early soteriology.

[193] "The plain scriptural notion of justification is pardon, the forgiveness of sins." *Justification by Faith* II.5.

[194] See Kenneth Collins discussion on final justification in *The Scripture Way of Salvation*, 191-204.

stressed present assurance upon one's sincerity: the integrity of the single intention. We begin with his correspondence to his mother in July 1725, "I am persuaded we may know if we are *now* in a state of salvation, since that is expressly promised in the Holy Scriptures to our sincere endeavors, and we are surely able to judge of our own sincerity."[195]

Later that fall he reminds his audience of the promise of God to provide for the needs of those who "sincerely seek the kingdom of God and his righteousness."[196] Some years later, when counseling a friend he again asserts, "The shield of faith will yet repel all his darts, if she can be taught to use it skillfully, if 'the eyes of her understanding can be enlightened to see what is the hope of our calling', to know that our hope is sincerity, not perfection, not to do well, but to do our best. If God were to mark all that is done amiss, who could abide?"[197]

A year earlier he told his mother, "If God be true, and I am sincere, then I am to hope; but God is true, and I am sincere (There is the pinch); Therefore, I am to hope."[198] Then, in 1733 Wesley gave his university audience the rationale for grounding assurance on one's sincerity, "God requires from man only what he can do and what grace provides, not impossibilities."[199]

This explanation receives fuller treatment in an unpublished sermon manuscript on the two covenants:

---

[195] JWL 7/29/25 (emphasis his). JW also writes in this letter, "We can never be so certain of the pardon of our sins as to be assured they will never rise up against us I firmly believe. We know that they will infallibly do so if ever we apostatize, and I am not satisfied what evidence there can be of our final perseverance, till we have finished our course." JW here affirms present forgiveness, but not unconditional eternal forgiveness.

[196] *Seek First the Kingdom* §11. Earlier that same year he told his mother, "I am persuaded we may know if we are *now* in a state of salvation, since that is expressly promised in the Holy Scriptures to our sincere endeavors, and we are surely able to judge of our own sincerity" (JWL 7/29/25).

[197] JWL 10/3/31.

[198] JWL 2/28/30.

[199] *The Circumcision of the Heart* II.6.

The Gospel of Holiness

> The covenant of God with man before the Fall was 'Do this and live.' ...This was the condition of that covenant, perfect obedience; to keep fully every law of God. But fallen man could no longer do this; a new covenant was therefore made, wherein God promised the same reward to man, but upon different conditions... 'Try to do this and live.' ...Use thy best endeavors to do everything which I command. Perfect obedience was made the condition of the first covenant; earnest, hearty obedience [the condition] of the second. 'Keep every law of God so far as thou canst'; obey every word of his mouth so far as thou art able; do the whole will of thy Creator in as full a manner as is in thy power: these were the conditions of the new. To those who perform these, he promises life; those who do not, have nothing to do with his promises. Observe that both the covenants agree in this, that both require man to do all he can.[200]

Like humility, sincerity was a cardinal virtue in Wesley's early system. In 1728 he devoted an entire sermon to the dangers of being insincere. Sincerity is said to be a "god-like virtue" possessing "beauty, honourableness, and wisdom."[201] This goes to the heart of Wesley's Gospel of Holiness. What God looks for is a single intention. This is the point, the moment when true religion begins in the heart. Where the single intention lives, real Christianity is to be found; where this intention is lacking, only a nominal faith exists. Therefore, the integrity of the single intention offers a sure foundation of God's final acceptance.

There is affinity between Wesley's early doctrine of assurance and that found in the contemporary evangelical church. The contemporary church in her evangelism places great emphasis upon sincerity as a basis for salvation assurance. All salvation tracts this author is aware of assure the seeker that if they truly

---

[200] *Sermons IV, Appendix C*; Works B 4:527-528.
[201] *On Dissimulation* P.3.

repent, and in faith pray with *sincerity* to receive Christ, they can have confidence they are saved (justified and born again). Often, scripture texts are shared that emphasize assurance upon the seeker's *sincere* decision.[202]

The point being made is not to challenge the validity of assurance upon one's sincerity, but to highlight a similarity between Wesley's Gospel of Holiness and the gospel message presented today. In a similar way, little weight is placed today on Wesley's doctrine of the Spirit's direct witness as the ground for assurance, even by many who claim his mantle. Could it be that in regard to assurance the church today has more affinity with early Wesley than with middle or late Wesley?[203]

So we see that Wesley's doctrine of assurance did not demand absolute perfection for one to have a confident hope of eternal life. First, the Holy Spirit imparts a "clear and cheerful confidence" to them that are "upright toward God."[204] Second, the benefits of the Lord's Table provide a precious sense of present forgiveness. Third, while Wesley held muddled views over the nature of present forgiveness in relation to sanctification, he did maintain a very clear position on sincerity as a ground for assurance of eternal life. Yet, as we will learn in the next chapter, all three of these supports failed him when he came face-to-face with the awesome power of a hurricane.

Perfection as Sole Pursuit

At the heart of the Gospel of Holiness is a spiritual awakening rooted in the single intention to attain perfection as the goal

---

[202] In the popular tract *Steps to Peace with* God (Billy Graham Evangelistic Association) Romans 10:13 and Ephesians 2:8-9 are quoted. The seeker is then asked, "Did you sincerely ask Jesus Christ to come into your life?" The other scripture text quoted is 1 John 5:12-13.

[203] I believe this is true even of the Holiness Movement and the churches that have formed out of it.

[204] *The Circumcision of the Heart* I.9.

of life. What Adam lost; Christ regains. What the serpent stole; Christ restores. We were created in God's image and likeness, but Adam's fall has effaced the beauty of our original, "pristine" righteousness. The human race now finds itself enslaved to various sinful passions and desires. The nature of our disease highlights the kind of redemption needed if we are to be reclaimed to perfection: the transformation of our dispositional nature. The essential character of our salvation revolves around the question of sanctification with perfection entailing inward holiness.

To this end Wesley developed an entire regimen for the cultivation of inward virtues within the heart. Life transformation became his motto as he pursued with vigor holiness of heart and life. Anything less than wholehearted devotion, marked by thoroughness of life transformation, was to be despised because only with the firmness of the single intention could the seeker attain the end for which he or she was created.

Wesley saw that to enter God's eternal kingdom one had to attain his righteousness.[205] Holiness thus became the "great end and design of all religion." He continually exhorts those under his care to jealously guard their souls so that no "mixture" would pollute their pure devotion to God.[206] There is only "one thing needful"…the "renewal of our fallen nature."[207]

Wesley often turned to the words of Jesus to make his point: if "our eye is single our whole body will be full of light, so, should it ever cease to be single, in that moment our whole body would be full of darkness."[208] This promise motivated him to tenaciously pursue holy tempers in every area of life, even to the point of obsession.[209] So concerned was he to be the best Chris-

---

[205] *Seek First the Kingdom* §7.
[206] *One Thing Needful* III.3.
[207] *One Thing Needful* I.2; *The Circumcision of the Heart* I.13.
[208] *One Thing Needful* III.2. JW's paraphrase of Matthew 6:23.
[209] In 1733-34 JW began an "exacter" diary to measure his religious temperament every hour of the day. See Heitzenrater, *The Elusive Mr. Wesley, Vol. 1*, 57.

tian he could be, that by 1735 he began to distinguish between the *almost* and *altogether* Christian.[210]

The almost Christian is nothing more than a "half" Christian, one whose heart is "double" in its devotion between God and the world; though such devotion in reality is an "abomination" in God's sight.[211]

The altogether Christian has but one business, one high calling, and one fixed intention: "to 'love the Lord thy God with all thy heart, and with all thy soul, and with all thy mind, and with all thy strength.'"[212] Thus love is the only motive that makes one an altogether Christian, and fills full (i.e. fulfills) the true intent of his early theology of perfection.

Love is all God wants. Or as Wesley put it, "To love God, and to be beloved by him, is enough."[213] This is the passion that awakened the heart of young John Wesley. Love became the single idea that would most powerfully guide the development of his doctrine of perfection toward its mature articulation. But this single idea, that our love can become perfect, finds its roots in the early years of Wesley's faith journey. At the time, when he experienced a profound spiritual awakening, when God's holy love captured his heart and his devotion, Wesley came to a new understanding of the gospel of Christ. A gospel, at its heart, rooted in holiness, and properly called—the Gospel of Holiness.

Assessment & Legacy

We can now pause and appraise Wesley's early gospel system, both its strengths and weaknesses. Even though numerous

---

[210] *The Preface to the Christian's Pattern* V.5, Works J 14:210. The *altogether* Christian will continue to be used as a synonym for Christian perfection (*The Almost Christian*, Works B 1:131; cf. JWL 8/17/60; 5/11/64).
[211] *Single Intention* II.3.
[212] *The Preface to the Christian's Pattern* V.5, Works J 14:210.
[213] *Single Intention* II.9.

remarks could be made, room allows for only an assessment of major aspects.

Starting in 1725, Wesley's theological views begin to grow through an ever-deepening evolution leading to his Aldersgate crisis thirteen years later. But through all the shifts and changes a single thread guides and controls the entire process. This thread, of course, is the doctrine of *imago Dei*. This core concept gave his theological system a coherence that fueled a program of holy living with divine energy and purpose. All beliefs, practices, and behaviors were measured by a single, common denominator: a renewed (perfect) heart.[214] This meta-narrative of redemption offered the reason or rationale for what was accepted and what was rejected in the program. This single idea determined for Wesley personally, and for the Methodist cause, their core values. The fruit of such a clear and powerful vision was an infatigable sense of mission. This single quality alone destined Wesley to become a great leader.[215]

The grand theme of renewal in God's image also empowered Wesley to build comprehensiveness within his theological system. Every aspect of life became connected to the core vision of perfecting the heart. As the vision touched more and more aspects of life, the doctrine's core values began to mold every facet of life.[216] These two qualities—comprehension and coherence—are the greatest strengths of Wesley's Gospel of Holiness. Together, they fused an organic whole that destined Wesley to

---

[214] As JW put it succinctly, the "great work," the "one thing needful, is the renewal of our fallen nature" (*One Thing Needful* I.2).

[215] All leadership materials today emphasize the critical importance for every human organization, including the church, to define its mission, vision, core values, and constituency if it is to be successful. In this regard JW's leadership ability has been clearly demonstrated by the number of people over time that was captivated by his vision of holiness.

[216] W. Stephen Gunter makes the same point when he writes that JW "had a rule to govern virtually every occasion, but he also had a general rule which governed them all: 'Whenever you are to do an action, consider how God did or would do the like, and you imitate His example'" (*The Limits of Love Divine*, 70). See his letter to his father Samuel JWL 12/10/34 §2.

shape his world in powerful ways. But as the saying goes— "Our greatest strength is often our greatest weakness"—this would also prove true for Wesley's Gospel of Holiness.

The primary weakness was a focus on the sanctifying process that ended up swallowing everything into it. Like a funnel, this lopsided tendency pulled everything into the process, even those truths that are not process oriented, like the forgiveness of sins. We saw earlier that Wesley maintained present forgiveness of sins, but he found it very difficult to articulate it with consistency. He failed to grasp the concept of divine gift, given at once, because *everything* was pulled into the process of gradual sanctification. This meant that even forgiveness was part of the sanctifying process; or, as Wesley favorably quotes Bishop Taylor, "'Pardon of sins in the Gospel is sanctification...a state of change."[217] This propensity to pull everything into the process, in the end, created a loss of balance that later forced a near collapse of his entire theological superstructure. When faced with the storms at sea, the consequence was personal despair and an urgent grasping for some kind of spiritual and theological life support. As a result, Wesley felt forced to do radical surgery on his theology upon his return to England in 1738.[218]

As he would later recognize, the source of imbalance was primarily due to a failure to distinguish between what God does *for* us from what he does *in* us.[219] In none of Wesley's extant early writings does he speak of present justification before God. That he did believe in present forgiveness of sins, we clearly saw,

---

[217] JWL 2/28/30; Works B 25:245. See the section above on assurance.

[218] I remind the reader that JW's theology is the doctrinal system, those beliefs and ideas, which gave the rational for his program of attaining perfection. The program begins with the decision of the single intention, empowering the practice of the appointed means of grace for the cultivation of inward virtues, leading to the perfection of the heart and character. As we will see in ch 2, Wesley's despair led him to question the validity of his program in attaining salvation as inward holiness. The loss of confidence in the program, in turn, forced him to reevaluate his theology.

[219] *Justification by Faith* II.1; *The New Birth* P.1.

but he never equates present pardon with present justification (as he will do later).

We further saw that he believed firmly in the indwelling presence of the Holy Spirit, offering comfort and assurance before God. But a close reading of his writings reveals, once again, that the motif of sanctification so controls the nature of this assurance that he never associates such assurance with present justification. Instead, the assurance which the Spirit proffers is interwoven with one's degree of progress in attaining inward holiness.[220] This single insight will provide rich dividends as we proceed with our study.

Parallel to the imbalance between the sanctifying process and present justification, is the void one feels in Wesley's early writings regarding the death of Christ. The lone exception is found in his sacramental theology. But, more importantly, the lack of references to Christ's death in his sermons and letters reveal exactly where his theology and faith went awry. He made sanctification the means to justification, instead of justification serving as the ground for sanctification. The consequence was a *wrong focus*. This became obvious upon his leave to America. Wesley's primary motive was not to serve his Lord; he went to save his own soul. He never appears to have grasped that justification is grounded solely on Christ's death. The Gospel of Holiness made justification the goal of the race, to be received at the final judgment. This single error led to several other imbalances.

We noted his continuing interest in the subject of saving faith. We corrected the wrong notion, held by many, that he only understood faith as rational assent. The simple truth is he did affirm, and at times with some clarity, a view of saving faith as trust and commitment. But again, we note his struggles to articulate this truth with precision. For when he does attempt to define faith in a

---

[220] In *The Circumcision of the Heart* I.9 JW specifically links the Spirit's witness to the fact he makes the believer's heart "upright toward God," and that their assurance is grounded upon the reality they are "now in the path which leadeth to life." So even here present assurance is based on the work of sanctification, not on the work of justification in Christ's death.

straightforward statement, he never once does so as trust. In his sermons he often appeals to the listener to exercise saving trust, and yet, theologically, he never articulates faith as trust. This confusion centered on the *object* of faith. When Wesley speaks of the object of faith his focus is nearly always on God's holiness, not Christ's atonement. Thus, early Wesley proclaimed a gospel of *holiness*, not a gospel of the *cross*. This truth alone divides the early period from his middle one.

Imbalance carried over into his doctrine of the new birth. We noted above that Wesley personally experienced a definite conversion, consisting of a single intention.[221] Since his holiness gospel was grounded on the motif of the *imago Dei*, regeneration became identified with the renewal process. In this way a dual message concerning the new birth was promulgated. As Henry Rack observes, "As used by Wesley it (new birth) often means not simply the moment of justification but the whole process by which the believer becomes transformed from sin to holiness."[222] While this comment was made concerning his post-Aldersgate teaching, it applies even more to his early period. The extant sermons from his early period abound with exhortations for his listeners to make a definite commitment, yet, theologically, he links regeneration to the unending process of sanctification in this life. Since some sin must always remain, the life transformation process is never complete or finished while we continue in this body.

This fostered a further lack of balance in his gospel. Since Wesley's holiness gospel tended to focus on the end of life—facing death and final judgment; or, as Albert Outler calls the *ars moriendi* motif, Wesley logically shortchanged the beginning of the faith journey. While affirming the life of holiness begins in a

---

[221] See the section "Spiritual Awakening." His mother recognized the "alteration" (*Letter 2/23/25*) and many years later JW remembered what transpired as a definite conversion (*Plain Account* 2:2). Only a conversion experience does justice to the sudden and deep changes that took place in JW's life in 1725 and thereafter.
[222] *Reasonable Enthusiast*, 394.

new birth, this message was muted due to his absorbing interest in the end of life. Therefore, during his early period Wesley is not remembered for his views on regeneration, his understanding of present forgiveness, his insights into the Spirit's indwelling, or his affirmation of faith as trust. What he is remembered most for is his rigorous program of practicing the means of grace, and his complete devotion to the ideal of Christian perfection realized in the article of death.

Between the start and finish of the believer's faith journey is where the means of grace fit in. Such means as communicating, prayer, scripture reading, fasting, fellowship, and charity became the locus of the Holy Club's ceaseless activity. Their primary purpose was to infuse holy dispositions within the heart, which in turn would lead to higher attainments of Christian perfection. Probably because of his personality and upbringing, Wesley became tenacious in maintaining and advocating the disciplines of the Club. In 1735 he wrote to George Whitefield to "press on, and not to faint" in keeping the spiritual disciplines.[223]

The wisdom of Wesley's program is that it offered the seeker specific, tangible and practical methods for the cultivation of spiritual growth and maturation. The glaring weakness was the program's tendency to promote reliance upon these methods, even though such reliance was officially repudiated.[224] Since Wesley's holiness gospel emphasized the attainment of holiness to the neglect of present justification, his entire system could easily slip into a works methodology. Again, this is exactly what his Oxford days are often remembered for. Following Aldersgate, Wesley contributed to this interpretation when he admitted to having been only an "almost" Christian:

---

[223] JWL 5/8/35; Works B 25:425. Whitefield replies he has increased his morning and evening devotions to two full hours, renewed his acts of resignation, and started to study and pray over the scriptures everyday.

[224] In the same letter JW had told Whitefield to "resume all the externals but not to depend on them in the least" (Henry Rack, *Reasonable Enthusiast*, 103).

> I did go thus far for many years, as many of this place can testify: using diligence to eschew all evil, and to have a conscience void of offence; redeeming the time, buying up every opportunity of doing all good to all men; constantly and carefully using all the public and all the private means of grace; endeavouring after a steady seriousness of behaviour at all times and in all places. And God is my record, before whom I stand, doing all this in sincerity; having a real design to serve God, a hearty desire to do his will in all things, to please him who had called me to 'fight the good fight', and to 'lay hold of eternal life'. Yet my own conscience beareth me witness in the Holy Ghost that all this time I was but 'almost a Christian'.[225]

This confession highlights the interest Wesley had in religious experience. It was a unique gift that he possessed the intuitive perceptiveness to focus his theological energy on those things essential to real life transformation. Fallen human nature has a tendency to absorb itself in trifling matters in the religious realm. All kinds of rituals and traditions have been, and are, perpetuated for insignificant reasons—reasons unrelated to spiritual renewal. The beauty of Wesley's early program was the theological rationale which undergirds it. His doctrine of *imago Dei* conveyed that every person is created for fellowship and communion with God. We all are designed to live in God's holy presence. Corresponding to this core vision is the Arminian belief in universal redemption: God's grace reaches out to every child of Adam.

---

[225] *The Almost Christian* I.13. JW here affirms his single intention, sincerity, and diligent practice of all the means, yet denies its saving value. But in 1784 JW recalls that it was in 1725 when he made the resolution to not be an almost, that is, nominal Christian (*In What Sense We are to Leave the World* §§ 23-24).

The Gospel of Holiness

But Wesley also held that free grace can be resisted and forfeited through willful sin.[226] The possibility of losing grace provides one reason Wesley was motivated to study the nature of religious experience. Even his early letters emphasize that spiritual counsel needs to grasp the pitfalls and dangers that can shipwreck the faith journey.[227] Much of what he learned was through trial and error. This is seen in how Wesley often unwisely measured himself by the state of his *feelings*.[228] When Susanna wrote to her sons about the benefits of communicating, John chastised himself for not "feeling" as he should.[229] It is a truism that we are often harder on ourselves than we are on others, and this can be seen in Wesley's evaluations of himself. On the flip side he often gave people the benefit of doubt because of their apparent holy feelings.[230] Therefore, one of the legacies from his early period is that Wesley's theological orientation forever contained an experiential locus. He personally maintained a deep interest in studying religious feeling.[231]

In keeping with the motif of *imago Dei*, the Gospel of Holiness was specifically designed to prepare the believer for death

---

[226] JW speaks of willful and presumptuous sin in *On Grieving the Holy Spirit* I.3.

[227] In many letters JW offers spiritual counsel. For example, see JWL 6/19/31; 10/3/31; 3/28/37; 3/29/37. For further study see ch 6.

[228] JW once referred to inward feeling the "most infallible of proofs" (JWJ 1/8/38) and then a year later he judged himself very harshly just because he did not *feel* he loved God as he should (JWJ 1/4/39; italic emphasis his).

[229] JWL 2/28/32; Works B 25:328. JW's words are, "though my understanding 'approved what was excellent', yet my heart did not feel it! Why was this, but because it was pre-engaged by those affections with which wisdom will not dwell? Because the animal mind cannot relish those truths which are spiritually discerned!" He then goes on to express his desire to acquire the mind of Christ and to renounce the world by setting his affections on higher things. He then openly acknowledges how "fast life flies away, and slow improvement comes" in the attainment of holiness.

[230] See JWJ12/2/44; *Plain Account* 19:44, 69, 98; 24:10-11; 25:37, 44-46, 73, 148.

[231] JW's mature theology had much interest in the subject. See *Plain Account* 19:44 note.

and eternity. Negatively, it appears this preoccupation with the "art of dying" had imbued his worldview with an inherent pessimism.[232] At times the glories of the eternal realm are painted in quite wonderful terms,[233] yet his descriptions of this life, even for the Christian, are much bleaker. Biographers look for a possible explanation in his upbringing and the personalities of his parents. Whatever the reasons, Wesley's *imago Dei* doctrine, as he then understood it, meant that a teleological focus would dominate his thought and practice; which, in turn, created an imbalance in his outlook. This eventually produced an inner tension within his theological perspective.

We learned that according to Wesley the fruit of holiness was threefold: happiness, divine fullness, and comfort in facing death.[234] Yet, it was the last expectation that finally drove him to despair over his spiritual state. Yes, Wesley had gone to America to "learn the true sense of the gospel;" and in God's sovereign way, totally unexpected by him, that is what this Oxford don discovered. It was the depths of despair that finally drove this ardent seeker of perfection to learn a new gospel, one based on the *cross*. But we are jumping ahead of ourselves. This is the subject of the next chapter.

What we learn from Wesley's early theological system is that many of his doctrines were still in their incubation stage. The immaturity of his system is reflected by the many imbalances it contains. Though the Gospel of Holiness held a coherent vision and was comprehensive enough to promulgate a definite lifestyle, it still lacked balance in relation to the totality of Christian experience; most notably, on the point of conversion and its con-

---

[232] Cf. JWS *Death and Deliverance*; *On Mourning for the Dead*; *The Trouble and Rest of Good Men*. What we saw of JW's perspective on persecution fits also confirms this same point.

[233] For JW's descriptions of heavenly bliss, see *Death and Deliverance* §§13-17; *The Promise of Understanding* III.3; *The Image of God* IV.2; *On the Resurrection of the Dead* II.1-4; *One Thing Needful* II.2, III.1, 3; *The Trouble and Rest of Good Men* II. 4-6.

[234] Cf. the section: The Fruit of Perfection; p 33.

comitants. Several of his doctrines were only in their beginning stages of development, notably, justification, faith, new birth, and assurance. Since it was the beginning moment of Christian experience, which primarily remained undeveloped at the time, other doctrines still in incubation—like prevenient grace and involuntary sin—reach maturity much later in his career.[235] Since his doctrine of perfection is intrinsically bound to these other doctrines, it too lacked balance and symmetry. This sets the stage for the impact of Aldersgate and the radical changes Wesley embraced in his "new" theology of perfection: the Gospel of Faith Alone.

We can begin to chart the development of Wesley's theology of perfection by highlighting and comparing key components of each gospel system:

<u>Gospel of Holiness</u>

Axiom:
Inward holiness

Ground:
Sanctification brings justification

Object of faith:
God & his promises

Focus:
Future salvation

Salvation by:
Faith in ordinances

Salvation is:
Lifelong process

---

[235] Cf. chs 4 and 10.

John Wesley's Theology of Christian Perfection

Assurance:
Sincerity, communicating & life transformation

Holiness complete:
Death

Faith complete:
Death

Christian complete:
Death

TWO
The Gospel of Faith Alone

When Wesley published his first journal extract in June 1740, he did so for two main reasons. First, he felt the need to respond to the sworn affidavit by Captain Robert Williams, accusing him of ill conduct during his time in America.[1] Wesley wanted to show he had faithfully fulfilled his ministerial responsibilities as expected by the Georgian trustees. But a second reason was no less on his mind: to explain what had taken place that would lead him to change his theology so drastically upon his return to England. Having been a missionary to a foreign land opened up many pulpit opportunities. But Wesley found after his return on February 1, 1738 that church after church closed their doors to what they must have considered was an enthusiastic message. Many of his friends expressed concerns about his extravagances, like praying extempore and not using notes when preaching.[2] Even some in his own family could not accept the enthusiasm of his "new" gospel. Samuel Wesley Jr., Wesley's older brother, complained more than once to his brother about practices he considered to be rank enthusiasm.[3]

Moreover, by 1740 the Methodist revival was in full swing and gaining national attention. Closely linked to the revival was the controversial practice of open air preaching. In the spring of 1739 Wesley joined George Whitefield in proclaiming the good news of present salvation by faith alone directly to the masses.

---

[1] JW's preface (§2) to Extract 1 of his *Journal*, Works B 18:121; see also Ward and Heitzenrater's comments in Works B 18:81.

[2] John Clayton told CW and JW that "few or none were edified by Mr. (John) Wesley's preaching, because they were offended with his manner." He then mentions JW not using sermon notes, being very emotional in his expressions, and seeking to focus the attention upon himself (JWL 5/1/38).

[3] Samuel sees the visions and JW's teaching on a sensible experience of divine assurance as dangerous, and leading the ignorant toward self-delusion (JWL 11/15/38). Cf. JW's response JWL 11/30/38.

John Wesley's Theology of Christian Perfection

With the success of huge crowds came even more scrutiny of Wesley's theology and message. Coupled with these events was the fractured nature of the revival. By the summer of 1740 Wesley formally broke ranks with the Moravians, and within months he would part paths with George Whitefield and the Calvinists. This historical context explains why the first journal extract ends as it does, with what can only be termed as a formal apology for his Gospel of Faith Alone wrapped in narrative format. Only by taking a fresh look at what transpired can we hope to understand *how* and *why* his theology of perfection took shape as it did during this pivotal period of spiritual formation.

Why the Gospel of Holiness Failed

One of the interpretive mistakes made concerning Wesley's early faith journey, and his theological evolution, is that he went to America to find inward certainty regarding his eternal salvation. We addressed this error in the last chapter and found it lacking precision when attempting to read Wesley's motives.[4] This error hinders one from grasping exactly what happened that led Wesley to do an almost about-face in his doctrinal system. After all, no one was more shocked over his lack of assurance than John Wesley himself! As we will soon discover, this was the single most important lesson he learned as a missionary to America. If we are to comprehend *why* Wesley lost his assurance, and *how* this became a catalyst for a radical overall of his doctrine of salvation and perfection, we must return to his Gospel of Holiness to find clues that will bring perceptive clarity to his many journal comments and self-reflections.

We saw in chapter one that his Gospel of Holiness was grounded on the meta-narrative of humanity's fall and subsequent renewal in God's image and likeness (*imago Dei*). This renewal centers on the attainment of a perfect heart in order to be fit and

---

[4] Cf. p 61 above.

ready for entrance into God's eternal kingdom. So absorbing was his vision to attain a holy heart that all other doctrines and interests were funneled through this core idea, thus fueling a clear sense of mission, core values, and a set program. The Holy Club's method called for the diligent practice of the means of grace in order to infuse holy tempers in the heart, which in turn would usher the seeker into higher levels of Christian perfection. The goal was deliverance from all sin, fully realized in the article of death.

We saw that while this absorbing vision was the greatest strength of his Oxford gospel system, it also became the source for its greatest weakness. The Gospel of Holiness focused so heavily on the end of life, that is, life's goal, that it shortchanged the commencement of salvation, commonly referred to as conversion. As a consequence, sanctification became the foundation and means to justification, regeneration, and assurance, instead of the latter serving as the ground for the former.

So while early Wesley believed in a present forgiveness of sins, he never equates it with present justification before God. Even though he uses the language of regeneration to describe the single intention, he still affirms no one to be a Christian, in the full sense of the word, until they attain perfection.[5] While he teaches a clear doctrine of assurance based on the Spirit's indwelling presence, this assurance is intrinsically conjoined with the life transformation process. If at some point the seeker of holiness becomes convinced that little or no change has transpired in their soul, all assurance crumbles into the abyss of nothingness. No amount of communicating at the Lord's Table or repeated affirmations of sincerity can overcome such empirical evidence. When we turn to Wesley himself, he was definitely of the mind to believe facts are facts. All of this will add insight into his quest for personal salvation and holiness; but for now we must turn our attention to another aspect of his holiness gospel if

---

[5] In June 1739 JW states unequivocally that he had never claimed to be a Christian while in America (JWJ 6/11/39). This question is discussed further below.

we are to unravel the mystery why Wesley converted to a new gospel.

A corollary of Wesley's doctrine of *imago Dei*, with its teleological focus, was his interest in the "art of dying." This serves as the controlling motif in his first written sermon, *Death and Deliverance*, and in his first published sermon ten years later, *The Trouble and Rest of Good Men*. Both sermons use the same text (Job 3:17) and emphasize the same theme: death delivers from remaining sin and ushers the believer into eternal happiness and glory.

The "art of dying" motif comes up again in the 1737 sermon *On Love*. In this homily Wesley admonishes his audience that one of the fruits of perfect love is peace and comfort when facing death. To illustrate this point, he shares the testimonies of two men who had attained a degree of perfect love in the article of death. The first was his father Samuel, the second a fellow Georgian, Mr. Henry Lascelles. According to Wesley, the beauty of the gospel is the radiant hope it offers to the single-minded Christian. As the heart is transformed by divine holiness, the single-minded Christian becomes fit and ready to dwell eternally in God's holy presence. This is how the gospel brings comfort and peace when facing death. Victory over fear in the face of death was jubilantly proclaimed by Wesley many times in the early period, including this sermon excerpt in 1732:

> (Death) is now disarmed, and can do us no hurt. It divides us, indeed, from this body awhile; but it is only that we may receive it again more glorious. As God, therefore, said once to Jacob, "Fear not to go down into Egypt, for I will go down with thee, and will surely bring thee up again;" so may I say to all who are born of God, "Fear not to go down into the grave; lay down your heads in the dust; for God will certainly bring you up again, and that in a much more glorious manner." Only "be ye steadfast and unmovable, always abounding in the work of the Lord;" and then let death prevail over, and pull down, this house

of clay; since God hath undertaken to rear it up again, infinitely more beautiful, strong, and useful.⁶

Wesley had many reasons to feel confident he would not fear death when the time came. After all, by the time he left for America he had spent ten years pursuing heart holiness and was actively employed in discipling others in the process. Consequently, upon the eve of his departure to America in October 1735, what was uppermost in his mind was not the question of personal assurance, but the desire to find an environment better suited for the perfecting of his soul.

Moving from one's comfortable surroundings into uncharted territory often brings out aspects of character one is unaware; and this proved true of John Wesley. While the little band of John, Charles, Benjamin Ingham, and Charles Delamotte busied themselves with the minutia of diet, devotions, writing and transcribing sermons, and ministering to their little flock aboard ship, God was moving in sovereign ways unbeknown to them. Soon after departing Downs, the winds began to increase which startled Wesley from his sleep. He later acknowledged his fear, "What manner of men those ought to be who are every moment on the brink of eternity."⁷ Nearly a month later he found himself filled with apprehension "by the tossing of the ship and roaring of the wind;" which, he adds "plainly showed I was unfit, for I was *unwilling* to die."⁸

Traversing the Atlantic in mid-winter can be no fun today, with our large ships, technology and weather forecasting equip-

---

⁶ *The Resurrection of the Dead* III.3.
⁷ JWJ 10/31/35.
⁸ JWJ 11/23/35. It is significant that JW mentions on three separate occasions during this voyage his *unwillingness* to die (11/23/35; 1/17/36; 1/23/36). Being unwilling to die revealed to JW just how unfit he was to face death, and logically, how unsanctified he must have been at the time. In the following summer JW faced a similar experience during a thunderstorm. He confessed at the time, "This voice of God, too, told me I was not fit to die; since I was afraid rather than desirous of it! O when shall I wish to be dissolved and to be with Christ? When I love him with all my heart" (JWJ 7/10/36).

ment. This was even truer in the eighteenth century. For a person, like Wesley, used to being settled in the cloister of a university environment, he now was clearly out of his element. By mid-January the storms were so severe that he wrote, "About nine the sea broke over us from stem to stern; burst through the windows of the state cabin...and covered us all over."[9] Being filled with apprehension, he questions whether he will see the next sunrise. With deep dissatisfaction he confesses shame over his *unwillingness* to die, "O how pure in heart must he be, who would rejoice to appear before God at a moment's warning!"[10] Wesley's self-doubt reveals much about his theology at the time.

In light of his present salvation beliefs we can sympathize with his exasperation. He now had spent several years preparing for the moment when he would face God and eternity. He had tenaciously practiced with all his might the means of grace, believing that holy dispositions were being infused within his heart and character. Wesley was confident he had made significant progress on the path toward perfection and inward holiness. The last thing he expected was to find himself dreading death. The irony of his ordeal is confirmed by his later journal comments.

On January 8, 1738 Wesley acknowledged he has a problem with pride, "I thought I had what I find I have not." In other words, he thought he had made great headway on the path toward perfection, but instead he found he only had "fair summer religion." How could such self-deception happen, over such a length of time, unless his heart was filled with pride? Since Wesley considered pride to be one of the cardinal sins of corrupt human nature, what else could he conclude except that he had made very

---

[9] JWJ 1/17/36.

[10] JWJ 1/17/36. Compare this statement with the testimony of Mr. Lascelles (JWJ 6/6-7/36), and Margaret and Rebecca Bovey (JWJ 7/8/36-7/10/36). In addition, we noted earlier JW's commitment to empirical evidence. Two years later when JW states unequivocally that his inward feelings are the "most infallible of proofs" (JWJ 1/8/38) we can understand why: his feelings indisputably revealed the inner state of his heart and the nature of his tempers. If JW were truly holy, as he thought he was, he would have *wanted* to die and to be with Christ.

The Gospel of Faith Alone

little progress on the faith journey. Simply stated, the storms and his resulting fears exposed the unsanctified state of his heart. John Wesley was confronted with the "most infallible of proofs": his own heart was not as transformed as he had previously judged it to be. When he later summarized his two-plus years in America, he openly acknowledged that this revelation was what he least expected to learn.[11]

If the above revelation wasn't enough, while aboard ship he came into contact with a group of Christians known as Moravians. Being impressed with their Christian demeanor, he was especially struck by their confidence when facing death:

> In the midst of the psalm wherewith their service began the sea broke over, split the mainsail in pieces, covered the ship, and poured in between the decks, as if the great deep had already swallowed us up. A terrible screaming began among the English. The Germans calmly sung on. I asked one of them afterwards, 'Was you not afraid?' He answered, 'I thank God, no.' I asked, 'But were not your women and children afraid?' He replied mildly, 'No; our women and children are not afraid to die.'[12]

Wesley's later conversation with Moravian pastor August Spangenberg only confirmed his plight. When asked if he knew Jesus Christ had saved him, the only response he could muster was a feeble profession in general terms, "I know he is the Savior of the world...I hope he has died to save me."[13] Spangenberg's questions pierced to the heart of Wesley's problem: he had placed his

---

[11] JW's words are, "It is now two years and almost four months since I left my native country, in order to teach the Georgian Indians the nature of Christianity: But what have I learned myself in the meantime? Why (*what I the least of all suspected*), that I who went to America to convert others, was never myself converted to God" (JWJ Ext. I Post-script; Works B 18:214; emphasis mine).
[12] JWJ 1/25/36.
[13] JWJ 2/7/36.

faith in the *wrong object*.[14] Instead of trusting in Christ alone to reconcile him to God, he had placed his faith in God, in his promises of perfection, and in his own sincere endeavors to attain holiness. Wesley had placed too much confidence in the means of grace to transform his heart. This led, at least implicitly, to a system of salvation by works. In 1739 when rumors spread around Bristol that he was secretly a follower of Catholicism, Wesley acknowledged that for ten years he had been a "papist, and knew it not."[15]

Peter Böhler's Solution

When Wesley met Peter Böhler on February 7, 1738 he made the following notation in his journal, "A day to be remembered." Böhler, while at the University of Jena, had been converted by Count Ludwig von Zinzendorf, the founder of the Moravian Church. He later became a minister and bishop in the church. Peter was in London on his way to America as a missionary to Georgia and Carolina. Since he had just arrived, Wesley found lodging for Böhler and his companions. A bond fast developed between the two men allowing Wesley to open up to Böhler

---

[14] "I fixed not this faith on its right object: I meant only faith in God, not faith in or through Christ" (JWJ 5/24/38 §11). JW records an interesting conversation with Spangenberg in which JW asks him to define faith. Spangenberg answers by quoting Hebrews 11:1 ("The substance of things hoped for, the evidence of things not seen;" KJV). This later became JW's favorite text when defining saving faith (JWJ MS 7/31/37; Works B 18:532).

[15] JWJ 8/27/39. Other factors, beside the storms and the Moravians, which contributed to his unrest, include the death and testimonies of Mr. Lascelles and the Bovey sisters (see n 8, 10 above), the entire Sophy Hopkey fiasco, the apathy of the Georgians response to JW's ministry, and the comfortable circumstances JW enjoyed. On July 23, 1737 JW confided to a friend, "How to attain to the being crucified with Christ I find not, being in a condition I neither desired nor expected in America—in ease, and honour, and abundance. A strange school for him who has but one business: To exercise himself unto godliness (1 Tim 4:7)"

The Gospel of Faith Alone

about his spiritual condition. It was from Peter Böhler that John Wesley learned what he would call his *new* gospel.

Böhler's solution was to first convince his troubled friend that salvation is by faith alone. Wesley's ingrained ideas of faith as an inward virtue (a temper of the heart) continually led to confusion in his mind when it came to seeing faith alone as a condition for salvation. To this Böhler exclaimed, "*Mi frater, mi frater, excoquenda est ista tua philosophia*—My brother, my brother, that philosophy of yours must be purged away."[16] What Böhler proclaimed, in sharp contrast to Wesley's holiness gospel, was that one either has or does not have saving faith. In other words, salvation is received as a complete package. If one does not have saving faith, that person is not a real Christian. As a consequence, Böhler's message left no room for degrees of faith as Wesley's Gospel of Holiness assumed. Finally, on March 5 Wesley was convinced of unbelief. He naturally concluded he needed to leave off preaching, "How can you preach to others, who have not faith yourself?" Böhler wisely counseled John to "preach faith *till* you have it; and then, *because* you have it, you will preach faith."[17]

A couple of weeks later, Böhler further "amazed" Wesley with his account of the immediate fruits of faith: happiness and holiness.[18] This, of course, struck a chord with Wesley's spiritual DNA. For a man who had committed himself so completely to the attainment of inward holiness, these fruits convinced him even more that Böhler's gospel was what his heart was truly seeking. The equation of inward holiness with salvation would

---

[16] JWJ 2/19/38.

[17] JWJ 3/5/38. Peter Böhler remembers the conversation somewhat differently, "I took a walk with the elder Wesley, and asked him about his spiritual state. He told me that he sometimes felt certain of his salvation, but sometimes he had many doubts; that he could only say this, 'If what stands in the Bible be true, then I am saved.' Thereupon I spoke with him very fully; and earnestly besought him to go to the opened fountain, and not to mar the efficacy of free grace by his unbelief" (Works B 18:228 n 49).

[18] JWJ 3/23/38.

become, as it was in his holiness gospel, an axiom in his faith-alone gospel.

A month later the two men got together, and this time Wesley had no objection to Böhler's definition of faith, or its twin fruits of happiness and holiness. He now understood that the proper object of faith was Christ alone, his death bringing forgiveness and reconciliation to the favor of God. This brings up another aspect of Böhler's gospel that contrasted sharply with Wesley's prior views: the ground of personal assurance. Whereas Wesley had emphasized sincerity, communicating, and the Holy Spirit's transforming presence, Böhler taught the Holy Spirit supernaturally bears witness to the reality of one's faith. This last truth logically led to another component of salvation by faith alone: instantaneous conversion. Since Böhler himself had experienced grace in a moment, he considered such conversion as normative. Wesley's response was to search the scriptures, especially the book of Acts, and there he found to his astonishment instantaneous conversion as the norm: "scarce any so slow as that of St. Paul, who was three days in the pangs of the new birth." But then, Wesley reasoned, God may have worked this way only in the first centuries, when the faith was young:

> But on Sunday, 23, I was beat out of this retreat too, by the concurring evidence of several living witnesses; who testified, God had thus wrought in themselves; giving them in a moment such a faith in the blood of his Son, as translated them out of darkness into light, out of sin and fear into holiness and happiness. Here ended my disputing. I could now only cry out, "Lord, help thou my unbelief!"[19]

---

[19] JWJ 4/23/38. Peter Böhler recollects that JW was not at first convinced by the "living witnesses." But while the group sang a hymn JW broke down and in a private meeting with Peter "wept heartily and bitterly." JW acknowledged "he was now satisfied of what I (Böhler) said of faith, and he would not question any more about it; that he was convinced of the want of it: but how could he help himself, and how could he obtain such faith?" (Lockmore, *Memorials*

The Gospel of Faith Alone

A few days later Wesley met with some friends and his brother Charles, and began to share his new understanding on the nature of saving faith and its fruits. He confessed that he did not believe he was presently a Christian. This produced a sharp reaction. Thomas Broughton felt Wesley must be a Christian to have done and suffered such things as he did in America. Charles became so angry he told his brother that such talk only stirs up "mischief."

By the end of April Wesley was "much confirmed" in the "truth that is after godliness" by the testimonies of two people who had received salvation in an instant, as "lightning falling from heaven."[20] Böhler finally departed London on May 4 to fulfill his commission in America. During mid-May Wesley confessed to having a spirit of heaviness concerning his spiritual condition.[21] At this time Böhler wrote an encouraging letter to John and Charles exhorting them to trust in Christ crucified for salvation. Peter counseled them to "taste and then see, how exceedingly the Son of God has loved you, and loves you still." These themes will echo in Wesley's testimony on May 24.[22]

In this way Wesley's new gospel became a radical departure from what he had believed and taught. Whereas he had believed salvation was the end result of a lifetime process through the infusion of holy habits by means of the means of grace (*via salutis*), he now proclaimed a gospel of present salvation by faith alone in Christ alone. The corollary of this new message was the

---

of the Life of Peter Böhler, 79). Luke Tyerman summarizes the "great doctrines" Böhler taught JW: (1) true faith brings dominion over sin (2) an abiding peace from being forgiven, and (3) saving faith is received in an instant (*Life and Times of the Rev. John Wesley* Vol. I, 177-178). Tyerman fails to mention the doctrine of the Spirit's witness. JW is clear in his journal comments on April 23 that he did learn from Böhler that one's assurance was grounded upon the Spirit's testimony.

[20] JWJ 4/28/38.
[21] JWJ 5/10-13/38.
[22] Charles also sought to experience a personal assurance of God's love at this time. Upon reading Martin Luther on Galatians ch 2 one evening, he wrote "I laboured, waited, and prayed to feel 'who loved *me*, and gave himself for *me*'" (CWJ 5/17/38).

bold idea that salvation is received in an instant, as a gift. Therefore, what Wesley learned from Peter Böhler can be summarized as follows:

> Salvation is by faith alone
> Faith is received in an instant, as a gift
> The object of faith is Christ alone
> The fruits of faith are happiness and holiness
> There are no degrees of faith; one either has it or not
> The Holy Spirit bears witness to the reality of one's faith

To see how Wesley's new gospel altered his theological system, we now turn to key documents of his Aldersgate era.

Salvation, Holiness and Faith

As May 24 approached, Wesley's journal records that he preached his new gospel in several churches, only to be told to not return. Everything was now coming to a head: with Charles' spiritual breakthrough on Pentecost Sunday, and John's building desperation to find faith at all cost. Finally, on Wednesday, May 24, Wesley took the time to write to a friend. We quote the letter in full because of the significant insights it offers concerning Wesley's perfection views at the time:

> O why is it, that so great, so wise, so holy a God will use such an instrument as me! Lord, 'let the dead bury their dead!' But wilt thou send the dead to raise the dead? Yea, thou sendest whom thou wilt send, and showest mercy by whom thou wilt show mercy! Amen! Be it then according to thy will! If thou speak the word, Judas shall cast out devils.
> I feel what you say, (though not enough,) for I am under the same condemnation. I see that the whole law of God is holy, just, and good. I know every thought, every

The Gospel of Faith Alone

temper of my soul, ought to bear God's image and superscription. But how am I fallen from the glory of God! I feel that 'I am sold under sin.' I know, that I too deserve nothing but wrath, being full of all abominations: And having no good thing in me, to atone for them, or to remove the wrath of God. All my works, my righteousness, my prayers, need an atonement for themselves. So that my mouth is stopped. I have nothing to plead. God is holy, I am unholy. God is a consuming fire: I am altogether a sinner, meet to be consumed.

Yet I hear a voice (and is it not the voice of God?) saying, 'Believe, and thou shalt be saved. He that believeth is passed from death unto life. God so loved the world that he gave his only-begotten Son, that whosoever believeth in Him should not perish, but have everlasting life.'

O let no one deceive us by vain words, as if we had already attained this faith! By its fruits we shall know. Do we already feel 'peace with God,' and 'joy in the Holy Ghost?' Does 'his Spirit bear witness with our spirit, that we are the children of God?' Alas, with mine He does not. Nor, I fear, with yours. O thou Saviour of men, save us from trusting in anything but Thee! Draw us after Thee! Let us be emptied of ourselves, and then fill us with all peace and joy in believing; and let nothing separate us from thy love, in time or in eternity.

A careful reading of this letter reveals (1) Wesley still maintains the axiom of his earlier gospel: salvation demands inward holiness. God's requirement has not changed, "every thought, every temper...ought to bear God's image and superscription." Perfection as inward holiness is still the requirement and expectation. (2) His failure to live up to this standard is stated in the sharpest of terms. He describes himself as being in an unsaved condition. This is in sharp contrast to his prior perspective, even up to the point of his return to England on February 1.[23] Credit must be given to Böhler who swayed Wesley to change his mind so drastically in regard to his eternal state. Wesley now embraces an all or nothing approach to salvation, collapsing perfection into the article of conversion.[24] (3) When he alludes to the means of grace he identifies them as a system of works, "all my works, my righteousness, my prayers, need an atonement." Before he had relied almost completely upon the means of grace to cultivate inward virtues within the heart; he now sees such efforts as trusting in himself to merit salvation. Wesley's confession says it all, "I am altogether a sinner, meet to be consumed." Yet, he hears the Spirit speaking, "Believe, and thou shalt be saved" (Acts 16:31). The new gospel is emphatic: salvation—meaning forgiveness, joy, assurance, and, most of all, holiness—comes by faith alone!

This letter, written only hours before his Aldersgate conversion, reveals exactly what John Wesley was expecting from his new gospel:

Salvation is inward holiness
Salvation is conditioned upon faith alone
Salvation is a complete package: one is saved or not saved
The means of grace is a system of works
Inward holiness comes by faith alone

---

[23] Cf. Appendix B: John Wesley's Confessions.
[24] Richard Heitzenrater concurs, "The English Moravians had, in Lutheran fashion, collapsed sanctification into justification and, in Pietist fashion, extended forgiveness of sins (imputed righteousness) into freedom from sin (imparted righteousness). This approach resulted in the expectation of a sinless perfection (including a full measure of the fruits of the Spirit) as the necessary mark or evidence of salvation (genuine conversion). This approach resulted in the expectation of a sinless perfection (including a full measure of the fruits of the Spirit) as the necessary mark or evidence of salvation (genuine conversion)" (*Wesley and the People Called Methodists*, 83).

The Gospel of Faith Alone

The Aldersgate Memorandum

It appears from Wesley's comments a year later that he wrote this record of his faith journey leading up to his conversion on May 24 shortly after the event itself.[25] Most likely the document was reworked before it was published in his second journal extract in October 1740. What can we learn about the principles of Wesley's new gospel from this testimony?

The memorandum begins with a series of short paragraphs outlining the gist of his spiritual upbringing and his views on salvation at each phase. He opens by saying he was about age ten when he lost the regenerating grace of his baptism. Summarizing his childhood development as one of outward strictness, Wesley saw his teenage and early college years in terms of a nominal faith when he was satisfied with mere perfunctory service, like reading the Bible, going to church, and saying his prayers. He reasoned at the time that since he was not as bad as other people he must be in a state of acceptance with God, even though he continued to indulge in known sin. As he tells his story the emphasis falls on his early ignorance of inward holiness, except for seasons when he struggled against sin.

The next several paragraphs focus on his spiritual awakening to inward holiness in 1725 and thereafter. He recalls the deep impression William Law's two books, *Christian Perfection* and *A Serious Call to a Devout and Holy Life*, made upon him:

> The light flowed in so mightily upon my soul, that every thing appeared in a new view. I cried to God for help, and resolved not to prolong the time of obeying Him as I had never done before. And by my continued endeavour to

---

[25] JW mentions that he shared his Aldersgate account with his mother, who approved of its contents. But sometime, later while John was in Germany, a copy was sent to a relative, who in turn shared it with his mother once again, but this time she became alarmed over its contents. JW had to set the record straight. This is a possible secondary reason why he published an official record of this memorandum in his second journal extract (cf. JWJ 6/13/39).

keep His whole law, inward and outward, to the utmost of my power, I was persuaded that I should be accepted of Him, and that I was even then in a state of salvation.[26]

As he pursued inward holiness, by means of the single intention and the ordinances, Wesley was confident he was in a state of salvation. Then came the storms at sea and the awful apprehension he was near death, "I could not find that all this gave me any comfort, or any assurance of acceptance with God" (§6). His ground of his assurance was eroding. The memorandum next traverses through his experiment with Christian mysticism, and how he later realized that all these efforts to gain salvation through personal holiness were only an attempt to establish his own righteousness before God. In this state of striving and failing, Wesley identifies with Paul's struggle in Romans chapter seven. He knows the law is spiritual and good, and that he delights in it, but he also knows he is enslaved to inward sin. Whereas before he had served sin willingly, he now served it unwillingly; yet, he still served sin.

At this point the narrative arrives at January 1738, when in the depths of despair he realizes that his fundamental problem is unbelief. The "one thing needful" is now to gain a "true, living faith."[27] He confesses, "But still I fixed not this faith on its right object: I meant only faith in God, not faith in or through Christ" (§11). Böhler had sensed this and provided the proper solution: faith alone in Christ alone. This set Wesley to seeking faith with a vengeance by renouncing all dependence upon his own righteousness. Though he describes himself as feeling indifferent, dull and cold, in reality his spirit was longing for the freedom of assurance and victory. In this mood he reluctantly agrees to attend a

---

[26] JWJ 5/24/38 §5.
[27] §11. Note the switch on the meaning of "one thing needful." Whereas in JW's GosH the phrase consistently referred to the renewal of our fallen humanity in God's image, now JW identifies it with saving faith. This reflects significant change in his soteriology. The GosFA was definitely a *new* gospel message.

The Gospel of Faith Alone

Moravian society meeting on Aldersgate Street, where he listened to Martin Luther's preface to the book of Romans be read. Wesley's now immortal words describes what transpired next:

> About a quarter before nine, while he was describing the change which God works in the heart through faith in Christ, I felt my heart strangely warmed. I felt I did trust in Christ, Christ alone for salvation: And an assurance was given me, that he had taken away my sins, even mine, and saved me from the law of sin and death.[28]

At long last Wesley found what he longed for: assurance before God and victory over all sin; or, as he often expressed it, happiness and holiness. John Wesley had finally attained perfection as inward holiness. At last, he now believed the "law of sin and death" was defeated.

Christ, Faith and Sin

We opened this chapter explaining why Wesley felt it necessary to acknowledge his spiritual failures in his first journal extract. This extract ends with a postscript that can only be classified as a formal apology for his new gospel message. Though written as a confession, theologically it serves as a defense. The changes from his *old* gospel to the *new* were so enormous, that Wesley's own evaluation of his spiritual state changed 180 degrees. Whereas he once thought of himself to have done very well in attaining inward holiness, he now considered all this supposed progress as dung.[29] We waited until now to examine this apology so we could first lay the foundation of Wesley's new gospel principles.

---

[28] JWJ 5/24/38 §14.
[29] Similar to the Apostle Paul's own faith journey; see Php 3:4-7.

When Wesley wrote the post-script is conjecture, but it is the opinion of this author that he probably did so soon after his Aldersgate conversion. What we do know from the document itself is that whenever Wesley composed the postscript it was written to serve as an apology for his faith-alone gospel. This becomes evident when we compare its contents to his other confessions written in January 1738.[30]

Wesley opens the apology/confession by affirming his unconverted condition while serving as a missionary to the Georgian Indians. By contrast, we learned above that he came to this conclusion *after* his return to England, when he came under the influence of Peter Böhler. When friends replied he must be insane for making such an assertion, Wesley's response was to quote the Apostle Paul, "'I am not mad,' though I thus speak" (Acts 26:25). It was hard for anyone who personally knew John Wesley, the life he lived, the sacrifices he endured, to believe he was at the time an unconverted person. These same people must have thought that if he was so mistaken on the point of his spiritual condition, what does this mean in regard to the *new* gospel he was now proclaiming?

Wesley then proceeds to make a point-by-point repudiation of his Holy Club program through a litany of short questions and answers:

> Are they read in philosophy? So was I. In ancient or modern tongues? So was I also. Are they versed in the science of divinity? I too have studied it many years. Can they talk fluently upon spiritual things? The very same could I do. Are they plenteous in alms? Behold, I gave all my goods to feed the poor. Do they give of their labour as well as of their substance? I have laboured more abundantly than they all. Are they willing to suffer for their

---

[30] Cf. Appendix B: John Wesley's Confessions. In this appendix a date from late April through June is offered as the most likely time when the post-script was initially written. JW probably reworked it before he inserted it in his journal for publication in May 1740.

brethren? I have thrown up my friends, reputation, ease, country; I have put my life in my hand, wandering into strange lands; I have given my body to be devoured by the deep, parched up with heat, consumed by toil and weariness, or whatsoever God should please to bring upon me.

Wesley's Holy Club had engaged in all these practices to perfect inward holiness in their lives. Through a second series of questions, he drives home the point that none of the above criteria can justify one before God, nor can they impart that "holy, heavenly, divine character." In the post-script Wesley offers lip service to the continuing use of the means of grace, but their salvific value is severely undercut.[31]

After this he plunges into a confession of personal sinfulness that easily matches his Aldersgate memorandum. What Wesley learned in America was that he had fallen short of God's glory, that his whole heart was "altogether corrupt and abominable," that being alienated from the life of God he is an "heir of hell." None of his good works can atone for this inherent sinfulness. His only hope is in Christ and in the righteousness of his atonement. Drawing upon categories found in his sermon *Salvation By Faith*, Wesley delineates between a true and false faith. A false faith includes both that which the demons hold and also what the pre-Calvary disciples possessed. A demonic faith is merely cold, intellectual, rational assent to the truths of the gospel. Such faith possesses no life. While the faith of the disciples acknowledged Jesus as the Jewish messiah and as a miracle-worker, it too was deficient. Such faith does not "overcome the world" by producing genuine inward holiness in the heart.

If rational assent and the affirmation of Jesus as a great teacher and miracle-worker cannot save, then what kind of faith

---

[31] Since JW's positive statement on the means of grace is included in parentheses, he is affirming their value, yet demoting their salvific value in light of the overall context.

does save? His answer reveals just how far he had moved from his earlier gospel principles:

> The faith I want is, "a sure trust and confidence in God, that, through the merits of Christ, my sins are forgiven, and I reconciled to the favour of God."[32] I want that faith which St. Paul recommends to all the world, especially in his Epistle to the Romans: That faith which enables every one that hath it to cry out, "I live not; but Christ liveth in me; and the life which I now live, I live by faith in the Son of God, who loved me, and gave himself for me." I want that faith which none can have without knowing that he hath it; (though many imagine they have it, who have it not;) for whosoever hath it, is "freed from sin, the" whole "body of sin is destroyed" in him: He is freed from fear, "having peace with God through Christ, and rejoicing in hope of the glory of God." And he is freed from doubt, "having the love of God shed abroad in his heart, through the Holy Ghost which is given unto him;" which "Spirit itself beareth witness with his spirit, that he is a child of God."

Saving faith now includes conscious union with Christ, freedom from the "whole body of sin," deliverance from doubt, filling the heart with God's love, being witnessed by the Holy Spirit. Christ alone is the sole object of this faith. Wesley says he lacked all these fruits upon his return to England. There was only one solution: conversion to Christ alone, by faith alone, in an instant alone, witnessed by the Spirit alone.

---

[32] *Homilies*: *Of Salvation,* Pt. III.

The Gospel of Faith Alone

Salvation By Faith

When Wesley mounted the pulpit at Saint Mary's Church on Sunday, June 11, less than three weeks following his evangelical conversion, he proclaimed what has become the quintessential manifesto of his Gospel of Faith Alone. The themes found in this homily had been stewing in his heart and mind for many weeks, and were now ratified by his own experience.[33] Accordingly, the thrust of *Salvation By Faith* is to declare audaciously the full extant of his new gospel: *sola fide* in *sola Christus*—salvation by faith alone in Christ alone. This salvation comes by mere grace: God's "free, undeserved favour." A favor, Wesley adds, that is "altogether undeserved, man having no claim to the least of his mercies" (P.1).

As he took to the pulpit his first order of business was to clarify in everyone's mind the true nature of saving faith. This was accomplished by means of contrast. Since his purpose was to persuade, Wesley identifies the kinds of faith his audience most likely had. He presents them in a fashion so his audience (and readers) could see where they stood on the faith journey path, and to know what they needed to do to find full salvation in Christ. The four kinds of faith enunciated are that of a heathen, a devil, the pre-Calvary disciples, and the apostles. In reality each class presents a different degree or level of faith, starting with the lowest (the heathen) and rising higher till the apostolic level is reached. But Wesley's purpose is to magnify the insufficiency of the first three levels in comparison to the last. So it is better to think of each category as a *kind* of faith rather than a *degree* of faith.[34] Let's look at each in turn.

---

[33] JW had been preaching the basic themes of this sermon numerous times over the last four months (JWJ 3/6/38; 3/19/38; 3/26/38; 3/27/38; 4/25/38; 4/26/38; 5/6/38; 5/7/38; 5/9/38; 5/14/38).

[34] The four categories of faith do infer a doctrine of prevenient grace, which implies a concept of degrees or graduating levels. But the reader must remember that JW's GosFA resists any acceptance of degrees when it comes to saving faith. As a consequence, JW does not argue for *degrees* of faith in *Salva-*

The faith of a heathen consists of a general belief in the being and attributes of the one God, along with the observance of a good moral life toward one's neighbor.[35] The next kind of faith includes all that a sincere heathen holds as true, but also affirms Jesus to be the "Son of God, the Christ, the Savior of the world" (I.2). Just as the demons know this truth, and at times tremble at it (Ja 2:19), so the person who has this kind of faith believes the scriptures to be God's holy word. Where this faith falters is in its lack of life transforming power. Such faith is only a mental assent to the truth.

The third kind of faith respects what the disciples of Jesus knew before Calvary. While this kind of faith draws one closer to saving grace, it still falls short of proper Christian salvation. Just as the disciples trusted in Christ's divine authority over disease and demonic power, so as to leave all and to follow him, a pre-Calvary faith knows enough of Christ to follow him with a single intention. In other words, this kind of faith follows Christ as one's pattern, the "grand Exemplar,"[36] not as a Savior crucified and risen. As Wesley now understands the faith journey, this is the kind of faith he had prior to his Aldersgate conversion. But he also knows that most of his audience probably has this kind of faith too. So he presses his argument to make it clear to everyone the exact nature of saving faith.

Saving faith is apostolic in nature. This alone is proper Christian faith. He then offers three reasons why this is so. For starters, apostolic faith has Christ for its object. This distinguishes such

---

tion By Faith, though his argument allows for it. At the time JW held to the position that any kind of faith other than apostolic faith is not saving. JW will later soften the line that separates apostolic faith from the other three kinds, leading to a view of graduating levels or degrees of saving faith (sermon: *On the Discoveries of Faith*). For this reason we will speak of *kinds* of faith, not *degrees* of faith.

[35] Later in life as JW was exposed to a variety of non-Christian faiths, he will recognize several sub-Christian levels of faith. See chapter 7.

[36] Plain Account 5:4. JW's early sermons often define the real believer in the language of a servant, possessing a single intention and real sincerity to serve God with the whole heart in every area of life (*Single Intention* P.1; I.2).

faith from that of a heathen, which is only a general belief in God and his moral goodness. Second, saving faith is a "disposition of the heart." This is diametrically opposite to the faith of a devil, which is a "speculative, rational thing, a cold, lifeless assent, a train of ideas in the head" (I.4). When describing saving faith Wesley uses the following terms—"trust," "full reliance," "recumbency," "closing" and "cleaving"—to illustrate his meaning. Saving faith is of the heart; devilish faith is of the head. While geographically the heart and head are only about a foot apart, Wesley now understood that in the realm of the spirit the distance can be many miles. Last, what specifically defines apostolic faith is that it "acknowledges the necessity and merit of (Christ's) death, and the power of his resurrection."[37] Thus, apostolic faith is distinguished from the faith of the pre-Calvary disciples. The latter only know Christ after the flesh, but apostolic faith knows Christ after the Pentecostal Spirit. Saving faith is a *living* trust in Jesus Christ, crucified and risen, a gift of divine grace, imparting spiritual life within the heart.

After pointing out what it means to be a true believer, Wesley moves to the task of clarifying the nature of salvation. It is here we see the contours of his faith-alone gospel standing in sharp contrast to his earlier gospel. Whereas before he had formerly held there was no perfection in this life—that sin always remains until the article of death—his message of salvation by faith alone proclaimed the exact opposite: The Christian life *begins* with victory over all sin. The disparity between the two gospels is further highlighted by their point of emphasis. Whereas the Gospel of Holiness stressed the end of life and the future kingdom, the Gospel of Faith Alone emphasizes the commencement of spiritual life and the present kingdom. Drawing on the homily's text, Ephesians 2:8, Wesley notes the present tense of the verb, "Ye *are* saved;" not "Ye *shall* be saved." He then presses home the nature of this present salvation.

---

[37] I.5. JW will later summarize that the Christian faith is grounded on the doctrines of original sin, justification and sanctification (new birth & holiness). These doctrines were at the heart of the evangelical revival.

John Wesley's Theology of Christian Perfection

In one word, salvation means *deliverance* from sin. Wesley finds this theme at the very beginning of the gospel, "You are to give him the name Jesus, because he will save his people from their sins." But to make his point even more clearly, Wesley asserts that Jesus saves from all sin: "original and actual, past and present, 'of the flesh and of the spirit.'"[38]

Three areas of deliverance are next identified. To begin, the Christian enjoys free *forgiveness*. Through a litany of scripture verses Wesley announces that faith in the merits of Christ's death takes away the curse and condemnation of the law, thereby justifying the believer before God. In contrast to the Gospel of Holiness, there is no need to wait until death to be declared righteous. Instead, the Gospel of Faith Alone proclaims that in the moment of heart-felt trust in the vicarious sacrifice of Christ the believer's record is wiped clean and nailed to the cross.

Having been saved from sin's guilt, the Christian is further delivered from its *fear*. Having peace with God and enjoying the presence of divine love within, the believer knows by the Spirit's witness they are accepted, no longer needing to fear divine punishment. But in consistency with his Arminian convictions, Wesley does add that one can lose saving grace through willful sin.[39]

Finally, and most significantly, salvation from sin means deliverance from its *power*. Wesley quotes 1 John 3:5-9 and 5:18 to show that the beginning of salvation includes freedom from sin's control. These verses became a staple in Wesley's faith-alone gospel.[40] But what does this freedom specifically entail? Wesley explains:

---

[38] Matthew 1:21 (NIV).

[39] Compare JW's early transcribed the sermon *On Grieving the Holy Spirit* (1732) with his post-Aldersgate sermon *The Great Privilege of those that are Born of God* (1739). In both sermons grace is only lost through conscious willful sin.

[40] It is significant that none of JW's extant sermons from his early period quote from these scripture passages. JW's first reference to them is on April 22, 1738 when he acknowledges being convinced that salvation comes by faith alone and wrestles with the idea of instantaneousness in the reception of sav-

The Gospel of Faith Alone

> He that is by faith born of God sinneth not, (1), by any habitual sin, for all habitual sin is sin reigning; but sin cannot reign in any that believeth. Nor, (2), by any wilful sin; for his will, while he abideth in the faith, is utterly set against all sin, and abhorreth it as deadly poison. Nor, (3), by any sinful desire; for he continually desireth the holy and perfect will of God; and any unholy desire he by the grace of God stifleth in the birth. Nor, (4), doth he sin by infirmities, whether in act, word, or thought; for his infirmities have no concurrence of his will; and without this they are not properly sins. Thus, 'He that is born of God doth not commit sin.' And though he cannot say he hath not sinned, yet now 'he sinneth not'. (II.6)

When saving faith takes root in the heart, perfection is attained. For to be justified, in the widest sense, "implies a deliverance from guilt and punishment, by the atonement of Christ actually applied to the soul of the sinner now believing on him, and a deliverance from the *whole body of sin*,[41] through Christ 'formed in his heart'." Wesley concludes that "he who is thus justified or saved by faith is indeed 'born again'."[42] Consequently, the Gospel of Faith Alone proclaims present salvation from all sin

---

ing grace. *Salvation By Faith* is the first sermon that JW quotes from 1 John 3:5-9 and 5:18, emphasizing present deliverance from committing sin. Peter Böhler obviously used these passages in his discussions with JW (Compare JWJ 3/26/38 with 4/22/38). William Law appealed to 1 Jn 3:9 in his *Practical Treatise on Christian Perfection* (ch 2). Law understood the verse to refer only to the believer's aversion toward sin, not a real and full freedom from its commission. JW was definitely following Böhler and not Law at this time.

[41] In 1771 JW editorially altered "the whole body of sin" to "the power of sin." This change in the text reveals (1) in 1738 JW did believe all sin was removed in conversion, and (2) he later changed his mind on this point. This change will be chronicled in ch 3.

[42] *Salvation By Faith* II.7 (emphasis mine). This passage demonstrates that JW's GosFA promulgated perfection in the article of conversion.

through instantaneous conversion. Inward holiness is attained the moment one becomes a real, altogether Christian.[43]

One further point should be noted. In *Salvation By Faith* no difference is drawn between the power of sin and the being of sin. This distinction will be made later. As a result, Wesley continues to fuse justification with sanctification. So the bottom line standard for salvation is still understood to be inward holiness. But the difference should be obvious to the reader: holiness now comes by "mere grace," as a gift. There is little, if any, room for works, not even for those works that the means of grace include.[44] Perfection is now attained in the article of conversion.

The Almost Christian

On July 25, 1741, John Wesley once again mounted the pulpit at St. Mary's Church in Oxford. Though this discourse was written over a year after he began teaching perfection as a second work of grace, it offers several insights into his faith-alone and holiness gospels; so we include it here in our study. The homily is built around two themes: the almost and the altogether Christian. Moreover, Wesley's purpose is to evangelize. His goal is to press his audience to see their need for a different *kind* of faith, not merely a different *degree*.[45] Consequently, though Wesley believes at the time that perfection is to be distinguished from the new birth (low degree) and justification, for argument sake he collapses perfection into the new birth and justification to drive home the point that his university peers have a glaring need to

---

[43] "These, while they trust in the blood of Christ alone, use all the ordinances which he hath appointed, do all the 'good works which he had before prepared that they should walk therein', and enjoy and manifest all holy and heavenly tempers, even the same 'mind that was in Christ Jesus'" (*Salvation By Faith* III.2).

[44] This will become obvious in the next chapter when we look at the stillness controversy.

[45] In *The Almost Christian* sincerity is a chief mark of the almost Christian while love is the chief mark of the altogether Christian.

embrace salvation by faith in Christ alone. In reality, the "almost" Christian is a critique of his prior gospel system.

Drawing upon the language of *Salvation By Faith*, he first defines the almost Christian in terms of heathen honesty. It is part of the universal conscience of the human race that certain virtues are promoted and their opposites rejected. No society, Christian or otherwise, can function unless people treat each other with integrity, justice, truthfulness, and the like. Wesley recognized that many of his university listeners belonged to this category when it came to their religion.

A second characteristic of the almost Christian is in maintaining a "form of godliness." This means keeping a sufficient measure of outward goodness, abstaining from excess (e.g. alcohol), keeping up with family prayer and using the other means of grace. In short, this kind of almost Christian has the appearance of a real Christian by doing "nothing outward which the gospel forbids," but still lacking the "one thing needful."[46] Coming closer to home, Wesley identifies the last mark of the almost Christian as sincerity in one's religion.[47] He is willing to grant that sincerity involves a "real, inward principle of religion," even a "real design" and a "hearty desire" to serve God, but he openly acknowledges from his own experience that such religion is completely insufficient to save:

> I did go thus far for many years, as many of this place can testify; using diligence to eschew all evil, and to have a conscience void of offense; redeeming the time; buying up every opportunity of doing all good to all men; constantly and carefully using all the public and all the private means of grace; endeavoring after a steady seriousness of behavior, at all times, and in all places; and, God is my record, before whom I stand, doing all this in sincerity; having a real design to serve God; a hearty desire

---

[46] *The Almost Christian* II.4.
[47] For a discussion on how sincerity serves as a ground for assurance in JW's GosH; see chapter 1 section: Assurance.

to do his will in all things; to please him who had called me to "fight the good fight," and to "lay hold of eternal life." Yet my own conscience beareth me witness in the Holy Ghost, that all this time I was but *almost a Christian*.[48]

In contrast, the *altogether* Christian is defined in terms of love: loving God with all one's heart, soul, mind and strength. Such love "engrosses the whole heart" and fills up the "entire capacity of the soul." The altogether Christian is dead to the world and finds joy, delight, and gratitude in God. Indeed, God is their sole desire. In a similar vein, the real Christian loves their neighbor as oneself. Every man, woman and child is considered one's neighbor and worthy of love. Wesley draws from 1 Corinthians 13 to magnify the purity of this believer's love.

Last, the altogether Christian is distinguished from the almost Christian by their faith. Everyone that believes is "born of God." Faith is the "ground," the spring from which flows the fullness of love to God and neighbor. In other words, real faith produces a "loving heart" that "obey(s) his commandments." When a person has a faith that purifies the heart from pride, anger, sinful desire, unrighteousness and all remaining sin, through the infilling of God's love, that person is "not almost only, but altogether, a Christian."[49]

This sermon draws the sharpest distinction between his two gospels. The Gospel of Holiness falls short in its promise to save from sin; while his new gospel, the Gospel of Faith Alone, proffers such liberty at the beginning of the faith journey. In other words, *The Almost Christian* places the disparity between the two gospels in the sharpest light to fix the listener's attention on the need for saving faith. The very best that nominal Christianity can offer is to rise to the level of a sincere servant of God. But the true gospel offers something more; in fact, much more. God de-

---

[48] *The Almost Christian* I.13.
[49] Ibid. II.6.

sires his people to know the fullness of his love poured out into their lives as true righteousness and holiness. Since salvation is a gift of divine grace, *sola gratia,* holiness is also a gift of divine grace, and is received instantaneously by faith alone, in Christ alone. Perfection is now synonymous with the new birth. The contrast between his two gospels can be stated as follows:

The Almost Christian = the Gospel of Holiness
The Altogether Christian = the Gospel of Faith Alone

The Almost Christian is not a real Christian
The Altogether Christian is a real Christian

The Almost Christian falls short of the perfect Christian
The Altogether Christian is the perfect Christian

I am not a Christian

We now come to one of the major paradoxes in Wesley's faith-alone theology: his confusing use of the term "Christian." As we will see in the next chapter, Wesley experienced several seasons of despair and doubt following his Aldersgate conversion. Many of these struggles were included in his published journal for specifically theological reasons (more on this point later). But for now our purpose is to observe how he used of the term "Christian" at the time.

On January 4, 1739, just four days after experiencing a fresh outpouring of the Spirit, Wesley wrote the following confession in his journal:

> My friends affirm *I am mad*, because I said "I was not a Christian a year ago." I affirm, I am not a Christian now. Indeed, what I might have been I know not, had I been faithful to the grace then given, when, expecting nothing less, I received such a sense of the forgiveness of my sins,

as till then I never knew. But that I am not a Christian at this day, I as assuredly know, as that Jesus is the Christ.[50]

Why would Wesley declare, only six months after his supposed evangelical conversion, he was not a Christian? A Christian, he says, has the fruits of the Spirit. But these he lacks: "I *feel* this moment, I do not love God; which therefore I *know,* because I *feel* it."[51] A Christian, he asserts, does not love the world. Yet he says, "I love the world. I desire the things of the world, some or other of them, and have done so all my life." At its root is the desire to find happiness in things like food and friends. Wesley then moves to the question of joy and peace in his life. But even here he feels within himself a level of instability. While his joy rises and falls, it lacks fullness and consistency. Wesley finds that his peace is deficient, "The peace I have may be accounted for on natural principles." While seeing himself having health, friends, financial security, and a balanced temperament, why wouldn't he have contentment and peace? He then begins to censure his past spirituality and the Holy Club program:

> Though I have given, and do give, all my goods to feed the poor, I am not a Christian. Though I have endured hardship, though I have in all things denied myself and taken up my cross, I am not a Christian. My works are nothing, my sufferings are nothing; I have not the fruits of the Spirit of Christ. Though I have constantly used all the means of grace for twenty years, I am not a Christian.

---

[50] JWJ 1/4/39; Works B 19:29. Many assume this is just another episode of JW wavering in his feeling of assurance. John Tyson argues against this view by suggesting that JW is acknowledging a temporary loss of saving faith (see Kenneth Collins, *Conversion in the Wesleyan Tradition*, 33 n 16). This solution is attractive. As we will see in the next chapter, JW does appear to hold for a time an intermittent view regarding perfection and its attainment.
[51] Emphasis his.

The Gospel of Faith Alone

When Peter Böhler convinced Wesley that salvation was by faith alone, Wesley realized that he personally lacked this kind of faith. And lacking this faith meant he was not a real Christian. Moreover, we have already seen that his faith-alone gospel continued to equate salvation with personal holiness. This logically led him to define a real Christian in terms of full salvation, complete deliverance from all sin. Simply stated, one is an altogether Christian or no real Christian at all. Logically, his faith-alone gospel necessarily conjoined being a Christian with perfection (inward holiness). This identification of a real Christian with perfection is a common thread that runs through both gospel systems.

To explain further, six months later Wesley remembers acknowledging in his pre-Aldersgate era, "I told all in our ship, all at Savannah, all at Frederica, and that over and over, in express terms, 'I am not a Christian; I only follow after, if haply I may attain it.'"[52] No amount of good deeds, personal sacrifice, or self-denial could define what is essential to true religion. A real Christian loves God with all the heart.[53] Therefore, John Wesley could only conclude that since he had not yet attained this level of love, he was not perfect, nor a real Christian. This explains his harsh judgment of himself in the above quotations, and why he felt he was not a Christian at the time. The simple truth is that as long as Wesley identified salvation solely in terms of perfect holiness, he would inevitability define a Christian in terms of perfection. For this reason the Gospel of Faith Alone taught:

---

[52] JWJ 6/11/39.

[53] JW's words are, "When they urged my works and self-denial, I answered short, 'Though I give all my goods to feed the poor and my body to be burned I am nothing.' For I have not charity. I do not love God with all my heart" (JWJ 6/11/39). Both JW's GosH and GosFA affirmed the same premise: salvation equals inward holiness. Therefore, JW was consistent in his confession that he was only a seeker of salvation when he knew his tempers were not yet transformed completely. Heitzenrater concludes from JW's confession on January 4 that the "genuine Christian is the perfect Christian" (*Wesley and People*, 91).

John Wesley's Theology of Christian Perfection

>   Salvation is perfection
>   Salvation is real Christianity
>   One must be a real, perfect Christian to be saved

Assessment and Legacy

Today, Wesley's Aldersgate conversion is much debated.[54] It is true that throughout his ministry he refers only a few times to the year 1738, with even fewer references to May 24. While scholars and historians continue to debate the details of the event, there can be no dispute concerning the epochal watershed the event had upon his theology and his doctrine of Christian perfection.[55]

The primary documents of the period show that Wesley continued to understand salvation as inward holiness, including the single intention. This sole point will become critical in understanding why his theology continued to develop in the direction it did in the aftermath of May 24. The most significant breakthrough for Wesley concerned the object of faith. Whereas before he had placed his trust primarily in God and in his promises to make him holy, he now placed his faith in Christ alone for justification and sanctification. In other words, salvation became *sola fide* in *sola Christus*—faith alone in Christ alone. In principle this was a radical departure from his Gospel of Holiness. For it meant that salvation was no longer only a future realization in the article of death, but a present gift bringing justification (peace and acceptance before God), new birth, adoption, full assurance, and perfection to the Christian. This truly was a gospel of instantaneous transformation—in a moment, when saving faith is exercised; the almost Christian is translated from the "kingdom of darkness

---

[54] For a purview of the range of opinions, see Kenneth Collins *John Wesley – A Theology Journey*; Kenneth Collins and John Tyson eds. *Conversion in the Wesleyan Tradition*; and Randy Maddox ed. *Aldersgate Reconsidered*.

[55] Cf. chapter 10: *Evolving Contours* and the *Plain Account* ch 7 end note.

The Gospel of Faith Alone

into the kingdom of his dear Son," and becomes an altogether Christian.[56]

Wesley now believed full salvation was realized in the article of conversion. This was a gospel with no degrees; it was all or nothing! And, in light of his new understanding of the gospel Wesley's continuing struggles with doubt and despair leading up to and following his Aldersgate conversion make sense.

In this all or nothing gospel, complete victory over sin begins with the first spark of regenerate life. As yet, Wesley had not learned to make important distinctions in his doctrine of sin. In his Aldersgate manifesto, *Salvation By Faith*, all manifestations of sin are placed under the single category of "power." While his new gospel did make a clear distinction between sin's guilt and sin's power, allowing him to proclaim present justification grounded solely on Christ's vicarious death, he still failed to delineate carefully between sin's power and being. This, too, is a carryover from his early period. Wesley's Gospel of Faith Alone still functioned with a unified, holistic concept of sin, which contributed to his later struggles over assurance.

Another radical departure concerned his doctrine of justification. Whereas the Gospel of Holiness only taught future justification, the Gospel of Faith Alone proclaimed present justification before God for everyone who believes. Justification forever replaced sanctification as the foundation for salvation in his gospel system. This was a real about-face in his soteriology. Nevertheless, he still continued to confound justification with sanctification. Before, sanctification served as the basis for justification; whereas now justification provided the foundation for sanctification. Yet, both were still so linked that to be justified meant also to be fully sanctified. The equation of salvation with inward holiness created unbearable imbalance and tension within his new gospel system; and, as we will soon see, in his personal life.

Simply put, Wesley's faith-alone gospel placed too much weight upon the God-moment of conversion. So much was ex-

---

[56] Colossians 1:14 (NIV).

pected from this single event, that even if divine power was at work in the moment of conversion it could not carry the weight. Wesley would find this out painfully in his own experience. Yet he was not alone. Böhler's pietistic soteriology proved to be incompatible with what many converts were experiencing. This is where Wesley's journal confessions come into play. But we are jumping ahead to the next chapter. To put this issue in New Testament terms, Wesley's faith-alone gospel collapsed the eschatological tension between the present and future ages.[57] Following the Moravians' lead, Wesley collapsed sanctification into justification. Again, to state the root problem, Wesley continued to assume that salvation equals perfection. This had proved to be the primary weakness in his holiness gospel; the same proved true of his faith-alone gospel.

This lack of balance created an "all or nothing" attitude in his new gospel. One was either an *altogether* Christian, or, at best, an *almost* one. There is no middle ground, no process, no levels, and no degrees. The person either has a faith that vanquishes all fear, doubt and sin, or one is not saved at all. This kind of perfectionism could only lead in one of two directions: self-incriminating despair or self-righteous denial, perpetual guilt or antinomian delusion, self-absorbed legalism or positional righteousness. Wesley suffered from the former; the Moravians, especially of the English variety, were caught in the web of the latter. What Wesley needed was *balance*.

But a major breakthrough concerned his understanding of faith as a divine work in the heart. Wesley lived for many years on a treadmill of works (though he was largely unconscious of

---

[57] This tension is often referred to as "already-not yet." James D.G. Dunn writes of Paul's theology, "The eschatological tension implicit in Paul's schema of salvation runs through all his soteriology...As the terms indicate, 'already-not yet' is a way of summarizing the recognition that something decisive has *already* happened in the event of coming to faith, but that the work of God in reclaiming the individual for himself is *not yet* complete" (*The Theology of Paul the Apostle*, 466).

The Gospel of Faith Alone

this).[58] The means of grace had been overrated. Too much weight had been placed on them to impart salvation. In light of his gospel principles we can understand why; but, nevertheless, Wesley learned during his time in America that the one thing he lacked—the "one thing needful"—was a "sure trust and confidence in God, that through the merits of Christ (his) sins were forgiven, and (he was) reconciled to the favour of God."[59]

We must remind ourselves that his basic goal did not change when he embraced his new gospel. But the means of attaining that goal had undergone radical alteration. Whereas before he believed salvation was attained through faith and good works (means of grace), with emphasis falling upon the latter, he now clearly saw that God offers salvation as a gift received *sola fide*, by faith alone. His initial reaction was to demote the salvific value of the means of grace.[60] But, as we will learn below, this will prove to be short lived. Yet, we must stress that Aldersgate did give Wesley a different kind of faith in regard to the instantaneous working of divine grace. He now saw that God intersects a person's path, touches the heart, and transforms the life in an moment. This became a gospel fit for revival; a gospel suited for the masses. This truly became a gospel of good news!

---

[58] One of the benefits of the "stillness" controversy was that it forever confirmed in JW's mind the critical importance the means of grace play in the spiritual development of the Christian. JW's mature theology connected the process of growth to the practice of the means of grace, and the crisis of instantaneousness to the gift of faith. See the *Plain Account* ch 17 end note, 1745 Q.9; also 18:13-16; 19:73-81; 25:75-79; 26:10-13.

[59] JWJ 2/1/38; Works B 18:215-16.

[60] This statement needs clarification. JW affirms in his May 24 memorandum that following his conviction he lacked saving faith and he continued to practice the means of grace as the way to attaining this faith (§12). This appears to imply a continuing belief in the importance of the means as necessary for receiving saving grace. This author takes JW at his word, but his new-found fascination with the instantaneous reception of grace inadvertently led to a diminution of the means as instrumental to receiving saving grace. This helps to explain JW being caught off guard by the stillness controversy in 1739.

John Wesley's Theology of Christian Perfection

Another area of significant change concerned the ground of assurance. We saw in chapter one that Wesley's holiness gospel provided a three pronged approach to personal assurance: (1) Holy Spirit's indwelling presence (2) communicating at the Lord's Table, and (3) the believer's sincerity of devotion (the integrity of the single intention). What evaporated Wesley's own sense of assurance were the storms at sea. Gripped with fear he realized how unwilling he was to die and to face God. Under his Gospel of Holiness system, the only reasonable conclusion was that his heart was still fundamentally unchanged. This brought shock waves to his conscience. How misguided could he have been to strive all those years for inward holiness only to find his heart fundamentally unchanged. As events unfolded in Georgia, this conclusion finally drove Wesley to his knees crying out for peace and assurance. This failure opened his heart to hear a different gospel message.[61] The new message promised assurance in an instant, with the Holy Spirit bearing witness of God's forgiveness and peace. Wesley's new gospel swung the pendulum to the opposite extreme, depreciating the value of sincerity and the means of grace. Over the next several decades he will continue to gravitate toward a more balanced position as he continues to grapple with these issues.[62]

Finally, how did these radical changes within his theological system affect his doctrine of perfection, defined as inward holiness? We have already seen that regarding its basic delineation, nothing really changed. Perfection was still the goal, and was still understood as holy tempers and dispositions. What changed were the means of attainment and the question of timing. Before, perfect love was attained through the disciplined practice of the means of grace infusing holy habits within the heart. Now, per-

---

[61] This point was argued in ch 1 and also earlier in this chapter. This author believes JW did not struggle with concerns over assurance as deeply, or as persistently, as many modern interpreters assert. I remind the reader that JW was surprised to find he was unwilling to die when faced by the storms at sea. Cf. ch 1, section: Assurance.

[62] Cf. ch 4: Aldersgate II.

fection was received instantly as divine gift. The logical corollary was that perfection is attained now, in this life, as a blessing of justification and the new birth. In other words, salvation *begins* with perfection, even salvation from the "whole body of sin."[63] This last element will soon change, as we will learn in the next chapter.

The question concerning the means of grace will go through further evolution as Wesley seeks to find balance between his two gospel systems. But the radical change from a perfection attained in the article of death, to one attained in the article of conversion, created a dilemma of its own. If it should prove that perfection is not attainable in the article of conversion, then when is it attained, if at all? This became the important question in light of Wesley's struggles following Aldersgate. While the answer is already known due to the ease of historical hindsight, we must look once more at the process by which Wesley's theology transitioned if we are to grasp the evolution of his doctrine of perfect love, and understand the *how's* and *why's* of his theological development.

What follows is the comparison chart highlighting the changes that took place in Wesley's theology of perfection:

Gospel of Holiness	Gospel of Faith Alone
Axiom:	
Inward holiness	Faith alone
Ground:	
Sanctification brings justification	Justification equals sanctification

---

[63] *Salvation By Faith* II.7. See JWJ 2/1/38 where JW adds the word "whole" to Rom 6:6, "whosoever hath it (saving faith), is 'freed from sin, the' whole 'body of sin is destroyed' in him." Both statements point to the belief that perfection, as deliverance from all sin, is attained in the article of conversion.

John Wesley's Theology of Christian Perfection

Object of faith:
God & his promises   Christ alone

Focus:
Future salvation   Present salvation

Salvation by:
Faith in ordinances   Faith alone

Salvation is:
Lifelong process   Instantaneous gift

Assurance:
Sincerity, communicating, Witness of the Spirit
& life transformation

Holiness complete:
Death   Conversion

Faith complete:
Death   Conversion

Christian complete:
Death   Conversion

THREE
The Gospel of Two Works of Grace

The evolution of John Wesley's theology of perfection in the aftermath of his Aldersgate conversion is best seen as a striving for balance between his two gospel systems—that of holiness and faith alone.[1] We learned in chapter one that inward holiness formed the core of Wesley's deep-seated beliefs, his spiritual DNA. This axiom drove his personal search for salvation and the development of his early theological system. It is a testimony of the change he experienced at Aldersgate that salvation by faith alone became the second axiom which would forge his theology in profound ways.[2] Thus these two axioms became the primary driving forces behind the integration of the *ordo salutis* within his theology of perfection. To repeat, that Wesley so soon struggles after Aldersgate, even very deeply, over questions of assurance and salvation, and yet never questions the validity of salvation by faith alone, is testimony to the depth of conviction he developed for this truth in such a short period of time (March through May 1738).

The quest for balance was mostly achieved through clarification of key doctrines and their relationship, like justification, new birth, assurance, sanctification, sin, faith and the means of grace. Yet one change in his *ordo salutis* would prove very critical to his Gospel of Two Works system: Wesley moved the single intention from the commencement of vital Christianity[3] to a second

---

[1] This comment refers to JW's entire future career and not just the period under consideration. See ch 8: Evolving Contours.
[2] Even Whitefield sympathizer and biographer Arnold Dallimore says of JW that the "great truth of 'justification by faith' had been burned into his soul" (*George Whitefield, Vol. II*; p. 22).
[3] At this point it would be misleading to use new birth language to communicate JW's position on the beginning moment of vital or real Christianity. As we will see below, JW's understanding of the new birth at the time was much more comprehensive of the total faith journey process.

moment on the faith journey path. This last point cannot be emphasized too strongly. It is true that Wesley never explicitly discusses this change when working out his theology or his understanding of Christian perfection as a second gift. But, as we will soon learn, credit must be given to this single change for the theological justification of a second work of grace. In both of Wesley's gospel systems we have studied thus far, the single intention is located at the beginning of spiritual life. We saw that Wesley's holiness gospel used the terminology of regeneration to describe the single intention. So early Wesley believed real Christianity began with the decision of the single intention. It is important to remember that this conviction did not change when he embraced his faith-alone gospel. Since justification and full sanctification were still associated and located in the same moment (conversion), the logical corollary was that the single intention must be an essential component of that event too. By moving the single intention to a second moment on the faith journey path, Wesley could more easily proclaim Christian perfection as a second work of grace.

The Cause of Wesley's Struggles

It is well known among students of Wesley of his continuing struggles following his Aldersgate conversion. Struggles over assurance persisted for several months (according to his journal and letters). This factor, plus the burgeoning needs of the recent converts, is what provided the climate out of which his theology of perfection continued to take shape. Yet, behind these struggles were implicit beliefs that more than contributed to his internal battles, they were the primary cause.

Our first clue is found in his bouts with doubt immediately following his conversion. Underpinning Wesley's self-reflective questioning was a theology that denied any room for doubt and fear to coexist with saving faith. This theology will later become known as "stillness."[4]

Our second clue is to look at *when* and *why* Wesley published his second journal extract. As Henry Rack observes, Wesley published his early journal extracts to "explain and justify the break with the Moravians" in the summer of 1740.[5] Wesley finished the preface for extract two on September 29, 1740, a little more than two months following the split, and only four months after the release of his first journal extract. If the reader remembers, extract two covers the period following his return to England. It details his meeting Peter Böhler, his conversion at Aldersgate, and ends with his travels to Germany to learn more about the Moravian faith. It was on this journey Wesley learned that the German Moravians did not agree with their English counterparts on aspects of justification, assurance, and degrees of saving faith. In the journal preface Wesley explains "it is my bounden duty to clear the (German) Moravians from this aspersion,"[6] meaning, the stigma of stillness. He then follows up with a concise summary of the issues involved in the controversy (as he saw them).

For starters, the English Moravians taught there are no degrees of saving faith. Justifying faith requires the person be "wholly freed from all doubt and fear" for acceptance before God. Further, a person is not considered justified until they have a "new, clean heart." At the time, this phrase served as a synonym for entire sanctification.[7] As Heitzenrater explains, the "English Moravians had, in Lutheran fashion, collapsed sanctification into justification and, in Pietist fashion, extended forgiveness of sins (imputed righteousness) into freedom from sin (in-

---

[4] Timothy Smith wrote in 1986, "Inattention to chronology has allowed scholars to minimize or ignore the connection between the Moravian controversy and Wesley's new view of entire sanctification" (*John Wesley and the Second Blessing,* Wesleyan Theological Journal, Vol. 21, 1986; 140).
[5] *Reasonable Enthusiast,* 203.
[6] Extract II, Preface (Works J 1:81).
[7] On the synonym "new, clean heart" see note 95 below.

fused righteousness)."[8] Therefore, perfection begins the faith journey, and serves as evidence for one's acceptance before God.

Stillness advocates argued against the use of the means of grace by anyone lacking saving faith. In December 1739 Wesley had a long discussion with Philipp Molther,[9] who was the real force behind the stillness controversy of 1740. In his journal Wesley explains Molther's rationale for being "still." Molther believed the way to receive justifying faith is to "wait" on Christ alone. He felt it is impossible to use the means of grace without trusting in them for acceptance.[10] When Molther arrived on October 18, he was appalled at the sight of society members sighing and groaning in the services. He was told these manifestations were the "'demonstration of the Spirit and of power'"[11] He interpreted such behavior as a groaning after salvation and proceeded to teach the members "free grace in the blood of Jesus." Molther saw such activity, combined with the practice of the means of grace, as diverting people away from Christ. He soon gained the people's trust and many within the Fetter Lane society stopped practicing the means of grace.

When Wesley returned in early November 1739 he found many of his converts "still" and doubting their prior sense of assurance. Being "still" meant to stop the following, like, going to church, partaking of communion, fasting, prayer, reading the Bi-

---

[8] *Great Expectations: Aldersgate and the Evidences of Genuine Christianity*, in Maddox, Randy ed. "Aldersgate Reconsidered" p. 68.

[9] Philipp Heinrich Molther (1714-1780) was educated in Jena where he underwent a spiritual conversion. Through teaching French to Count Zinzendorf's son, Renatus, he came into contact with the Moravians and became a traveling companion of the Count. He was appointed to serve in Pennsylvania and waited in London for several months for a boat. During this time James Hutton introduced him to the Fetter Lane Society. Molther was a noted composer of music and translated many Moravian Hymns into French (Works B 19:119, n. 2).

[10] Charles wrote of the stillness advocates, "The unjustified, say they, are *to be still*; that is, not to search the Scriptures, not to pray, not to communicate, not to do good, not to endeavor, not to desire; for it is impossible to use means with out trusting in them" (CWJ 4/25/40).

[11] Rack, *Reasonable Enthusiast*, 203.

ble, and works of compassion.[12] Again, from Molther's perspective to continue such means while seeking salvation in Christ only diverted the heart away from Christ. One need only to *wait* for God's justifying grace to be freely bestowed.

This meant that salvation comes as a complete package—meaning justification, sanctification, new birth and assurance. But this also implied there could be no degrees and shades of saving faith. One either has faith or does not have faith. It is all or nothing. Salvation is by Christ alone, through faith alone, witnessed by the Spirit alone, in an instant alone. As we will now see, the very principles Wesley will abhor in 1740 were the ones he innocuously digested under the tutelage of Böhler two years earlier.

Wesley's Continuing Struggles

On the evening of May 24, 1738 Charles Wesley was still recovering from his illness when towards ten his brother came bustling into his room with a group of friends triumphantly declaring, "I believe!" Charles records their exuberance as they sang a "hymn with great joy and parted with prayer." And so John's "new gospel" was ratified by his own experience. He now had an assurance that his sins were washed away and he was saved from the "law of sin and death."[13] Wesley believed he would now always conquer.[14] Yet, within hours he began to be buffeted with

---

[12] JWJ 12/31/39. Molther asserted from his private discussions with the members that many did entertain doubts over their salvation (Podmore, *The Moravian Church in England, 1728-1760*, 63).
[13] JWJ 5/24/38, §14; Rom 8:2.
[14] JWJ 5/24/38, §16. Only a few days later JW told everyone at the Hutton's home that he had not been a Christian before his Aldersgate conversion. When Mr. Hutton balked JW proceeded to tell his host and guests that only when they had "renounced every thing but faith, and then got into Christ," had they "any reason to believe (they) were Christians" (Benham, *Memoirs of James Hutton*, 34). Since "every thing" included the means of grace this also confirms that JW had imbibed stillness principles from Böhler.

all kinds of doubts over the reality of his faith. He confessed to lacking joy and feeling depressed, due to the number of temptations. Only five days after his exhilarating heart-warming conversion, he traveled with another recent convert of Böhler's ministry, Shepherd Wolf. Wolf's testimony appeared so superior to his that Wesley began to question whether they shared the same kind of faith at all.

The struggles persisted. Old bosom sins began to lift their head. Wesley speaks of being "troubled" for grieving God's Spirit. On June 6 he became deeply perplexed over a letter he received that asserted "no doubting could consist with the least degree of true faith; that whoever at any time felt any doubt or fear was not *weak in faith*, but had *no faith* at all; and that none hath any faith till the law of the Spirit of life has made him *wholly* free from the law of sin and death."[15] Wesley went to prayer "begging God" to direct him. Opening to 1 Corinthians 3, he read Paul's description of the Corinthian's behaving as "babes" in Christ because of their worldliness. Down a few verses these same believers are referred to as God's temple and building; thus concluding in Wesley's mind, at least for the moment, one can have a *degree* of saving faith even though it might be *weak*. But he could not find any lasting peace. We need to ask, why?

Feeling spiritually "sawn asunder," Wesley decided to travel to Germany to converse with those who were "living witnesses of the full power of faith."[16] He was confident such men would have the patience to help someone, like himself, who was weak in faith. Initially, Wesley must have felt greatly disappointed when these "holy men" barred him from the Lord's Table. They considered him to be *homo perturbatis*, a perturbed person who lacked full assurance.[17] Upon his return from Germany Wesley continued to be plagued with doubt, all due to the stillness principles he had digested. In October he wrote to a friend concerning

---

[15] JWJ 6/6/38.
[16] JWJ 6/7/38.
[17] Cf. Heitzenrater, *Great Expectations*, 67; Benham, *Memoirs of James Hutton*, 40.

The Gospel of Two Works of Grace

the "state of those who are 'weak in faith.'" The response he received threw him into a tailspin. Though the letter has not survived, from Wesley's reaction we know the thrust of its contents: justifying faith cannot coexist with the least degree of doubt.

A little more than a month later he was in communication with his close friend Charles Delamotte. Charles had been a travel companion to America and knew Wesley well. John opened his heart and shared his struggles to find full assurance. His journal records the substance of Delamotte's response:

> In this you are better than you was at Savannah. You know that you was then quite wrong. But you are not right yet. You know that you was then blind. But you do not see now.
>
> I doubt not but God will bring you to the right foundation. But I have no hope for you, while you are on your present foundation. It is as different from the true, as the right hand from the left. You have all to begin anew.
>
> I have observed all your words and actions, and I see you are of the same spirit still. You have a simplicity. But it is a simplicity of your own. It is not the simplicity of Christ. You think you do not trust in your own works. But you do trust in your own works. You do not yet believe in Christ.
>
> You have a present freedom from sin. But it is only a temporary suspension of it, not a deliverance from it. And you have a peace. But it is not a true peace. If death were to approach, you would find all your fears return.[18]

Obviously, Charles discerned that his friend's predicament stemmed from a continued trust in oneself, not in Christ. According to stillness theology, remaining doubt must be interpreted ac-

---

[18] JWJ 11/23/38; In Works B 25:597 Frank Baker lists this as a letter JW wrote to Charles Delamotte. But in JW's journal (11/27/38) he lists it as Delamotte's last conversation to him. From JW's response in his journal this letter could not have been written from him to Delamotte.

cordingly. So in Delamotte's eyes, his friend's apparent victory over sin was a delusion since his peace was not consistent. The fact Wesley still had doubt pointed to only one conclusion: he did not have saving faith. We begin to see how Wesley's struggles were rooted in the stillness principles inherent in his faith-alone gospel.

Several days later he wrote to the society in London inquiring of their spiritual state. From the tone in his journal one gets the impression he was fishing for some kind of encouragement. William Fish wrote back extolling the richness of God's saving grace. He testified of God's love filling the heart, destroying all self-love, thus saving him from sin's dominion. He shared how he was born of God in an instant, with the gift of full assurance flooding his heart so that the "whole bent" of his will was toward Christ day and night—even in his dreams! A second letter (now anonymous) tells a similar story. The author experienced new birth, assurance of present forgiveness, complete union with Christ, and the witness of the Spirit over the expanse of three days.[19] These letters were inserted into Wesley's journal because they testify to the power and fruit of saving faith in Christ; a faith that is evidenced by full assurance and complete deliverance from all sin. Yet, the corollary must also be true: such faith leaves little, if any, room for doubt to coexist with justifying faith.

Wesley's testimony, by contrast, must have appeared to his colleagues as very defective. Still seeking to find a peace that would vanquish all fear and doubt, on December 16 he examines himself once again. He concludes the "old heart of stone" still remains in him. Confessing a "carnal heart," Wesley openly acknowledges his lack of a "single eye," at least, with consistency. Questions over the newness of his desires persist, only to be answered in the negative. Wesley recognizes he has a "great desire" for Christ to be formed within him, yet he admits to numerous "little" desires sneaking in and stealing his devotion. He finally

---

[19] JWJ 12/3/38. These are among the first testimonies of Christian perfection in JW's Journal. See Appendix C.

The Gospel of Two Works of Grace

concludes he is in a *mixed* state: "my love is only partly spiritual and partly natural." Around this time he opened his heart to Isaac Lelong:

> Do not think, my dear brother, that I have forgotten you! I cannot forget you, because I love you. Though I can't yet love anyone as I ought, because I can't love our blessed Lord, *as I ought*. My heart is cold and senseless. It is indeed a heart of stone. O when will he take out of the midst of me, and give me a heart of flesh? Pray for me, and let all your household pray for me, yea, and all the brethren also, that our God would give me a broken heart, and a loving heart, a heart wherein his Spirit may delight to dwell.[20]

Having imbibed stillness principles Wesley's faith could not break free and get traction. Finally, like icing on the cake, on January 4 he exclaims, "I am not a Christian," simply because he was not a *perfect* one. He then affirms a second stillness principle, "Though I have constantly used all the means of grace for twenty years, I am not a Christian." Implicit in this reasoning is that the means of grace have purpose so long as there are degrees of faith. But if, as Wesley's faith-alone gospel affirmed, saving faith is a gift received instantly by the Holy Spirit, then to what purpose does the constant practice of attending church, reading scripture, fasting and prayer serve in attaining this faith? Wesley's persistent struggles reveal just how much he had digested stillness principles without knowing it.

Let us pause and assess the significance of what this means. First, we have to acknowledge that Wesley's faith-alone gospel contributed to the stillness controversy that later erupted in the fall of 1739. This is the only explanation that makes sense as to why many of Wesley's converts so easily embraced Molther's message. Molther merely took the inherent principles of the re-

---

[20] JWL 12/31/38, or possibly 11/22/38 (see Works B 25:584).

vival message—salvation by faith alone, in Christ alone, through the Spirit alone, in an instant alone—to their logical conclusion. If salvation is received instantly as a complete and finished package, then to what purpose do the means of grace serve in attaining salvation? After all, how can there be any degrees to a faith that comes instantly, in a complete package, from the divine Spirit? Even John Wesley, the high church sacramentarian he was, could find little room for the means of grace in his new gospel.[21]

Second, the stillness controversy played a central role in the evolution of Wesley's perfection theology. For it was in response, or better, in reaction to stillness ideas and principles that Wesley began to forge his own doctrine of perfection as a second gift. Early Wesley had grounded salvation on the sanctification process; thereby placing much emphasis on the principle of degrees.[22] The goal of this system was to attain complete (perfect) holiness in the article of death, preparing the believer for final justification at the last judgment. At Aldersgate the pendulum swung to the opposite extreme. Justification, inward holiness, and full assurance were now gifts to be received at the commencement of the faith journey. The key to finding balance was to inte-

---

[21] After JW accepted his new gospel he made a number of negative comments regarding the salvific value of the means of grace. A good example is the testimony he recorded on September 30, "One who had been a zealous opposer of 'this way' sent and desired to speak with me immediately. He had all the signs of settled despair, both in his countenance and behaviour. He said he had been enslaved to sin many years, especially to drunkenness; that *he had long used all the means of grace*, had constantly gone to church and sacrament, had read the Scripture, and used much private prayer, and yet was nothing profited. I desired we might join in prayer. After a short space he rose, and his countenance was no longer sad. He said, 'Now I know God loveth me and has forgiven my sins. And sin shall not have dominion over me, for Christ hath set me free.' And according to his faith it was unto him" (JWJ 9/30/38, emphasis mine; see JWJ 5/24/38 §§6-10, 1/4/39).

[22] In making this point the reader is reminded that JW did have an understanding of instantaneousness in his early period, in the sense that the single intention began at a specific moment in time. The point being made is that his early theological system gravitated heavily toward a progressive emphasis.

grate these two gospel systems at this point. Reaching back to his holiness gospel Wesley incorporated the principle of degrees; from his faith-alone gospel he retained the principle of instantaneous reception. In this way Wesley's Gospel of Two Works combined both process (degrees of faith) and instantaneous reception (divine gift) to form a new gospel system.

Third, the stillness controversy explains why Wesley openly shared his post-Aldersgate struggles before the entire world, and why he dropped the subject after January 4, 1739. The journal became an effective way to refute stillness teaching among Wesley's readership. To make the point, Wesley used his own story to illustrate the truth that weak faith is genuine, justifying faith. He did this in two ways. (1) He attributes his continuing struggles to the infection of stillness principles within his thinking, thus exposing the dangers of ingesting this kind of teaching. In each episode of his recorded struggles, stillness theology is the root cause behind his doubts. He drops the subject after January 4 because there was no need to continue the exercise. Simply put, his point was made. Focus shifts to the new period of his life: field preaching and the revival.[23] (2) Wesley records a lengthy section in his journal on the teachings of Christian David, and the testimonies of other German Moravians, affirming degrees of saving faith. These testimonies contradict what the English Moravians taught, undercutting their stillness message. Besides refuting stillness, these testimonies played an additional role helping Wesley develop his Gospel of Two Works of Grace. To this we now turn.

Marienborn & Hernhuth

Wesley informs us that he made the decision to visit the Moravian community in Germany in the wake of his deep struggles

---

[23] See JWJ 3/28/39 for a lengthy insert explaining this change of direction in his life and ministry.

John Wesley's Theology of Christian Perfection

over his lack of assurance. As we saw above, he felt himself being "sawn asunder" as to whether his weak faith was saving or not. Moreover, since his first encounters with the Moravians in America, he had desired to visit the source of this faith community. So Wesley and his companions sailed from England on June 14 and arrived at Marienborn and Count Zinzendorf's place on July 4. After recovering from a short illness, Wesley's excitement grew over the opportunity to live among those who were "living proofs of the power of faith: persons 'saved from inward as well as outward sin', by 'the love of God shed abroad in their hearts'; and from all doubt and fear by the abiding 'witness of the Holy Ghost given unto them.'"[24]

The next day John wrote to both his brothers extolling the virtues of his Moravian hosts. To his brother Samuel John exclaimed, "I am with a church whose conversation in heaven, in whom is the mind that was in Christ, and who so walk as he walked."[25] John was finally living among people who were living expressions of his faith-alone gospel. Then to Charles he celebrated the "everlasting truth" that real faith brings peace with God, freedom from sin, and full renewal as a new creation in Christ. These letters offer significant insights into Wesley's present frame of mind, and confirm his theological leanings at the time. The letters reveal his firm conviction in his faith-alone gospel that he learned from Peter Böhler and the English Moravians. But the letters also reflect stillness theology: salvation is viewed as a complete package received in a single work of grace.

Several days later Wesley took part in a gathering for visitors. One person from Frankfort asked Count Zinzendorf, "Can a man be justified, and not know it?" Wesley eagerly wrote down the Count's response:

1. Justification is the forgiveness of sins.
2. The moment a man flies to Christ he is justified.

---

[24] JWJ 7/6/38.
[25] JWL 7/7/38. See *Plain Account* ch 5 for JW's definition of perfection as the mind and walk of Christ.

3. And has peace with God, but not always joy.
4. Nor perhaps may he know he is justified till long after.
5. For the assurance of it is distinct from justification itself.
6. But others may know he is justified by his power over sin, by his seriousness, his love of the brethren, and his 'hunger and thirst after righteousness', which alone proves the spiritual life to be begun.
7. To be justified is the same thing as to be born of God.
8. When a man is awakened, he is begotten of God; and his fear and sorrow and sense of the wrath of God are the pangs of the new birth.[26]

Wesley immediately recognized a marked difference between Zinzendorf's perspective and his English counterparts. Whereas the Count acknowledged that a new convert's joy can fluctuate and assurance can often lag behind justifying faith, Böhler taught no one could have peace with God and power over sin apart from full assurance. Böhler made full assurance a necessary concomitant of the saving event; whereas the Count allowed a temporal distinction between justification and assurance. After several more days with the Count, Wesley, along with his companions, set out for Hernhuth.

Arriving in early August, Wesley had the privilege of listening four times to Christian David, the carpenter turned Moravian preacher and bishop.[27] Time would show the degree of influence David would have on the development of Wesley's perfection

---

[26] JWJ 7/12/38. Concerning #7 see ch 4 *Aldersgate II*. In #8 the phrase "pangs of the new birth" was later used in the revival to explain the physical manifestations that erupted (Dallimore *George Whitefield*, 326; e.g. JWL 7/2/39 Works B 25:665, l. 14).

[27] JW includes a lengthy excerpt of Christian's life story and faith journey (Work B 18:273-281; Tyerman, 1:200).

theology.[28] From Wesley's notes we learn Christian taught there was more than one state of grace. Three of David's messages dealt specifically with the questions swirling in Wesley's mind over faith, assurance, and salvation from sin.

David began by expounding on the Beatitudes in Matthew's Gospel. Those weak in faith are identified with the poor in spirit. Since the text affirms that the kingdom of God is already given to the poor in spirit (weak in faith), David reasons they must already be saved. Then, using the individual Beatitudes as markers, David describes the stages which the immature believer passes through until they are filled with righteousness, attaining purity of heart from "all self and sin," becoming like their heavenly Father, merciful as he is merciful.[29] In his second sermon David draws upon Romans chapters seven and eight. He explains how believers pass through an "intermediate state," between the legal bondage described in chapter seven to the "full glorious liberty of the children of God" described in chapter eight.[30] In the third homily David clarifies the nature of the intermediate state by looking at the disciples' faith journey between Christ's crucifixion and Pentecost. Jesus declared the disciples "clean" (Jn 15:3) and prayed that their faith might not fail (Lk 22:32). So, David concludes, the disciples already had a degree of saving faith prior to Pentecost. Yet, he did not believe they were "properly *converted*," delivered from "the spirit of fear," or had "*new hearts*" until they received the "gift of the Holy Spirit" at Pentecost.[31]

These three expositions began a process in Wesley that would eventually lead to an understanding of salvation that embraces two works of grace. David carefully discriminated between justi-

---

[28] Ward and Heitzenrater write, "The sheer space given by JW to Christian David's preaching and autobiography testifies to the impact which they made" (Works B 18:273 n. 98). Cf. note 44 below.

[29] Works B 18:270; Lk 6:36.

[30] Works B 18:270. The reader should note David's acceptance of degrees of faith and a view of the new birth as progressive.

[31] Works B 18:271 (emphasis his). It is no accident Christian David was touching on these subjects. Many believers were wrestling with the same questions JW was asking.

The Gospel of Two Works of Grace

fication and sanctification, identifying the former as a first work of grace and the latter as a second work. He made a clear distinction between a faith that is weak, yet justifying, and a faith that is strong, filled with God's fullness. Moreover, in these messages justification serves as the foundation or ground for sanctification and the believer's journey toward Christian perfection. Here was a gospel where both the power of faith alone and the demand for inward holiness worked in tandem.

In a fourth message David addressed the proper ground for faith and reconciliation. Wesley was so impressed with this message he wrote down the substance of it. David opens by affirming salvation is not by works but "'wholly and solely by the blood of Christ.'" He goes on to explain that in the preparatory stages, when the person is seeking salvation and faith, they often feel deep remorse and contrition. Contrary to Molther and other stillness advocates, David does not demean this preparatory stage in the salvation process. Instead, he affirms these emotions are part of the Spirit's work preparing the seeker for saving faith. But he cautions that these feelings are not a proper ground for acceptance before God:

> The right foundation is, not your contrition (though that is not your own), not your righteousness, nothing of your own; nothing that is wrought in you by the Holy Ghost; but it is something without you, viz., the righteousness and the blood of Christ.[32]

David's teaching on the preparatory work of the Spirit directly contradicted the stillness principles inherent in Wesley's faith-alone gospel and Böhler's message. Stillness doctrine placed little value on the preparatory work of the Spirit. Collapsing justification, sanctification, new birth and assurance into a single package, which was received supernaturally in a moment of faith, meant the preparatory work of prevenient grace had little to no

---

[32] JWJ 8/10/38.

value. As a consequence, all means of grace could, and should, be set aside until the gift of saving faith is received. David reaffirmed for Wesley the inherent value of practicing the means of grace in preparation for the gifts of justifying and sanctifying grace.

David then finishes his message by reiterating that salvation is by faith alone. Keeping in step with his pietistic Lutheranism, he affirms that justifying faith must be of the heart:

> The faith of the head, learned from men or books, is nothing worth. It brings neither remission of sins or peace with God. Labour then to believe with the whole heart. So shall you have redemption through the blood of Christ. So shall you be cleansed from all sin. So shall ye go on from strength to strength, being renewed day by day in righteousness and all true holiness.[33]

Christian David's last message did much to confirm in Wesley's mind the convictions of his Aldersgate experience, yet pointed the way out of the quagmire he had found himself stuck.

But David's influence was not limited to his sermons. Wesley carefully records his lengthy testimony, which covers several pages in his journal.[34] Our purpose is to not dwell on the sum of David's story, but to isolate the theology that left an indelible mark on Wesley's doctrinal development. The following excerpt highlights several important doctrinal seeds that Wesley will later incorporate into his own theology of perfection:

> I saw not then that the first promise to the children of God is, "Sin shall no more reign over you;" but thought I was to *feel* it in me no more from the time it was forgiven. Therefore, although I had the *mastery* over it, yet I often *feared* it was not forgiven, because it still *stirred in me*,

---

[33] Works B 18:272.
[34] Works J 1:120-127; Works B 18:273-281.

The Gospel of Two Works of Grace

> and at some times "thrust sore at me that I might fall." Because, though it did not *reign*, it did *remain* in me; and I was continually *tempted*, though not *overcome*. This at that time threw me into many *doubts*; not understanding that the devil tempts, properly speaking, only those whom he perceives to be escaping from him. He need not tempt his own...Neither saw I then that the "being justified" is widely different from the having the "full assurance of faith." I remembered not that our Lord told his apostles before his death, "Ye are clean;" whereas it was not till many days after it that they were fully assured, by the Holy Ghost then received, of their reconciliation to God through his blood.[35]

Christian explains how he first believed all sin was removed in justification, so he would not even *feel* it any longer. Yet he soon learned that though sin was no longer his *master*, it still *stirred* within him. Although sin no longer *reigned*, it did *remain*. At first, his weak faith was thrown into many *doubts* and *fears*, by many *temptations* "thrust sore at me that I might fall." This whole experience taught David there are two works of grace, not one; and two distinct levels of faith: justifying and full assurance.

David's testimony goes on to explain how he came to reject Calvin's doctrines of unconditional election and limited atonement. This next excerpt, though lengthy, tells how David came to balance both justification and sanctification within his theology:

> In the meantime we found a great remissness of behaviour had crept in among us. And indeed the same was to be found in most of those round about us, whether Lutherans or Calvinists, so insisting on *faith* as to forget, at least in practice, both *holiness* and *good works*.
>
> Observing this terrible abuse of preaching Christ given for us, we began to insist more than ever on *Christ*

---

[35] Works B 18:274 (emphasis Wesley).

living in us. All our exhortations and preaching turned on this; we spoke, we writ, of nothing else. Our constant inquiries were: 'Is Christ *formed* in you? Have you a *new heart*? Is your soul *renewed in the image of God*? Is the *whole body of sin destroyed* in you? Are you *fully assured*, beyond *all doubt* or *fear*, that you are a *child of God*? In what manner and at what *moment* did you receive that full assurance?' If a man could not answer all these questions, we judged he had no true faith. Nor would we permit any to receive the Lord's Supper among us till he could.

In this persuasion we were when I went to Greenland five years ago. There I had a correspondence by letter with a Danish minister, Hans Egede, on the head of justification. And it pleased God to show me by him that we had now *leaned* too much to this hand, and were run into another extreme: that '*Christ in us*' and '*Christ for us*' ought indeed to be *both insisted on*, but first and principally 'Christ for us', as being the *ground* of all. I now clearly saw we ought not to insist on anything we *feel*, any more than anything we *do*, as if it were necessary previous to justification or the remission of sins. I saw that least of all ought we so to insist on the *full assurance of faith*, or the *destruction of the body of sin*, and the *extinction of all its motions*, as to exclude those who had not attained this from the Lord's Table, or to deny that they had any faith at all. I plainly perceived this full assurance was a *distinct gift* from justifying faith, and often not given till *long after* it; and that justification does not imply that sin should not *stir* in us, but only that it should not *conquer*.[36]

Here was a gospel grounded on two works of grace. After running to extremes in both directions, first toward justification and

---

[36] Works B 18:279-280 (emphasis Wesley).

The Gospel of Two Works of Grace

then toward sanctification, David learned to balance both with an emphasis on justification as the *ground*, and full assurance (of a perfect heart) as a *distinct gift*. In addition, David calls these two distinct works of grace: *Christ for us* and *Christ in us*. The first gift brings forgiveness of sins, release from sin's reign, and adoption into God's family. The second gift—Christ living in us—brings full assurance from all fear and doubt, the destruction of the whole body of sin, Christ formed within, and renewal in the image of God. As to timing David acknowledges the second gift is "often not given till long after" the first.

To show the influence David had on Wesley's theological development, let us reconstruct the basic contours of the faith journey according to Christian David:

> *Stage One: Nominal Faith.* For those born in a Christian nation, they grow up baptized in the church and learn the external forms of Christianity, but lack personal awareness of the gospel's power to save from sin's guilt and power.
>
> *Stage Two: Awareness of Need.* The faith journey properly begins with the Holy Spirit awakening the heart to a personal need for redemption. The seeker begins to mourn over their sin and to feel their need for forgiveness and a new heart. In this condition the seeker must be cautioned to not place trust in oneself, in any feelings of remorse, or in their repentance.
>
> *Stage Three: The First Gift.* The seeker then looks to Christ dying and rising for them. God gives the gift of faith for the seeker to trust in Christ alone for forgiveness and acceptance before God. God declares the believer clean in his sight. The Holy Spirit imparts assurance bringing peace and freedom over sin. This is the first work of grace.

Stage Four: There are three phases to this stage of spiritual development:

A. Peace, Then Struggle. In the days, weeks, and months that follow, the Christian rejoices in the work God has wrought in the heart. But soon the journey takes a turn for the worse. Temptations arise that bring fears that the heart is not truly transformed. The stirrings of sin begin to be felt. The believer's faith weakens as doubts begin to fill the mind. In this state the believer lacks assurance their heart is really changed, thereby raising questions in the mind concerning one's acceptance before God.

B. Sin Remains. At this time the Spirit instructs the immature believer about the nature of the sin that remains. God gives comfort by assuring the believer that though their faith is weak; it is real and acceptable to their heavenly Father. The believer sees that while sin no longer *reigns* over them, it does *remain* in them. The Christian is humbled and begins to mourn over their sinful heart.

C. Sanctifying Grace. God then prepares the seeking heart for the second gift: Christ living in them. The promise of full assurance draws the Christian to hunger and thirst after righteousness and true holiness of heart. They long for full renewal in the image of God, even for the whole body of sin to be destroyed. Longing for inward holiness, the believer looks to Christ for a second work, a gift distinct from justification.

Stage Five: The Second Gift. God then does what only he can do. He touches the heart a second time. In a *moment* the believer receives the gift of full assurance. The Holy Spirit comes to dwell permanently, thereby bringing

Christ's life into the very depths of their being. The heart is purified from all self-will and sin. Christ is now formed within. The heart is now made new. The whole body of sin is destroyed.

From the above description Christian David's influence on Wesley's doctrinal development is evident, even upon a cursory reading of Wesley's writings. On a conceptual level, David's description of both works of grace dovetails with Wesley's own explication of perfect love; for Wesley will later delineate the faith journey using the same contours as David did. Wesley will later integrate much of David's terminology within his own message. For instance, David delineates between sin's *reign* and the sin that *remains*. Twenty-five years later Wesley will use the same terminology to describe the stages of freedom from sin: "He (the believer) is saved from sin; yet not entirely: It *remains*, though it does not *reign*."[37] Moreover, Wesley's later homilies on the Sermon on the Mount follow the same train of thought as David's first sermon.[38] Finally, as David made much use of "Christ *for us*" and "Christ *in us*" (his emphasis), Wesley will later use this same terminology to clarify the distinction between justification and the new birth:

> But what is it to be 'justified'? What is 'justification'? This was the second thing which I proposed to show. And it is evident from what has been already observed that it is not the being made actually just and righteous. This is *sanctification*; which is indeed in some degree the immediate *fruit* of justification, but nevertheless is a distinct gift of God, and of a totally different nature. The one implies what God *does for* us through his Son; the other what he *works in* us by his Spirit.[39]

---

[37] *On Sin in Believers* IV.3; cf. III.8; IV.12; V.2; *Repentance of Believers* I.2, 10, 11.
[38] Compare with sermons #21-23 *Sermon on the Mount* I, II, III.
[39] *Justification By Faith* II.1 (emphasis his).

John Wesley's Theology of Christian Perfection

As Wesley will later describe sanctification as a *distinct gift* from justification, so David taught a second gift of "full assurance." Though Wesley will later distinguish full assurance from the gift of perfect love,[40] he does come to see salvation from all sin along similar lines as David taught. Note what David's constant inquiry was:

> Is Christ formed *in you*?
> Have you a new heart?
> Is your soul renewed in the image of God?
> Is the whole body of sin destroyed in you?
> Are you fully assured, beyond all doubt or fear, that you are a child of God?
> In what manner, and at what moment, did you receive that full assurance?[41]

These questions parallel Wesley's own theology of perfection. As his Gospel of Two Works proclaimed full deliverance from all sin, so David taught explicitly that the second gift of full assurance brought "the destruction of the body of sin, and the extinction of all its motions." Wesley even embraced David's perspective concerning the timing of perfection. Christian taught that the gift of full deliverance did not often come until "long after" justification. Nearly thirty years later Wesley will write to his brother Charles, "As to the manner, I believe this perfection is always wrought in the soul by faith, by a simple act of faith; consequently in an instant...As to the time, I believe this instant generally is the instant of death...But I believe it may be ten, twenty, or forty years before death."[42]

The parallels between the two men's theologies also pertain to other areas. Both embraced universal redemption and rejected

---

[40] See *Plain Account* 8:1 for JW's use of the same language when describing perfection. Later, we will see that JW did come to identify full assurance with spiritual adolescence and perfection with adulthood.
[41] Works B 18:279.
[42] JWL 1/27/67; see *Plain Account* 25:130 n.

The Gospel of Two Works of Grace

Calvin's notion of unconditional election.[43] The above similarities explain why so much space is devoted to Christian David in Wesley's journal.[44]

Wesley recorded the testimonies of ten other men. For the most part, these testimonies only confirm what Wesley learned from Christian David. Michael Linner and David Nitschman share how they experienced two saving events in their faith journey. Albinus Feder testifies of his failure to find salvation through his best endeavors to practice the means of grace; confirming, once again, the weakness of Wesley's Gospel of Holiness. Augustine Neisser shares how full assurance "grew up" in him "by degrees." The two other Neisser brothers and their cousin testify to receiving the gift of full assurance and freedom from all doubt and fear. The last testimony Wesley wrote down was that of a Swede, Arvid Gradin. Wesley recorded many years later that this was the first account he ever heard of a person attaining Christian perfection.[45] Arvid's testimony differs from the other men in that he describes receiving the peace of forgiveness and freedom from all sin in one, single, powerful event. Gradin calls his experience the "witness of his Spirit":

'Requies in sanguine Christi. Firma fiducia in Deum et persuasio de gratia divina; tranquillitas mentis summa, atque serenitas et pax; cum absentia omnis desiderii carnalis, et cessatione peccatorum etiam internorum. Verbo, cor quod antea instar maris turbulenti agitabatur, in summa fuit requie, instar maris sereni et tranquilli.' [46]

---

[43] For David's testimony on the matter see Work B 18:275-76.
[44] In Works J 11 pages; in Works B 11 1/2 pages. Compare to JW's Aldersgate memorandum on 5/24/38: Works B 10 pages; Works J 6 1/2 pages. More space is devoted to David than to his own testimony on May 24.
[45] *Plain Account* 8:3.
[46] Works B 18:291; Note: This is apparently Gradin's own statement in Latin, as taken down by Wesley and translated by him; although it may possibly be a quotation from some other author.

John Wesley's Theology of Christian Perfection

Here is Wesley's translation:

> 'Repose in the blood of Christ. A firm confidence in God, and persuasion of his favour; serene peace and steadfast tranquility of mind, with a deliverance from every fleshly desire, and from every outward and inward sin. In a word, my heart, which before was tossed like a troubled sea, was still and quiet, and in a sweet calm.'[47]

Wesley Returns from Germany

The change in Wesley's views became apparent immediately upon his return to England in mid-September 1738. Whereas before, seen in his correspondence to his family, Wesley espoused one single salvific event bringing full justification and complete sanctification; he now begins to acknowledge degrees of faith in the life transformation process. In a letter to Arthur Bedford (late September) he distinguishes between assurance of salvation and assurance of faith. He even separates saving faith from the assurance of faith by describing the latter as a "distinct gift of the Holy Ghost," thus incorporating Christian David's terminology in his response. In the next paragraph we find Wesley defining, for the first time upon his return from Germany, what he understands full assurance to be:

> I believe is neither more nor less than hope; or a conviction, wrought in us by the Holy Ghost, that we have a *measure* of the true faith in Christ, and that as he is already made justification unto us, so if we continue to watch and strive and pray, he will gradually become "our sanctification here, and our full redemption hereafter." This assurance, I believe, is given to some in a smaller, to

---

[47] Compare with the same passage in *Plain Account* 8:2.

others in a larger *degree*; to some also sooner, to others later, according to the counsels of his will. But since it is promised to all, I cannot doubt but it will be given to all who diligently seek it.[48]

Over the next several months Wesley began to transition theologically in a new direction. The Gospel of Faith Alone had declared freedom from all sin in the event of justification. This left little, if any, room for the means of grace to have any significant role in the attainment of salvation. This theology inadvertently fed stillness thinking in the converts. But the dye had now been cast; Wesley was beginning to move theologically in a new direction.

When he begins his third journal extract, he picks up the story upon his return from Germany. We noted above the letter he received in October that threw him into a tailspin. This letter prompted Wesley to examine himself in light of 2 Corinthians 5:17, "If any man be in Christ, he is a new creature: Old things are passed away; behold, all things are become new."[49] Of course, by "all things are become new" Wesley understood to mean perfection. It is not important for our purpose to walk through all six categories by which he examined himself. What is significant is the conclusion that he had a "measure of faith, and that he felt 'accepted in the Beloved,'" even though he still lacked a "full assurance of faith." In other words, Wesley was now confident he was justified and reconciled to God, but he still lacked the second gift: full renewal as a new creation in Christ.

A couple of weeks later he communicated as much to his brother Samuel:

> By a Christian I mean one who so believes in Christ as that sin hath no more dominion over him. And in this obvious sense of the word I was not a Christian till May 24

---

[48] JWL 9/28/38 (emphasis mine).
[49] JWJ 10/14/38.

last past...What sins they were which till then *reigned* over me, and from which by the grace of God I am now free...If you ask by what means I am made free (though not perfect, neither infallibly sure of my own perseverance), I answer, by faith in Christ; but such a sort or degree of faith as I had not till that day...Some measure of this faith...I now enjoy by his free mercy...this witness of the Spirit I have not, but I patiently wait for it. [50]

As Wesley continued to share his heart with friends and reflect upon his spiritual state, he remained on the roller coaster of believing one moment he had saving faith, and in the next entertaining doubts over his salvation. Earlier we looked at his confession on January 4, 1739 in which he scolds himself for his lack of assurance. This was the last time Wesley publicly acknowledged his struggles over assurance. From this point forward his journal and surviving letters reflect a change in tone as the revival enters a new phase. During the early months of 1739 his ministry begins to mushroom as his audiences' number in the several hundreds.[51] His correspondence with his brother Samuel reveals a growing awareness in his assurance of salvation.[52] And, finally, at the same time, he comes to realize his calling as an evangelist and revival leader.[53]

On January 25, 1739 Wesley reflects in his journal on the many adults he had lately baptized. Only one was "born again, in the full sense of the word," meaning, a "thorough, inward change, by the love of God filling her heart." Most, he acknowledged, were born again in a "lower sense," having received the gift of justification. Some had not even received this gift. So, by late January, just eight months after his Aldersgate conversion,

---

[50] JWL 10/30/38.
[51] JWL 2/26/39.
[52] JWL 4/4/39; 5/10/39.
[53] JW told John Clayton that he looked upon "all the world" as his parish (JWL 3/28/39).

The Gospel of Two Works of Grace

Wesley was beginning to embrace a gospel in which the new birth involves more than just one God-moment.

The Life and Death of Thomas Halyburton

In February Wesley published *An Abstract of the Life and Death of the Reverend Learned and Pious Mr. Thomas Halyburton*, in which he attached a preface outlining his present perfection views.[54] The theme of the preface is the inward kingdom of God, and opens with a brief account of how God sets up his reign in the heart.[55] The journey begins with prevenient grace awakening the sinner and drawing them to cast all their sins upon Christ. The believer then receives a "true, living faith"—peace is given, joy is imparted, and deliverance from the dominion of sin begins. God's love is poured out "producing all holiness of heart." So God does save from all sin and fills the believer with the fullness of his love. Of interest to us is how Wesley labels this process a single "work of God in the soul of man." That is, both justification and sanctification are united together in one "glorious liberty" of divine working in the heart—the new birth.

In this preface Wesley begins to more carefully nuance the liberty that is ours in Christ. Whereas in *Salvation By Faith* freedom from various categories of sin are lumped together under the single heading of "power," he now more carefully delineates between sin in its "proper sense"—that is, committing sin—and sin "improperly termed" as "sins of infirmity." This latter category includes those "numberless weaknesses and follies" that drop off

---

[54] Works J 14:212-214; 2nd edition 1741.
[55] This is the earliest post-Aldersgate account by JW describing the faith journey from the unconverted state to the attainment of Christian perfection. Other like descriptions can be found in *Hymns and Sacred Poems II* (1740; Works J 14:322-327), *Thoughts on Christian Perfection* (1759; Plain Account 19:68-75), *Scripture Way of Salvation* (1765; Works B 2:155-169). A comparison of these accounts of the faith journey reveals development in JW's theology of perfection.

John Wesley's Theology of Christian Perfection

in physical death, while Scripture promises deliverance from sin in this life. Sin is now classified as proper and improper.

Wesley quotes 1 John 3:9 and 5:18 to define sin and salvation's true nature:

> "Whosoever is born of God doth not commit sin;" (unless he lose the Spirit of adoption, if not finally, yet for a while, as did this child of God) "for his seed remaineth in him, and he cannot sin, because he is born of God." He cannot sin so long as "he keepeth himself;" for then "that wicked one toucheth him not."

Wesley here appears to embrace a concept of intermittent perfection. Mr. Halyburton experienced perfect love intermittently; that is, he "sometimes fell back from the glorious liberty he had received into a spirit of fear, and sin, and bondage." Several paragraphs later Wesley speaks of multiple "relapses" by the weak Christian. Under this system the new birth introduces the believer into perfect love, but the believer is not yet confirmed or established. They swing back and forth between sin and bondage on one hand, and obedience and victory on the other, until they are "fully freed from sin."[56] Significantly, perfection is here understood as not committing sin, even to the point the person "cannot sin," thereby becoming fully born of God. The condition of waning between sin and holiness Wesley refers to as a "child" and as "weak" in faith. These titles will later play a significant role in the development of his perfection theology. The immature believer is justified, but has not yet learned to "abide in Christ" and to "cleave to Him with all his heart."

Wesley's theology of perfection in early 1739 is best described as a single work of grace—defined as a new birth from sin to holiness—yet containing two distinct moments of deliver-

---

[56] Charles G. Finney's position on Christian perfection can be summarized as being similar to JW's beliefs at this point. Perfection according to Finney is becoming established or confirmed in a pattern of consistent obedience (*Lectures on Systematic Theology* 2:782-788).

ance: new birth in a lower sense and in a full sense.[57] But these twin moments remain blurred and required further clarification.

Revival Enthusiasm

On April 2 Wesley took the momentous step of preaching in the open fields at Bristol. The surge in converts turned his attention to their spiritual development. In response Wesley's message began to change. Over the next several months his favorite text was 1 Corinthians 1:30, "Christ, made of God unto us, wisdom, and righteousness, and sanctification, and redemption." Most significant is that this passage gives equal emphasis on justification

---

[57] Several years later JW will represent the new birth as comprehending the total renewal process:

> Q.3. Is not every believer a new creature?
> A. Not in the sense of St. Paul, 2 Cor 5:17, "All old things are passed away in him who is so a new creature and all things become new."
> Q.4. But has every believer a new heart?
> A. A great change is wrought in the heart or affections of every one as soon as he believes; yet he is still full of sin, so that he has not then a new heart in the full sense.
> Q.5. Is not every believer born of God, a temple of the Holy Ghost?
> A. In a low sense he is. But he that is in the proper sense born of God cannot commit sin.
> Q.7. Does this (perfection) imply that he who is thus perfect cannot commit sin?
> A. St. John affirms it expressly. He cannot commit sin because he is born of God (1 Jn 3:9). And, indeed, how should he, seeing there is now none occasion of stumbling in him?
> 1744 Minutes (Outler, *John Wesley*, 140-41)

Cf. Appendix D: The Evolution of the New Birth.

and sanctification.[58] Another favorite text was the Beatitudes, with its emphasis on holy living.[59]

The revival generated many excesses: swooning, convulsions, fits, and the like. As expected, these became controversial among revival supporters and their critics. Many within the revival interpreted these effects as the "pangs of the new birth, the work of the Holy Ghost, casting out the old man."[60] Wesley himself considered these "signs" as God's approval upon his ministry. In this heightened revival atmosphere the hearts of young converts were fertile soil for the message of perfection.

That Wesley was teaching perfection by June 1739 is confirmed by a conversation he had with a Quaker. The Quaker objected to Wesley's strictness and his emphasis on perfection. Instead, he defended the idea there is "no harm in costly apparel, provided it was plain and grave."[61] During this same month enthusiasm erupted at the Fetter Lane society demanding Wesley's leadership and counsel. Charles informs us of the inroads the French Prophets were making within the society.[62] A prophetess,

---

[58] JWJ 4/10/39; 6/14/39. JW preached on this text numerous times during 1739.

[59] JWJ 4/1/39. Christian David had preached on this text when JW was there in August 1738. The Beatitudes were preached by JW numerous times in 1739, thus reflecting his deep interest in the subject of sanctification at this time.

[60] John Cennick, in Dallimore, *George Whitefield* I:326. JW's letters and journal include many references to this phenomenon; e.g. see JWJ 4/21/39, 4/30/39, 5/1/39, 5/2/39, 5/21/39, 10/23/39, 10/25/39; JWL 2/26/39, 4/9/39, 7/2/39, 10/27/39. The last letter expresses JW's position on the phenomenon: "I believe nature might have a part in those fits, as well as Satan, raging before he is cast out; but that the Holy Spirit, deeply convincing them of sin, is the chief agent in most of those who are seized with them."

[61] JWJ 6/15/39.

[62] Concerning the French Prophets, Ward and Heitzenrater write, "When the revocation of the Edict of Nantes in 1685 removed the concessions made to the French Prophets they sought refuge in many parts of Europe, and Huguenot communities developed in England. The fanatical Camisards who revolved against Louis XIV during the first decade of the eighteenth century similarly came over, bringing with them many emotional excesses, so that most religious people shunned the 'French Prophets'. Bristol was one of their strong-

The Gospel of Two Works of Grace

by the name of Lavington, gained much attention with her bizarre behavior and extravagant prophecies. She began advocating "absolute perfection" as an attainable state in this life.[63] Charles denounced her claims but to little avail. John finally arrived on June 13 and after a several days quieted the situation down. The main leaders of the society agreed to disown the prophetess and to heal their division over the matter.[64] Wesley exhorted all to follow after holiness, and to avoid as fire any teacher or prophet who did not speak according to the "Law and Testimony." Nevertheless, this outbreak of enthusiasm shows the extant to which perfection ideas were pregnant in many minds, along with the penchant for religious fanaticism.[65] This outbreak also reveals that the society was already moving toward an antinomianism fitted for the blatant stillness theology of Philipp Molther later that year.

The problems at Fetter Lane only confirmed for Wesley the need for a gospel grounded on two divine moments. Revival fire was leading young converts to over-inflate their spiritual attainments. By July Wesley found it necessary to caution young converts against "fancying they had 'already attained, or were al-

---

holds" Works B 25:658 n 1. On 4/22/39 CW had a discussion with the Count over visions, dreams and motions. Both were in agreement against them.

[63] CW records one such episode, "Many of our friends have been pestered by the French Prophets, and such-like *pretenders* to inspiration. J. Bray is the foremost to listen to them, and often carried away with their delusions. Today I had the happiness to find at his house the famous Prophetess Lavington. She was sitting by Bowers; and Mrs. Sellers on the other side. The Prophet Wise asked, 'Can a man attain perfection here?' I answered, 'No.' The Prophetess began groaning. I turned, and said, 'If you have anything to speak, speak it.' She lifted up her voice, like the lady on the tripod, and cried out vehemently, 'Look for perfection; I say absolute perfection!' I was minded to rebuke her; but God gave me uncommon recollection, and command of spirit, so that I sat quiet, and replied not" (CWJ 6/7/39).

[64] JWJ 6/16-6/22; JWL 7/2/39. Podmore informs us that another prophet by the name of Wise was cohabitating with Lavington (*The Moravian Church in England, 1728-1760,* 55).

[65] Other divisive issues were lay preaching, membership in the church, predestination, visions and dreams, screaming, groaning, and raptures in the Holy Spirit (CWJ 4/1/39, 4/15/39, 4/22/39, 5/16/39, 6/4/39, and 6/6/39).

ready perfect.'"[66] Drawing from Mark 4:26, he preached on the gradual increase of the kingdom of God. Nearly three decades later Wesley would again caution young converts against the notion that justifying faith eliminates all sin:

> How easily do they draw the inference, 'I *feel* no sin; therefore I *have* none.' It does not *stir*; therefore it does not *exist*: it has no *motion*; therefore it has no *being*. But it is seldom long before they are undeceived, finding sin was only suspended, not destroyed.[67]

Two States and the New Birth

During the summer of 1739 Wesley found it necessary to defend the revival against its critics. Henry Stebbing, a well-known champion of Anglican orthodoxy, published an anti-Methodist tract on the new birth. Toward the end of July Wesley took time to reply to Stebbing's criticisms.

Wesley published his response in his journal (7/31/39). He describes the new birth as that "great and mighty change" from the "old man" to the "new man." It is a "change of heart, an inward renewal in the spirit of our mind." The old man is clarified as the "evil heart of unbelief," which is "corrupted by pride and a thousand deceitful lusts." The new man is a "good heart, which after God is created in righteousness and true holiness." Such a heart is "full of that faith which, working by love, produces all holiness of conversation" (§3).

Wesley describes the transformation produced in the new birth as a change of "states" (§4). In the new birth, the person moves from the former state, the old man, to the latter state, the new man. As we saw above (and will see below), Wesley's pre-

---

[66] JWJ 7/23/39; Php 3:12.

[67] *Scripture Way of Salvation* I.5-6; emphasis his. Note JW's use of Christian David's terminology in this passage.

sent views regard the new birth as comprehending the entire renewal process from conversion to perfect saint.

The one condition of the new birth is a "living faith." Such faith looks to Christ and his vicarious death for salvation. It becomes a "spring" for God's love, joy, peace, and all the other fruits of the Spirit. The believer begins to "feel" the working of God's Spirit within, thereby witnessing to the reality of his love and acceptance. As Jesus does in John 3, Wesley likens the work of the Spirit to the wind: "As you hear the wind, and feel it too, while it strikes upon your bodily organs, you will know you are under the guidance of God's Spirit the same way" (§7). In the new birth the Christian becomes sensibly aware of the operations of God's inward reign.

Justification, Sanctification and the New Birth

Wesley's understanding of justification had gone through major changes over the past couple years. Under his holiness gospel, justification formally took place at the last judgment and was grounded on one's full sanctification.[68] When Wesley embraced his faith-alone gospel, the relationship between justification and sanctification took a complete about-face. Justification now served as the ground for sanctification. This is testimony to the impact that Aldersgate made on his heart and theology. When in November 1738 he rediscovered his Church's Homilies on justification, Wesley immediately published an extract of their essential parts. Justification by faith alone in Christ alone became the primary axiom of his faith-alone gospel and profoundly shaped his spiritual DNA. As Wesley renewed his commitment to degrees of faith, distinguishing between two works in the faith journey, it became logically necessary to formally separate justi-

---

[68] I say formally because in ch 1 we saw that JW did believe in the present forgiveness of sins, he just never identified this with present justification.

fication from sanctification. By mid-September 1739 Wesley made this important breakthrough.

In a conversation with a fellow clergyman,[69] Wesley was given the opportunity to state precisely where he differed from other Anglican clergy who dissented from the revival.[70] He begins by affirming he did not disagree with any clergyman who believed and taught the Church's Prayers, Articles and Homilies. But with the rest he clearly spells out the differences:

> First, they (dissenting clergy) speak of justification, either as the same thing with sanctification, or as something consequent upon it. I believe justification to be *wholly distinct* from sanctification, and necessarily antecedent to it.[71]

Wesley then clarifies that Christ's death and resurrection are the "whole and sole cause" of our justification, and along with faith the condition and ground for good works before God.

He next defines sanctification and the new birth as inward transformation. The distinction between the two is subtle, but significant. Both are said to be an "inward thing," with sanctification emphasizing more the process side of salvation and new birth the idea of instantaneous change. The latter encompasses an "entire change of our inmost nature from the image of the devil (wherein we are born) to the image of God." Here, the new birth comprehends the whole of sanctification, but with the stress falling on the instantaneous element.

Wesley draws upon concepts from his early period to explain his meaning more fully. The new birth is a change in one's tempers and affections. It is the transformation of "earthly, sensual affections" into "holy and heavenly" ones. This was a central

---

[69] Ward and Heitzenrater identify the clergyman as perhaps Eden Howard, Chaplain of East India Company (Works B 19:96 n. 34).
[70] JWJ 9/13/39.
[71] JWJ 9/13/39; emphasis mine.

theme in *The Circumcision of the Heart*.[72] Wesley furthermore identifies the new birth and perfection to angelic nature.[73]

The step Wesley took at this time was momentous in the development of his two-works gospel. For it illustrates how far he had come theologically in little more than a year. In agreement with his faith-alone gospel, the new birth and perfection continue to be associated: the new birth is that change (renewal) which makes one perfect in holiness and love. We saw above he had recognized degrees of faith as early as January of 1739.[74] But through the ensuing months what settled in his mind was the conviction that justification is not only connected in timing with the new birth (in the "lower sense"), but also that justification is "wholly distinct" as a work of God from sanctification and the new birth. Justification became a separate, distinct work; no longer confused with sanctification. This change was a breach with both prior gospel systems (holiness and faith-alone), and became a major step in the formation of a new gospel system, emphasizing two works of grace. From this point forward, Wesley never confuses justification (what God does *for* us) with sanctification and regeneration (what God does *in* us). This clarification must have left a deep impression on him since in less than a month he most likely wrote and preached the sermon *Justi-*

---

[72] "In general we may observe it is that habitual *disposition* of soul which in the Sacred Writings is termed 'holiness', and which directly implies the being cleansed from sin, 'from all filthiness both of flesh and spirit', and by consequence the being endued with those virtues which were also in Christ Jesus, the being so 'renewed in the image of our mind" as to be 'perfect, as our Father in heaven is perfect'" (1.1; emphasis mine).

[73] A theme found in his GosH: *Guardian Angels* (1726) I.2; II.6; *In Earth as in Heaven* (1734); *One Thing Needful* (1734) I.2, 5.

[74] JWJ 1/25/39. I would remind the reader that JW started to recognize degrees in his extant writings upon his return from Germany in September 1738. Yet, his continuing personal struggles reveal that he had not come to a settled position on the matter. In January 1739 JW ceased to struggle over personal assurance and he openly acknowledged degrees of new birth in those he baptized.

fication By Faith.[75] In this sermon he draws once more on Christian David's teachings to make his point:

> What is 'justification'? This was the second thing which I proposed to show. And it is evident from what has been already observed that it is not the being made actually just and righteous. This is sanctification; which is indeed in some degree the immediate fruit of justification, but nevertheless is a *distinct* gift of God, and of a *totally different* nature. The one implies what God does for us through his Son; the other what he works in us by his Spirit.[76]

Wesley is beginning to clarify the primary stages on the faith journey path. Whereas before, under his faith-alone gospel, two states were identified—sinner and (perfect) saint—now three are recognized: unsaved, justified (new birth in low degree) and perfect (new birth in full sense). As multiple states were recognized within his gospel system, Wesley was able to clarify and to more sharply distinguish between outward and inward holiness. This distinction is an outgrowth of formally separating justification from sanctification, and of delineating his differences with other clergy who taught that sanctification and the new birth are "outward thing(s)."[77] During the fall and winter of 1739/40 Wesley began to use more often the terminology of outward and inward to define holiness and sin.[78]

---

[75] "At five in the evening I explained to about a thousand people the nature, the cause, and the condition or instrument of justification" (JWJ 10/6/39). See sermon #5 Works B 1:181-199. Ward and Heitzenrater note, "apparently the sermon upon that text which was first published in 1746" (Works B 19:102 n. 69).

[76] *Justification by Faith* 2:1 (emphasis mine).

[77] JWJ 9/13/39. JW lists this as the major difference between himself and the other Anglican clergy over the doctrines of justification, sanctification and new birth.

[78] JWJ 10/9/39; 10/23/39; 1/25/40. JW had listed four kinds of sin in *Salvation By Faith* (habitual, willful, inward desire and infirmity), but had placed these all under the single heading "power." It should be noted JW did distinguish the

The Gospel of Two Works of Grace

The Stillness Controversy

When Wesley returned to London in early November 1739, he found the society under the spell of Philipp Molther. The first person he met was a woman he had known for her strong faith and good works. She informed Wesley "Mr. Molther had fully convinced her, she never had any faith at all; and had advised her, till she received faith, to be still, ceasing from outward works."[79] By the next day Wesley was aware that stillness teaching had spread further than he realized. Having a long conversation over the matter with Moravian pastor, Augustus Spangenberg, ended to no avail. On November 17 Wesley records in his journal that he explained at Bristol "the nature and extent of Christian perfection," and the next morning he taught on the nature of indwelling sin. These journal notes confirm that the needs of the converts continued to play a role in shaping Wesley's doctrine of the second blessing.[80]

On December 31 Wesley sat down with Molther to discuss the matter fully. Afterwards, he went home and carefully wrote down the position of both parties. Wesley placed the differences under five headings. For starters, Molther believed there are no degrees to justifying faith. Instead, justification is associated with full, complete renewal in holiness and assurance, and an unwavering awareness of Christ living within. In contrast, Wesley asserted there are degrees of saving faith. A "state" of justification

---

latter group as not being "properly sin." Several months later he made an even sharper distinction between willful sin and sins of infirmity in his *An Extract of the Life and Death of Mr. Thomas Halyburton*. Since during the fall and winter of 1739/40 JW makes several notations in his Journal addressing the subject of inward and outward holiness, and inward and outward sin, it is safe to assume he was acquiring greater clarity on these subjects during this time.

[79] JWJ 11/3/39.

[80] Timothy Smith believes this was the time when JW first preached his sermon *Christian Perfection*, which was later written and published in early 1741. Though this is possible, this author holds to a later date for the composition of this sermon because it reflects further development in JW's views, specifically his use of 1 Jn 2:12-14 to identify stages of renewal.

does exist before "all things in him are become new,"[81] that is, before perfect holiness and full assurance are attained. Salvation is not received as a complete package. There are a series of stages or "states" in the believer's faith journey toward full renewal.

Concerning the "way to faith," both men disagreed very sharply. For Molther, the way to faith is through Christ alone, apart from any other means, like prayer, Bible reading, attending church or the sacraments. Concerning these disciplines the seeker must be "still." Wesley believed just the opposite. For him the seeker must be still, but in a different sense. Instead of ceasing from the means of grace, which are the normal channels by which God imparts spiritual life (grace), they must be "still" in the sense of not trusting in these things so as to merit acceptance before God; but not in the sense of stopping them altogether. It is likely that in some degree both men were simply talking past each other.

The implications for Wesley's own theological evolution are obvious, and reflect just how far he had traveled down the path to a gospel embracing two works of grace. His faith-alone gospel had imbibed much of the stillness principles Molther taught. The real difference is that Wesley had held these ideas more implicitly, whereas Molther taught them explicitly. Like Molther, Wesley had believed salvation to be a complete package: one has saving faith or one does not; there are no degrees or shades to faith; to be justified is to be sanctified fully; to be born again is to possess a full assurance of faith. Wesley now knew better. He had seen many converts duped by this theology into believing they had attained levels of great spiritual heights when he knew they were still spiritual infants.[82] Wesley had come to believe justification is "wholly distinct" from sanctification and a separate

---

[81] 2 Corinthians 5:17. The reader should be reminded that JW's doctrine of the new birth incorporated perfection in the inward change. Hence, all scripture texts that refer to the new birth were understood by JW as teaching attainable perfection. In this passage the phrase "all things become new" is seen as meaning perfection: full, complete renewal in God's image.

[82] This is the significance of the Fetter Lane Society schism six months earlier.

The Gospel of Two Works of Grace

"state" from perfection. Degrees of faith now appeared obvious to him while Molther's message looked more and more like a *new* gospel.

The stillness controversy finally settled in Wesley's mind the salvific value of the means of grace. While he continued to profess a belief in the ordinances, his faith-alone gospel had undercut their saving value. Wesley could now see the seriousness of this error. Since he now reaffirmed degrees of faith, he could also assert that the ordinances play a valuable, even critical, role in the *ordo salutis*. So the faith journey does require due diligence in practicing the means of grace.[83] By drawing upon both gospel messages Wesley was able to synthesize a new gospel that stressed both salvation by faith alone in Christ alone, and the demand for inward holiness as preparation for eternity.

The clincher that reveals how much Wesley's thought had evolved over the one and a half years since Aldersgate is when he labeled the stillness teaching a "new gospel."[84] This is rather ironic. If the reader remembers, when Wesley learned the gospel of faith alone from Peter Böhler, he labeled it a "new doctrine" and a "new gospel." He now spoke of his two-works gospel as the "old path"[85] and the "old way."[86] This "way" taught salvation by faith alone, but also proclaimed that the ordinances are the means of grace in the attainment of conversion and perfect love.

---

[83] In 1745 JW answered the following question, "How should we wait for the fulfilling of this promise? A. In universal obedience; in keeping all the commandments; in denying ourselves, and taking up our cross daily. These are the general means which God hath ordained for our receiving his sanctifying grace. The particulars are,—prayer, searching the Scriptures, communicating, and fasting" (*Plain Account* ch 17 end note Q.9).

[84] JWJ 4/25/40.

[85] JWJ 1/2/40; 7/4/40. Cf. JWJ 3/6/38 & 5/24/38 §11 when he labels his faith-alone gospel as a "new doctrine" and a "new gospel."

[86] JWJ 6/22/40. On this date JW also refers to his early period as the "new path of salvation by faith and works," and his GosTW as the "old way of salvation by faith only." Thus JW's 1740 remarks about the "new" gospel included both his message prior to Aldersgate and Molther's no-degrees gospel.

John Wesley's Theology of Christian Perfection

Christian perfection was becoming a well-defined second work of grace.

The Wilderness State

Through the ensuing winter months of 1740 Wesley continued to press his doctrines of new birth and salvation from all sin as the stillness controversy continued to brew.[87] At the end of March he took the time to describe a fourth state:

> From these words, 'Then was Jesus led by the Spirit into the wilderness, to be tempted of the devil,' I took occasion to describe that *wilderness state*, that state of doubts, and fears, and strong temptation, which so many go through (though in different degrees) after they have received remission of sins.[88]

Of course, the wilderness state is closely alloyed to the justification state, yet distinguished from it. Wesley admits that not all go through this phase, but all do pass through the justification stage. As a result, the wilderness state became, at least implicitly, a fourth spiritual state in Wesley's two-works system.[89] It also became the explanation for his personal struggles following Aldersgate. What he himself personally went through, he knew many converts were facing. Stillness had promised to save people from the struggle to find inner peace and full assurance, but in reality it led many to lose all confidence in their spiritual standing.

---

[87] JWJ 1/17/40; 3/5/40. Charles listed the wilderness state the prior summer (CWJ 8/25/39).

[88] JWJ 3/28/40 (emphasis mine).

[89] The four states identified so far: unconverted (natural man), justification, wilderness, and perfection. On 10/23/39 (JWJ) JW did divide the unconverted state into that of "nature" and of "bondage." These could be called "states" if one chooses. My focus is on those attainments beginning with justification and which JW referred to as a "state."

The Gospel of Two Works of Grace

By April 1740 many confided in Wesley they were "greatly troubled by this new gospel, and thrown into the utmost heaviness." Wherever Wesley went he found that this teaching produced nothing but "grievous confusion."[90] Stillness advocates became even bolder. Wesley's old friend, Mr. Stonehouse, told him "no one has any degree of faith till he is 'perfect as God is perfect.'"[91]

Finally, toward the end of June Wesley decided to confront the issues head on. Over the course of several days he taught on one topic after another related to the stillness controversy. This process brought further clarification to the nature of the wilderness state. Those weak in faith suffer from mixed feelings, especially fear and doubt. Probing deeper, in the wilderness state the heart is not yet "fully purified" from all its idols. The believer lacks consistency in devotion. Wesley concludes that he finds "almost all believers to be, within a short time after they have first peace with God," to be in this weak state.

Yet, the scriptures declare this weak faith to be justifying. Wesley pointed to Romans 14:1; 1 John 2:12-14; Matthew 8:26, 14:31; Luke 22:32 and John 15:3 to press his point. All these passages speak of a faith that is weak, yet genuine and acceptable to God.

Two days later he took up the topic once more to encourage those suffering under the weight of stillness doctrine. Wesley reminds them that though they feel doubt, fear, temptation and the "body of sin" within (Rom 6:6), these were not definite signs that they lack saving faith. Reaching back to what he had learned from Christian David (two years earlier) Wesley told his audience, "Sin does 'remain' in one that is justified, though 'it has not dominion' over him. For he has not 'a clean heart' at first, neither are all things as yet 'become new'. But fear not, though you have an evil heart. Yet a little while, and you shall be endued with power from on high, whereby you may 'purify yourselves, even

---

[90] JWJ 4/25/40.
[91] JWJ 4/30/40.

as he is pure', and be 'holy, as he which hath called you is holy.'"[92] Thus, the faith journey is marked by highs and lows, and consists of four basic states: unconverted, justified, wilderness and a new, clean heart (perfection).

Sacred Hymns and Poems II[93]

In the spring of 1740 the Wesley brothers published their second volume of hymns. In the preface John offers for the first time a much more complete description of his Gospel of Two Works. The theme is the "glorious liberty from the bondage of corruption." Wesley's text is Ephesians 2:8, "By grace ye are saved through faith." This "gracious gift," which is "begun on earth, but perfected in heaven," is said to be none other than the "image of God fresh stamped upon our hearts." After briefly acknowledging there is no absolute perfection in this life, Wesley reminds his reader that those fully born of God are not perfect in comparison to what they shall be. But this is not the heart of his message, nor the emphasis of this preface. The good news is that God now saves from sin, including doubt and fear. The believer is saved from fear when they are justified and from doubt when the Spirit testifies of God's acceptance.

But Wesley's "first principle" is to declare, once again, the grand privilege of every believer: "Whosoever is born of God, doth not commit sin. For his seed remaineth in him, and he cannot sin, because he is born of God."[94] The new birth delivers from committing sin and introduces those fully born of God into the liberty of "full salvation." Wesley is careful to clarify that full salvation is not given all at once. He now acknowledges there are two works, one gradual and the other instantaneous, along with two God-moments in the process. Wesley personally knows a "cloud of witnesses" that can testify to receiving in one moment

---

[92] JWJ 6/24/40.
[93] Works J 14:323-327.
[94] 1 Jn 3:9 (JW's translation).

The Gospel of Two Works of Grace

both justifying faith and the abiding witness of the Spirit. But he does not know of a single case in which one has received in the same moment justifying faith, the Spirit's witness, and a "new, clean heart." At the time this latter phrase served as a synonym for Christian perfection in Wesley's writings.[95]

Wesley next lists six liberties arising from the new birth (in full sense). All of them deal directly with the inner person. The first liberty is freedom from the root of sin itself: pride. Those born of God feel "all their sufficiency is of God." The opposite of pride is humility, which was always placed at the head of Wesley's early lists on the faith journey.[96] The second liberty is freedom from self-will. The perfect believer continually breathes the prayer, "Father, thy will be done." Third, is freedom from evil thoughts. Such thoughts cannot even enter the mind of one whose heart is fully renewed in God's likeness, since they are "full of God." The fourth blessing is freedom from wanderings in prayer. Since nothing remains that can hinder sweet communion with God, the mind is free to reflect and commune with the Most High. The next freedom involves the removal of all spiritual darkness. Since the heart is clean and pure, the mind's eye is single in its focus and the whole life basks in the fullness of God's light.[97] Last, there is liberty from temptation, but only in "one sense." Temptations that use to buffet and trouble the newborn believer in Christ now find no room to take root. The heart is clean, fully renewed, and in continual communion with God.

What follows is a lengthy elaboration of the faith journey, much longer than the one found in his *Life of Halyburton*. The

---

[95] The phrase is found in this preface (Spring/40) and in JWJ 6/24/40; 7/20/40; 9/29/40 (Preface for Extract 2); 5/2/41; and 8/8/41. In *Christian Perfection* II.29 JW quotes Ezek 36:25-27, which speaks of being *cleansed* with water and having a *new heart*. This is the probable source for the phrase. The term is also found in JWJ 8/10/38 introducing Christian David's sermons. This appears to be an editorial comment from 1740, not in 1738, because all of JW's other uses of the term are found in 1740 and 1741.

[96] *The Circumcision of the Heart* (1733) I.2-5; *Preface to The Christian's Pattern* (1735) II.4-5.

[97] Matt 6:22-23.

general way God works commences with the awakening of a careless sinner to their need for God. Coming under conviction and realizing their inner poverty and certain damnation, the seeker comes to Christ crying out for forgiveness. God "shows them he hath taken away their sins, and opens the kingdom of heaven in their hearts." All fear and sorrow flee away as God's forgiving love pours into the heart. The believer now knows they are justified by faith alone in Christ alone. In this state they may remain for days, weeks, or even months, supposing the war within is over and all sin is gone. But soon "bosom-sins" flare up and "assault" the child of God. Out of this conflict arise fears and doubts that cloud the heart and cause the believer to mourn. This is the wilderness state. God then sends the Spirit to witness to their adoption. This outpouring of God's love melts the heart into a spirit of meekness and resignation. After a season of brokenness and comfort God begins to reveal the depths of pride and self-will hidden within the heart. While continuing to witness to their adoption, this revelation creates an "inexpressible hunger" for full deliverance from sin. God then "remembers his holy covenant, and he giveth them a single eye and a clean heart." The believer is then fully born of God and enjoys the liberties described above. Here is process and moment intertwined in one holistic gospel: one good news with two distinct works of grace.

This preface is clear on another matter: *the single intention no longer initiates the faith journey of vital Christianity*. Only in a second moment, when the heart is cleansed, is the single intention fully realized. As stated before, while this conviction was a necessary corollary of his two-works gospel, this single change proved momentous in the evolution of his perfection theology. By placing the single intention at a second moment on the faith journey path it forever burned the bridge of going back to either of his prior gospels. This insight cannot be emphasized too strongly. Both prior gospel systems had located the single inten-

The Gospel of Two Works of Grace

tion at the commencement of the faith journey.[98] Wesley was clearly forging a new gospel system.

Before we move on, two more insights should be noted about the above preface. Once again, we see the imprint of Christian David's influence in that Wesley incorporates a number of themes from the Beatitudes. David had used the Beatitudes to teach his own version of two works in the summer of 1738. By the spring of 1739 Wesley was expounding on the same text within the societies to teach Christian perfection as a second work of grace.[99] Further, the preface contains the seeds to his later use of 1 John 2:12-14, which identifies three levels of Christian development: children, adolescents, and adults. We learned earlier that this text was first used in June 1740. Since this preface was penned shortly before those events, we should not be surprised to find the language of 1 John missing it. Yet, three levels of attainment are specified in the preface: forgiveness (child), abiding witness of God's Spirit (adolescence), and a new clean heart (adult). This three-fold division forms the basic framework for his *ordo salutis* from conversion to perfection.

When we compare this preface to the one a year earlier (*Life of Halyburton*) we see other developments in his theology of perfection. Concerning the earlier preface we noted Wesley's apparent intermittent view on the new birth and perfection. Since only two states were then stressed—unconverted and perfect, with the latter defined as not committing sin—those weak in faith were viewed as vacillating between sin and (full) obedience. The inherent reason for their vacillation was their lack in being established and confirmed in their devotion. But in 1740 Wesley's

---

[98] By "commencement" is meant the start of real or vital Christianity in the heart. In the GosH this moment is the decision of the single intention. In the GosFA this moment is the faith-conversion, which implies the single intention is included in the event.

[99] JWJ 6/15/39: JW's discussion of perfection with a Quaker demonstrates he was already proclaiming perfection as an attainable state. The fact JW was preaching on the Beatitudes in April points also to the probability he was proclaiming perfection as a second blessings as early as April 1739.

theological understanding had changed, or should we say, sharpened. While still viewing the new birth as that change from entire sinfulness to entire holiness, Wesley now nuances more carefully between justification and sanctification. These two works are seen as *wholly distinct* from each other. The new birth and sanctification are still identified, but forgiveness is a distinct gift in its own right. This clarification allowed for a separate, distinct work to follow: Christian perfection.

Christian Perfection

In 1765 when Wesley penned *A Plain Account of Christian Perfection* he remembers, "In the latter end of 1740, that I had a conversation with Dr. (Edmund) Gibson, then bishop of London, at Whitehall. He asked me what I meant by perfection. I told him without any disguise or reserve. When I ceased speaking, he said, 'Mr. Wesley, if this be all you mean, publish it to all the world. If any one then can confute what you say, he may have free leave.' I answered, "My Lord, I will."[100] If Wesley's memory is correct, then it was in early 1741 when he wrote and published the landmark sermon *Christian Perfection*.[101] Once more, our interest is not to rehearse all his arguments, nor to just summarize the substance of the homily, but to identify developments in his theology of perfection.

Wesley opens with an acknowledgment that his message of attainable perfection in this life is what "many cannot bear" (P.1). So, the sole purpose of the sermon is to clarify in what sense Christians can and cannot be perfect in this life. Up to this time,

---

[100] *Plain Account* 12:1-3.
[101] See Works B 2:97-124 for the sermon's text. JW's early gospel systems each had a landmark sermon which encapsulated its core message: Holiness: *The Circumcision of the Heart*; Faith Alone: *Salvation By Faith*; Two Works: *Christian Perfection*. His later period will have several critical homilies due to the nature of his theological development. These include *The Scripture Way of Salvation, The New Creation,* and *On Working Out Our Own Salvation.*

The Gospel of Two Works of Grace

Wesley had not made this distinction in writing, thereby adding fuel to his critics' claim he was promoting a sinless, even an absolute perfection.[102] Five limitations are acknowledged.

First, believers are said to remain imperfect in their knowledge of God, our world, and of the Scriptures except in matters relating to salvation in Christ. In a similar vein, Christians are never free from mistakes in this life. This logically follows the first qualification. Wesley then explains himself on the question of mistakes:

> The best and wisest of men are frequently mistaken even with regard to facts; believing those things not to have been which really were, or those to have been done which were not. Or suppose they are not mistaken as to the fact itself, they may be with regard to its circumstances; believing them, or many of them, to have been quite different from what in truth they were. And hence cannot but arise many farther mistakes. Hence they may believe either past or present actions which were or are evil to be good; and such as were or are good to be evil. Hence also they may judge not according to truth with regard to the characters of men; and that not only by supposing good men to be better, or wicked men to be worse, than they are, but by believing them to have been or to be good men who were or are very wicked; or perhaps those to have been or to be wicked men who were or are holy and unreprovable. (I.4)

Wesley's admission of our continual proneness to mistake in the moral realm will later play a crucial role in the development of his doctrine of sin.[103] Closely related is the fact of human "infirmity." By infirmity Wesley did not mean sin, either outward or inward, but "all those inward and outward imperfections which

---

[102] George Whitefield's letters to JW on 3/26/40 and 9/25/40 show that many thought this of his doctrine.
[103] Cf. ch 5.

are not of a moral nature."[104] Two years earlier he had made the important distinction between committing sin and so-called "sins of infirmity."[105] A fourth qualifier relates to temptation. Wesley's position has now changed from the prior spring. Whereas before he believed perfection did deliver from temptation in "one sense," he now strongly limits such freedom to a "season" following one's reception of forgiveness, when the emotions are high. In due time these strong emotions subside and temptation returns, introducing the immature believer to the wilderness state.

Last, Wesley responds to the criticism that he teaches absolute perfection. He now reaffirms his principle of "degrees." Just as there are degrees of faith, so there are degrees of perfection. Wesley now sees perfection to be only another "term for holiness" (I.8). He concludes that even those who are perfect still need to grow daily in grace.

It was during the stillness controversy of 1740 that Wesley first introduced the terminology of 1 John 2:12-14. Drawing upon the apostle's delineation of little children, young men and fathers (2:12-14), Wesley identifies each group with specific attainments in the faith journey process. It is worth quoting him at this point:

> 'I write unto you, little children', saith the Apostle, 'because your sins are forgiven you'; because thus far ye have attained, being 'justified freely', you 'have peace with God, through Jesus Christ'. 'I write unto you, young men, because ye have overcome the wicked one'; or (as he afterwards adds) 'because ye are strong, and the word of God abideth in you.' Ye have quenched the fiery darts of the wicked one, the doubts and fears wherewith he disturbed your first peace, and the witness of God that your sins are forgiven now 'abideth in your heart'. 'I write unto you, fathers, because ye have known him that is from the beginning.' Ye have known both the Father and the Son

---

[104] Cf. *Plain Account* 19:23-34; especially v 23 n.
[105] In the preface to *Extract of the Life of Mr. Halyburton*.

The Gospel of Two Works of Grace

and the Spirit of Christ in your inmost soul. Ye are 'perfect men, being grown up to the measure of the stature of the fullness of Christ'. (II.1)

The states of childhood, adolescence and adulthood added further clarification to his understanding of the faith journey by identifying specific attainments at each stage of spiritual development (forgiveness, the abiding witness of the Spirit, a new clean heart[106]). Whereas in the earlier preface (*Sacred Hymns and Poems II*) forgiveness and assurance remain confusingly associated in relation to timing, he now plainly distinguishes between these two blessings.[107] He demarcates three distinct attainments instead of two. Childhood continues to be identified with the first gift, the forgiveness of sin, while the next level of attainment concerns overcoming fear and doubt through the abiding witness of God's Spirit. This state now marks the adolescent.[108] Last is the second gift, the attainment of adulthood; or as Wesley puts it—the "fullness of Christ" in a "new, clean heart." What precedes, transpires between, and follows these states is the gradual work of renewal in God's image.

We also see Wesley's doctrine of sin taking shape. Let's briefly retrace our steps. In chapter two we learned the Gospel of Faith Alone proclaimed that all sin is vanquished in the moment of conversion. All sin, even the "whole body of sin," is removed through Christ indwelling the heart.[109] By early 1739 Wesley took the important step by emphasizing even more the distinction between sin and human weakness. Then by the fall and winter of 1739/40 Wesley started articulating holiness and sin in terms of "outward" and "inward." This distinction finally moved Wesley

---

[106] Works J 14:326; §9.
[107] JW's wording in the preface, "We know, a cloud of witnesses, who have received, in one moment, either a clear sense of the forgiveness of their sins, or the abiding witness of the Holy Ghost" (§9). In *Christian Perfection* these two gifts are separated between the child and the adolescent.
[108] I'm using the language of JW's journal here.
[109] *Salvation by Faith* II.7 (original edition).

to view perfection as more than the commission of sin. As a result, Wesley moved away from the intermittent view he appears to have espoused in early 1739. At the time perfection was viewed simply as not committing sin.[110] A year later (spring 1740) freedom from sin was defined in terms of both (1) not committing sin, and (2) freedom from sinful dispositions; like pride, self-will and evil thoughts.[111] But at the time he did not spell out the exact relationship between the two kinds of sin. Now, in 1741 Wesley clarifies that deliverance from sin is realized in two separate works of grace. He did this by distinguishing between the commission of sin (outward sin) and sinful dispositions (inward sin).

Wesley declares in *Christian Perfection* that even those newly born of God are perfect in the sense of not committing *outward sin* (II.4). Having been "planted together in the likeness of the death of Christ" and "born again in the lowest sense" they do not "continue in sin" (II.3). Sin's reign has ceased. The believer's life is transformed to not deliberately transgress God's moral law (II.4). Wesley goes through an extended section demonstrating that all true believers have ceased from sin in this sense. But it can only be said of adult Christians that they overcome *inward sin*:

> It is only of those who 'are strong in the Lord', and 'have overcome the wicked one', or rather of those who 'have known him that is from the beginning', that it can be affirmed they are in such a sense perfect as, secondly, to be freed from evil thoughts and evil tempers. (II.21)

---

[110] But see JW's letter to Mrs. Anne Dutton, dated 6/25/40 by Frank Baker (but possibly earlier; see Baker's notes). In this letter JW defines perfection once again as not committing sin, "We do not say that we have no sin *in us*, but that we do not *commit sin*. And so the Apostle himself says, [1 John] 3:9. Yea, he says that he that is born of God cannot sin!...I could bring many other arguments to prove this also." Essential to grasping JW's position is his doctrine of the new birth. See Appendix D *The Evolution of the New Birth*.

[111] Preface, *Hymns and Sacred Poems II*; §§6-7.

The Gospel of Two Works of Grace

Sinful thoughts and dispositions are the source behind sinful actions (outward sin) and are identified by Wesley as the "evil nature, the body of sin" (II.25). In the attainment of spiritual adulthood, the tempers of pride, self-will and anger are finally "purified" and the body of sin decisively "destroyed."[112] The entirely sanctified can testify to being crucified and risen with Christ.[113] Wesley concludes, "Thus doth Jesus 'save his people from their sins': and not only from outward sins, but also from the sins of their hearts; from evil thoughts and evil tempers."[114] The closing paragraphs contain a bold proclamation of present deliverance from all sin, both inward and outward.[115] Along with a sprinkling of scripture texts, Wesley offers the hope of full salvation to the hungry seeker culminating in the eschatological promise that we will be "delivered from the bondage of corruption into the glorious liberty of the sons of God" (Rom 8:21).

Retrospect

Wesley's basic paradigm of the faith journey is now in place. His gospel evolved from (1) a message of holiness realized in the article of death, to (2) a message of full salvation received instantly by faith, to (3) a message incorporating the best of both: a gospel grounded on two works of grace. The process was not easy, and at times personally painful. Not only did Wesley go through many months of deep struggle, but he also found himself making friends to only later part paths with them. Since his own views were continually evolving and taking shape, much of the

---

[112] This is JW's choice of terms II.26.
[113] Galatians 2:20 is quoted by JW in the homily at this point.
[114] II.27; Matthew 1:21.
[115] JW offers one of his most important qualifications concerning his perfection doctrine at the end of this homily, "It remains, then, that Christians are saved in this world from all sin, from all unrighteousness; that they are now in such a sense perfect as not to commit sin, and to be freed from evil thoughts and evil tempers" (II.28). JW here defines what he understands to be full salvation from all sin (PA 12:44).

responsibility lies with himself. For example, Wesley became fast friends with the Moravians and embraced much of their principles, yet he later parted paths because his owns views kept changing while their beliefs remained more constant. Still, he owed much to them. Wesley was a man on a search. Through the fires of personal struggle and revival he began to forge a theology all his own, a theology that will be called *Wesleyan*.

Consistent in each of Wesley's three gospels is the identification of the new birth with perfection. In chapter one, we saw that Wesley used the language of new birth when speaking of the single intention. With the doctrine of the *imago Dei*, he identified the new birth with the attainment of perfection in the article of death. When he embraced his "new" gospel of faith alone, the new birth continued to be linked with perfection. But now both were collapsed into one event: the article of conversion. As the new birth was understood as given in an instant, so was full salvation. In July 1739 Wesley specified the new birth as a change of "states"—from the old man to the new man. A couple months later, in mid-September, he further spelled out the nature of the new birth by identifying the change with one's inward tempers, "I believe it to be an inward thing; a change from inward wickedness to inward goodness; an entire change of our inmost nature from the image of the devil (wherein we are born) to the image of God...in a word, a change from the *tempers* of the spirits of darkness to those of the angels of God."[116] Thus, the new birth ushers the earnest seeker into a state of perfect love and devotion.

This same position can be found in his preface to *Hymns and Sacred Poems II* and in the sermon *Christian Perfection*. In the latter work only those who are "fathers" are said to be "properly Christians."[117] In 1750 this phrase was changed by Wesley to "perfect Christians," thus reflecting further development in his thought. It would take another nine years for his position on re-

---

[116] JWJ 9/13/39.

[117] II.2. Albert Outler comments, "Taken literally, this would mean that none but the perfect are 'proper Christians'. In 1750 and thereafter, Wesley altered this to read, 'these only are perfect Christians' (Works B 2:105 n 57).

The Gospel of Two Works of Grace

generation to solidify in the sermon *The New Birth*. In this sermon regeneration is distinguished from baptism (IV.1),[118] and surprisingly from sanctification (IV.3). The new birth is a "part of sanctification, not the whole; it is the gate of it, the entrance into it." Then to clarify he adds, "When we are born again, then our sanctification, our inward and outward holiness, begins." So it took a couple decades for Wesley to finally separate his doctrine of regeneration from that of perfection within his *ordo salutis*.[119]

One of the tools Wesley found most helpful to clarify his views was the concept of *states*. This concept facilitated distinguishing core doctrines that had previously been blurred in his thinking. Like pieces to a jigsaw puzzle, the idea of states served to define justification, sanctification, assurance, inward and outward sin, and new birth as individual pieces of the *ordo salutis* puzzle. In this way Wesley stopped confusing these core doctrines. Structuring the faith journey into different levels of maturation further facilitated this process. Now the various components of the faith journey could be firmly placed at specific points along the path toward full renewal.

Along with this theological process were the practical needs of the converts. Wesley learned the hard way that the Moravian gospel he had imbued just did not fit the needs of his followers. Most of them did not experience salvation as a complete package. In the heat of revival, when emotions are running high, many believed they had experienced all that was promised. But as their emotions settled, such professions evaporated into thin air. This explains the rampant enthusiasm within the societies in 1739. Physical manifestations were thought to be a sign from God that

---

[118] But see Ole Borgen's masterful study of JW's sacramental theology. How JW relates the new birth to baptism is more nuanced and complex than what the homily *The New Birth* implies.

[119] In II.5 of *The New Birth* JW does come close to his earlier language of equating regeneration with Christian perfection. It is referred to as "that great change," but a close reading picks up a fundamental difference. Regeneration is clearly linked to being brought to life. This is a marked difference from JW's statements about the new birth during the period under present study. Cf. Appendix D.

the kingdom had fully arrived. Even Wesley for a while accepted these manifestations as divine testimony of his message and ministry. Nevertheless, over time enthusiasm cooled and most people realized they were still living in a fallen world with sinful human tendencies remaining. Wesley was perceptive enough to see through the revival smoke and call for a second, deeper work of the Spirit. In this way he could affirm what God had done in the first work, while calling believers to higher levels of Christian holiness.

Behind the needs of the converts was the fundamental premise of Wesley's two-works gospel: gradual process punctuated by instantaneous God-moments. Wesley was able to fashion a path that includes gift and work, faith and ordinance, instant and process, God and human cooperation—working together under the leadership of divine grace, calling, and empowerment.[120] This is the genius of Wesley's two-works gospel.

The Wesleyan path is a particular understanding of the faith journey.[121] In theology this comes under the heading of soteriology, the doctrine of salvation. The Wesleyan perspective sees the goal as the recovery of the image of God lost by Adam in the garden. Unable to save ourselves, the human race now stands in need of redemption and salvation. The foundation is God's unbounded grace, but this grace is conditioned upon human response, that is, faith expressed in obedience and love. The faith journey is the inward kingdom of God,[122] with God setting up his reign in the human heart. According to Wesley, the faith journey can be demarcated as follows:

---

[120] Randy Maddox's illustration of a dance offers a good illustration of the divine/human synergism. God leads and the believer responsively follows, but together they both create a beautiful work (*Responsible Grace*, 151).

[121] The soteriology JW forged is what led to him to part paths with Calvinists, Moravians (Lutherans), and many in his own church. This eventually led to the (Wesleyan) Methodists forming their own denomination and their own theological tradition.

[122] *Preface to an Extract on the Life of Mr. Halyburton*; §1.

The Gospel of Two Works of Grace

Prevenient Grace: God awakens the seeker to his love and their need for reconciliation. Coming under conviction, the seeker feels their spiritual poverty[123] and by faith looks to Christ for forgiveness and salvific healing.

Child of God: This is the first gift: justification. Having been forgiven by faith in Christ's sacrificial death, the newborn believer is filled with peace and joy that can last for weeks or even months. Having been born again (in a low sense), the child of God is now set free from sin's reign (outward sin), and is renewed in the heart to serve God in love and obedience through the practice of the means of grace (works of piety and mercy).

Wilderness State: After a time the old enemies, those bosom sins that so easily beset, arise to assault the believer. This shakes the immature believer's confidence by instilling fear and doubt. Causing unrest within, the child struggles over questions like, "Will I be able to persevere?" "Will I falter?" "Was I deceived when I thought God forgave me?" "Am I really God's child?" "Did my emotions deceive me, since sin still remains in me?" In this state of doubt, even deep despair, the believer is often tempted to give up practicing the means of grace.

Adolescence: But it isn't long before God reassures his "mourning"[124] child by witnessing to their acceptance and forgiveness. The adolescent grabs hold of God's promises

---

[123] We saw above JW first learned his GosTW from Christian David, who used the Beatitudes in Matthew ch 5 as a primary text. Starting in April 1739 there are numerous references in JW's Journal of him preaching from this text. The themes of the first five beatitudes are also imbedded in the description of the faith journey described in the preface to *Hymns and Sacred Poems II*.

[124] In the preface to *Hymns and Sacred Poems II* JW identifies the second beatitude with the wilderness state and as leading to and preparing the child for the adolescent state. The third beatitude is identified with attaining the adolescent state (Works J 14:327).

John Wesley's Theology of Christian Perfection

and by faith overcomes the fiery darts of the evil one. Having overcome, the Spirit's witness becomes abiding, bringing renewed hope and assurance, thus giving strength and encouragement to diligently practice the means of grace, knowing this is God's path to full salvation—holiness of heart and life.

Hunger after Full Righteousness: Even with God's abiding testimony the work of renewal remains unfinished. God reveals to the believer the depths of their heart, uncovering pride, self-will, anger and other sinful dispositions and attitudes[125] that pollute their love to God and neighbor. Even though the adolescent sinks under the weight, such revelation produces meekness, resignation, and the desire[126] for nothing else but God's full reign within, bringing full deliverance from remaining sin.

Adulthood: This is the second gift: full salvation. By faith in Christ's cleansing work on the cross, the body of sin is destroyed and the evil nature of pride, self-will, and anger is replaced with the nature of Christ: perfect love. With the heart fully renewed to love God and neighbor wholeheartedly, the believer's communion with God is sweet and blessed. Prayer becomes their breath and God's word their food. Christ makes the heart his permanent dwelling, witnessed by his Spirit who fills as an artesian well springing up with his full fruits. Spiritual adulthood is now attained.

Continued Maturation: Now that the adult believer is perfect in their love, they still need to continue growing in their knowledge of God and his salvation. Their continued

---

[125] JW's terminology in *Christian Perfection* is evil (sinful) thoughts and tempers.

[126] JW links the fourth and fifth beatitudes to the seeker's preparation for perfection.

The Gospel of Two Works of Grace

maturation of character brings greater strength and discernment in the face of temptation and trial, empowering the believer to overcome weaknesses inherent in one's character and personality. Nonetheless, this process of growth never ends, for even in eternity we will be ever learning the fullness of God's ways.

The Gospel of Two Works of Grace laid out a path that was realistic in its goals, yet visionary in its appeal. By offering a second moment—when all willful sin is vanquished and consistent obedience in love attained[127]—the believer is given a realizable goal; yet, one that stretches the believer to the limits of their spiritual potential. The blending of instant and process, attainment and goal, Spirit empowerment and human endeavor, into a single system of spiritual development is what believers need to remain encouraged and motivated in their faith journey, and in their usefulness for the kingdom.

Over the next two decades Wesley's two-works gospel will continue to develop as (1) the question of assurance is further clarified[128] and (2) his Arminian principles conclude that even perfecting grace can be lost through willful disobedience.[129] As Wesley ages his role as spiritual father emerges in his letters.[130]

---

[127] JW's conceptual models during this period are committing sin and holy tempers. We can paraphrase these concepts by stating that adult believers attain consistency in their obedience of love.

[128] By July 1747 JW came to the position that justifying faith is not always accompanied with a sense of pardon (JWL 7/31/47). Randy Maddox writes, "He (JW) now maintained that such an awareness of pardon was possible, indeed the 'common privilege of real Christians,' but denied that its accompaniment was essential to justifying faith. His earlier publications that had conjoined these two in absolute terms were now judged to be contrary to both Scripture and experience" (*Responsible Grace*, 126).

[129] In the *Plain Account* JW wrote, "It (perfection) is amissible, capable of being lost; of which we have numerous instances. But we were not thoroughly convinced of this, till five or six years ago" (26:9; see also 19:99; 25:64-69, 102-104; 26:14). JW wrote the above statement in 1764. Counting back 5 to 6 years leads to 1758-59.

[130] This is the subject of ch 6.

John Wesley's Theology of Christian Perfection

But this is the subject of the next section when we learn how his theology of perfection continued to evolve from the 1760's into the 1780's.

We now return to the comparison chart highlighting the similarities and differences between Wesley's three gospels:

Gospel of Holiness	Gospel of Faith Alone	Gospel of Two Works
Axiom:		
Inward holiness	Faith alone	Inward holiness & Faith alone
Ground:		
Sanctification brings justification	Justification equals sanctification	Justification begins sanctification
Object of faith:		
God & his promises	Christ alone	Christ alone & God's promises
Focus:		
Future salvation	Present salvation	Present & future salvation
Salvation by:		
Faith in ordinances	Faith alone	Faith alone & ordinances
Salvation is:		
Lifelong process	Instantaneous gift	Gift and process
Foundation of Assurance:		
Sincerity, communicating, & life transformation	Witness of the Spirit	Witness of Spirit & life transformation
Holiness complete:		
Death	Conversion	Adulthood
Faith complete:		
Death	Conversion	Adulthood
Christian complete:		
Death	Conversion	Adulthood

Section Two

Mature Enlargements in John Wesley's Theology of Christian Perfection

I know many who love God with all their heart, mind, soul, and strength. He is their one desire, their one delight, and they are continually happy in him... But these souls dwell in a shattered, corruptible body, and are pressed down thereby, that they cannot exert their love as they would.

Letter to Elizabeth Hardy, December 26, 1761

FOUR
Aldersgate II

By the mid-sixties Wesley's theology of perfection began to enter a new phase. The decade proved to be very turbulent for Methodism and for John Wesley personally. A perfection revival broke out early in the decade that quickly slipped into open schism among some Methodist ranks. But out of the turmoil and conflict new contours began to emerge in Wesley's thought that would powerfully shape his perfection theology over the next two-plus decades. To tell this story we begin by assessing where Wesley's theology was at in the middle of the decade. In two successive years he wrote and published what would later be regarded as landmark works on his perfection theology. The first was the sermon *The Scripture Way of Salvation* and the second was *A Plain Account of Christian Perfection*.[1]

In a number of ways, as *Salvation By Faith* served as the manifesto for his faith-alone gospel and began what Wesley historians refer to as his middle period (1738-1765), *The Scripture Way of Salvation* serves as the manifesto for his late period (1765-1791). Both *Salvation By Faith* and *The Scripture Way of Salvation* use the same text and follow the same general outline, but contain marked differences when depicting the faith journey. We have covered the former sermon and its theology, so we need only to highlight the theological shifts found in the latter. We start by noting in *The Scripture Way* that the focus remains on salvation as present blessing, just as in *Salvation By Faith*. Only now, twenty-seven years later, Wesley realizes the faith journey is more complex. Beginning in the first moments when preventing grace enlightens the heart to God and his claims, the faith journey progresses through several stages until "entire sanctifica-

---

[1] *The Scripture Way* was published in 1765 and the *Plain Account* in early 1766 (see his letter to John Newton 2/28/66 and the Introduction to Volume One of this series).

tion" is attained: "full salvation from all our sins, from pride, self-will, anger, (and) unbelief." Only then does "perfect love" fill the heart and take up the "whole capacity of the soul" (I.9).

But in contrast to his faith-alone gospel, Wesley's two-works gospel sharply distinguishes between justification and sanctification. *The Scripture Way* labels both as the "general parts" of our present salvation from sin. Justification is defined as pardon, the forgiveness of sins and "our acceptance with God" (I.3). At the same time we are born again. Wesley refers to the latter as a *real* change, while the former is a *relative* change.[2] In the new birth the seeds of every virtue are planted in the heart and develop to the degree that sin is removed. This is in sharp contrast to his Gospel of Faith Alone, which so identified justification with full salvation that both were collapsed into a single God-moment.[3]

Once again, it was the needs of the converts that prompted Wesley to articulate his theology as he did. Out of the great revival in the early sixties,[4] many converts assumed (just as they did in 1739[5]) they were instantly delivered from all sin in the moment of the new birth. Wesley cautions them that just because sin "does not stir" they should not assume it "does not exist." Just because sin appears to have no "motion," they should not conclude it has no "being."[6] In reality, sin is only "suspended" not "destroyed." What lies between is the wilderness state: that season when new converts struggle with questions of assurance and bosom sins.[7] What had most notably changed since 1741 when

---

[2] This distinction is identical in thought to what Christian David made in the summer of 1738. David spoke of "Christ *for* us" and "Christ *in* us."
[3] The GosFA linked justification, new birth, full assurance, and entire sanctification into one experience of instantaneous faith. Cf. ch 2.
[4] 1759-1763. Cf. *Plain Account: Introduction, Why Wesley Wrote*.
[5] This is a common characteristic of both transitional periods (which I refer in this chapter and in chapter 10 as Aldersgate I and Aldersgate II). Both spiritual crises JW faced were connected to intense periods of revival.
[6] *The Scripture Way* I.5. Note the similarity in language to what Christian David used in 1738.
[7] In the late 50's and early 60's JW published a series of sermons which contributed significantly to the mature articulation of his two-works gospel. One

John Wesley's Theology of Christian Perfection

Wesley penned his last manifesto on holiness (*Christian Perfection*) is that now he distinguishes regeneration from sanctification,[8] and more clearly delineates sin's bondage as threefold: guilt, power and being.[9]

But his doctrine of faith had evolved too. Wesley now draws a sharper line between faith and assurance, and gives a much larger role to repentance than before. In 1738 saving faith had been defined by contrasting it to the other faiths—a heathen, a demon, and the pre-Calvary disciples. Foremost in Wesley's thought at the time was the object of faith, meaning Christ's atonement and resurrection. Times had changed and so had Wesley. He now defines faith in terms of Hebrews 11:1, a divine "evidence of things not seen."[10] This evidence, or conviction, is a "kind of spiritual *light*," a "supernatural *sight*" to see the truth of God. Faith is fun-

---

of these was *The Wilderness State*, published in 1760. In this homily JW outlines the loss of faith, love, joy, peace and spiritual power caused by spiritual darkness resulting from renewed sins of commission and omission (Works B 2:202).

[8] In *The New Birth* (1759) JW formally separates the two. He strongly disagrees with William Law's position that treats both as speaking of the same divine work in the soul, "It (Law's tract) all along speaks of regeneration as a progressive work carried on in the soul by slow degrees from the time of our first turning to God. This is undeniably true of sanctification; but of regeneration, the new birth, it is not true. This is a part of sanctification, not the whole; it is the gate of it, the entrance into it" (IV.3). See Appendix D.

[9] Back in 1738 sin was categorized as guilt and power (*Salvation by Faith* II.2, 3, 5). By the early sixties sin was divided into three categories, "The *guilt* is one thing, the *power* is another, and the *being* yet another" (*On Sin in Believers* IV.4).

[10] Heitzenrater identifies CW as the first one to use Heb 11:1 as a definition for saving faith in *Awake, Thou That Sleepest* I.11 (1742; *Great Expectations*, 84, n 178). See Outler's notes on this passage. Apparently, JW's first use of this text to define saving faith was in *Earnest Appeal* §6 (1743), and then the following year in *Scriptural Christianity* I.2. It is possible that his 1746 published sermon *Justification By Faith* (IV.2) draws from an earlier use of the text, since the roots of that sermon possibly go back to Sept/Oct 1739 (JWJ). What we do know is that the first recorded use of Heb 11:1 to define saving faith is in JWMSJ 7/31/37 (Works B 18:532) by the Moravian brethren to JW's questions.

damentally a spiritual sense by which we know and relate to God and the spiritual realm. This move from the object of faith to its psychological working will prove to have important bearings on Wesley's personal faith journey and on his theological development.[11]

Just as his concept of faith evolved, so did the role of repentance within his gospel system. While faith continued to serve as the immediate and necessary condition for justification and sanctification, repentance now plays a larger role by becoming linked more tightly to prevenient grace and the means of grace. As grace initially enlightens the heart to God, so the seeker is responsible to "cease to do evil" and to "learn to do well."[12] In a similar manner, following one's justification the process of repentance continues regarding *remaining* sin. While the believer's first repentance deals with sin's guilt (forgiveness) and power (outward sin), their second repentance focuses on rooting out inward sin, which continues to pollute the Christian's devotion to God. This latter repentance is defined as a "conviction of our helplessness, of our utter inability to think one good thought, or to form one good desire…to speak one word aright, or to perform one good action but through his free, almighty grace" (III.8). Wesley then links repentance to the means of grace and the practice of good works:

> First, all works of piety, such as public prayer, family prayer, and praying in our closet; receiving the Supper of the Lord; searching the Scriptures by hearing, reading, meditating; and using such a measure of fasting or abstinence as our bodily health allows.
> Secondly, all works of mercy, whether they relate to the bodies or souls of men; such as feeding the hungry,

---

[11] Faith as a spiritual sense has a long history in JW's understanding of faith. It is mentioned as early as 1733 in *The Circumcision of the Heart* (P.2), and plays a major role in JW's explication of the new birth in *The Great Privilege of Those that are Born of God* I.1-5. We will return to this subject in ch 7.

[12] Isaiah 1:16-17. JW quotes this passage in the sermon.

> clothing the naked, entertaining the stranger, visiting those that are in prison, or sick, or variously afflicted...This is the repentance, and these the fruits meet for repentance, which are necessary to full sanctification. This is the way wherein God hath appointed his children to wait for complete salvation. (III.9-10)

Here several themes or concepts coalesce: repentance, works of piety and mercy, good works, and sanctification (inward holiness). By linking repentance to the entire faith journey, from the first inklings of grace to the fullness of perfect love, Wesley moves his gospel to encompass the entire work of God in the human soul—a more universal gospel. By conjoining good works to the means of grace (works of piety and mercy), he formally reaffirms the role of good works in his gospel system. Within five years this renewed emphasis will raise the ire of the Calvinists to a new level.

But no less important in explicating his gospel of two divine moments was the writing and publishing of *A Plain Account of Christian Perfection*. At the time this book served to ground his doctrine of perfection historically and theologically by including excerpts of several writings from the past thirty years.[13] All aspects of his two-works gospel are addressed and reaffirmed. Central to the book's message is the inclusion of two more recent tracts, *Thoughts on Christian Perfection* (1759) and *Farther Thoughts on Christian Perfection* (1763). These twin tracts proved very important to the maturation of his two-works gospel by conceptually delineating sin into two categories: voluntary and involuntary. The former category had been part of Wesley's vo-

---

[13] W. Steven Gunter refers to the *Plain Account* as "piecemeal apologetics" (*Love Divine*, 212). This author holds a more positive view. JW's primary purpose in writing was to show by what he had taught over several decades that he had been consistent in his teachings on the subject. See volume one of this series *John Wesley's 'A Plain Account of Christian perfection' The Annotated Edition.*.

cabulary since the early thirties.[14] The latter had developed slowly through the decades and recently took on a more visible role within his perfection doctrine.[15] Wesley now declares the persistent reality of involuntary sin, even in the "most perfect;" meaning, that *all* Christians continue to transgress God's holy standard for which they need *daily* forgiveness.[16] This opened the door wider for further sanctification and growth following one's perfection in love. In other words, Christians can be perfect regarding their dispositional nature (tempers) and still fall short of God's absolute standard of Adamic righteousness.[17]

Another significant change in Wesley's views was over the idea that one could lose their perfection. As Wesley once held to the concept of intermittency in attaining inward holiness (early 1739), he again embraces the belief that seekers of perfect love often fluctuate in and out of pure devotion before becoming established in the experience.[18] As the years passed this became more and more a concern for Wesley.[19]

So, to summarize, by the mid-sixties the Gospel of Two Works embraced a faith journey of continual progress punctuated by two divine moments of instantaneous renewal. These twin moments were identified with stages in the physical life—childhood and adulthood— and were witnessed by the Spirit's testimony and fruits.[20] When it comes to stating explicitly and

---

[14] JWL 6/19/31. See also *Salvation By Faith* II.6 (1738), *Preface to An Extract of the Life and Death of Mr. Halyburton* §5 (Work J 14:212), and *Plain Account* 19:6-25 (1759, 1765).

[15] In 1759 JW wrote *Thoughts on Christian Perfection* and published it the following year.

[16] *Plain Account* 19:12.

[17] JW's words in *Farther Thoughts on Christian Perfection* are, "But Adam fell; and his incorruptible body became corruptible; and ever since, it is a clog to the soul, and hinders its operations. Hence, at present, no child of man can at all times apprehend clearly, or judge truly…Consequently, no man is able to perform the service which the Adamic law requires" (PA 25:8).

[18] *Plain Account* 25:103. This change took place in 1758-59.

[19] *Plain Account* 25:103 n. Chapter 6 addresses this issue in full.

[20] *Plain Account* 25:49-51. Since the chief feature of the adolescent state is a full assurance that eliminates all doubt and fear, it is somewhat surprising JW

John Wesley's Theology of Christian Perfection

concisely what Christian perfection meant to John Wesley at this time, there is no better statement than his own eleven-point summary written in 1764:

1. There is such a thing as perfection; for it is again and again mentioned in Scripture.
2. It is not so early as justification; for justified persons are to 'go on unto perfection.' (Heb 6:1)
3. It is not so late as death; for St. Paul speaks of living men that were perfect. (Php 3:15)
4. It is not absolute. Absolute perfection belongs not to man, nor to angels, but to God alone.
5. It does not make a man infallible: None is infallible, while he remains in the body.
6. Is it sinless? It is not worth while to contend for a term. It is 'salvation from sin.'
7. It is 'perfect love.' (1 Jn 4:18) This is the essence of it; its properties, or inseparable fruits, are, rejoicing evermore, praying without ceasing, and in everything giving thanks. (1 Th 5:16-18)
8. It is improvable. It is so far from lying in an indivisible point, from being incapable of increase, that one perfected in love may grow in grace far swifter than he did before.
9. It is amissible, capable of being lost; of which we have numerous instances. But we were not thoroughly convinced of this, till five or six years ago.
10. It is constantly both preceded and followed by a gradual work.

---

never formally identified this as a third instantaneous moment. His theology implicitly made room for such an experience since most received the gift of full assurance in a moment. The same could be said of the servant state, as we will learn below. Since the servant state is entered into instantaneously, being connected to justification, it would point to a fourth divine moment in the Wesleyan scheme of the faith journey. See chs 9 and 10.

11. But is it in itself instantaneous or not? In examining this, let us go on step by step. An instantaneous change has been wrought in some believers: None can deny this. Since that change, they enjoy perfect love; they feel this, and this alone; they 'rejoice evermore, pray without ceasing, and in everything give thanks.' Now, this is all that I mean by perfection; therefore, these are witnesses of the perfection which I preach.[21]

Thus Wesley appears to have finally settled in his theological views regarding perfection. We can say this with a fair amount of certainty. The *Plain Account* was issued several more times in his life and each time the subtitle was changed to read the most recent year.[22] Signifying, as later editor Thomas Jackson notes, that Wesley's theology of perfection did not materially change for the rest of his life.[23] The great achievement of Wesley's two-works gospel is found in its sense of balance. As a system it combined and held in tension: instant and process, faith and ordinance, voluntary and involuntary (sin), first and second repentance, partial and full renewal. And it held out to seekers specific milestones of attainment along the faith journey path—childhood, adolescence, adulthood. Plus, Wesley grounded the entire process on the transformation of the tempers toward complete renewal in the image and likeness of God. Hence, at each milestone a greater transformation of the dispositional nature is attained, with the Holy Spirit bearing witness to each state or level. Each one of these themes and motifs remained constant in his two-works gospel system. Could it be that after harmonizing his prior two gospel systems—holiness and faith alone—John Wesley finally found his theological resting place?

---

[21] *Plain Account* ch 26.
[22] The last time was in 1777.
[23] Works J 11:366.

John Wesley's Theology of Christian Perfection

Aldersgate II

The era we commonly refer to as "Aldersgate" was a very turbulent season in the life of John Wesley. We saw in chapter two that 1738 proved to be a time of deep personal reevaluation and inner struggle. As he looked in the mirror of self-reflection, he became acutely aware of his spiritual deficiencies. This prompted Wesley to be sharply critical of his prior faith journey up to that point in time. In the months leading up to and following his evangelical conversion on May 24, 1738 Wesley had gone through severe struggles over his faith, his level of spiritual attainment, and the doctrines he had believed in so strongly.

Besides the struggles, Aldersgate proved to be a season of enormous theological change. His theological system looked much different after Aldersgate than before. Both students and historians of Wesley have looked hard for the time when he passed through a second change, when he personally attained perfect love; but to no avail.[24] Wesley never left any record outlining such an experience. As late as 1767 he acknowledged to the Lloyd's Evening Post, "I have told all the world I am not perfect." And then a little later in the same letter he adds in reference to his tract *The Character of a Methodist*, "I tell you flat I have not attained the character I draw."[25]

Even if we cannot pinpoint a time when Wesley personally experienced the second blessing, we can identify a second Aldersgate-like period in his life. This period parallels the first Aldersgate era in so many ways that this author has dubbed it "Aldersgate II." Just as Aldersgate I radically altered Wesley's perspective on his life and doctrine; this crisis produced deep soul-searching and profound theological reevaluation. Three decades earlier, Aldersgate I developed out of Wesley's deep dissatisfaction over his spiritual development. In a similar way, this crisis sprang from personal discontent over his faith journey after 1738.

---

[24] See W. Stephen Gunter *Aldersgate, the Holiness Movement, and Experiential Religion* in Maddox, Randy ed. *Aldersgate Reconsidered*, 121-131.
[25] JWL T 3/5/67.

Aldersgate II

As Aldersgate I led to fundamental changes in Wesley's theological system; like sound waves Aldersgate II would over time reverberate throughout his entire doctrinal system. But, and most importantly, this crisis alone explains why Wesley reversed his journal confessions made in 1738. To understand Aldersgate II we must begin by looking at the great perfection revival and schism of 1759-1763 and its aftermath.

The Great Perfection Revival

To understand both Aldersgate I and II, including why they happened, we must first appreciate the deep-seated belief Wesley had in the idea of perfection. Simply put, perfection was the core conviction of his spiritual DNA. Under the tutelage of his mother and father, his spiritual constitution had been largely shaped around the concept of perfection.[26] When he experienced his conversion to a single intention in early 1725, it was to the ideal of perfection as freedom from the "tyranny of sin" that captivated his heart and devotion.[27] Even when he later passed through the dark night of the soul and at last cried out, "I went to America to convert the Indians; but Oh! who shall convert me,"[28] the entire orientation of his thought was still toward attaining perfection.[29] One of the constants throughout Wesley's life and ministry is that the demand for inward holiness was "burned into his soul."[30] This explains Charles' remark to him many years before the great perfection revival broke out:

---

[26] JWJ 5/24/38 §1; Roy Hattersley, *The Life of John Wesley*, 27-30.
[27] *Death and Deliverance* §14.
[28] JWJ 1/24/38.
[29] JWJ 1/25/38 memorandum §1. JWJ 2/1/38 post-script, "I want that faith which…whosoever hath it is 'freed from sin'; 'the whole body of sin is destroyed' in him."
[30] Dallimore, *George Whitefield* 2:22.

> Your day of Pentecost is not yet fully come; but I doubt not it will: And you will then hear of persons sanctified, as frequently as you do now of persons justified.[31]

When John recalled these words in 1762 he records in his journal, "Any unprejudiced reader may observe, that it was now fully come." When hundreds began professing the experience of perfect love Wesley felt deep inner satisfaction. The revival appears to have first sprouted in 1758 and continued into 1763. When enthusiasm began to raise its ugly head we can understand why Wesley moved with such slowness to suppress it.[32] Thomas Maxfield and George Bell became the primary ringleaders of a movement promoting "angelic" perfection. According to these schismatics, perfection lifts a person above the consequences of Adam's sin and fall. Eschatological perfection had arrived. Those perfected would not taste physical death, nor would they need face temptation or pain. Also espoused was a return of the charismata of the Spirit, including faith healing, speaking in tongues, prophecy, and the gift of spiritual discernment. The movement quickly peaked in December 1762 when George Bell pronounced that the world would end in less than three months (on February 28). The prophecy, of course, failed and the schism exhausted itself in a split from Wesley and his societies, with Bell and Maxfield pulling a couple hundred people away.[33] Wesley's response to the schism was primarily two-fold: to articulate his doctrine of involuntary sin, thus cutting off any hope of an eschatological perfection in this life, and to emphasize the fruits of the Spirit as the final arbiter for attainment of perfect love.[34]

While we are far removed from these events, it is important to grasp the enormous emotional impact they had on John Wesley. Reginald Ward and Richard Heitzenrater note of the schism and

---

[31] JWJ 10/28/62.
[32] See *Plain Account*, Introduction: Why Wesley Wrote.
[33] *Plain Account* ch 22 and notes.
[34] See *Plain Account* 25:88-100. In the PA the Spirit's fruit (indirect witness) even takes precedence over the direct witness.

separation, "'Some who knew Mr. Wesley well, have declared that this was the heaviest trial that ever befell him.'"[35] It was at this time that Wesley lost some of his "choicest friends" due to the separation. The perfection revival and the ensuing schism (and separation) only fueled further questions and criticisms of Wesley's perfection teachings.

Continuing Struggles over Perfection

In the years following the revival and schism Wesley penned a number of letters to his brother Charles regarding the question of perfection within the societies. These letters reveal the struggle that transpired between the brothers (and others) over the viability of the doctrine. Only a year after Maxfield formally severed ties with Wesley, John wrote of the "frightful stories" coming from London instilling apprehension in the other circuit preachers to not even mutter a word about perfection.[36] This withdraw caused Wesley to tell George Merryweather, "Where Christian perfection is not strongly and explicitly preached there is seldom any remarkable blessing from God, and consequently little addition to the Society and little life in the members of it."[37] In the same month he pleaded with his brother, "We must, we must, you and I at least, be all devoted to God!"[38] Charles had become very disenchanted with the whole doctrine. John's frustration is evident:

> That *perfection* which I believe, I can boldly preach, because I think I see five hundred witnesses of it. Of that *perfection* which you preach, you do not even think you see any witness at all...I wonder you do not, in this arti-

---

[35] Works B 21:438 n 90.
[36] JWL T 5/25/64.
[37] JWL T 2/8/66.
[38] JWL T 2/28/66.

cle, fall in plumb with Mr. Whitefield. For do not you, as well as he, ask, "Where are the perfect ones?"[39]

While Wesley continued to press his followers to seek the second blessing, Charles persisted in dragging his feet by promoting a gradual perfection not fully realized in this life. John tries to reason with him, "I still think, to disbelieve all the professors amounts to a denial of the thing. For if there be no living witness of what we have preached for twenty years, I cannot, dare not, preach it any longer. The whole comes to one point: Is there, or is there not, any instantaneous sanctification between justification and death? I say, Yes. You (often seem to) say, No."[40] Finally, John's emotions boil over:

> I am at my wit's end with regard to two things, — the Church, and Christian perfection. Unless both you and I stand in the gap in good earnest, the Methodists will drop them both. Talking, will not avail.[41]

As we put the pieces of a puzzle together, what begins to emerge from Wesley's extant writings is a picture of an encroaching spiritual crisis looming in the near horizon. Times of testing and trial often lead to soul-searching; which in turn can move a person to question even their deepest convictions. With Wesley's core beliefs—his very DNA—being challenged by those closest to him, and in whom he put the most trust (his brother), John must have felt the entire gamut of emotions from grief and discouragement to frustration and anger. From the emotional highs of revival, through the lows of schism and separation, to the quagmire of controversy over his most beloved doctrine, the weight had to take a toll leading to profound questions. It was in this climate that John Wesley began to reexamine his faith journey from a new perspective.

---

[39] JWL T 7/9/66 (emphasis his).
[40] JWL T 2/12/67.
[41] JWL T 5/14/68.

Aldersgate II

A Plain Account of Christian Perfection

The *Plain Account* has come down to us as a spiritual classic. It continues to be reissued in a variety of formats and serves as the most comprehensive statement by Wesley on his doctrine of Christian perfection. This perfection consists of "no wrong temper, none contrary to love, remains in the soul; all the thoughts, words, and actions, are governed by pure love."[42] While both scholar and student continue to mine the book for the slightest nuance in Wesley's doctrine and its development, what is often missed is the book's historical significance in relation to Wesley's own faith journey. The *Plain Account* has the privileged position, among his many published writings, as being the first to speak in *positive terms* of his pre-Aldersgate faith journey.[43] Up to this point in time Wesley had consistently maintained he had been in an unconverted state before his Aldersgate conversion in May 1738.[44]

---

[42] *Plain Account* 19:5.

[43] The letter to John Newton on May 14, 1765 was written earlier than the *Plain Account* (see JWJ) but wasn't published until 1769, over three years after the *Plain Account*. Therefore, the *Plain Account* is the earliest public record of JW stating 1725 as his conversion to vital religion.

[44] JW was consistent on this point. Beginning in October 1738 JW told his older brother he was not a Christian before May 24 (JWL 10/30/38). In 1741 he declared he was only an "almost Christian" before the university (*Almost Christian* I.12-13). In 1751 he wrote Bishop Lavington concerning his January 1738 confessions, "I am here describing the thoughts which passed through my mind when I was confessedly an unbeliever" (Works B 11:401). Again in 1758 JW told Elizabeth Hardy, "I myself was so a few years ago. I felt the wrath of God abiding on me. I was afraid every hour of dropping into hell. I knew myself to be the chief of sinners. Though I had been very innocent in the account of others, I saw my heart to be all sin and corruption. I was without the knowledge and the love of God, and therefore an abomination in His sight" (JWL 5/58; Telford 4:20). Another line of evidence involves the histories of Methodism written by JW. In 1749 he penned *A Plain Account of Methodists* in which he begins the story in 1739, the year after Aldersgate. In 1765 he wrote *A Short History of Methodism* and began the story in 1729, his Oxford era. Finally, in 1781 JW published *A Short History of the People Called Methodists,* which also began the story in 1729. When we note when these histories

John Wesley's Theology of Christian Perfection

In the first volume of this series it was pointed out the close parallel that exists between the opening chapters of the *Plain Account* and Wesley's letter to John Newton on May 14, 1765 (JWJ). In both Wesley briefly tells the story how he came to embrace the doctrine of heart holiness. Two corollaries follow: First, the date of the letter points to the time when Wesley began to write the *Plain Account*.[45] Second, the contents of the letter confirm that by May 1765 Wesley was already in the process of reinterpreting his pre-Aldersgate faith journey. This is how Wesley states it in the *Plain Account*:

> In the year 1725, being in the twenty-third year of my age, I met with Bishop Taylor's "Rule and Exercises of Holy Living and Dying." In reading several parts of this book, I was exceedingly affected; that part in particular which relates to purity of intention. Instantly I resolved to dedicate all my life to God, all my thoughts, and words, and actions; being thoroughly convinced, there was no medium; but that every part of my life (not some only) must either be a sacrifice to God, or myself, that is, in effect, to the devil. (2:1-3)

To repeat, this is Wesley's first public record following Aldersgate in which he speaks of his early period in positive terms.[46] In

---

were written, we see that those penned in the sixties and later ground the story in the early period. And the history written in the latter forties begins after Aldersgate. This author finds the evidence convincing that JW probably changed his mind when he began to reflect on when he embraced perfection in his life. The only evidence that points to this time is in the spring 1765 when he wrote to John Newton and he started writing the *Plain Account*. See note 86 below.

[45] See volume one of this series: *A Plain Account*, 5-8.

[46] There is no mention of JW's Aldersgate conversion in the *Plain Account* (see PA ch 7 end note for a brief discussion of this subject). One possible explanation is that by 1765 JW did not believe his Aldersgate conversion contributed anything of significance to his understanding of perfection. This is possible, even likely. But what we do know is that by 1765 JW had already

the *Plain Account* he uses the terminology of conversion to describe his experience in 1725. This is accomplished by referencing the event to his mind, will and emotions. Wesley testifies of being "exceedingly affected." In an "instant" he made the epochal decision to commit his entire life to God. In keeping with his evangelical theology of the new birth, he underscores the impact made on his life at the time. Simply stated, he no longer served the devil by living for himself. Instead, from that moment he pursued living for God with a single intention—with all his "thoughts, and words, and actions." The power of conversion explains Wesley's passion for inward holiness.

When we compare this description from 1765 with those of his earlier Aldersgate era it becomes obvious that his views had changed. Even though Wesley describes in his now famous Aldersgate memorandum how his early faith journey had been marked with earnestness to seek a new life (§4); just a few paragraphs later he states he was the whole time in legal bondage to sin (§9), lacking saving faith (§11). This is confirmed by Wesley's confession a year later, "I was (fundamentally) a papist and knew it not,"[47] Two years later his opinion had not changed, since he confesses to have been only an "almost Christian." His faith had been sincere, but salvifically defective.[48] In contrast, the *Plain Account* paints a very different picture. Vital Christianity began not in 1738, when he embraced his new gospel of salvation by faith alone, but in 1725 when he was powerfully converted to the gospel of inward holiness.

---

changed his mind about when he was his converted to vital religion and inward holiness. See note 41 above.

[47] JWJ 8/27/39.

[48] In *Almost Christian* I.13 JW says that for "many years" he sought a (1) "conscience void of offence," (2) disciplined his use of time for the promotion of good, (3) consistently practiced the means of grace with all sincerity and seriousness of devotion, (4) had a "real design to serve God," and (5) was eager to please him in all things. Yet, JW says in 1741 that all this time his "conscience beareth (him) witness in the Holy Ghost" that he was "but *almost a Christian*." This is a strong criticism of his holiness gospel. By 1767-68 he was affirming that the above description applied to the Christian!

John Wesley's Theology of Christian Perfection

To summarize, Wesley's writing of the *Plain Account* in 1765, along with his letter to John Newton that same year, involve a fresh reevaluation of his faith journey, leading to a radically new assessment of his spiritual state prior to and following his Aldersgate conversion in 1738.

John's Letter to Charles

The *Plain Account* was published in the early months of 1766. Wesley's extant letters through the first half of that year reveal that the subject of perfection was uppermost in his mind. Yet, as we noted above, his brother was moving in a different direction. Charles was embracing more and more a progressive view of perfection that so exalted the experience that no one could attain it in this life.[49] While Wesley and George Whitefield were patching up their relationship at this time, the latter continued to misrepresent Wesley's doctrine of holiness by calling it that "monstrous doctrine of sinless perfection." He then spoke of the teaching as turning its "deluded votaries into temporary monsters."[50] Luke Tyerman summarizes the situation well, "Thus was Wesley between two fires; Whitefield setting the doctrine too low, and Charles Wesley setting it too high; and both of them ready to ridicule what Wesley called its witnesses." Just as the storms at sea thirty years earlier had awakened Wesley to deeper spiritual need, God was now using the storms of schism and conflict to move him to feel once more a deep need in his spirit.

On June 27, 1766 John opened up to Charles:

In one of my last (letters) I was saying I do not feel the wrath of God abiding on me; nor can I believe it does. And yet (this is the mystery), I do not love God. I never did. Therefore I never believed, in the Christian sense of the word. Therefore I am only an honest heathen, a prose-

---

[49] JWL T 7/9/66. Charles was embracing a view more in harmony with JW's Gospel of Holiness.
[50] Tyerman 2:562.

lyte of the Temple, one of the God-fearers; (Acts 13:16). And yet to be so employed of God; and so hedged in that I can neither get forward nor backward! Surely there was never such an instance before, from the beginning of the world! If I ever have had *that faith*, it would not be so strange. But I never had any other evidence of the eternal or invisible world than I have now; and that is none at all, unless such as fairly shines from reason's glimmering ray. I have no direct witness (I do not say that I am a child of God) but of anything invisible or eternal.

And yet I dare not preach otherwise than I do, either concerning faith, or love, or justification, or perfection. And yet I find rather an increase than a decrease of zeal for the whole work of God and every part of it. I am so swept along I know not how that I can't stand still. I want all the world to come to what I do not know myself. Neither am I impelled to this by fear of any kind. I have no more fear than love. Or if I have any fear, it is not of falling into hell, but of falling into nothing.

Wesley's heirs have not known exactly how to understand this confession. Richard Heitzenrater refers to it as an "unusual bearing of his soul." He adds, "Here we see him, in a moment of honest introspection, despairing of his own faithlessness, sensing a loneliness in his predicament, and relying upon the meager consolations of reason."[51] Wesley biographer Henry Rack is even more taken back, "This astonishing confession seems at first sight to be a throwback to the dark days of self-doubt and self-excoriation in the months immediately following his (Aldersgate) conversion."[52] Both of these esteemed Wesley historians acknowledge that this confession has disturbed and baffled Wesley's admirers. Thomas Jackson, early editor of Wesley's Works, apparently excised this confession from his edition of

---

[51] *JW and the People Called Methodists*, 224.
[52] *Reasonable Enthusiast*, 546.

Wesley's letters.[53] As Albert Outler explains, "One of the remarkable features of Wesley's career after 1739 is the steadiness of his mood and the near total absence of emotional depressions. This letter reveals one of the most striking exceptions, and carries us back to the patterns of the pre-Revival past...It reminds one of the old anxieties about the groundlessness of existence that had been so acute in 1738, before and after 'Aldersgate.'"[54]

It is true Wesley was going through one of his toughest times in regard to his marriage. We could add that the upcoming annual conference was shaping up to be difficult since the question of separation from the established Church was on the table. And, as mentioned above, the ongoing controversy over the viability of his perfection doctrine within the societies continued to weigh upon him. The letter also reveals another weight on Wesley's heart: he was feeling much exasperation over Charles' withdrawal from the societies.

But we ask, do these factors alone explain this unusual confession? Rack responds by probing into Wesley's past, concluding that Aldersgate must have been only a passing phase. He feels Wesley never did experience the kind of emotions his followers did, leading to seasons of self-doubt.[55] While conceding that Wesley's temperament probably did not lend itself to much feeling, we must conclude there is more at play here than his emotional makeup. Interestingly, the letter offers us several clues.

Wesley opens by alluding to an earlier letter in which he expresses many of the same sentiments. So this is no momentary lapse of suffering the "blues." But what should catch our attention is *how* Wesley describes his present spiritual state. He sees himself in a *pre-new birth* condition; yet, and this is most surprising, simultaneously in a *post-justification* state. Let's look at each in turn:

---

[53] Compare the letter in Works J 12:130 to Telford 5:15. The controversial section is excised in Works J.
[54] *John Wesley*, 80 n 1.
[55] *Reasonable Enthusiast*, 546-550.

Aldersgate II

> And yet (this is the mystery), I do not love God. I never did. Therefore I never believed, in the Christian sense of the word. Therefore I am only an honest heathen, a proselyte of the Temple, one of the God-fearers; (Acts 13:16)... I have no direct witness (I do not say that I am a child of God).[56]

Wesley here portrays himself as lacking that faith and love which comprise the new birth; or, should we say, that characterize the new birth experience. Taken at face value this confession says he lacks saving faith. We can say this because he identifies his present faith to that of a heathen, or to that of a proselyte. We saw in chapter two that the Aldersgate manifesto *Salvation By Faith* sharply contrasts saving faith to that of a heathen. Three years later his university sermon, *The Almost Christian,* came to the same conclusion: the faith of a heathen, though sincere, falls short of proper Christian faith. In this letter Wesley places himself in the same category as a heathen, proselyte, or God-fearer.[57] He verifies this by confessing, "I do not love God. I never did." Since genuine love to God is foundational to his doctrine of the new birth, Wesley must have meant by this statement he did not believe he was presently born again.[58] Confirming this conclusion is his acknowledgment that he lacks the witness of adoption. Consequently, Wesley rationally concludes he is presently in a *pre-new birth* spiritual condition.

However, this is not all the letter construes. For he also declares:

---

[56] The parts in parentheses were in shorthand in the original letter.
[57] God-fearer is taken from Acts 10:2; 13:16.
[58] JW's concept of the spiritual senses being awakened in the new birth implies that in the new birth genuine love for God takes root in the heart, thereby awakening the believer to God and his grace (Compare *Marks of the New Birth* III.1; *The Privilege of Those that are Born of God* I.8; *The New Birth* I.1, II.1-5).

John Wesley's Theology of Christian Perfection

> I do not feel the wrath of God abiding on me; nor can I believe it does… I find rather an increase than a decrease of zeal for the whole work of God and every part of it. I am so swept along I know not how that I can't stand still. I want all the world to come to what I do not know myself. Neither am I impelled to this by fear of any kind. I have no more fear than love. Or if I have any fear, it is not of falling into hell, but of falling into nothing.

Taken at face value this statement concludes that Wesley considered himself to be in a *post-justification* state. Just as he did in January 1738, Wesley relies upon infallible evidence: inward feelings.[59] Though he lacks the *direct witness* of the new birth,[60] to his surprise he does not *feel*, nor can he *believe*, he is under God's condemnation. To bolster his argument Wesley affirms in no uncertain terms that he feels no fear. Now lacking fear was interpreted within Wesley's doctrinal system as a fruit of the justified state.[61] So Wesley concludes he must be saved (i.e. justified). Moreover, he *feels* within an increasing zeal for God's work. This desire is so strong that it sweeps him along like a strong current of water. How could this be if he was presently void of spiritual life?

---

[59] In JWJ 1/8/38 inward feeling is said to be the "most infallible of proofs."

[60] The direct witness is defined by JW as "an inward impression on the soul, whereby the Spirit of God directly witnesses to my spirit, that I am a child of God" (*Witness of the Spirit I*, I.7). The indirect witness is a "good conscience toward God" and an "inward consciousness" of the fruit of the Spirit in one's life (*Witness of the Spirit II*, II.6). In this letter JW denies having the former testimony but not the latter. This is another characteristic of the servant state (PA 19:69; 25:70).

[61] E.g. *Salvation by Faith* II.4. JW identified freedom from fear and doubt with assurance of salvation. Full assurance (adolescent state) includes overcoming all fear and doubt; in other words, a consistent state of ongoing assurance before God. In the letter under study, JW lacks any fear of divine wrath, which is a definite mark of being in the justified state.

Aldersgate II

A New Gospel Emerges

To briefly recap, the great perfection revival and ensuing schism compelled Wesley to rethink aspects of his perfection doctrine. We see this process unfolding in his eleven-point summary (1764), the sermon *The Scripture Way of Salvation* (1765) and the *Plain Account* (1766). During this same period his doctrine of involuntary sin began to emerge as a major component in his doctrinal system.[62] The idea that all believers continue to fall short of God's holiness and yet remain in his favor (justified) opened the door for Wesley to revisit his doctrine of justification. The schism left a huge wake in its path. As the subject of perfection continued to brew turmoil within the societies, and between the Wesley brothers, John was compelled to ask hard questions regarding his perfection beliefs and his faith journey up to that time.

This created a climate, similar to the one thirty years earlier, in which his faith was tested and found wanting. He now realized he had previously judged his pre-Aldersgate faith journey much too harshly. In fact, when it came to explaining how he had come to embrace his core conviction of heart holiness, he now saw he had received it through a powerful conversion back in 1725. This new perspective of his pre-Aldersgate faith led him to reevaluate his post-Aldersgate faith journey. This is where John's letter to his brother becomes so revealing. Besides all the arguments as to whether this was a momentary dip in mood or of something more profound (and I would argue for the latter), the theology in this letter is so radical compared to anything he had written since Aldersgate. The implication is clear: Wesley now judges himself to be in a *pre-new birth* condition, yet a *post-justification* state. Logically, this meant severing temporally justification from the new birth, not just distinguishing between the two as he had done before.[63] This became a new development within his gospel sys-

---

[62] In *Thoughts on Christian Perfection* (1759).
[63] The point here is critical if we are to understand the evolution of JW's doctrine of perfection. Most evangelical communities today, including the au-

tem; one that added more degrees to the faith journey process. This new understanding of the gospel broadened his understanding of the faith journey, from a focus on the *ordo salutis* beginning with the new birth and ending with physical death (the post-new birth path), to spotlight what transpires *prior* to the new birth (the pre-new birth path). Theologically, Wesley's path is now set to embracing a gospel that celebrates more fully the universality of God's holiness.

Wesley records in his journal entry for December 1, 1767 how this new understanding of justification changed his views on salvation:

> *Tuesday*, DECEMBER 1. Being alone in the coach, I was considering several points of importance. And thus much appeared clear as the day: — That a man may be saved, who cannot express himself properly concerning Imputed Righteousness. Therefore, to do this is not necessary to salvation.
>
> That a man may be saved, who has not clear conceptions of it. (Yea, that never heard the phrase.) Therefore, clear conceptions of it are not necessary to salvation: Yea, it is not necessary to salvation to use the phrase at all.
>
> That a pious Churchman who has not clear conceptions even of Justification by Faith may be saved. Therefore, clear conceptions even of this are not necessary to salvation.
>
> That a Mystic, who denies Justification by Faith, (Mr. Law, for instance,) may be saved. But if so, what becomes of *articulus stantis vel cadentis ecclesiae?*—The grand doctrine by which a church stands or falls.

---

thor's (The Church of the Nazarene), distinguish between justification and the new birth, but link both together in relation to time. JW now separates the two in relation to time: the servant is justified, but not born again. The child is justified and born again, signified by the witness of the Spirit of adoption.

If so, is it not high time for us *Projicere ampullas et sesquipedalia verba;* (To lay aside big words that have no determinate meaning) and to return to the plain word, "He that feareth God, and worketh righteousness, is accepted with him?" (Acts 10:35)

What is being debated here involves much more than just semantics. At stake is when salvation (justification) begins. Two years earlier in the sermon *The Scripture Way of Salvation* Wesley made clear the synonymous meaning of the terms justification, forgiveness and acceptance.[64] Just as in 1738, when his own struggles served as the existential testing ground through which his theology was being forged, we now see the same pattern developing in the mid-sixties. A couple of points follow.

For openers, Wesley begins with the casual comment of finding time to reflect on "several points of importance." Justification before God, and its corollary doctrine of assurance, was again uppermost in his mind. When the storms at sea eroded his sense of assurance under his holiness gospel, he sought to find solace in the instantaneous moment of divine witness. But over time even this proved insufficient, as his letter to Charles testifies. So another ground for assurance, other than the Spirit's witness, had to be found. To this we can add his letter to John Newton and his comments in the *Plain Account* concerning his 1725 conversion. In both Wesley testifies to receiving spiritual life prior to his Aldersgate conversion. The implication necessarily follows that justification and new birth do not always happen in the same moment. Therefore, a new ground for the timing of justification had

---

[64] The connection between justification and acceptance was made by JW as early as in 1733 when he wrote *The Circumcision of the Heart* (P.3), though then JW identified both with the final judgment. Thirteen years later the same link is made in *Justification By Faith* (II.5). In 1745 justification, forgiveness, pardon and acceptance are all conjoined in *A Further Appeal to Men of Reason and Religion* I.2, which was reaffirmed in a letter to Mr. Horn in 1762 (Works B 11:443). This should convince all that when JW says the servant is accepted by God he means they are justified.

to be found. This explains why Wesley appears eager to find a place of quiet to think and reflect on these issues. Since he records that some points were "clear as the day," he must have had a real desire to reach some kind of conclusion. These questions were agitating his mind and needed resolution.

The solution Wesley reached that day proved to have far reaching ramifications for his gospel system. Concerning the question of timing, justification before God is no longer inseparably linked to the new birth. Though Wesley continued to ground the new birth on personal faith in Christ's death and resurrection, he now finds it necessary to locate a more basic level of faith for justification. Once again, he reaches back to his pre-Aldersgate era for the solution. Since he now believes he was genuinely converted in 1725, he could also affirm that his pre-Aldersgate faith must have been acceptable, that is, justifying before God. The Gospel of Holiness had grounded saving faith in God, in his eternal nature, holy character and the promises of renewal in his image.[65] Hence, the moment of acceptance was found in the decision of the single intention; that is, in the sincere endeavor to become holy as God is holy. As in his early period, this became the "bottom line" standard for vital religion and real Christianity. When he penned his New Testament commentary in the mid-fifties, he noted that even before Cornelius had heard the good news of salvation in Christ, God had already accepted (justified) him because of his reverence toward God and his practice of the means of grace.[66] Acts 10:35 became the foundation to add another spiritual state to his *ordo salutis.*

---

[65] See chapter one.

[66] Acts 10:34-35 KJV: Then Peter opened his mouth, and said, "Of a truth I perceive that God is no respecter of persons: But in every nation he that feareth him, and worketh righteousness, is accepted with him."

Aldersgate II

The Servant State

The change in Wesley's views was immediate. Just three months following his December journal entry, Wesley responds to Thomas Rutherforth's variety of charges about being evasive and contradictory.[67] He admits to changing his views during the "latter part" of forty-plus years of ministry (meaning the 1760's). Concerning assurance Wesley acknowledges several levels. The highest degree relates to perseverance, which he calls the "full assurance of hope." He concedes that very few experience this level of confidence. The next is "being now in the favour of God as excludes all doubt and fear." While adults in the faith could possibly feel the former degree of assurance, Wesley typically identified this level with adolescents. The next level of assurance is simply the "consciousness of being in the favour of God," and could be intermittent with seasons of doubt and fear. But significant to our study is that Wesley labels this lower level as the "common privilege of Christians *fearing God* and *working righteousness*."[68] A Christian is now defined, not by the new birth, but by this lower *pre-new birth* standard (Cornelius in Acts 10:35). This is substantively the same standard Wesley affirmed of himself in his letter to his brother Charles in June 1766.[69]

Several days later in correspondence with Ann Bolton, Wesley uses the title *servant* to identify this pre-new birth, post-justification state, "He (God) has already given you the faith of a servant. You want only the faith of a child."[70] A couple of years later he again encourages Miss Bolton by clarifying what the servant state entails:

---

[67] JWL T 3/28/68; Works J 14:347.
[68] The italics mine for emphasis.
[69] Nearly a year earlier JW had begun to define a Christian as such, "I see no objection to your marrying one that fears God and is seeking salvation through Christ. Such an one is not an unbeliever in the sense wherein that word is taken in 2 Corinthians 6:14" (JWL 4/20/67). This confirms that JW was going through a major overhaul in his understanding of salvation and justification.
[70] JWL T 4/7/68.

> My Dear Sister, 'He that feareth God,' says the Apostle, 'and worketh righteousness,' though in a low degree, is accepted of Him; more especially when such an one trusts not in his own righteousness but in the atoning blood. I cannot doubt at all but this is your case; though you have not that joy in the Holy Ghost to which you are called, because your faith is weak and only as a grain of mustard seed.[71]

Let us summarize. The servant state, we have seen, developed (1) out of Wesley's own change of mind concerning the time when he was first converted to vital religion, and (2) when he realized that he still lacked the assurance of the new birth (the direct witness of the Spirit). These twin factors moved him to revisit his doctrine of justification and to reconsider the point in time when God initially accepts a person. His solution was to posit a state *prior* to the new birth when one is justified and accepted by God, yet still lacking the standing of a child of God. This delineation between the servant and child proved exceedingly helpful to Wesley in understanding his own faith journey. For he had now come to believe he had experienced two moments of conversion: one in 1725; the other in 1738. How to reconcile the apparent contradiction?

By the mid-seventies Wesley worked out a solution. In chapter two we saw that he closes his first journal extract with a confession that is scathing toward his prior faith journey. He now returns to this same post-script and includes several footnotes correcting the views contained therein. When in 1738 he had written, "I who went to America to convert others, was never myself converted to God." He now acknowledges, "I am not sure of this." Before, Wesley described himself as void of saving faith and consequently a child of divine wrath.[72] He now disclaims

---

[71] JWL T 8/12/70.
[72] JW draws upon Eph 2:3 here.

these affirmations, "I had even then the faith of a *servant*, though not that of a son" (emphasis his). If we remember, by April 1738 Wesley had been fully convinced that Peter Böhler's gospel of instantaneous salvation by faith alone was correct. Logically, at the time he concluded he was in an unsaved condition. For example, when Wesley shared his new gospel with Thomas Broughten, the Delamotte family, and with Charles in April 1738, Thomas objected. Wesley summarizes his response "He could never think that I had not faith, who had done and suffered such things." In 1738 and thereafter[73] Wesley believed he had lacked saving faith before his Aldersgate conversion. Now in the 1770's he saw things differently, "He (Mr. Broughton) was in the right. I certainly then had the faith of a *servant*, though not the faith of a son."

Let's look at one more example. In his Aldersgate memorandum Wesley rehearses his faith journey from childhood up to the present (1738). When referencing his salvation hope during his Oxford period Wesley acknowledged, "I was persuaded that I should be accepted of him, and that I was even then in a state of salvation" (§5). We have already learned that in 1738 this view of assurance was rejected as being grounded upon works, and hence self-righteousness. In 1775 Wesley reverses this prior judgment when he writes, "And I believe I was" (i.e. saved).

Over the years many interpretations have been offered to explain the paradox of Wesley's two conversions and his many comments relating to them. Distinguishing between the servant and child helped John Wesley to understand his own faith journey. Accordingly, what transpired at Aldersgate on May 24, 1738 was his spiritual birth from above, when he became a child of God and overcame the power of outward sin.[74] But his spiritual

---

[73] See note 44 above.

[74] Therefore, all views that see Aldersgate as the time when JW experienced perfection are wrong. Equally so are the views that merely identify it with JW receiving assurance or as just another step in the faith journey process. JW interpreted it differently: this was the time when he became born again, a child of God.

awakening in 1725 was no less important, for that was when he found favor and acceptance with God. By the late 1780's the servant state had become formally another stage in the Wesleyan *ordo salutis*:

> Indeed nearly fifty years ago, when the preachers commonly called Methodists began to preach that grand scriptural doctrine, salvation by faith, they were not sufficiently apprised of the difference between a servant and a child of God. They did not clearly understand that even one 'who feared God, and worketh righteousness, is accepted of him.' In consequence of this they were apt to make sad the hearts of those whom God had not made sad. For they frequently asked those who feared God, 'Do you know that your sins are forgiven?' And upon their answering, 'No', immediately replied, 'Then you are a child of the devil.' No; that does not follow. It might have been said (and it is all that can be said with propriety) 'Hitherto you are only a servant; you are not a child of God.'[75]

The central characteristic of the servant state is a faith that fears God and pursues righteousness and goodness. God *accepts* this person whether they know Christ or not.[76] In this sense Wesley can say the servant is truly a "blessed" state before God.[77] Nevertheless, the servant still lacks the birth of the Spirit, which brings personal assurance of salvation, the impartation of God's love in the heart, power over sin's dominion, and an awareness of union with Christ in his death and resurrection.[78]

---

[75] *On Faith* §11 (1788); see also *Discoveries by Faith* §§13-14.

[76] 1770 Minutes, Works J 8:337, "(1.) Who of us is now accepted of God? He that now believes in Christ with a loving and obedient heart. (2.) But who among those who never heard of Christ? He that, according to the light he has, 'feareth God and worketh righteousness.'" See also *On Living Without God* §14.

[77] JWL T 11/16/70.

[78] *On Faith* I.12. This explains why JW referred to the servant as "partially" accepted.

Aldersgate II

Works Reintroduced

As Wesley's two-works gospel matured it moved more and more in the direction of his earlier holiness gospel without abandoning the fundamental principles of his faith-alone gospel. This led to greater appreciation of the means of grace within the faith journey process. We saw at the beginning of this chapter how in *The Scripture Way of Salvation* Wesley linked the means of grace with repentance and good works. This began a process of reaffirming works in his gospel system at a more significant level. As Wesley worked through his own questions of faith, assurance and the point of acceptance before God, leading to a new category within his *ordo salutis* (the servant), he was also implicitly providing a basis for works in the salvation process to a degree not considered before. Since the servant is accepted because he or she "fears God" and "works righteousness," the logical question became: how does "working righteousness" serve in justifying one before God? By 1770 Wesley was ready to answer this question and to reassert works within his gospel program:

> We said in 1744, "We have leaned too much toward Calvinism." Wherein?
> A. (1.) With regard to man's "faithfulness." Our Lord himself taught us to use the expression: Therefore we ought never to be ashamed of it. We ought steadily to assert upon his authority, that if a man is not "faithful in the unrighteous mammon, God will not give him the true riches."
> (2.) With regard to "working for life," which our Lord expressly commands us to do. "Labour," *ergazesthe*, literally, "*work*, for the meat that endureth to everlasting life." And in fact, every believer, till he comes to glory, works *for* as well as *from* life.
> (3.) We have received it as a maxim, that "a man is to do nothing in order to justification." Nothing can be more false. Whoever desires to find favour with God, should

"cease from evil, and learn to do well." So God himself teaches by the Prophet Isaiah. Whoever repents, should "do works meet for repentance." And if this is not in order to find favour, what does he do them for?
Once more review the whole affair:

(1.) Who of us is now accepted of God?
   He that now believes in Christ with a loving, obedient heart.
(2.) But who among those that never heard of Christ?
   He that, according to the light he has, "feareth God and worketh righteousness."
(3.) Is this the same with "he that is sincere?"
   Nearly, if not quite.
(4.) Is not this salvation by works?
   Not by the merit of works, but by works as a condition.
(5.) What have we then been disputing about for these thirty years?
   I am afraid about words, namely, in some of the foregoing instances.
(6.) As to merit itself, of which we have been so dreadfully afraid: We are rewarded according to our works, yea, because of our works. How does this differ from, "for the sake of our works?" And how differs this from *secundum merita operum*? which is no more than, "as our works deserve." Can you split this hair? I doubt I cannot.[79]

The Calvinists were outraged the moment these minutes were published. The doctrinal controversy lasted for several years. Lady Huntingdon told those in her college they should quit unless they were willing to disavow the minutes.[80] Tracking the contro-

---

[79] Works J 8:337 (emphasis his).
[80] Tyerman, III:73.

Aldersgate II

versy is interesting but we leave that to Wesley historians; our concern is the evolution of his perfection theology.[81]

To begin, consider how Wesley's holiness gospel and his servant theology permeate the above document. The central motif is that eternal life comes to those whose religion is vital and alive, motivating reverence (fear) toward God and holy living (righteousness), even if one does not know Christ. In addition, consider how little faith is mentioned. And even when it is expressed, the focus has shifted by the addition of the phrase "with a loving, obedient heart." The weight of the entire document is on the central truth: without holiness "no man shall see the Lord."[82] Faith in Christ is not even essential since those who do not know him are justified and saved as long as they have holy tempers—they "feareth God and worketh righteousness" (Acts 10:35).

Wesley's theology is now shifting to a center oriented around his original core conviction: salvation demands inward holiness. In chapter one, we saw that this single conviction was the axiom of his holiness gospel, fueling a disciplined program of life transformation through the cultivation of holy tempers. Wesley's faith-alone gospel rejected this program as salvation by works. But by rejecting Moravian stillness and reaffirming degrees of faith (and various stages on the faith journey), the means of grace as works of piety and mercy were found once again to play a crucial role in the life transformation process. After this it was only a small step to formally link the means of grace with repentance and good works, thereby reinserting works into the salvation process. Does this mean Wesley abandoned salvation by faith? Not so, as we will soon see.

Accordingly, the 1770 Minutes reassert the link between salvation and holy tempers. Sincerity, another mark of Wesley's holiness gospel, is once again reaffirmed as a ground for assurance. Finally, the strong emphasis on the believer working for their

---

[81] See Heitzenrater, *Wesley and the People Called Methodists*, 240-241.

[82] Hebrews 12:14. My point is not to insinuate that JW had not espoused holy living as the legitimate fruit of saving faith. But as a point of emphasis we see a definite trend developing in his perfection theology.

salvation implies the necessary practice of the means of grace, just as in his Oxford days. Wesley's gospel is moving in the direction of becoming more universalistic. Not in the sense that all people will be eternally saved irregardless of their response, but that final salvation is becoming more accessible to those who do not know Christ.[83]

Nevertheless, we still see aspects of Wesley's faith-alone gospel in the Minutes. While salvation by faith is diminished, it is present. Meaning, Wesley did not abandon his maxim of *sola fide*. Salvation by faith alone continued to shape his thought, theology and understanding of the faith journey,[84] but with a twist. Beginning with the servant state Wesley will continue to expand his understanding of degrees of faith by affirming other pre-new birth, pre-Christian states.

In a similar vein, works still do not merit salvation. The 1770 Minutes do not assert salvation by self-effort and self-reliance. What they do affirm is the basic truth: faith without works is dead (Ja 2:26). Works serve as a "condition," as long as there is time and opportunity for them. Wesley later explains that when he spoke of salvation in the Minutes he was referring to "final salvation." He then adds, "Who can deny that both inward good works (loving God and our neighbor) and outward good works (keeping his commandments) are a condition of this? What is this more or less than '*Without holiness no man shall see the Lord*'?"[85] Wesley's two-works gospel is well on the way to becoming the Gospel of Universal Holiness.

Assessment and Legacy

The mid-sixties was a climate well suited for a spiritual crisis in Wesley's life. The great perfection revival unraveled into a schism that compelled him to rethink what he believed about sin,

---

[83] This subject is developed in chapter 7.
[84] This point is confirmed by the several sermons on faith in the latter 80's.
[85] JWL T 7/10/71.

Aldersgate II

holiness, the faith journey and perfection. To state it differently, it was the climate of perfectionism and schism that moved Wesley to restate what he believed regarding perfection and salvation, and how he came to believe in them. This is where the *Plain Account* offers important insights into Wesley's state of mind at the time. This is the first publication in which he openly acknowledges an earlier conversion other than his Aldersgate heart-warming in 1738. The roots to this change of perspective can be traced to the spring of 1765 when he wrote to John Newton explaining how he came to believe in Christian perfection. The parallels between this letter and the opening chapters of the *Plain Account* show (1) this was the time when Wesley began to write the *Plain Account* and (2) Wesley was in the process of reevaluating his own faith journey.[86] This is confirmed by the fact that in the *Plain Account* Aldersgate literally fades into the background and disappears as irrelevant to the purpose of the book.[87]

The same year he wrote the *Plain Account*, he also wrote and published *The Scripture Way of Salvation*, offering his mature thoughts on his two-works gospel. In this homily justification is

---

[86] When we compare JW's description of his 1725 awakening in the letter to John Newton to that in the *Plain Account*, the latter reflects more advanced language than the former. In the letter he simply says he was "struck" and "felt a fixed intention" to give himself to God. Note the passivity in this description. In the *Plain Account* JW uses stronger language. He was "exceedingly affected" and "instantly...resolved to dedicate all (his) life to God," including "all (his) thoughts, and words, and actions." The terminology is sharpened, made stronger, and reflects further reflection and thought on the subject. This difference in language supports the interpretation that JW was working through his reinterpretation of his faith journey in the spring to summer of 1765. If JW had already formed his opinion regarding his 1725 conversion by 1765, then what he wrote in the letter would have been more similar in tone to what he wrote in the *Plain Account*.

[87] We can never know for sure why he left it out. The probable reason is that in 1765 JW no longer felt Aldersgate contributed anything significant to his doctrine of Christian perfection. This notion is strengthened in light of the point made in the prior note. If JW was in the process of reevaluating his faith journey and coming to different conclusions than what he held before, then he probably did not see any reason to include it.

defined as forgiveness and acceptance before God. The latter term is what provided the breakthrough for Wesley to reinterpret his pre-Aldersgate faith journey. What happened next was inevitable. If Wesley was already "saved"—that is, justified and accepted by God—before his Aldersgate conversion, then what really happened on that May evening in 1738?

Over the next several months Wesley spent enough time reflecting on his faith journey *following* Aldersgate to conclude that his experience was seriously deficient, "I do not love God. I never did. Therefore I never believed in the Christian sense of the word." Though not as severe as the one he faced in 1738, Wesley was in the midst of a spiritual crisis that would generate significant changes within his theological system.

Within two years Wesley was advocating a pre-new birth state, which he called the *faith of a servant*. This state lacked the witness of adoption, along with the awareness of God's love in Christ filling the heart; but the person was still justified and accepted by God. At the heart of this change in his gospel system was the reaffirmation of his lifelong conviction that vital religion is grounded in holy tempers, not correct doctrine. By spring 1768 Wesley began counseling seekers according to his new understanding of the faith journey. When he published his complete Works in the 1770's, he added footnotes to his 1738 journal correcting his earlier confessions that declared he lacked salvation prior to Aldersgate. He now grasped that justification is not always temporally linked to the new birth. While both blessings are often received simultaneously, this is not always the case.[88] What counts before God are holy tempers living in the heart and a sincere pursuit of divine truth as God gives spiritual light.[89]

There are several similarities and contrasts between the two crises. In both Wesley's dissatisfaction with his present spiritual experience is what moves him to seek emotional relief through a new God-moment. In Aldersgate I (1738) Wesley was negative

---

[88] JW continued to link justification and the new birth in relation to time (JWL T 1/2/70).

[89] The 1770 Minutes make this point very clear.

Aldersgate II

toward his early faith journey causing him to accept a radically "new" gospel message. In Aldersgate II (1766) he frowns upon his post-Aldersgate faith journey causing him to reclaim much of his earlier gospel. Both crises led to change, not only in his theological system, but also in how he did ministry. In Aldersgate I Wesley began telling seekers that salvation is received by faith alone in Christ alone, witnessed by the Spirit alone. Aldersgate II led him to counsel seekers that justification is not always received in the moment of the new birth.

Both Aldersgate I and II served to shape how Wesley understood the life transformation process. Aldersgate I emphasized the instantaneous moment over everything else. In the years following Aldersgate I, Wesley expended theological energy developing the *ordo salutis* between the new birth and physical death. Aldersgate II broadened the *ordo salutis* by including states that are pre-new birth. What transpired was that through both crises Wesley's gospel system developed greater wholeness and balance.

Very significant is how Aldersgate I and II served to ground Wesley's personal faith. Following Aldersgate I he consistently looked to his conversion on May 24 as the beginning of spiritual life. Therefore, he deemed his prior state as unsaved.[90] By contrast, Aldersgate II led him to ground his faith journey not in 1738, but in 1725. We can outline this change as follows:

Aldersgate I:
    1738 is the foundation of his spiritual life
    1738-50's: Critical of pre-Aldersgate faith journey

Aldersgate II:
    1725 is the foundation of his spiritual life
    1765-67: Dissatisfied with his post-Aldersgate faith journey

To those who might question the central argument of this chapter—that Wesley experienced a spiritual crisis in the mid-

---

[90] See note 44 above.

sixties—they must explain in a satisfactory manner why Wesley changed his mind as to when he was saved. That he did so is certain, but why? When the pieces of the puzzle are put together this author believes only one conclusion offers a sufficient explanation: Wesley experienced a powerful spiritual upheaval in the years 1765-1767, and this crisis compelled him to change his mind regarding his early faith journey, the time when he received salvation (justification), and his understanding as to what really happened at Aldersgate in 1738.

After Aldersgate II, Wesley continued to look back to his early period with fondness. Since he now identified more with his early period, a certain romantic longing often came over him. In 1772 he told his brother:

> I often cry out, *Vitae me redde priori!*[91] Let me be again an Oxford Methodist! I am often in doubt whether it would not be best for me to resume all my Oxford rules, great and small. I did then walk closely with God and redeem the time. But what have I been doing these thirty years?[92]

Both Aldersgate I and II were transitional phases in the evolution of Wesley's theology of perfection. Both eras represent periods of time when Wesley went through a spiritual crisis of sufficient magnitude to alter his views of himself and his gospel system. As we look back we see other shifts occurring. In the years following Aldersgate I Wesley expended most of his theological energy developing the faith journey that *follows* the new birth.[93] By the mid-sixties this aspect of the faith journey had reached maturity

---

[91] The editor translates: "Horace's epistles, I. Vii. 95: 'Give me back my former life.'"
[92] JWL T 12/15/72.
[93] This is evidenced by the development of the three main states of the Christian's journey: childhood, adolescence, adulthood. See ch 8.

Aldersgate II

and remained constant thereafter.[94] During Aldersgate II a major shift in focus took place. For the next couple decades the unique contribution to his theological system was the development of the servant state and other aspects of prevenient grace, which are *pre-new birth* in focus.[95] In this way Wesley's *ordo salutis* was enlarged to cover the entire faith journey of renewal in God's image; from the first spark of spiritual awareness to complete perfection in the article of death (and beyond).[96] A time chart summarizes this point succinctly:

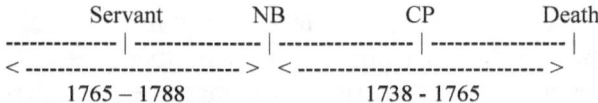

If the conclusions of the first four chapters are accurate, a Wesleyan theology must take into consideration the entirety of Wesley's theological journey. While each period has its own unique contribution and emphasis; in many ways, the late period (1765-1791)[97] attains the balance Wesley personally sought by drawing from his early and middle periods to formulate a gospel proclaiming the universalism of God's holiness and grace. Therefore, only as we understand how Wesley's two-works gospel continued to take shape in his later years can we fully appreciate his mature doctrine of perfect love, and in this way build a theology that can be faithfully called *Wesleyan*.

---

[94] This is confirmed by the publishing of *The Scripture Way of Salvation* and the repeated release of *A Plain Account of Christian Perfection*.
[95] To learn more about JW's servant theology see Appendix E.
[96] Chapter 7 picks up the story at this point and develops this theme in its fullness.
[97] In this study the late period is usually stated as beginning in 1768, not 1765. I here choose the earlier date to include the homilies *The Scripture Way of Salvation* and *The Repentance of Believers*, and the *Plain Account*. It is difficult to place a single year as the definitive moment when JW's theology moved from its middle period to its late period, unlike the transition from his early to middle periods.

FIVE
Sin in the Ordo Salutis

In any study on Christian perfection, no matter whose perspective is being examined, the question of defining sin becomes central. Since the coherence of Wesley's doctrine of perfect love revolves around the question of how much sin can be removed in this life, it becomes imperative that we grasp how he structurally organized his doctrine of sin. To fail here is to misread Wesley. But just as his doctrine of perfection is multi-faceted, so is his teaching regarding sin. Both of these doctrines, perfection and sin, evolved along parallel paths as his Gospel of Two Works attained maturity in the 1760's. Besides his sermons, the twin publications *Thoughts on Christian Perfection* (1759) and *Farther Thoughts on Christian Perfection* (1763) offer critical insights we will not want to miss.[1] Below we will mine these writings to outline structurally what Wesley's mature doctrine of sin looked like. But first let us survey how his understanding of sin developed up to the 1760's.

Chronological Perspectives

With the decision to enter holy orders in early 1725, and the spiritual awakening that soon followed, Wesley's interest in the subject of sin intensified.[2] This interest was a natural corollary to his single intention to attain perfection. If to be "'perfect, as our Father in heaven is perfect'" is the goal, then it behooves the

---

[1] The sermons written during this same period that contributed to the maturation of JW's GosTW are *Original Sin* (1759); *The New Birth* (1760); *The Wilderness State* (1760); *Wandering Thoughts* (1762); *On Sin in Believers* (1763); *The Scripture Way of Salvation* (1765); *The Repentance of Believers* (1767).

[2] In JWJ 5/24/38 §§2-3 JW acknowledges he previously had only a casual concern when it came to sin.

seeker to be "cleansed from sin, 'from all filthiness both of flesh and spirit.'"[3] We saw in chapter one that early Wesley focused on the restoration of humanity's pristine nature lost by Adam (*imago Dei*). Sin was typically viewed as corruption deeply implanted in fallen human nature. In his first written sermon Wesley identified this inward corruption as "infirmities" that become the "law of our members," continually warring against the "law of our mind."[4] These infirmities were later called in *The Circumcision of the Heart* our "corrupted nature" (I.2), the "sinfulness and helplessness of our nature" (I.2), and "inbred pollution" (I.11). Thus early Wesley held to a robust doctrine of original sin.

But early Wesley's doctrine of sin was not limited to the sub-volitional. His well-known definition of sin as a "voluntary breach of a known law" was first expressed in a letter during his Oxford period.[5] Voluntary sin was divided further into the twin categories of "habitual" and "single acts." Regarding the former, perfection is available in this life; but concerning the latter even the Apostle Paul had to trust in the gospel promise of moment-by-moment forgiveness.[6] Interestingly, the latter category is also referred to as "all that is done amiss." Wesley then affirms that apart from God's mercy no one could abide God's holy judgment. So we here see the beginning of what will later become the categories of voluntary and involuntary sin. Sin as deliberate volition is rooted in his understanding of Adam at the beginning. Mankind was created good and possessed the capacity to choose. Along with the wicked angels Adam abused his liberty and willfully sinned against God.[7] His posterity have followed suit. Just as there can be no virtue without voluntary choice,[8] so there can

---

[3] *The Circumcision of the Heart* I.1; Matt 5:48; 2 Cor 7:1.
[4] *Death and Deliverance* §14; Rom 7:23.
[5] JWL 10/3/31.
[6] JW's words are, "He knew who had promised to forgive these, not seven times but seventy times seven (Matt 18:22). Nay, a thousand times a thousand, if they sincerely desire it, shall all sins be forgiven unto the sons of men."
[7] *The Image of God* P.4.
[8] *On Guardian Angels* I.5.

John Wesley's Theology of Christian Perfection

be no sin, "strictly speaking," without the engagement of the will.[9] Therefore sin, according to early Wesley, can be summarized as (1) disease of nature[10] and (2) willful acts. Even a cursory reading of his early sermons demonstrates that the former category was the controlling motif in his early theological system. So we can understand why early Wesley did not believe Christian perfection was fully attainable in this life.

When we move to the Aldersgate era sin becomes more carefully nuanced. This is evident in his new gospel manifesto *Salvation By Faith*. This homily divides sin into two general categories—guilt and power, with the former referring to one's past sinfulness and the latter to sin's present reign.[11] Sin's power is further subdivided into the three subcategories of habit, willful, and desire (II.6). Wesley's perfection views come into play here. Those born of God do not sin habitually, since to do so means that sin still reigns, which is a mark of the non-Christian. Neither do they sin willfully given that the will is now set on living for Christ. Last, they do not sin by desire because their hearts have been thoroughly transformed to desire only God's perfect will. What is implied in this description is that these three subcategories make up the general category of voluntary sin.

In addition, Wesley speaks of "sin by infirmities." Since infirmities involve no "concurrence of (the) will," such deviations—whether in word, thought, or deed—are not "properly" sin. So Wesley confidently concludes that those born of God do not commit sin. Moreover, he declares the believer is now saved from "all their sins," both actual and original (II.2, 7). Though still rudimentary in organization, Wesley's thought is moving in a definite direction. Central to his doctrine of sin is the plumb line of human volition and the core conviction that our innate perversity is due to original sin. The theological premises in *Salvation*

---

[9] JWL 10/3/31, Works B 25:318 *l*.27.
[10] *The Trouble and Rest of Good Men* II.5.
[11] II.3, 5. In this sermon JW also addresses the subject of fear due to sin's guilt. Though the context makes it clear he does not view this as another category.

Sin in the Ordo Salutis

By Faith are two-fold: first, Adam's sin entails on his posterity sinful desire and human infirmity. Second, our personal sinfulness leads to bondage by habit and choice. In this homily the subtle linking of original sin to sinful desire and infirmity offers important insights into how Wesley's doctrine of sin will evolve. Below, we will explore the inner workings of this relationship.

Moving to the winter of 1739 we find a similar distinction made between sin as infirmity and volition:

> What do you mean by the word "sin?" those numberless weaknesses and follies, sometimes (improperly) termed sins of infirmity? If you mean only this, we shall not put off these but with our bodies. But if you mean, "It does not promise entire freedom from sin, in its proper sense, or from committing sin," this is by no means true, unless the Scripture be false; for thus it is written: "Whosoever is born of God doth not commit sin;" (unless he lose the Spirit of adoption, if not finally, yet for a while, as did this child of God;) "for his seed remaineth in him, and he cannot sin, because he is born of God." He cannot sin so long as "he keepeth himself;" for then "that wicked one toucheth him not." (1 John iii. 9; v. 18.).[12]

By the 1740's Wesley's theology of perfection had moved from a single work of full instantaneous sanctification (spring-summer 1738), to a single work encompassing degrees of attainment until instantaneously completed (fall 1738-summer 1739), to a gospel proclaiming two distinct works of grace (fall 1739 and thereafter). By 1741 Wesley was classifying sin according to the categories inward and outward.[13] Once again, we look to the landmark

---

[12] *Preface to An Extract of the Life and Death of Mr. Thomas Halyburton* §5; Works J 14:212.

[13] It appears JW first learned to use the terms "inward" and "outward" from the Moravians. When JW was in Germany (1738) he recorded several testimonies, of which two used the terminology of inward and outward to describe their deliverance from sin (David Schneider and Arvid Gradin). This same

sermon *Christian Perfection*. Here, outward sin refers to the outward act, which Wesley calls an "outward transgression" of the law (II.4). Outward sin is just another term for committing sin (II.7, 20). Inward sin lies deeper in human nature and refers to sinful thoughts and tempers, like pride, unbelief, self-will, and anger (II.21-26). Only those who are *fathers* (adults) know by experience this fuller deliverance. Thus, voluntary sin became more sharply nuanced between the external act and the inner disposition. Outward and inward became one of the most common terms Wesley uses to categorize sin (and holiness). To give one example, the Conference Minutes of 1744 classify sin as outward and inward. Outward sin is vanquished at justification, while inward sin is only suppressed until full salvation is realized.[14] Also, these same minutes reaffirm our original sinfulness as children of Adam, having been born with a "sinful, devilish nature."[15] Wesley obviously saw a link between innate sinfulness and inward sin (more on this later).

Two years later, in *The First Fruits of the Spirit*, Wesley discusses our deliverance from sin under the headings of *past* (guilt), *present* (another word for outward), *inward* (corruption of nature), *infirmity* (involuntary failings), and *sins of surprise* (impulsive or reactive responses).

Essential to his discussion was the question concerning the concurrence of the will:

---

language was next used by JW in his *Rules of the Band Societies* (12/25/38; Works B 9:77). The terminology seems to have been next used in his letter to Dr. Henry Stebbing in mid-summer 1739. JW describes the new birth by contrasting outward change to inward transformation (JWJ 7/31/39). Such language is next put to use in early October (JWJ 10/9/39). Thereafter, JW began to use the categories, inward and outward, to clarify which sin is removed in the new birth and in the moment of perfect love (JWJ 1/25/40; *Christian Perfection*). Though this language is included in JW's Aldersgate memorandum (§§1-3), this author believes he probably incorporated these terms after he went to Germany that summer.

[14] Q. 7; Works J 8:276.
[15] Q. 15.

Sin in the Ordo Salutis

> We cannot say, either that men are, or that they are not, condemned for sins of surprise in general: But it seems, whenever a believer is by surprise overtaken in a fault, there is more or less condemnation, as there is more or less concurrence of his will. In proportion as a sinful desire, or word, or action, is more or less voluntary, so we may conceive God is more or less displeased, and there is more or less guilt upon the soul. (II.11)

So central for Wesley was the concurrence of the will in the commission of sin that in 1748 he repeated his now famous definition of sin as an "actual, voluntary transgression of the law...acknowledged to be such at the time that it is transgressed."[16] Thus sin, properly speaking, rests on the person's liberty of deliberate choice. Of interest is how Wesley views the inter-relationship between outward and inward sin. In *The Great Privilege of Those that are Born of God* (1748) he explains through a nine-step process how sin can once again gain dominion over the Christian. Let us look at his argument.

Sin gains access through temptation. The Spirit warns but the believer succumbs. If the choice to sin persists then the Spirit becomes grieved, and the believer's faith is weakened. The Christian's love for God then begins to grow cold. In response the Holy Spirit convicts and points the wayward believer to repentance. At this point a critical decision is made. If the Christian rejects the inner voice of the Spirit by listening to the tempter's voice, then "evil desire begins and spreads" in the soul until the light of divine faith and love flickers out. At this point God's power departs and the person becomes "capable of committing outward sin" (II.9).

In this context outward sin refers to the commission of *habitual* sin—a mark of the religiously nominal state.[17] In other words, the loss of saving faith begins with outward sin, that is, a

---

[16] *The Great Privilege of Those that are Born of God* II.2.
[17] E.g. *Salvation by Faith* II.6; JWL 10/30/38, Works B 25:575, *ll.*11-15.

John Wesley's Theology of Christian Perfection

deliberate choice, yet the backsliding continues because of inward sin, finally to issue in habitual sin. Sin as choice leads to sin as desire resulting in sin as habitual.

For the most part, Wesley's vocabulary on sin is now set in place. His often-used terms are outward, inward, habitual, commission, infirmity, voluntary (and involuntary) and willful. One should keep in mind another whole set of terms for original sin.[18] In relation to personal guilt the plumb line is whether the human will is engaged. While early Wesley worked primarily with two categories of sin (disease of nature and willful act), middle Wesley diversified and expanded his concept of sin. Sin became more complex, reflecting change in his understanding of the human predicament and the stages of renewal in his *ordo salutis*.

The next major development came a decade or so later. The perfection revival and schism of the early sixties forced Wesley to qualify his doctrine of sin even more. In response to his critics, Wesley introduces the language of "being" to identify inward sin.[19] When we remember that twenty-five years earlier Wesley had classified willful sin and sinful desire under the single title of "power," this step proved significant to his theological system. For it sharply distinguished between the two works within his gospel scheme by delineating more precisely which kind of sin is overcome in each work of grace. So as his two-works gospel reached maturity, so did his doctrine of sin.

This distinction could be stated another way. We saw in chapter three Wesley learned from Christian David that sin no longer *reigns*, but it does *remain*. Now in the mid-sixties Wesley taught that sin is *suspended* but not *destroyed*. Viewed from the scripture principles of flesh and Spirit, sin continues to struggle for dominion in the Christian's heart and life.[20] Only in a second sanctifying moment is this cancer finally removed and full salvation realized: "love excluding sin; love filling the heart, taking up

---

[18] E.g. see *Plain Account* 18:6 n.
[19] *On Sin in Believers* IV.4 (1763).
[20] *The Scripture Way of Salvation* I.6.

the whole capacity of the soul."[21] Yet, critical to Wesley's teaching of "love excluding sin; love filling the heart" was the formal categorization of sin as voluntary and involuntary developed in the tracts *Thoughts on Christian Perfection* (1759) and *Farther Thoughts on Christian Perfection* (1763). This fundamental distinction, rooted in his early conviction on the liberty of the will, makes it possible for his mature doctrine of sin to be structurally organized in a Wesleyan way. To this structure we now turn our attention.

Wesley's Doctrine of Sin

A little background first. In April 1758 Wesley responded to the fears that Elizabeth Hardy felt over the extreme views some young Methodist preachers had regarding perfection. Apparently, these preachers were telling people they were still in a state of damnation until they were made perfect in love. Wesley, of course, repudiated such claims. At the annual conference in August these young preachers were exhorted to keep to a general description when preaching full salvation and not become entangled in minute details over the doctrine.[22] As he did with Miss Hardy, Wesley stressed to the conference that even those who are perfect still have continual need for forgiveness regarding mistakes that lead to transgressions of the perfect law.

The next year he repeated this same message to the conference. But now Wesley says that perfection is entered into instantaneously and can be lost.[23] His critics did not relent. So he authored a tract with thirty-eight questions and answers, hoping to satisfy his detractors. Of course, it did not work. But this tract, *Thoughts on Christian Perfection*, did make significant progress at formally organizing his doctrine of sin in a structural manner. Four years later he published the sequel *Farther Thoughts on*

---

[21] *The Scripture Way of Salvation* I.9.
[22] Outler, *John Wesley*, 177.
[23] PA 25:102-104; 26:9, 14; JWL 5/18/57; Maddox, *Responsible Grace*, 183.

John Wesley's Theology of Christian Perfection

Christian Perfection. Though this larger tract includes much material of a pastoral nature, in the opening series of questions and answers Wesley gives his doctrine of sin structural grounding by drawing upon the Reformed concept of two covenants. The concept of covenants offered Wesley two distinguishable standards by which to define sin (and perfection). By reading these two tracts in light of other key sermons on the subject (like *Christian Perfection* and *On Sin in Believers*), the structural organization of Wesley's mature doctrine of sin becomes apparent. Another factor in this process was the schism led by Thomas Maxfield and George Bell.[24] Their excesses compelled Wesley to emphasize even more the limitations of attainable perfection. This in turn contributed to Wesley's mature doctrine of sin.

In what follows is the structural organization of Wesley's mature doctrine of sin by use of the following classifications: category, standard, subcategory, time of deliverance, and state (stage). After this we will summarize how his concept of original sin fits into the picture. We now turn to *Thoughts on Christian Perfection* to see how Wesley organizes his doctrine of sin into two basic categories[25]:

> 1. and 2. Not only sin, properly so called, (that is, a voluntary transgression of a known law,) but sin, improp-

---

[24] PA *Introduction*; chs 20-22; 25:105-167.

[25] The following six points are answers are to six questions:

> 1. Is there anything besides sin that would expose to eternal damnation?
> 2. Is there any thing besides sin that needs the atoning blood?
> 3. Is there no such perfection in this life as absolutely excludes all sin?
> 4. If we do not allow this, do we not contradict ourselves in talking of sinless perfection?
> 5. Can a person be filled with the love of God and yet be liable to sin, to transgress the perfect law?
> 6. How can we call such a transgression of the perfect law, as without the blood of atonement would expose us to eternal damnation, any other than sin?"

erly so called, (that is, an involuntary transgression of a divine law, known or unknown,) needs the atoning blood, and without this would expose to eternal damnation.
3. I believe there is no such perfection in this life as excludes these involuntary transgressions which I apprehend to be naturally consequent on the ignorance and mistakes inseparable from mortality.
4. Therefore "sinless perfection" is a phrase I never use lest I should *seem* to contradict myself.
5. I believe a person filled with the love of God is still liable to these involuntary transgressions.
6. Such transgressions you may call sins, if you please. I do not for the reason above mentioned.[26]

We learned above that the two categories, voluntary and involuntary, are rooted in Wesley's early period when he distinguished between habits and single acts of sin. Gradually, by Aldersgate his views evolved to see sin as volition, desire and infirmity. By 1759 the language of voluntary and involuntary were being coupled to distinguish between sin "properly so called" and sin "improperly so called." We must remember that for Wesley the dividing point between these two categories is the plumb line of volition (the engagement of the will). Coupled with this is the belief sin requires personal awareness of the moral standard ("known law"). In other words, voluntary sin involves deliberate choice; involuntary sin does not. Below we will define more precisely the nature of involuntary sin. What the above quotation clarifies is that involuntary transgressions are inseparably connected to human mortality. Even though he subtitled it "sin, improperly so called," Wesley maintains that such sin is still a transgression of the divine law and needs the atonement of Christ to save from divine wrath. Consequently, even the most perfect are "still liable to these involuntary transgressions." Wesley's

---

[26] Outler, *John Wesley*, 287.

mature doctrine of sin can be divided into two basic categories, with the one much more serious than the other.

We begin to visually chart Wesley's doctrine of sin as follows:

```
                          Sin
                         /    \
Category:        Voluntary Sin       Involuntary Sin
                sin properly so called   sin improperly so called
```

One of the marked differences between these two categories regards the standard each references. Scott Jones explains that "Wesley's dispensational view is in keeping with traditional Reformed interpretation...There the Puritan divines distinguish between two covenants, a covenant of works which applies to before the Fall and one of grace which applied after Adam's sin."[27] In *Farther Thoughts on Christian Perfection* these two covenants are worked out through the parallel concept of two categories of law. Adamic law[28] was "given to Adam in innocence" and in substance is the same as given to the angels in heaven. Being "created free from any defect...his (Adam's) body was then no clog to the mind; it did not hinder his apprehending all things clearly, judging truly concerning then, reasoning justly." As a consequence, the law of Eden "required that he should always think, always speak, and always act precisely right, in every point whatever."[29] This view of humanity's original perfection is one of the constants in Wesley's theological system.[30]

---

[27] Scott Jones, *John Wesley's Conception and Use of Scripture*, 58.
[28] In *Farther Thoughts* JW uses the following names/titles for Adamic law: Mosaic law, angelic law, law of works, and perfect law.
[29] PA 25:4, 5, 7.
[30] See the sermons *The Image of God* (1731); *Justification by Faith* (1746); *Original Sin* (1759); and *The Fall of Man* (1782).

Sin in the Ordo Salutis

But with the coming of Christ, Wesley understood that another law had essentially replaced the law given to Adam. The law of faith says, "not everyone that doeth, but everyone that believeth, now receiveth righteousness...he is justified, sanctified, and glorified."[31] Instead of being fulfilled by perfect performance (i.e. works), this law is satisfied by love: "Faith working or animated by love is all that God now requires of man. He has substituted love...in the room of angelic perfection."[32] This alone is the standard for Christian perfection.

Of special interest is how Wesley integrates these two standards in his theology of perfection:

> Q. 13. But if Christ has put an end to that law, what need of any atonement for their transgressing it?
> A. Observe in what sense he has put an end to it, and the difficulty vanishes. Were it not for the abiding merit of his death, and his continual intercession for us, that law would condemn us still. These, therefore, we still need for every transgression of it.[33]

What Wesley means is that Adamic law, the law of works, is still in *full force*. Christ did not abolish this law; instead, by his death he covers the believer's transgressions so that this law no longer condemns. As we will soon see, the Christian, even the most perfect, can live only on the basis of God's forgiveness imparted daily through the perpetual intercession of our heavenly high priest Jesus Christ.[34] So there are two standards, both of which hold us accountable before the divine tribunal. Only through the

---

[31] PA 25:11.
[32] PA 25:14.
[33] PA 25:41.
[34] Significantly, by stressing the importance of Christ's *continual intercession* in relation to sin, JW links the resurrection of Christ to our justification (Rom 4:25b). Thus, in his death Christ provided atonement and in his resurrection he forever lives to intercede for our voluntary and involuntary sin (PA 19:23; 25:41).

gospel is there hope of salvation. Significant to Wesley's system is that voluntary sin pertains to the law of faith and is fulfilled by love; involuntary sin pertains to transgressions of the perfect law given to Adam in the garden.

We can chart this as follows:

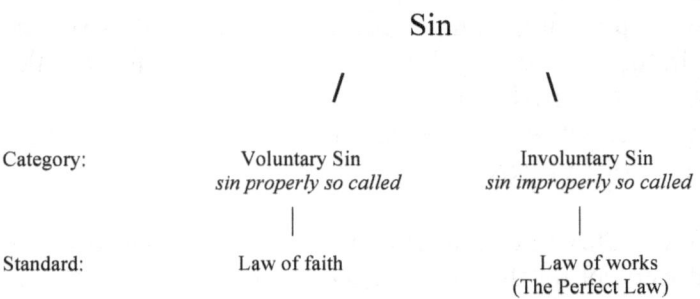

We now proceed to take a deeper look at these two foundational categories. At the height of the perfection schism Wesley wrote a definitive homily explaining the nature of voluntary sin in the life of the born again believer. In response to a publication that linked sin's guilt and power to its being, he now used the opportunity to distinguish between them, "The *guilt* is one thing, the *power* another, and the *being* yet another."[35] Voluntary sin is now subdivided into three groups. These three subcategories match his earlier grouping of sin as guilt, outward and inward.[36] Wesley is consistent in his two-works gospel: sin's guilt is dealt with in justification; sin's power (outward sin) is broken in the new birth. Sin no longer *reigns* but it still *remains*. But only in adulthood is the being of sin (inward sin) removed. Only then does the believer taste perfect love. So the timing of deliverance is clear: justification removes sin's guilt; the new birth breaks sin's power; perfect love vanquishes sin's being.

Our chart now looks like this:

---

[35] *On Sin in Believers* IV.4.
[36] E.g. *Christian Perfection* (1741).

Sin in the Ordo Salutis

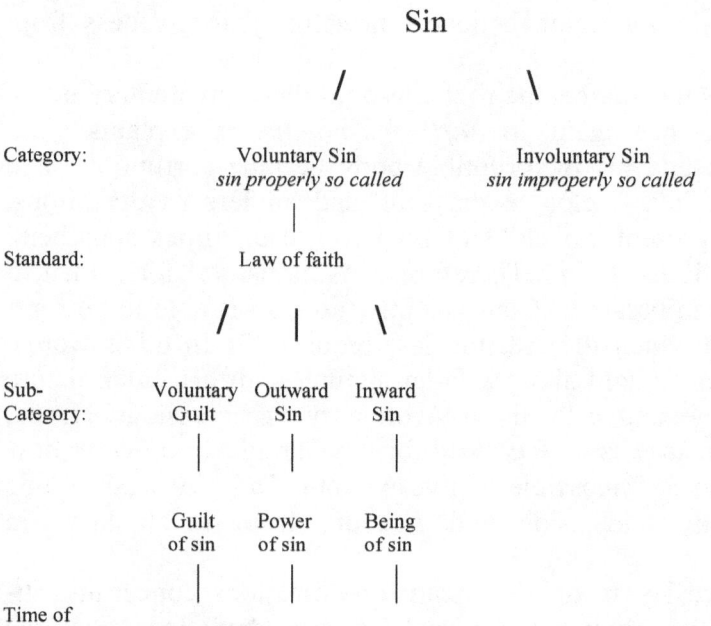

When we turn to the subcategories of involuntary sin we see a marked difference from the ones under voluntary sin. Wesley consistently spoke of this kind of sin as weakness and folly,[37] mistake and infirmity.[38] He explains himself more fully, "By 'sin's of infirmity' I would mean such involuntary failings as saying a thing we believe true, though in fact it prove to be false; or hurting our neighbor without knowing or designing it, perhaps when we designed to do him good."[39] This gives insight into what Wesley understood by an involuntary transgression. Even the most perfect fall short of the absolute standard of God's holiness by inadvertently hurting other people. These "mistakes in practice" bring legal guilt that exposes to divine judgment, which requires Christ's atonement and intercession. Wesley taught that

---

[37] *Preface to the Life and Death of Mr. Halyburton* §5 (1739).
[38] *Christian Perfection* I.4, 7 (1741).
[39] *The First-fruits of the Spirit* II.8; see also *The End of Christ's Coming* III.3; *The Fall of Man* II.2.

even entirely sanctified believers need daily forgiveness from God.[40]

What is the source, the root cause, of these involuntary transgressions? Once again, in *Farther Thoughts* he explains, "But Adam fell; and his incorruptible body became corruptible; and ever since, it is a clog to the soul, and hinders its operations. Hence, at present, no child of man can at all times apprehend clearly, or judge truly...Therefore, it is as natural for a man to mistake as to breathe...Consequently, no man is able to perform the service which the Adamic law requires."[41] In other words, Adam's sin brought about a fallen nature, and this fallen nature serves as the source for these involuntary transgressions. Hence, culpable mistake is now *natural* for the Christian, no matter how perfect, and is impossible to live without. Only in death is this mortal body laid aside and freedom from involuntary sin ceases.[42]

Yet, Wesley made significant qualifications concerning involuntary sin. Though these mistakes are "deviations from the holy and acceptable and perfect will of God;" yet he maintains "they are not properly sin" for three reasons. First, since they are done inadvertently; that is, they do not defile the conscience. Second, these sins do not break the Christian's fellowship with God. And third, such sins are not inconsistent with living in and under the Spirit's control.[43]

We can now chart Wesley's doctrine of sin:

---

[40] *Thoughts*, PA 19:11-12; JWJ 7/24/61.
[41] PA 25:8.
[42] This is the same position JW held in his early period when he *denied* perfection was possible in this life (*The Trouble and Rest of Good Men* II.4-6). As with other aspects of JW's mature theology, he essentially returns theologically to his early period, though he will articulate that position differently. He continues to use the language and categories developed after Aldersgate but in many ways he gravitates back to his early position (see chapter 7).
[43] *The First-fruits of the Spirit* II.8.

Sin in the Ordo Salutis

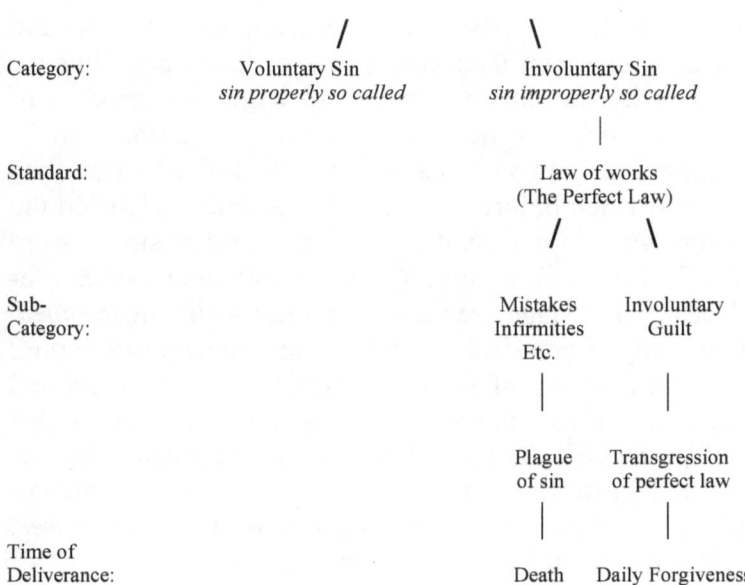

Our next step is to identify the stages of the faith journey that match up to these subcategories. Let us retrace our steps. Wesley understood sin to be either voluntary or involuntary. Voluntary sin is grounded on the New Testament standard of faith and love in Jesus Christ and deals with people's intentional responses. In addition to sin's guilt, Wesley often refers to inward and outward sin to highlight the nature of voluntary sin. Outward sin (sin's power) refers to the outward act, while inward sin (sin's being) points to the inner disposition and temper. By contrast, involuntary sin includes all inadvertent failures to keep God's absolute standard given to Adam in his pristine purity. Since the human race is now fallen, such failures bring legal guilt that requires forgiveness, but does not defile the conscience or one's fellowship with God. These infractions are of a much less serious nature than voluntary sin.

Wesley believed and proclaimed that our guilt for voluntary sin is dealt with in justification; sin's power in regeneration, sin's being in entire sanctification, but involuntary sin in physical death. It is at this point that Wesley's *ordo salutis* comes into

John Wesley's Theology of Christian Perfection

play. For a correlation exists between each subcategory and Wesley's stages of renewal in God's image. In chapter four we discovered that by the late sixties he had begun the process of temporally separating justification from the new birth. That is, even if someone had not yet received the Spirit of adoption they could still be justified before God. This stage Wesley labeled the *faith of a servant*. From 1 John 2:12-14 three other stages were identified: *children, adolescents* (young men), and *adults* (fathers).[44] These three stages represent specific states in the *ordo salutis*. Last, only in physical death does involuntary sin expire. Thus, Wesley's doctrine of sin is structurally organized around his understanding of the stages of renewal and sheds light on his theology of perfection. As the believer grows in greater degrees of renewal and inward transformation, they progress in greater degrees of salvation from sin: first is sin's *guilt*, then sin's *power*, after this sin's *being*, and last sin's inherent *plague*.

Let's see how our chart looks like now:

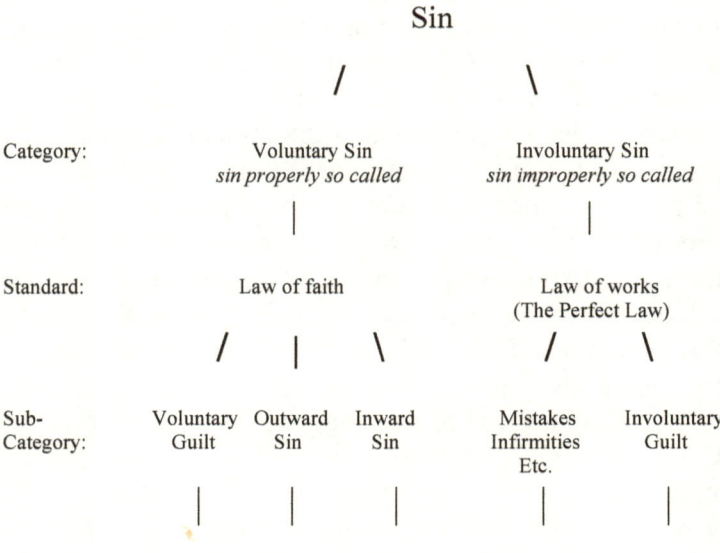

---

[44] *Christian Perfection; NT Notes* 1 Jn 2:12-14; PA 12:9, 29.

Sin in the Ordo Salutis

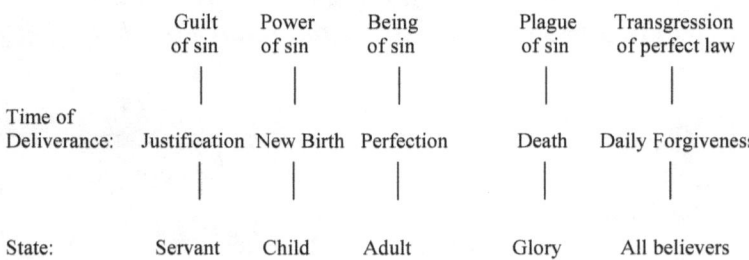

So what can we conclude about Wesley's doctrine of sin, especially in relation to his theology of perfection? It is evident he believed in two kinds of perfection. When asked if those perfect were still sinners, Wesley once responded, "Explain the term one way, and I say, Yes; another, and I say, No."[45] Though using somewhat different language than we have been using, Harald Lindström clarifies both kinds of perfection by placing them in conjunction to each other:

> *Adamic*: *Based* on the covenant of works: man must fulfill the law of works.
> *Christian*: *Based* on the covenant of grace: man must fulfill the law of faith.
>
> *Adamic*: *Signifies* perfect obedience to every point in this law. This holiness must be perfect in degree and continue without intermission throughout the whole of life.
> *Christian*: *Signifies* perfect obedience in so far as this is attainable in the present circumstances of man. It means perfect love. This holiness is a perfection of motive, not of degree. It concerns man's will and intention.
>
> *Adamic*: This is perfect fulfillment of the law (of works) and perfect deliverance from sin *in the absolute and objective sense*.

---

[45] JWL 9/15/62.

John Wesley's Theology of Christian Perfection

Christian: This is perfect fulfillment of the law (of faith) and perfect deliverance from sin *in the relative and subjective sense*.

Adamic: Therefore in order that he may not suffer damnation for his sin and guilt, he is every moment dependent on the merit and intercession of Christ.
Christian: Yet in order to remain perfect he is every moment dependent on the merit and intercession of Christ.[46]

In some sense Wesley's theology of perfection teaches that all regenerated believers are perfect according to their stage of development.[47] Yet, upon the whole, he reserved calling perfect only those who attained spiritual adulthood. Nonetheless, Wesley did hold that all believers remain imperfect in this life; that every Christian needs to confess their failings and ask for daily forgiveness from God. This dual emphasis inevitably led to confusion over his views on perfect love. The question revolves around which standard is being referred to, and which category of sin is being referenced.

In either case, Wesley's mature doctrine of sin can be charted as follows:

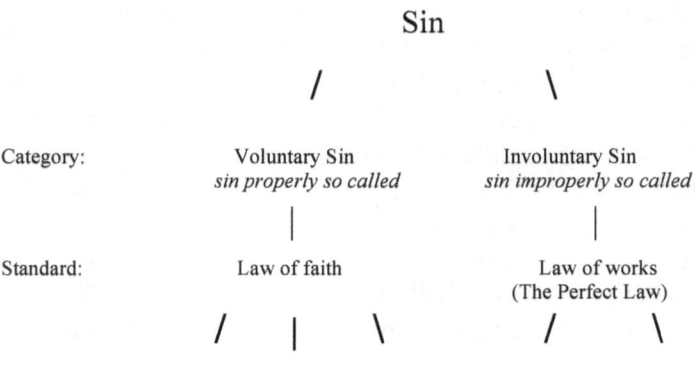

---

[46] Lindström, *Wesley & Sanctification*, 153-54.
[47] *Christian Perfection* II.2.

Sin in the Ordo Salutis

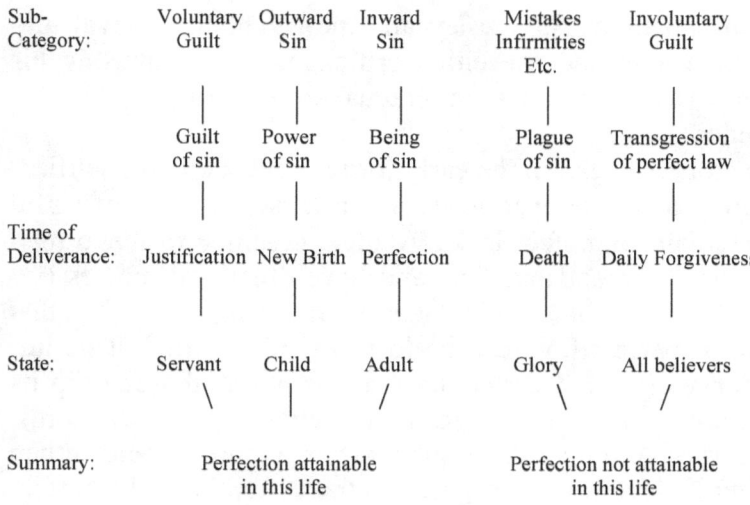

Original Sin in Wesley's Doctrine of Sin

We now turn to the question of original sin. How do Wesley's views on original sin fit into the above structure? What is the relationship between original sin, voluntary sin, and involuntary sin? Is original sin removed in the gift of perfect love? Or, did Wesley believe our deliverance from inbred sin is only realized in the article of death?

How Wesley answers these questions differs from one period to another. Early Wesley believed our innate corruption was vanquished only in the article of death.[48] At Aldersgate the pendulum swung to the opposite extreme. Freedom from original sin begins in the article of conversion.[49] In light of his own struggles and those of his converts, Wesley soon became convinced that freedom from *all* sin transpires in stages. By late 1739 he was teaching two primary moments in the faith journey, with both involving a salvation from sin: outward sin at conversion and inward

---

[48] See *Death and Deliverance* (1725) and *The Trouble and Rest of Good Men* (1735).
[49] *Salvation by Faith* II.2, 7; JWJ 12/7/38; 1/4/39 Works J 1:165-169, 170-172.

sin at full salvation. As Wesley and the Methodist revival matured, with friend and foe either criticizing and/or abusing his views on perfect love, we see a gradual softening in his doctrine of perfection.

This process began in the early forties when certain qualifications were put on the experience. Even those cleansed of sinful tempers remain imperfect in knowledge, continue to make mistakes in judgment and practice, and have other weaknesses (infirmities).[50] By the late fifties Wesley was acknowledging that the grace of perfect love can be lost (and regained).[51] This implies a concession that perfecting grace is not as thorough in its transformative power as was formerly believed. In other words, the remains of Adam's fall (original sin) are more tenacious than was earlier believed at Aldersgate and thereafter. With the perfection revival in the early sixties, and with many claiming angelic perfection,[52] Wesley felt it necessary to once again qualify his doctrine of perfection by stressing the continuing reality of involuntary sin. Now, even the most perfect were being taught to pray *daily* for forgiveness.[53]

All these changes were shaped by many factors, but one that is least noticed is how Wesley related original sin to infirmities and inward sin at different periods in his career. We saw that early Wesley closely identified original sin with human infirmity and weakness.[54] This meant, logically, that any deliverance from inherited sinfulness could not be attained apart from the believer being freed from these infirmities. As Wesley acknowledged to his university audience, "perfect holiness is not found on earth" since "some remains of our disease will ever be felt," so only "death will deliver us" from pain, folly, infirmity, and hence,

---

[50] *Christian Perfection* I.
[51] Footnote 23 above.
[52] PA chs 20-22; see also *Cautions and Directions Given to the Greatest Professors in The Methodist Societies* (1762; Outler, *John Wesley*, 298-305).
[53] JWJ 7/24/61; PA 19:12.
[54] See *Death and Deliverance* §14; JWL 10/3/31 (Works B 25:318, *ll*.22, 29-32).

sin.[55] But early Wesley also associated original sin with inward sin. Through his entire early corpus inbred sin is the source behind sinful dispositions and tempers.[56] Thus, original sin, infirmity and inward sin were organically related in Wesley's early theology, and perfection attainable only in the article of death.

At Aldersgate a fundamental shift takes place. Wesley began to draw a sharper distinction between infirmities and sinful desires (inward sin). Emphasis is now placed on the instantaneous moment and the power of grace to inwardly transform the will and desires (tempers). Infirmities are relegated to a separate category. While still acknowledged, their diminutive status is evident: such deviations are no longer sin "properly speaking." The tighter Wesley linked original sin to inward sin, the more optimistic his theology of perfection became. Since inward sin is removed in the article of conversion, it logically followed that inbred sin is also removed in the same moment.[57] This optimism was shattered over the next several months as Wesley personally struggled with questions of assurance and victory over sin.

Over the next two decades Wesley gradually moved back to a position that acknowledged the tenacious reality of infirmity as involuntary sin.[58] This admission required that original sin must persist in some manner throughout this earthly life. Since he maintained a definite distinction between involuntary sin and inward sin, Wesley's teachings imply that original sin is at the same time removed and not removed in those made perfect in love. In other words, by the mid-sixties Wesley's theology of per-

---

[55] *The Trouble and Rest of Good Men* P.; II.3-4.
[56] *Death and Deliverance* §14; *The Circumcision of the Heart* I.1-2, 4, 10, 11; *The Trouble and Rest of Good Men* P.; II.5; *Single Intention* II.9.
[57] JW's Aldersgate memorandum is a testimony of salvation from inward sin: "I felt I did trust in Christ, Christ alone for salvation: And am assurance was given me, that he had taken away *my* sins, even *mine*, and saved *me* from the law of sin and death." See chapter two for a full discussion of JW's GosFA.
[58] This development began with the problems encountered at the Fetter Lane Society in June 1739 and the stillness controversy in 1740 (see chapter 3). JW first put into writing his thoughts in 1741 with *Christian Perfection*. The process culminated in 1759 with *Thoughts on Christian Perfection* (PA 19:7-25).

fection held that adult believers are free from original sin in one sense but not in another. Of course, this fed confusion in how his views were understood, then and now. Yet, to his death Wesley affirmed both truths: the adult believer is simultaneously perfect and imperfect. They have tasted freedom from all sin; yet need daily forgiveness for transgressions of the perfect law. This soteriological tension is never resolved by Wesley.

Original Sin as Inward Sin

To show the connection between original sin and inward sin (sinful tempers) we turn to Wesley's *A Plain Account of Christian Perfection* (1766). We note several links between the two. Chapter nine includes several lines from *Hymns and Sacred Poems I* (1739). In these poetic prayers perfection involves a change of nature that alters one's dispositions and actions. By linking perfection to a change of nature Wesley identifies original sin to inward sin:

Turn the full stream of nature's tide;
Let all our actions tend
To thee, their source; thy love the guide,
Thy glory be the end (v 2)

Heavenly Adam, life divine,
Change my nature into thine;
More and spread throughout my soul,
Actuate and fill the whole (v 5)

Chapter twelve includes selections from the sermon *Christian Perfection*. In this significant homily inward sin is called our "evil nature" and "the body of sin."[59] Wesley proceeds to contrast our sinful tempers with the nature of Christ, who according to

---

[59] PA 12:32.

Sin in the Ordo Salutis

Christian tradition (and Scripture) did not have any original sin. In the same paragraph Wesley argues from 1 John 1:7 that Christians can be cleansed from *all* sin, and that no unrighteousness remains.

Chapter eighteen offers several excerpts from *Hymns and Sacred Poems IV* (1749). Though these two volumes were written by Charles, and that John did not approve of every sentiment found therein, the ones included in the *Plain Account* surely met with his approval:

> *From this inbred sin deliver;*
> *Let the yoke now be broke;*
> *Make me thine for ever.*
>
> *Partner of thy perfect nature,*
> *Let me be now in thee*
> *A new, sinless creature* (vv 6-7)

Here, "inbred sin," "perfect nature," and a "new, sinless creature" demonstrate an unambiguous link between original sin and Christian perfection (the cleansing of inward sin). In chapter nineteen (*Thoughts on Christian Perfection*) "inbred sin" is said to be gradually mortified until the believer "experiences a total death to sin." Then the holy temper of perfect love (19:5) reigns uncontested in the heart (19:68, 71). Several paragraphs later, Wesley identifies this remaining sin as the "sinful nature" (19:83). In these examples Wesley uses several synonyms of original sin to refer to the kind of sin that the holy temper of perfect love replaces. This signifies that a strong identification between original sin and inward sin is evident in Wesley's theology.

We now turn to another key doctrinal sermon: *On Sin in Believers* (1763). While the central theme is to enunciate that sin remains in the born again Christian until perfected in love, several statements show that Wesley saw inward sin as an expression of original sin. He begins with a quotation from his church's articles, "Original sin is the corruption of the nature of every man, whereby man is in his own nature inclined to evil, so that the flesh lusteth contrary to the Spirit" (P.3). Original sin is here understood by Wesley to mean inward sin: "any sinful temper, passion, or affection; such as pride, self-will, love of the world...any disposition contrary to the mind which was in Christ" (II.2). Inward sin is further called the "flesh" and that "evil nature" which opposes the Spirit, "even in believers" (III.1). According to Wesley sin exists as guilt, power and being, with the latter just another term for inward sin (IV.4). He then summarizes the sermon's central message, "That, although we are renewed, cleansed, purified, sanctified, the moment we truly believe in Christ, yet we are not then renewed, cleansed, purified altogether; but the flesh, the evil nature, still *remains*, (though subdued) and wars against the Spirit" (V.2; emphasis his). Thus inward sin is closely linked to the sin inherited from Adam. Our sinful tempers find their source in that corruption of nature that is corrected in the sanctifying moment of full salvation.

Original Sin as Involuntary Sin

We turn again to the *Plain Account* since this document includes the tracts *Thoughts on Christian Perfection* (ch 19) and *Farther Thoughts on Christian Perfection* (ch 25). In chapter nineteen we find the subject of involuntary sin discussed in sufficient detail. While Christian perfection is strongly affirmed in this chapter, so is the reality of culpable mistakes and shortcomings (19:7-12). Wesley links these culpable shortcomings with the "natural consequence of the soul's dwelling in flesh and blood" (19:8). He further explains that since our inner person functions through the medium of bodily organs it becomes inevitable that we will at times think and act wrong. In other words, Wesley acknowledges that an eschatological tension remains in this life, even for those perfected in love. While the new age has dawned in the death and resurrection of Jesus Christ, believers still live in this present evil age. Simply put, our redemption is not yet complete. We remain fallen due to depravity inherited from Adam.[60]

In chapter twenty-five Wesley gives one of his most definitive theological explications of his perfection doctrine. Utilizing the covenant concept of two laws, he proceeds to describe the pristine perfection Adam first enjoyed and then lost (25:2-8). In the wake of Adam's transgression his posterity was left in a condition that makes it as "natural for a man to mistake as to breathe; and he can no more live without the one than without the other." Wesley summarizes, "Consequently, no man is able to perform the service which the Adamic law requires" (25:9). The human race is now fallen, unable to live as Adam did in the garden. Even the perfection attained in full salvation cannot overcome this debilitating condition. Human nature continues to have failures and shortcomings that bring legal guilt that must be atoned for (19:11-12; 25:41). Involuntary sin remains an everyday reality.[61] So pervasive is this condition that Wesley refers to it as "natural" (25:9).

What we learn is that the source behind these involuntary failures is that corruption of nature inherited from Adam. Original sin not only contaminated humanity's dispositional nature (inward sin), but also so distorted the human condition that none of us can think, judge or act in a manner that fully satisfies God's holy standard:

> Mistake as well as ignorance is, in our present state, inseparable from humanity. Every child of man is in a thousand mistakes, and is liable to fresh mistakes every moment. And a mistake in judgment may occasion a mistake in practice, yea, naturally leads thereto. I mistake, and possibly cannot avoid mistaking, the character of this or that man. I suppose him to be what he is not; to be better or worse than he really is. Upon this wrong supposition I

---

[60] See *Original Sin* (1759).
[61] *The Fall of Man* II.2; JWJ 7/24/61.

behave wrong to him, that is, more or less affectionately than he deserves. And by the mistake which is occasioned by the defect of my bodily organs I am naturally led so to do. Such is the present condition of human nature, of a mind dependent on a mortal body. Such is the state entailed on all human spirits while connected with flesh and blood![62]

Wesley ties original sin to our mortal state. Because of this a soteriological tension remains in his doctrine of sin. With a dual emphasis on original sin, as both inward sin and involuntary sin, the inevitable consequence is that adult believers are both perfect and imperfect at the same time. This tension was mentioned above and will be explored more fully in the last chapter.

We now chart Wesley's doctrine of original sin as follows:

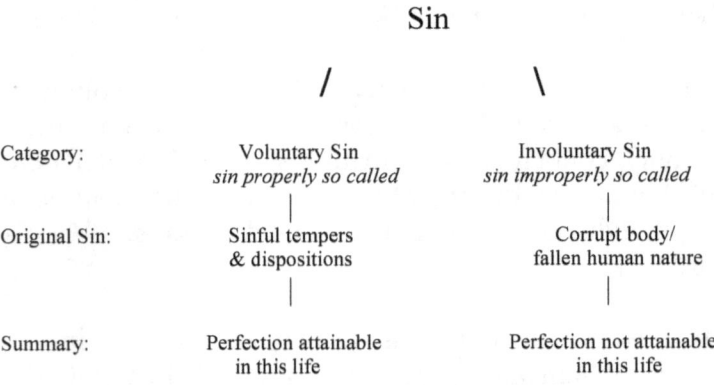

We have now structurally organized Wesley's doctrine of sin according to category, standard, subcategory, and state. We have identified which kind of sin is removable in this life, its timing of removal, and which kind of sin persists until the article of death. By charting Wesley's doctrine of sin we see that his views on sin are inherently conjoined to his *ordo salutis*. That is, different

---

[62] *The Fall of Man* II.2.

Sin in the Ordo Salutis

stages of deliverance from sin parallels stages of renewal in God's image.

The chart is now complete and looks as follows:

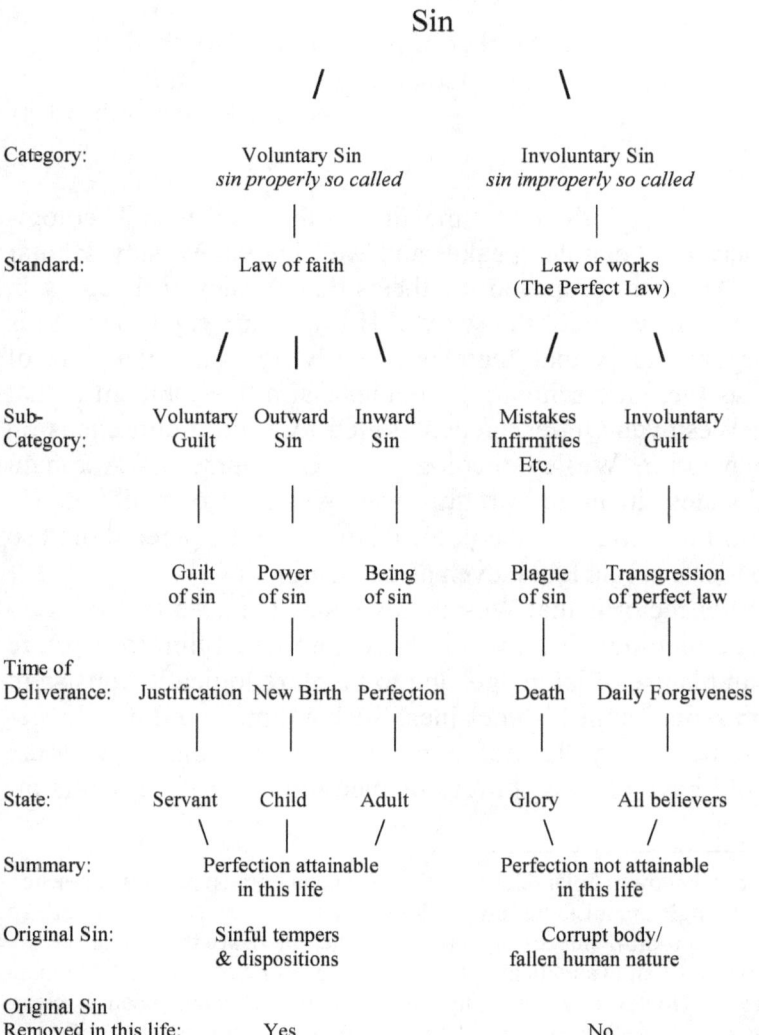

SIX
Spiritual Father

"You are the elder brother of the American Methodists;
I am, under God, the father of the whole family."
John Wesley to Francis Asbury

At the thirty-ninth annual meeting of the Wesleyan Theological Society the keynote speaker and well-known Wesley scholar William Abraham proposed the thesis that Wesleyan theology in its contemporary mode is now over. If I read him right, one of his basic arguments is that there are nearly as many versions of Wesley as there are scholars.[1] Another claim by Abraham is that the neo-Wesleyan/Outler agenda[2] failed to build a consensus on how to position Wesley theologically. Of course, as Abraham himself states, in large part this was Wesley's own doing. He drank from far too many theological streams to be pigeonholed so easily under a single label, even as an Arminian.[3]

Another factor is that Wesley never saw the need to produce a systematic theology. This would have compelled him to be more precise in his use of language, and to be more logically consistent in the presentation of his doctrines. Such a tome could have once-for-all settled many debates over his own theological contours and would have allowed him to nuance himself before others at-

---

[1] Abraham tells how scholars define JW as a fundamentalist holiness preacher, a revivalist Anglican, a Liberation theologian that is either wobbly, soft or just a proto, or as a proto-Pentecostal theologian. Then there are those who see JW as some flavor of an evangelical, whether it is a catholic or a liberal. Abraham summarizes, "However we draw up the typology, one conclusion is clear: there are as many Wesley's as there are Wesley scholars" (*The End of Wesleyan Theology*, WTJ 40:1:13).

[2] Abraham, WTJ 40:1:8-12

[3] E.g. JW's atonement views are more Calvinistic than many Arminian-Wesleyans who followed him.

Spiritual Father

tempted the task. But Wesley prided himself as a man of the people—one among the "bulk of mankind."[4] Yet, more importantly, was Wesley's immersion in the revival. He disdained flowery language and the niceties of philosophical speculations and reasonings.[5] Instead, he professed to teach "plain truth for a plain people." This meant he never bothered to sharpen his terminology with razor-edge precision. It was the needs of the common people under his care that concerned him most. As Abraham concludes, even today Wesley continues to serve his posterity as *spiritual father* rather than as an epochal theologian of Protestantism.[6]

In the entire Wesley corpus it is his letters that show this side of his character and ministry. They are theologically rich in content and need to be studied alongside his journal, sermons and other published writings. Yet, it is in his letters we see Wesley come forth as spiritual father. For in his mail he enters into personal relationship with scores of people as he counsels them regarding their spiritual development. And, I would add, his letters offer important insights into the evolution of his thought and theology. Up to this point in our study we have often turned to them to ascertain specific transition points in the evolution of his perfection theology. We now turn to his later letters (from the late fifties on) to point out further maturation in his two-works gospel.

Several areas of interest arise. For starters, in a number of letters the question of degrees or levels within the experience of Christian perfection are addressed. Moreover, beginning in the late fifties Wesley's correspondence often discusses in detail how to attain and retain the experience. His spiritual fatherhood becomes most evident in several letter series in which he counsels seekers of full salvation over an extended period of time. His fatherly advice and tender counsel is what attracted many to his person, while offering us further clarification of several aspects

---

[4] *Preface,* Works J 5:1.
[5] *Preface*, Works J 5:2.
[6] In contrast to the likes of Luther, Calvin, Schliermacher, and Barth.

of his theology. Therefore, a full rounded understanding of Wesley's theology of perfection necessitates a careful look at this correspondence.

The Gospel of Two Works

In chapter three we charted the course by which Wesley developed his two-works gospel system. In this system the faith journey is grounded on a life transformation process that incorporates specific God-moments at critical thresholds of spiritual attainment. Behind the twin parameters of process and moment are the axioms of inward holiness and salvation by faith alone. These maxims represent the core values that informed his mature *ordo salutis*, and, as we will see, his later correspondence. As with all his letters, Wesley's mail is situational; which means we cannot expect a single letter, or even a group of them, to spell out fully his two-works theology. But what we do see over the existing body of correspondence is that his two-works theology did permeate his thought and the counsel he gave to his addressees.

Wesley often refers to both God-moments within a single letter. Dorothy Furly is told she had received the "first fruits of the Spirit" through God changing her heart in "some measure." Now, she only needs to "earnestly wait for the great change" when "every root of bitterness" will be "torn up."[7] In another letter he identifies the first work as the "former change" and the second as the "latter change."[8] In a similar vein, Hester Roe is reminded of the difference between the "first love" and a "pure love," for the former empowers one to live above the power of the "root of sin," yet only the latter can take it away.[9]

Wesley once explained this distinction to a nobleman:

---

[7] JWL 6/18/57.
[8] JWL 6/27/60.
[9] JWL 5/3/76.

Spiritual Father

I have frequently observed that there are two very different ranks of Christians, both of whom may be in the favour of God, a higher and a lower rank. The latter avoid all known sin, do much good, use all the means of grace, but have little of the life of God in their souls, and are much conformed to the world. The former make the Bible their whole rule, and their sole aim is the will and image of God. This they steadily and uniformly pursue, through honour and dishonour, denying themselves, and taking up their cross daily; considering one point only, "How may I attain most of the mind that was in Christ, and how may I please him most?"[10]

In other correspondence Wesley distinguishes what God does *for* us from what he does *in* us.[11] God is the one who justifies and afterwards sanctifies.[12] The first work involves a "taste" of salvation from sin, followed by a gradual work leading to a "farther instantaneous change."[13] Wesley draws upon the parable of the talents to make his point, "When we are justified, He gives us one talent; to those that use this He gives more. When we are sanctified, He gives, as it were, five talents. And if you use the whole power which is then given, He will not only continue that power, but increase it day by day."[14]

Here is Wesley's two-works gospel: the first work is followed by degrees of growth leading to a second moment, only to be followed by another process of growth and development.[15] Yet, as

---

[10] JWL T 1/1/70.
[11] See *Justification By Faith* II.1 and *The Great Privilege of Those That are Born of God* P.2 for this terminology in his sermons.
[12] JWL 12/22/56; 2/8/66; 12/28/70; 3/9/82.
[13] JWL 12/15/63.
[14] JWL 6/3/74.
[15] JW told Miss Furly "You are right in looking for a further instantaneous change, as well as a constant gradual one" (JWL 12/15/63). And to Miss March he wrote, "Every one, though born of God in an instant, yea, and sanctified in an instant, yet undoubtedly grows by slow degrees, both after the former and the latter change" (JWL 6/27/60).

we saw above, Wesley was very aware the move from the first work of grace to the second was no smooth transition.

The Wilderness State

From his own struggles with doubt following his Aldersgate conversion, Wesley learned just how deep these conflicts could be. By 1740 he refers to these struggles as the wilderness state.[16] On the heels of the great perfection revival in the early sixties,[17] Wesley encourages miss March there is "very frequently a kind of wilderness state, not only after justification, but even after deliverance from sin."[18] Just a few years prior Wesley had published a sermon on the same topic. Yet in his letters we see a personal side to the struggles his converts faced as they worked out their salvation with fear and trembling.[19] What were their struggles? How did their struggles following justification and new birth compare with those following full salvation? We turn to his letters for answers.

Wesley's correspondence abounds with advice to those wrestling to confirm their spiritual standing. He reminds one convert that following justification a direct witness from the Holy Spirit is often felt, only later to become intermittent.[20] This intermittency is compounded by numerous inner struggles. Wesley confronts one preacher about his prejudice, ingratitude, uneven temper, lack of self-control with his tongue, and lack of brotherly love. Though this man was greatly used by God, at times his poor choice of words and demeanor had caused Wesley to "tremble."[21]

---

[16] Cf. page 158.
[17] For a fuller description of this period see vol 1 *Introduction: Why Did Wesley Write A Plain Account?*; and chs 20-22.
[18] JWL 10/13/64.
[19] Php 2:12-13.
[20] JWL 1/30/62.
[21] JWL T 12/86.

Spiritual Father

When we turn to his other mail we find a whole host of issues these seekers of perfect love encountered. Common issues include, as Wesley calls them, "unprofitable reasonings" and "wanderings" of the imagination. In their place he counsels one seeker to practice the peace of God which guards the heart, mind, affections and passions as a "garrison keeps a city."[22] Other problems were envy, gossip, vanity, depression, ("occasions of heaviness and dejection"), weariness and faintness of mind, weakness of nerves, passions of resentment, conflicting emotions and many afflictions over health.[23] With many of these trials Wesley gives credit to Satan and his minions[24] or to our fallen condition.[25] The following is a good example of the kind of conflicts that plagued many Methodists, and the role as spiritual father Wesley supplied:

> You say, "I know not whither I am going." I will tell you whither. You are going the straight way to be swallowed up in God. "I know not what I am doing." You are suffering the will of God, and glorifying Him in the fire. "But I am not increasing in the divine life." That is your mistake. Perhaps you are now increasing therein faster than ever you did since you were justified.[26]

As we found in other parts of our study, the primary cause of these ailments is sinful tempers; and the primary disposition is pride. Wesley warns one dear sister, "There is a mountain that stands in the way; and how you will get over it, I know not: I

---

[22] JWL 12/14/85.
[23] JWL 11/9/87; 5/3/76; 11/23/83; 1/20/58; 7/14/81; 6/17/74.
[24] JWL 6/23/74; 11/9/87. To Ann Bolton JW wrote, "Undoubtedly Satan, who well understands the manner how the mind is influenced by the body, can, by means of those parts in the animal machine which are more immediately subservient to thinking, raise a thousand perceptions and emotions in the mind, so far as God is pleased to permit" (JWL 9/27/77).
[25] JWL 1/18/74.
[26] JWL 3/9/82.

mean pride."[27] Self-importance was the root cause behind one preacher's prejudice and other vices.[28] It feeds a desire for vanity and an unhealthy desire for approval from other people. Pride further imprisons one to fear the rejection of others.[29] Yet, Wesley acknowledges that distinguishing between right and wrong tempers can be as difficult as discerning truth from error.[30]

This led many to seek his counsel and advice. To one lady he explains the difference between "heaviness" and "darkness of soul." Heaviness is due more to our mortal condition whereas darkness is often caused by "our own fault." What did he advise? "It seems your trial was of the latter kind (i.e. heaviness)...But of whatsoever kind it was, you may profit thereby: It need not leave you as it found you."[31] To another who suffered from nervous disorders Wesley advises several of his Oxford rules: early sleep (never later than ten o'clock), early rising, awareness of Satan's schemes to afflict doubt, and seeking counsel from trusted advisors.[32] Wesley could be terse and to the point, as he is to this fellow minister, "Suffer me now to speak a word between you and me. Is not the reason of your preaching so languidly and coldly, that you do not feel what you say? And why not? Because your soul is not alive to God."[33] But to close confidants he was always very patient and encouraging.

One such confidant was Ann Bolton. Forty years Wesley's junior, Ann experienced a spiritual awakening in the summer of 1762. The following February she joined the Methodist society and began a lifelong pilgrimage to attain holiness of heart and life. It is good to remember that the only requirement Wesley placed on joining a society was the desire to "flee from the wrath

---

[27] JWL 9/7/87.
[28] See note 21 above.
[29] JWL 5/3/76; 12/1/86; 9/7/87.
[30] JWL 7/13/71.
[31] JWL 6/17/74.
[32] JWL 3/25/81.
[33] JWL 10/25/86.

Spiritual Father

to come."[34] This requirement fit her early faith journey. Ann shares it was in "June 1763, when the Lord deepened his work…and the true light began to shine upon my dark soul."[35] Through the late sixties Ann's spiritual temperature would ebb and flow, alternating between periods of dryness and seasons of hope. John Banks says of Bolton's faith journey:

> This was to be the pattern of Ann's life. She had a doubtful, timorous spirit and was much given to 'reasoning' herself into fear and unbelief. She needed constant support, and perpetual proof before she could say: Be gone my needless fears, and doubts no longer mine.[36]

Wesley probably met Miss Bolton in early 1764 while on his regular preaching tour. The earliest extant letter we have from his pen to the young maiden is four years later when he advises her on a marriage proposal. Soon a deep friendship developed between them.[37] A couple months later Wesley wrote to encourage her faith and to remind her that she already has the faith of a servant. She only needs the faith of a child:

> Look up, my sister, my friend! Jesus is there! He is ever now interceding for *you*! Doubt not of it! Doubt not his love! Forget yourself, a poor, vile, worthless sinner. But look to Jesus! See the Friend of Sinners! *Your* Friend; your ready and strong Savior![38]

---

[34] "There is one only condition previously required in those who desire admission into these societies, 'a desire to flee from the wrath to come, to be saved from their sins' (*General Rules of the United Societies* §4, Works B 9:70).
[35] John Banks, *Nancy Nancy*, 12.
[36] Banks, 15.
[37] Banks mentions that JW's extant correspondence to Ann totals 117 letters, and that he published 22 letters from her to him in the Arminian Magazine (*Nancy, Nancy*, 2).
[38] JWL 4/7/68.

The struggles Ann faced were common among early Methodists. She confides in Wesley of her struggles with pride. In response John counsels her to distinguish between pride and a temptation to pride, "Then you may trust that all the motions you feel tending to pride or vanity...are not sin, but temptation."[39] In a desire for the abiding witness of the Spirit, Ann, like so many others, sought Wesley's wisdom concerning various emotions and perceptions.[40] With his continual urging to seek perfect love, she wrestled with issues of marriage, handling disappointments, physical faintness and weariness, and discerning God's leading in her life.[41] Through it all Wesley reminds her of his godly jealousy, "Perhaps I shall find faults in you that others do not; for I survey you on every side. I mark your every motion and temper; because I long for you to be without spot or blemish."[42] Is it little wonder that Ann never married until Wesley had passed?

Through the years Ann remained a faithful society member and class leader, yet we never sense from Wesley's correspondence that she attained perfect love while he was alive. Her affection and appreciation for Wesley ran deep. When he passed on March 2, 1791 Miss Bolton came several days later to meet with friends and to attend the funeral service. On March 12 she wrote to a friend, "No words can possibly give you any idea of my feelings from our late loss. From a letter I had lately read from our dear beloved pastor and *father*."[43] For many, like Ann, there was no greater tribute than to remember John Wesley as their spiritual father.

---

[39] JWL 11/7/71.
[40] JWL 9/27/77; see note 24 above.
[41] JWL 8/31/84; 3/28/85; 1/9/89.
[42] JWL 12/5/72.
[43] Banks, *Nancy, Nancy*, 92; emphasis mine.

Spiritual Father

Attaining Full Salvation

It is well known that Wesley considered full salvation to be the "grand depositum" which God entrusted to the Methodists.[44] The corpus of his mail breathes with continual longing to see his people receive all that Christ purchased on the cross.[45] We have noted several times how inward holiness, full salvation from sin, became early in his life the DNA of his faith and character. When bursting out in frustration to his brother Charles, "I am at my wit's end in regard to two things,—the Church, and Christian perfection,"[46] John was revealing the depth of passion and conviction he felt towards this scripture truth. While through the later sixties he felt compelled to fight for the doctrine and its accompanying experience, in his correspondence we see continual exhortations and encouragements for his followers to seek perfection in their love to God and neighbor.

One of the strongest themes in his letters is that perfection is available now, even today, "One part of your work is to stir up all who have believed, to go on to perfection, and every moment to expect the full salvation which is received by simple faith."[47] If the promise is to be received now, as Wesley asserts, preachers must "expect the blessing while (they) speak."[48] Telling people they must wait until they die, or until a "year hence, or a week hence" only becomes a hindrance to receiving the blessing. Instead, the seeker must desire and press after it.[49] Believers need to hunger and thirst after perfection if they are to retain what they have already received, "Indeed, if they are not thirsting after this, it is scarce possible to keep what they have."[50]

---

[44] JWL 9/15/90.
[45] *Plain Account* 16:4.
[46] JWL 5/14/68.
[47] JWL 12/19/73.
[48] JWL 4/26/72.
[49] JWL 5/18/57; 1/18/61.
[50] JWL 3/29/66.

John Wesley's Theology of Christian Perfection

When it came to *how* a Christian is to attain perfection, Wesley was not short on counsel. He warns Miss Furly against the danger of looking inward too much, "You are hindered chiefly by not understanding the freeness of the gift of God. You are perpetually seeking for something in your self, to move him to love and bless you. But it is not to be found there; it is in Himself, and in the Son of his love."[51] In his later years Wesley never tired of exhorting his followers to look to Christ for full salvation:

> Has not Christ done and suffered enough for you? The purchase is made; the price is paid already; you have only to believe, and enter into rest; to take the purchased possession; all is ready; and to-day is the day of salvation! Why should you not now be all love? all devoted to Him that loves you? Is it not the language of your heart?[52]

Looking to Christ reflects the impact that Aldersgate made on Wesley, and expresses the fundamental difference between his holiness and his faith-alone gospels. Salvation by faith alone became the second axiom that profoundly shaped his two-works gospel. Wesley's mail breathes with an atmosphere of looking to Christ alone for full salvation from inward sin. The primacy of faith in receiving the gift of sanctification is seen in his use of the phrase "simple faith." While the phrase is found little in his published writings, in his letters it pops up a number of times, "Certainly simple faith is the very thing you want; that faith which lives upon Christ from moment to moment…Fear not; only believe, and enter into rest."[53] Central to Wesley's faith-alone conviction is the immediacy of the second gift, "Full salvation is nigh, even at the door. Only believe, and it is yours."[54] To press

---

[51] JWL 2/9/58.
[52] JWL 11/20/67; cf. 7/1/68; 7/13/68; 9/1/71.
[53] JWL 9/1/71; 1/19/82; 6/16/85.
[54] JWL 3/17/71.

home the availability of the gift, Wesley, at times, employs the biblical language of Christ's parousia:

> See that you hold fast the beginning of your confidence steadfast unto the end! And how soon may you be made a partaker of sanctification! And not only by a slow and insensible growth in grace, but by the power of the Highest overshadowing you, in a moment, in the twinkling of an eye, so as utterly to abolish sin, and to renew you in his whole image![55]

Besides seeking the divine blessing by faith alone, Wesley's Gospel of Two Works incorporated the methodology of his holiness gospel. It was here that the means of grace took on a critical role.

We turn once again to his correspondence with Miss Furly. Wesley counsels her that the way to increase one's sense of God's love is to (1) not commit sin (2) not omit any duty (3) not give place to any inward sin (4) remain constant in prayer and (5) not give way to spiritual sloth.[56] In an earlier letter he reminds her that by remaining faithful to "all works of piety and mercy" she is "waiting on God in the old scriptural way."[57] While instantaneous change comes in response to faith; only through the constant practice of works of piety and mercy, as the means of grace, can the believer develop Christ-like character: "All who expect to be sanctified at all, expect to be sanctified by faith. But, meantime, they know, that faith will not be given but to them that obey."[58]

One of the principal ways Wesley encouraged his people toward perfection was by applying the methodology of the Bands within his correspondence. The Bands were small groups that met

---

[55] JWL 9/24/85; See also JWL 9/1/71; Paul's language in Php 4:5 "The Lord is at hand" (JWL J #732; #803).
[56] JWL 5/18/57.
[57] JWL 12/22/56.
[58] JWL 8/19/59.

John Wesley's Theology of Christian Perfection

for the sole purpose of instilling inward holiness in the participants. D. Michael Henderson informs us that the Bands were the original mode of Methodism from which the other aspects of the societies sprang.[59] Their methodology was very specific. The group gathered at an appointed time and opened with prayer and song. Each member took turns sharing how their past week went by answering a series of questions related to present assurance, temptations and sins encountered, whether victory was found, and whether the person was transparent and open for advice.[60] So effective was this method for spiritual development that Wesley uses it often in his correspondence:

> Perhaps the best way to examine your own growth is, first, to consider whether your faith remains unshaken. Do you continually see Him that is invisible? Have you as clear an evidence of the spiritual as of the invisible world? Are you always conscious of the presence of God, and of his love to your soul? In what sense do you pray without ceasing? Are you never in a hurry, so as to dim the eye of your soul, or make you inattentive to the voice of God? Next, consider your hope. Do you thereby taste of the powers of the world to come? Do you sit in heavenly places with Christ Jesus? Do you never shrink at death? Do you steadily desire to depart, and to be with Christ? Do you always feel that this is far better? Can you in pain and trouble rejoice in hope of the glory of God?[61]

To Sarah Ryan Wesley inquires:

> Do you find no interruption or abatement at any time of your joy in the Lord? Do you continually see God; and that without any cloud, or darkness, or mist between? Do you pray without ceasing, without ever being diverted

---

[59] *John Wesley's Class Meeting*, 112.
[60] Works B 9:77-78.
[61] JWL 6/30/73.

from it by anything inward or outward? Are you never hindered by any person or thing? by the power or subtlety of Satan or by the weakness or disorders of the body pressing down the soul? Can you be thankful for everything without exception? And do you feel all working together for good? Do you do nothing, great or small, merely to please yourself? Do you feel no touch of any desire or affection but what springs from the pure love of God? Do you speak no words but from a principle of love, and under the guidance of his Spirit? O how I long to find you unblamable in all things, and holy as He that hath called you is holy![62]

The above inquiries reveal much how Wesley understood Christian perfection. One of the principal scripture texts he often appeals to formulate his inquiries is 1 Thessalonians 5:16-18. As Paul exhorted the Thessalonians to "rejoice evermore; pray without ceasing; in every thing give thanks," so Wesley believed the essence of perfect love to revolve around these three qualities.[63] In the end, Wesley envisioned Christian perfection to be a deeper transformation of the dispositional nature, resulting in full and consistent communion and identity (union) with God.[64]

Before we move on, one final means of attaining perfection requires our attention. Wesley encouraged his people to view all things as a means to grow in God's perfect love, and this includes physical suffering. It is common knowledge that Wesley wrote a popular manual on medicine, for which he received criticism for

---

[62] JWL 11/22/57; cf. JWL 12/14/57; 1/28/58; 2/20/58; 3/18/60; 5/30/65; 4/12/70; 11/3/89.

[63] *Plain Account* 26:7; JWL 4/5/58; 6/25/71.

[64] "The essence of Christian perfection is this: God can so transform your dispositional nature that his love, even his perfect love, can become the natural and habitual characteristic of your life. Added to this, God can do this work of grace in this life, which is so characterized by ignorance, mistake, temptation, and trial – all the human frailties that are inescapable in this life" (*Plain Account*, 15).

many of his remedies.[65] His use of electricity to treat various ailments is widely known.[66]

We saw above that many of his converts faced health issues that tend to produce a variety of doubts over their spiritual attainments. Wesley pressed his followers to see their sufferings as God's appointed path toward full salvation. John Banks informs us of Ann Bolton's problems with sleep insomnia, fits of weeping, severe headaches, dental neuralgia, and even contemplations of death.[67] Wesley's fatherly advice bears quoting in full:

> I wanted much to know how your soul prospered. I could not doubt but the god of this world, the enemy of all righteousness, would use every means to move you from your steadfastness. Blessed be God, you are not moved! That all his labour has been in vain! Hitherto hath God helped you; and, fear not, he will help you to the end. He gives you health as a token for good: He can trust you with it, while you give him your heart. And O stand fast in the glorious liberty wherewith he has made you free! You are not called to desire suffering. Innocent nature is averse from pain; only, as soon as his will appears, yours is to sink down before it. Hark! What does he say to you now? "Lovest thou me more than these?"[68]

---

[65] Banks, 55.

[66] "On Tuesday July 30th 1771 Ann (Bolton) wanted to go to Marston to see JW about her eyes, but her brother would not take her. She wrote the next day to Miss Eden asking her to obtain JW's opinion on electricity for her eyes. Among Ann's papers, also, was a letter of 1784 from a G. Clark which shows that other people believed what JW believed. 'It is a pain to my mind to write to you at this time, and on this occasion, as I cannot give you that consolation I could wish in regard to your Brother. I have had many come to me from the Faculty when they could do them no more service in that desperate disorder. Yet I know of two that got benefit from electricity. To both of these I gave small shocks once a day, from the corners of each eye to the back of the head in a direction from each eye, and then from the corner of each eye through the ball'" (Banks, 57).

[67] Banks, 58-59.

[68] JWL 5/2/71; cf. 6/15/71.

Spiritual Father

Wesley believed that God wisely chooses the right path for each of his children. The believer must learn to submit and to patiently trust in their heavenly Father to lead them to a rest that is "perfect and entire, wanting nothing."[69] As Wesley reminds Miss Furly, "There is a wonderful mystery in the manner and circumstances of that mighty working, whereby he subdues all things to himself, and leaves nothing in the heart but his pure love alone." He then points to God's purpose, "Meantime, he designs, by this weakness of body, to keep your soul low, as a weaned child."[70] The path to perfection is not always easy, nor does it come immediately for every child of God. Often, only in the fires of deep personal trial does one learn to surrender their all and to fix the eyes of the heart on Christ alone.[71]

The Fruits of Perfect Love

In 1733 Wesley penned his most enduring definition of perfection as that "habitual disposition of soul which in the Sacred Writings is termed 'holiness', and which directly implies the being cleansed from sin, 'from all filthiness both of flesh and spirit', and by consequence the being endued with those virtues which were also in Christ Jesus, the being so 'renewed in the image of our mind' as to be 'perfect, as our Father in heaven is perfect.'"[72] His later correspondence reveals that his views had not materially changed. The primary fruit of pure love continued to

---

[69] James 1:4.
[70] JWL 3/6/59.
[71] To Miss March JW shared this important qualifier, "You seem to think pain, yea, much pain, must go before an entire cure. In S. R— it did, and in a very few others. But it need not: Pain is no more salutary than pleasure. Saving grace is essentially such; saving pain but accidentally. When God saves us by pain rather than pleasure, I can resolve it only into his justice, or sovereign will. To use the grace we have, and now to expect all we want, is the grand secret." (JWL 10/13/65).
[72] *The Circumcision of the Heart* I.1.

be salvation from unholy tempers,[73] yet he concedes "whether there be any soul clothed with flesh and blood which enjoys every right temper."[74] This concession is due to Wesley's mature understanding of involuntary sin, "Undoubtedly, as long as you are in the body," he told Mrs. Marston, "you will come short of what you would be; and you will see more and more of your numberless defects, and the imperfections of your best actions and tempers."[75] Wesley continued to maintain that all believers, even the most perfect, need the advocacy of Christ for daily forgiveness.[76]

In a similar manner, Wesley repeatedly declares that scripture perfection conveys freedom from pride, anger and evil desire.[77] This is the essence of deadness to the world[78] and freedom from inbred sin.[79] On the positive, perfect love casts out fear,[80] imbues the believer with the dispositional nature (mind) of Christ,[81] and empowers the Christian to love God with the whole heart.[82] One of Wesley's favorite qualifiers for full salvation is "humble, gentle, patient love of God."[83] This terminology, found so often in his letters, corresponds to the trinity of sinful tempers that comprise inbred sin: pride, anger and evil desire.[84]

---

[73] JWL 4/5/58; 9/15/62; 10/13/62; 10/5/70.
[74] JWL 7/6/70.
[75] JWL 8/11/70.
[76] JWL 5/8/58; 12/26/61; cf. JWL 10/5/70; PA 19:23-25.
[77] JWL 9/25/57; 2/21/59; 7/22/66. JW once told Samuel Furly that to be cleansed from all sin meant liberty from "all pride, anger, evil desire, idolatry, and unbelief" (JWL 9/15/62).
[78] JWL 7/10/64.
[79] JWL 3/15/70.
[80] JWL 7/1/57.
[81] JWL 2/21/59; 11/22/69.
[82] JWL 5/12/63; 12/28/70.
[83] JWL 1/27/67; for the development and use of this terminology in part or in full, see JWL 6/14/57; 1/5/72; 10/5/72; 10/23/72; 7/18/73; 6/17/74; 11/30/74; 4/12/82. See the PA 25:130.
[84] This author first noticed the connection between humble, gentle and patient with pride, anger and self-will when writing the annotated edition of the Plain Account.

Regarding other blessings to becoming an "altogether Christian,"[85] probably the most significant is being fit and ready to enter eternity. Wesley reminds Elizabeth Hardy, "Till you are saved from unholy tempers, you are not ripe for glory."[86] In chapter one, we learned this was the primary goal of his holiness gospel. But this theme was not lost to the elderly Wesley, "It is well if the great change be wrought in a soul even a little before it leaves the body," for then the saying becomes true that "precious in the sight of the Lord is the death of his saints!"[87] Perfection prepares one for glory since it casts out sin and renews one in God's image.[88] Hence, full salvation is the one thing needful,[89] the essence of authentic religion;[90] and, as Wesley saw it, the central purpose of his ministry.[91] No wonder he continued to exhort his preachers to press their people to seek after this blessed experience.[92]

Wilderness State II

We have seen that believers usually pass through a season of testing and struggle following the first work of grace; but what about the second blessing? From the exalted language Wesley employed to describe the experience, one could reason that to be sanctified entirely would end all inner struggles. Wesley, how-

---

[85] This is another synonym of perfection in JW's letters: JWL 5/11/64; 3/29/66.
[86] JWL 4/5/58.
[87] JWL 8/31/71.
[88] JWL 1/8/74; 9/9/69.
[89] JWL 9/24/85.
[90] "'What then is religion?' It is happiness in God, or in the knowledge and love of God. It is 'faith working by love;' producing 'righteousness, and peace, and joy in the Holy Ghost.' In other words, it is a heart and life devoted to God" (JWL 5/2/86).
[91] JW told Mr. Walker, "I have one point in view, to promote, so far as I am able, vital, practical religion; and by the grace of God to beget, preserve, and increase the life of God in the souls of men" (*Second Letter to the Rev. Mr. Walker,* Works J 13:197).
[92] JWL 2/25/74; 1/19/82; 3/7/83.

ever, saw it differently, "There is very frequently a kind of wilderness state, not only after justification, but even after deliverance from sin."[93] What were these struggles? How did Wesley counsel these believers?

To begin, fully sanctified believers appear to wrestle with what Wesley calls "evil reasoning." He refers to this as a "second darkness"—a wilderness state that compares to the one following justification and new birth. Again, we turn to his correspondence with Miss March to probe his thoughts. So serious was evil reasoning that at the height of the perfection revival in the early sixties, Wesley believed it alone was the cause for seventy-five percent of professors losing the blessing.[94] This malady appears primarily to be the tendency to see perfection as something more than what the believer experienced, causing needless doubts to cloud the mind.[95] Such reasoning distorts the "simplicity" of perfection as a "free gift" received by "simple faith."[96] This "bad disease" undermines the "first principles" that "according to the plain Bible account" perfection is nothing more than "pure love reigning in the heart and life."[97] What is the remedy? Obvious to Wesley is the need to rightly divide the testimony of the Bible. But no less important is that "there cannot be a lasting, steady, enjoyment of pure love, without the direct testimony of the Spirit."[98]

Other struggles surface in Wesley's letters. Some professors of perfect love ran into problems undervaluing God's grace while overvaluing the approval of friends and loved ones.[99] Others suffered from bouts of "heaviness" (discouragement) whereby one did not feel God was very near, or that one's love for God was

---

[93] JWL 10/13/64.
[94] JWL 10/13/64; 7/24/69.
[95] JWL 6/24/64; 6/3/74.
[96] JWL 6/13/70.
[97] JWL 6/27/70.
[98] JWL 6/3/74.
[99] JWL 3/14/68.

that "warm."[100] Wesley acknowledges that many "wanderings" and "deficiencies" are consistent with full salvation. Believers wrestle with what to call the experience and often struggle with feelings of unworthiness.[101] This shows the tendency for many early Methodists to focus inwardly too much.

In response, Wesley encouraged his followers to keep their eyes set on Christ and to maintain a simple faith in him. This requires guarding oneself against the temptation to reason too much over feelings that will only darken the soul.[102] Again, one of Wesley's methods is to ask a series of probing questions:

> Do you hold fast what God has given you? Do you give Him all your heart? And do you find the witness of this abiding with you? One who is now in the house with me has not lost that witness one moment for these ten years. Why should you lose it any more? Are not the gifts of God without repentance? Is He not willing to give always what he gives once? Lay hold, lay hold on all the promises.[103]

Wesley was persistent to remind everyone that sinful tempers can take root again, so the Christian must remain alert to the tactics of the enemy.[104] Moreover, he believed the sanctified believer must continue to deal with involuntary sin. This admission meant prac-

---

[100] JWL 8/23/63.
[101] JWL 7/25/67; 5/30/69.
[102] JWL 7/27/70.
[103] JWL 4/12/70.
[104] "They are all love; yet they cannot walk as they desire. 'But are they all love while they grieve the Holy Spirit?' No, surely; they are then fallen from their steadfastness; and this they may do even after they are sealed. So that, even to such, strong cautions are needful. After the heart is cleansed from pride, anger, and desire, it may suffer them to re-enter: Therefore I have long thought some expressions in the Hymns are abundantly too strong; as I cannot perceive any state mentioned in Scripture from which we may not (in a measure, at least) fall." (JWL 12/26/61).

tically that no believer could always practice right tempers.[105] As long as we are in this body, we are prone to mistakes, human weakness, and "ten thousand wandering thoughts, and forgetful intervals, without any breach of love, though not without transgressing the Adamic law."[106] Of course, this means that even the most perfect are dependent on Christ for inward holiness. Quoting from his *Plain Account* Wesley clarifies to Joseph Benson:

> "None feel their need of Christ like these; none so entirely depend upon him. For Christ does not give light to the soul separate from, but in and with, himself. Hence his words are equally true of all men, in whatever state of grace they are: 'As the branch cannot bear fruit of itself, except it abide in the vine; no more can ye, except ye abide in me: Without' (or separate from) 'me, ye can do nothing.' For our perfection is not like that of a tree, which flourishes by the sap derived from its own root; but like that of a branch, which, united to the vine, bears fruit; but severed from it, is 'dried up and withered.'"[107]

In addition to reminding professors of the continuing reality of involuntary sin and their need for Christ, Wesley pressed home there are "innumerable degrees" of perfection, so the believer should not expect too much of oneself. Bottom line, full salvation entails having "one desire" and "one design" governing the heart and life.[108] Wesley felt the need to keep before seekers, and those who believe they had attained, a clear idea what perfection is and is not. "Always remember," Miss March was told, "the essence of Christian holiness is simplicity and purity; one design, one desire; entire devotion to God."[109] Once again, the single intention serves as the bottom line for the second work of grace.

---

[105] JWL 7/6/70.
[106] JWL 6/16/72; also 6/7/61; 7/25/67.
[107] JWL 10/5/70; Works J 12:413.
[108] JWL 3/14/68.
[109] JWL 4/14/71.

Spiritual Father

Retaining the Experience

What might surprise many who are less familiar with Wesley's ministry was his admission that most who attain the blessing usually lose it at a later point. In the aftermath of the perfection revival Wesley spoke of over four hundred in London who professed the experience, only to surmise that nearly half lost it later.[110] Five years later he acknowledged "although many taste of that heavenly gift, deliverance from inbred sin, yet so few, so exceeding few, retain it one year later; hardly one in ten; nay one in thirty."[111] He then reminisced how hundreds in London had been partakers of the blessing over a period of sixteen to eighteen months, only now to confess doubt whether twenty still retained it. This had led many to question whether perfection could be enjoyed for longer periods of time.

Two things became certain for Wesley. First, there is no state from which anyone cannot fall.[112] Second, such a consequence is avoidable.[113] Professors who believed they had lost the gift were encouraged to seek the blessing again.[114] Therefore, attaining and losing the blessing is what many Methodists faced as they sought after the blessing.

Of uppermost importance, according to Wesley, is the witness of the Holy Spirit. For only the witness can confirm one's attainment of full salvation. He cautions believers to not look to the experiences of other seekers; nor to rely solely on the feeling that all sin is gone.[115] Instead, believers are exhorted to seek the direct and immediate witness of the Holy Spirit. Only an "abiding witness" of the Spirit can secure the gift from being lost little by little.[116] An especially strong testimony is when the direct witness

---

[110] JWL 10/13/65.
[111] JWL 3/15/70.
[112] JWL 9/29/64.
[113] JWL 5/8/70.
[114] JWL 6/25/68; 5/30/69; 6/10/81; 4/29/89.
[115] JWL 10/12/64.
[116] JWL 8/23/63.

is combined with the fruit (indirect witness) of the Spirit, "for there can be no stronger proof that we are of God."[117] Since the witness can be intermittent, believers must ask their heavenly Father to give them an *abiding* witness that the work is complete.[118] For one of the great truths is that there "cannot be a lasting steady, enjoyment of pure love, without the direct testimony of the Spirit."[119]

Wesley was careful to distinguish between an assurance of sanctification and an assurance of final perseverance. The former is essential for perfect love, but not the latter.[120] In fact, a "plerophory (or full assurance) of hope" is at times given to one not yet perfected in love, as in the case of William Grimshaw.[121] But the elderly Wesley conceded that the assurance of hope generally attends only those who enjoy the gift of pure love.[122]

A corollary of the Spirit's testimony is the due diligence required of those believing they have tasted the heavenly gift. The sanctified Christian needs to learn to discern between pride and a temptation to pride.[123] Implied here is the acknowledgment that it can be very difficult to read the state of one's own heart. The root cause is spiritual conflict. Satan uses human weakness due to humanity's fallen condition to cloud the mind in its judgments and emotions.[124] The result is evil reasoning—those rationalizations and emotional impressions that confuse many concerning the nature of perfect love. The perfect Christian needs to keep growing in wisdom and attain greater heights of inward holiness.[125]

---

[117] JWL 3/31/87.
[118] JWL 1/30/62; JWL J #733 (no date).
[119] JWL 6/3/74.
[120] JWL 10/6/78.
[121] Ibid.
[122] JWL 4/10/81; cf. 1/19/73.
[123] JWL 11/7/71.
[124] JWL 9/27/77.
[125] Though the perfect Christian was pure in their devotion and love, JW's doctrine of involuntary sin meant they still committed culpable mistakes due to human ignorance and weakness. Hence, growth in wisdom was essential so

Spiritual Father

Degrees of Growth

We have already noted that innumerable degrees comprise the sanctified state. The idea of degrees becomes obvious in light of the wilderness state that often follows moment of perfecting grace and from the sober reality that so many fail to retain the experience for any length of time. When we add Wesley's doctrine of sin, which openly affirms the continuing reality of involuntary sin, it becomes evident there must be degrees within the perfection state. This is in keeping with Wesley's two-works gospel.

As we saw in chapter three, in 1740 this gospel viewed the faith journey as a lifelong process punctuated by two divine moments—new birth and full salvation. By the mid-forties Wesley's soteriology began to imply a third moment: full assurance.[126] Over time, as his gospel system continued to evolve, a fourth God-moment began to emerge: the *faith of a servant* (justification). As a result Wesley's *ordo salutis* began to look more like a progressive journey punctuated by two greater God-moments (new birth[127] and perfection), along with two somewhat lesser moments, experientially speaking (justification and full assurance). Wesley labeled each moment with its own title: servant, child, adolescent, and father.[128] In this way, he came to understand and articulate his own version of the faith journey. More important, what this inherent structure implies is that growth continues following the threshold of perfect love.

---

as to not commit these mistakes as before. This became the primary need in the life of the sanctified.

[126] I say "implied" because JW never formally made receiving full assurance into a third divine moment in the faith journey process. Yet, his doctrine of the Spirit's witness meant it was received in an instant, just as the new birth and perfection, thus implying a third divine moment in his *ordo salutis*.

[127] By the late sixties the servant state was identified with justification and the new birth with the witness of the Spirit.

[128] In the next chapter this pattern will develop even more as JW develops further stages in his *ordo salutis*. See JW's homilies on the Sermon on the Mount for his delineation of the faith journey in the 1740's.

John Wesley's Theology of Christian Perfection

Wesley repeatedly confirmed that one design and desire is the lowest level of spiritual adulthood.[129] This is what he called the "essence of Christian holiness...entire devotion to God."[130] From this foundation he built his understanding of degrees in the life of the sanctified, which, for the most part, remained vague and undefined, especially in his published sermons and writings. But in his letters we can identify several aspects of this maturational process.

In early 1781 Wesley began corresponding with Ann Loxdale, the later wife of Thomas Coke. Ann was suffering from an illness which Wesley felt was providentially granted for her spiritual development. As she shares her experience with Wesley, he reminds her of the possibility to have her heart and mind "continually stayed upon God."[131] Wesley believed Ann had tasted such devotion in the past, but due to a variety of reasons she had lost the blessing and needed to receive it again. A month later he praises her progress in recovering a "measure" of what she once enjoyed. He was now confident she would attain all she had lost.

Still suffering from her "sickness," Wesley advised humble resignation patterned after Christ. By August he was counseling her to "hold fast," since he believed she once again "tasted of the pure love of God.[132]" In the months ahead he admonishes her to rely not upon the judgments of others in evaluating her spiritual state; but, instead, to trust in the light which the Spirit gives. She also faced continuing trials, which Wesley felt were God's means of calling her to deeper levels of resignation and surrender. "You know," Wesley wrote, "our blessed Lord himself, as man, 'learned obedience by the things that he suffered.'"[133] It appears from the meager correspondence that remains, Ann passed through her own wilderness state through the first half of 1782. Wesley's loving support and counsel kept pointing her to Christ's

---

[129] JWL 9/15/62; 3/14/68.
[130] JWL 4/14/71.
[131] JWL 6/10/81.
[132] JWL 8/15/81.
[133] 12/15/81; Hebrews 5:8.

prayer in the garden— "Not as I will, but as thou wilt" —and he advised her to meditate on 1 Corinthians 13, the love chapter. He then encourages her to read his *Plain Account*, which, he assures her, describes the highest religion possible this side of heaven.[134] Most important, Ann needed to grow in resignation, and in that love which is humble, gentle and patient.[135]

While Ann would once again lapse from the mountaintop of pure love,[136] her correspondence with Wesley reveals just how difficult it was to retain the gift; and further, to continue growing in the experience. When she did regain a profession in the summer of 1781 Wesley refers to her as a "babe" in the state.[137] This offers another insight into how Wesley understood the faith journey following perfect love. Just as newborn believers in Christ need to become established through the witness of the Spirit, newborn Christians in the sanctified state need the same confirming work. Only the abiding witness of the Spirit can finally remove all the doubts that plague the newly sanctified.[138] Part of this process is for professors to learn to accept the limitations of their fallen humanity and not become overly critical of themselves due to such weaknesses. As full salvation from sin was understood to be primarily a deeper transformation of the dispositional nature, Wesley saw further growth entailing the cultivation of right tempers: "There is so close a connexion between right judgment and right tempers, as well as right practice that the latter cannot easily subsist without the former."[139]

This meant the believer must discern between sin and temptation. As Wesley once told one believer, "What you feel is cer-

---

[134] JWL 6/10/81; 4/12/82.
[135] JWL 4/12/82.
[136] JWL 10/8/85.
[137] "I do not see any reason to doubt, but that you have tasted of the pure love of God. But you seem to be only a babe in that state, and have, therefore, need to go forward continually" (JWL 8/15/81). This shows how fluid JW's language could be, since he almost always used the term "babe" to describe the new birth.
[138] JWL 8/23/63.
[139] JWL 7/6/70.

tainly a degree of anger, but not of sinful anger."[140] The fully sanctified Christian needs to discern not just between temptation and sin, which is difficult enough, but between voluntary and involuntary sin.[141] Such theological hair-splitting was a lot to expect from the average Methodist who had no formal theological training. For while Wesley could tell Elizabeth Hardy that he knew many who loved God with all their heart, he also acknowledged these same believers do not always think, speak or act right.[142] This created a gap between profession and experience that for many was impossible to bridge. But for those under Wesley's fatherly care this meant pressing forward toward greater spiritual maturity in how one thinks, speaks and acts as sanctified believers.[143]

Wesley saw that believers need to grow in other areas, like communion with God and the nurturing of their faith.[144] Fully sanctified believers still need to rely on Christ's heavenly intercession for their involuntary sin, and for God to breathe perpetual holiness within the heart.[145] While "lower degrees" of perfection include the power to always cleave to God,[146] higher degrees involve the gradual ripening of love, in which communion with the triune God never ceases. In the end, what Wesley desired most for his people was nothing less than complete union with God, where the "plenitude of the presence of the ever-blessed Trinity" is enjoyed in ceaseless praise.[147]

---

[140] JWL 5/31/71.
[141] JWL 12/26/61.
[142] Ibid.
[143] JWL 9/15/62.
[144] JWL 6/25/71; 7/1/72.
[145] JWL 10/5/70; 9/1/74.
[146] JWL 9/15/62.
[147] The full quote is, "Tell me, my dear Hetty, do you experience something similar to what Mr. De Renty expresses in those strong words: 'I bear about with me an experimental verity, and a plenitude of the presence of the ever-blessed Trinity?' Do you commune with God in the night season? Does He bid you even in sleep, Go on? And does He "make your very dreams devout?" (JWL 6/2/76; cf. JWL 6/16/77; 12/17/87).

Spiritual Father

The Axioms of Holiness

We round off this chapter by returning to the axioms that grounded Wesley's two-works gospel. In 1771 he rehearsed how he developed his core convictions with the Countess of Huntingdon. In the 1720's, Wesley "saw that 'without holiness no man shall see the Lord.'"[148] He thereafter began "following after it." A decade later he saw by divine grace "how to attain" this holiness; namely, by "faith in the Son of God." This then became his message: "We are saved from sin, we are made holy, by faith."[149] As we chronicled in earlier chapters, the belief that salvation demands inward holiness and is attained by faith alone became more than a message, these convictions formed the DNA of his character and spiritual temperament.

These maxims could be stated in other ways. To the young Philothea Briggs, Wesley retorts, "None are or can be saved but those who are by faith made inwardly and outwardly holy."[150] So important were faith and holiness to Wesley that along with original sin, these three truths serve as the grand doctrines of Holy Scripture.[151]

Wesley's correspondence reveals just how deep he believed in these maxims. In the early seventies, when the Calvinists were enraged over the 1770 Conference Minutes, Wesley remained adamant that we are justified by faith, not works; but that our works do serve as a condition for our second justification at the final judgment. Yet even here it is only by faith in the "righteousness and blood of Christ that we are enabled to do all good works."[152] So while the Calvinists celebrated salvation by faith alone, Wesley could not embrace their particular message. Holiness ran too deep in his psyche to agree with Calvinism on this point, "It is far better for our people not to hear Mr. Hawksworth.

---

[148] Hebrews 12:14.
[149] JWL 6/19/71.
[150] JWL 8/31/72.
[151] JWL 4/6/61.
[152] JWL 3/1/74.

Calvinism will do them no good."[153] So strong did John feel about these matters that he told his brother Charles:

> If we duly join faith and works in all our preaching, we shall not fail of a blessing. But of all preaching, what is usually called Gospel preaching is the most useless, if not the most mischievous: A dull, yea, or lively, harangue on the sufferings of Christ, or salvation by faith, without strongly inculcating holiness. I see, more and more, that this naturally tends to drive holiness out of the world.[154]

As Wesley battled the Calvinists throughout the 1770's over the relationship between faith and works with salvation, the maxim of holiness continued to grow in strength within his own thought. As he entered into the last decade of his life these changes began to appear more in his sermons than in his letters. The motif of universal salvation rooted in his servant theology, along with the theme of universal holiness, moved Wesley's Gospel of Two Works into new contours. How this evolution took shape is the subject of the next chapter. But before we move on we would be amiss to ignore one of the most significant letters in the entire Wesley corpus on the subject of Christian perfection.

In the aftermath of the perfection revival in the early sixties, we saw that John and Charles drifted apart over the nature of perfection, along with how and when full salvation is realized. John's letters to his brother during this period reflect just how deep holiness was stamped on his character. One can feel the anguish as he asks his brother whether the Methodists should give up full salvation in their preaching.[155] Yet, only six months earlier Wesley penned one of his most precise statements on Christian perfection. When the letter was written also appears to have played a role in settling his mind on the subject following the per-

---

[153] Ibid.
[154] JWL 11/4/72.
[155] JWL 6/14/68.

fection revival and schism.[156] The letter remains in two forms with only minor differences.[157] That this letter proved significant is confirmed by the fact Wesley later edited and published it in the Arminian magazine with only slight variations (which makes a third edition). Here is that latter version:

> Some thoughts occurred to my mind this morning concerning Christian perfection, and the manner and time of receiving it, which I believe may be useful to set down.
>
> 1. By perfection I mean the humble, gentle, patient love of God, and our neighbour, ruling our tempers, words, and actions.
> I do not include an impossibility of falling from it, either in part or in whole. Therefore, I retract several expressions in our Hymns, which partly express, partly imply, such an impossibility. And I do not contend for the term sinless, though I do not object against it.
>
> 2. As to the manner. I believe this perfection is always wrought in the soul by a simple act of faith; consequently, in an instant.
> But I believe a gradual work, both preceding and following that instant.

---

[156] See the introduction to volume one of this series, *John Wesley's 'A Plain Account of Christian Perfection' – The Annotated Edition*.

[157] Telford placed one letter in 1762 and the other in 1767. Through personal correspondence with Randy Maddox, he ponders that possibly one is a copy of the other, since the Wesleys often made copies of their letters for themselves. They also would copy letters to send them on to other people. After a careful side by side comparison of both letters this author is convinced that the one placed by Telford in 1762 was a draft (first?) and the second (?) was the one sent to Charles. The general reason for this conclusion stems from the fact that the majority of differences deal with punctuation and sentence structure. In this author's opinion this rules out the idea of one letter being a copy of the other.

3. As to the time. I believe this instant generally is the instant of death, the moment before the soul leaves the body. But I believe it may be ten, twenty, or forty years before.

I believe it is usually many years after justification; but that it may be within five years or five months after it, I known no conclusive argument to the contrary.

If it must be many years after justification, I would be glad to know how many. Pretium quotus arroget annus?[158]

And how many days or months, or even years, can any one allow to be between perfection and death? How far from justification must it be; and how near to death?[159]

---

[158] "This quotation from Horace is thus translated by Boscawen:— 'How many years give sanction to our lines?'" (Thomas Jackson, Works J 11:446)
[159] Works J 11:446.

SEVEN
The Gospel of Universal Holiness

We now pick up where chapter four ended. To retrace our steps, by the mid-sixties Wesley's two-works gospel had attained maturity; meaning, his *ordo salutis* between the new birth and physical death was fully delineated and did not materially change thereafter.[1] Three convictions define this gospel: the twin instantaneous moments of new birth and perfection, the faith journey patterned after the natural life-development process (childhood, adolescence, adulthood), and the formalization of two basic categories in his doctrine of sin (voluntary and involuntary). Yet, while the contours of the faith journey between new birth/adoption[2] and physical death were set in place, the spiritual crisis Wesley faced did lead to a broadening of his *ordo salutis* in other areas, thereby generating further evolution in his theology of perfection.

First, and foremost, this broadening led Wesley to reevaluate the point in time when justification is received. The result was for

---

[1] See JW's apologetic sermon for the revival and Methodism, *On God's Vineyard* (1787), for a later summarization of his GosTW: (1) Justification is simultaneous to new birth. (2) New birth is the gate to sanctification. (3) New birth and sanctification involve inward transformation in the dispositional nature (tempers). (4) Faith journey involves both instant and process. (5) Equal stress on justification and sanctification. JW's linking of justification with the new birth does not negate his distinction between servant and child. JW understood that for the majority of Englishman justification would be received at the same time as the new birth. The servant state made room for believers, like JW in the mid-60's, who lacked the witness of the Spirit (new birth) yet knew they had peace with God.

[2] JW identified adoption with the new birth (#106 *On Faith* I.10-12). To lack the direct witness of adoption (Spirit) normally meant one was not a child (born again), but only a servant (justified). See ch 4 for a full discussion of this distinction. Cf. Scott Kisker *Justified But Unregenerate? The Relationship of Assurance to Justification and Regeneration in the Thought of John Wesley.* WTJ 28:44-58.

John Wesley's Theology of Christian Perfection

justification to be formally separated from the new birth (and adoption) in point of time. This opened the door for Wesley to develop his *ordo salutis* in the pre-Christian states of prevenient grace; and to clarify, at least for himself, the relationship between his 1725 awakening and his 1738 evangelical conversion. In a nutshell, by the mid-seventies Wesley concluded, concerning his own faith journey, that he was justified as a *servant* in 1725, but born again as a *child* in 1738. Thus, from this time on he gave greater attention to those stages that are pre-new birth and pre-Christian.[3]

A parallel trend was a reemphasis on the role that good works play in salvation itself (as works of mercy and piety). The 1770 Conference Minutes infuriated the Calvinists resulting in a heated pamphlet war between the two camps.[4] What we see happening in the seventies and eighties is Wesley returning to his Gospel of Holiness principles and integrating them more thoroughly into his two-works gospel system.[5] Accordingly, as we will soon see, a

---

[3] In this chapter "pre-Christian" is used to identify non-Christian religious faiths. For JW this group primarily included heathen, Moslem, Jew, and John the Baptist's pre-Christian movement (in the time of Christ). "Pre-Christian" was chosen over "non-Christian" because it reflects better JW's robust doctrine of prevenient grace in the 1770's and 80's. See JW's sermon *On Faith* (#106) in which differing levels of pre-Christian faith are listed (including the above examples).

[4] W. Stephen Gunter writes, "Prior to 1770 Wesley was content to insist that works would necessarily flow from saving faith, but he did not attempt to work out a formal theological explanation for how works fit into the *ordo salutis*" (*Love Divine*, 261). Gunter offers a good discussion of the controversy (cf. ch 4 n 79).

[5] Many of JW's later sermons pick up themes and motifs found in his early period. Some of these are *On a Single Intention* (single intention is the foundation of vital religion); *Human Life a Dream* (early JW used the dream-life to highlight the shortness of life); *The Imperfection of Human Knowledge* (picks up the motifs in #140 *The Promise of Understanding*); *God's Approbation*; *Of Good Angels* (See JW's early angelology in ch 2); *On Redeeming the Time* (a reemphasis on his Oxford disciplines); *Constant Communion* (a publishing of his 1732 homily); *On the Wedding Garment* (holiness is the means and assurance of eternal life). This confirms that late JW developed a renewed appreciation of his Oxford period, "I often cry out, *Vitæ me redde priori!* (My former

The Gospel of Universal Holiness

stronger emphasis on holy tempers begins to emerge once again as the bottom-line standard for final salvation. And, most significant, these changes allowed for a broadening of the benefits of salvation within Wesley's soteriology to a degree not seriously considered before. Salvation now becomes available to those who have a pre-Christian faith. By the mid-seventies Wesley was well on his way to embracing a gospel of universal holiness grounded on the power of prevenient grace to produce holy tempers, resulting in acceptance before God. We begin by looking how Wesley's theology began to move in the direction of universal salvation.

Universal Salvation

One of the themes running through Wesley's later sermons is that God's saving mercy extends even to those who are pre-Christian in their faith. Hints of this can be found in earlier writings, most notably in his explanatory notes regarding Cornelius' present acceptance before God.[6] In chapter four we saw that by the late sixties Acts 10:35 became the wedge that temporally severed justification from the new birth.[7] This text became Wesley's primary argument for the servant state. At first he applied the servant state to himself and other seeking Christians who consciously lacked the witness of the Spirit (assurance of adoption as God's born again child). But by the mid-eighties this argument was expanded to openly address the status of those who have a pre-Christian faith:

---

happy life restore) Let me be again an Oxford Methodist! I am often in doubt whether it would not be best for me to resume all my Oxford rules, great and small. I did then walk closely with God, and redeem the time. But what have I been doing these thirty years?" (JWL 12/15/72). The source for this trend is found in his mid-60's spiritual crisis. For a full discussion see ch 4.
[6] NT Notes Acts 10:35; see also 1770 Minutes Q.77 (Works J 8:337).
[7] JWJ 12/1/67.

> But it may be asked: 'If there be no true love of our neighbour but that which springs from the love of God; and if the love of God flows from no other fountain than faith in the Son of God; does it not follow that the whole heathen world is excluded from all possibility of salvation? Seeing they are cut off from faith; for faith cometh by hearing. And how shall they hear without a preacher?' I answer, St. Paul's words, spoken on another occasion, are applicable to this: 'What the law speaketh, it speaketh to them that are under the law.' Accordingly that sentence, 'He that believeth not shall be damned,' is spoken of them to whom the gospel is preached. Others it does not concern; and we are not required to determine anything touching their final state. How it will please God, the Judge of all, to deal with them, we may leave to God himself. But this we know, that he is not the God of the Christians only, but the God of the heathens also; that he is 'rich in mercy to all that call upon him', 'according to the light they have'; and that 'in every nation he that feareth God and worketh righteousness is accepted of him.'[8]

Several insights into Wesley's universal-holiness gospel can be detected here. The central truth Wesley now builds his broadened soteriology on is the universal fatherhood of God; who, after all, is God of both Christian and pre-Christian alike. Since God has revealed his merciful disposition in the gospel of his Son, Wesley concludes he will be rich in mercy to *all* who call upon him in sincerity according to the spiritual light they possess. After all, as Wesley already argued, our heavenly Father accepts everyone who in true reverence pursues a life of righteousness in order to please him (Acts 10:35). Two implications necessarily follow. First, final salvation[9] ultimately rests on the possession of holy

---

[8] *On Charity* (1784) I.3.
[9] By final salvation I mean what many Wesley scholars refer to as second justification, which takes place at the last judgment.

tempers (inward holiness), not on faith alone. Second, whereas middle Wesley held that holy tempers are attained through faith in Christ's sacrifice as the expression of God's love,[10] he now makes room for prevenient grace to produce these holy tempers. While both points are interrelated, let's begin with the first one.

Throughout Wesley's ministerial and theological career he distinguished sharply between religion of the heart and of the head. A couple examples will suffice. In the tract *The Character of the Methodist* (1742) he made the point very clear: "The distinguishing marks of a Methodist are not his opinions of any sort...all opinions which do not strike at the root of Christianity we 'think and let think'" (§1). In this tract he proceeds to describe the Methodist in terms of holy tempers ruling the heart. By the time Wesley is done with his description, even his critic is exclaiming that these "marks" are only the "common, fundamental principles of Christianity" (§17). In the mid-seventies Wesley repeated the same point, "Persons may be quite right in their opinions, and yet have no religion at all; and, on the other hand, persons may be truly religious, who hold many wrong opinions."[11] So for Wesley the chief mark of saving faith are holy tempers and good works.[12] In the 1740's only this kind of faith was considered by Wesley as properly Christian and saving. But as Wesley became more open to the idea that pre-Christians can be saved without ever personally believing in Christ, he began to sever holy tempers from a proper Christian faith. No longer would faith in Christ be necessary or essential for pre-Christians to attain holy tempers and acceptance before God.

This broadened soteriology takes center stage in the landmark sermon: *On Working Out Our Own Salvation* (1785). The pri-

---

[10] JW's favorite text to make this point was 1 Jn 4:18 "We love because he first loved us." During his middle period JW argued from this text that holy tempers can only arise from experiencing God's love in the cross of Christ. Hence, the new birth was the foundation for the faith journey of developing holy tempers.

[11] *On the Trinity* §1.

[12] See *On The Wedding Garment*.

John Wesley's Theology of Christian Perfection

mary purpose of this homily is to clarify the role of good works in salvation. But as Wesley depicts the path of preventing, convincing, justifying and sanctifying grace, the overall emphasis falls on the acquisition of holy tempers for salvation. In sharp contrast to his faith-alone and two-works gospels, these tempers now begin *before* one has a proper Christian faith.[13] No longer is faith in Christ necessary to begin inward holiness; prevenient grace is sufficient. Over the next several years as Wesley's mind was drawn to contemplate the being of God, the eternal realm, and his own preparation for eternity,[14] he came to believe more and more that since "there is one God, so there is one religion and one happiness for all men."[15] The fundamental Christian belief in one God now emerges as another core axiom informing Wesley's perfection theology.[16] When asked about the nature of this one true religion, his response was straightforward, "True religion is right tempers toward God and man."[17]

While throughout his entire ministerial career Wesley taught the primacy of inward holiness, what becomes evident during his last decade is the tendency to ground final salvation more and

---

[13] JW's exact words are, "Salvation *begins* with what is usually termed (and very properly) 'preventing grace'; including the first wish to please God, the first dawn of light concerning his will, and the first slight, transient conviction of having sinned against him. All these imply some tendency toward life, some *degree* of salvation, the beginning of a deliverance from a blind, unfeeling heart, quite insensible of God and the things of God" (II.1; emphasis mine). Let me add, JW's earlier gospels (faith alone & two works) proclaimed the beginning of holy tempers in the gift of regeneration. JW's servant theology changed this position and led the evolution to the formation of his universal holiness gospel which affirmed the gift of holy tempers in prevenient grace.

[14] Among the many late sermons on these themes, see especially *On Living without* God and On *Faith* (#132).

[15] *The Unity of the Divine Being* §1.

[16] See *On Eternity* (1789); *God's Approbation of his Works* (1782); *On Predestination* (1773); *The General Spread of the Gospel* (1783); *What is Man?* (#103; 1787); *On the Omnipresence of God* (1788); *The Unity of the Divine Being* (1789).

[17] *The Unity of the Divine Being* §16.

more on the attainment of holy tempers. Once again, this theme comes through in the sermon *The Wedding Garment*:

> Choose holiness by my grace, which is the way, the only way, to everlasting life. He cries aloud, Be holy, and be happy; happy in this world, and happy in the world to come. 'Holiness becometh his house for ever!' This is the wedding garment of all that are called to 'the marriage of the Lamb'' Clothed in this they will not be found naked: 'they have washed their robes and made them white in the blood of the Lamb.'[18]

Does this mean Wesley abandoned his prior maxim of salvation by faith alone? As believed and taught in his faith-alone gospel, we must answer in the affirmative. Yet, our response must be more nuanced in regard to his later years. For starters, Wesley did not jettison his belief in salvation by faith alone, for he certainly continued to teach and preach his two-works gospel of salvation by faith alone in Christ alone. Nevertheless, his later sermons do reflect a softening on salvation by faith alone compared to his middle period. Wesley continued to believe those under the hearing of the gospel must meet the conditions of the gospel, which is faith in Christ. On this point he never wavers. For example, in the same sermon quoted above he reminds his listeners, "By faith we are saved and made holy." And then he adds, "The imagination, that faith *supersedes* holiness, is the marrow of Antinomianism."[19] These quotations typify what we find in this period. Still, we must conclude that the weight given to inward holiness as the "only way" to eternal life is greatly heightened in the 1780's, and did diminish, in some degree, the importance that a proper Christian faith plays in salvation. When we put side by side these later sermons to those from the 1740's the differences are striking. The

---

[18] *On the Wedding Garment* (1790) §19.
[19] *The Wedding Garment* §18 (emphasis his).

differences reveal that his theology of perfection did evolve over time.

To remember, Wesley's Gospel of Holiness emphasized the progressive acquisition of inward holiness through the practice of the means of grace. At Aldersgate the pendulum swung to the opposite extreme with salvation by faith alone through Christ alone informing his message of instantaneous salvation and holiness. After Aldersgate Wesley struggled to find balance between these two gospel systems but eventually formed a soteriology grounded on two instantaneous works of grace within a continuum of progressive growth and development. As the elderly Wesley and the Methodist movement faced new challenges in the later decades of the eighteenth century, Wesley gravitated toward his earlier holiness gospel to make room for the servant state and a robust doctrine of prevenient grace.

By the 1780's Wesley's servant theology was moving him to build his *ordo salutis* on the central Christian truth of the universal fatherhood of God as Creator, Provider and Redeemer. While this new maxim did not negate his prior gospel maxims—the demand for inward holiness and salvation by faith alone—it did open the door for the benefits of eternal salvation to be given to those who had not yet tasted the gospel of Jesus Christ. In other words, what evolved in his theology was the idea that pre-Christian seekers of God can attain a degree of holy tempers without ever personally knowing Christ by faith. Their salvation still rests on faith, but a degree of faith according to their level of moral and spiritual light. Such is the power and sufficiency of prevenient grace in Wesley's Gospel of Universal Holiness!

So sure was Wesley of these principles that he told his audience at Rotherham, "Nor do I conceive that any man living has a right to sentence all the heathen and Mahometan (Moslem) world to damnation. It is far better to leave them to him that made them, and who is 'the Father of the spirits of all flesh'; who is the God

The Gospel of Universal Holiness

of the heathens as well as the Christians, and who hateth nothing that he hath made."[20] He then proceeds to explain himself further:

> I believe the merciful God regards the lives and tempers of men more than their ideas. I believe he respects the goodness of the heart rather than the clearness of the head; and that if the heart of a man be filled (by the grace of God, and the power of his Spirit) with the humble, gentle, patient love of God and man, God will not cast him into everlasting fire prepared for the devil and his angels because his ideas are not clear, or because his conceptions are confused.[21]

While Wesley had specifically in mind such Christian doctrines as original sin, justification by faith and Christ's atonement when he wrote the above paragraph, yet in principle he was also opening the door for other pre-Christian faiths to attain eternal life.

In the end *holiness alone* became what ultimately counts before God, leading to eternal life. At its foundation, the axiom of the Gospel of Universal Holiness is one God as Creator and Father of all creation, who loves and desires to save all he has created. Since there is only one God, there is in reality only one way to heaven: God graciously accepts *everyone* who gives him sincere reverence and a life of authentic holiness (Acts 10:35). The servant state is now broadened to include other pre-Christian faiths. Logically, this meant faith in Christ was no longer the sole determinative factor for final salvation. Since holiness was now available to *all* people through prevenient grace, final salvation was now opened up for them too.

What is more, this *new* gospel (using Wesley's Aldersgate terminology) also called for a broadening in Wesley's concept of faith. The Gospel of Faith Alone defined saving faith in clear terms: saving faith is the faith of regeneration, the faith of new

---

[20] *On Living without God* §14.
[21] *On Living without God* §15.

birth. Any other faith was sub-Christian, at best only an "almost" faith.[22] With the personal crisis of 1766 and the birth of the servant state within his gospel system, Wesley could no longer maintain regeneration as the bottom-line standard for saving faith. He now realized that a lower level of saving faith must be acceptable to God. This lower level of faith became explicit in the 1780's.

In April 1788 Wesley put the finishing touches on a sermon that Albert Outler calls the most "explicit statement of his vision of *universal saving grace* than anything else in the Wesley corpus."[23] The scripture text is Hebrews 11:6, "Without faith it is impossible to please him." Once again, Wesley uses a text grounded on the maxim of God's universal fatherhood. Since he already believes those in the servant state are accepted by God, it logically follows they must also possess a degree of faith that is pleasing. In this sermon Wesley describes several "sorts" of faith in an ascending order, beginning with the lowest level and rising to the evangelical threshold. These can be listed as materialist, deist, heathen, Moslem, Jew, Roman Catholic, and Protestant. After chiding the whole idea that the faith of a Catholic or Protestant will avail any better before God than that of a Moslem, heathen, or even that of a materialist—if it is merely mental assent to official church doctrine—Wesley goes on to assert that saving faith, even in its "infant state," enables one to "fear God and work righteousness" (Acts 10:35). He then adds, "Whosoever, in *every nation*, believes thus far, the Apostle (Peter) declares, is 'accepted of him.' He actually is, at that very moment, in a state of acceptance."[24]

So over time Wesley came to see the lowest denominator of saving faith is not faith in Christ, but a faith that reverences the

---

[22] See *The Almost Christian* for confirmation of this point.

[23] *On Faith* (April, 1788), Works B 3:491 (emphasis mine).

[24] *On Faith* I.10 (emphasis mine). The reader should note that the "infant state" is no longer identified with regeneration, as previously held, but now with the servant state. This is an important insight into JW's thinking at the time.

one true God and produces righteousness in one's life (Acts 10:35). This level of faith centers on the maxims of one God and the necessity of inward holiness to enter the eternal kingdom.[25] We should note what did remain consistent in Wesley's gospel system throughout the later decades: justifying faith leads to holy tempers. Only now, under the Gospel of Universal Holiness, prevenient grace is sufficient to generate these affections and justifying faith. The hope for final salvation is now available even to those whose faith is pre-Christian.

We need to underscore another aspect on faith that contributed to Wesley's new standard for salvation. In the early forties Wesley began to define faith by Hebrews 11:1, "Now faith is the substance of things hoped for, the evidence of things not seen." Over time he began to see faith as a spiritual sense (evidence or inner conviction) by which the believer sees, touches, tastes, hears, and, significantly, *feels* the realities of the invisible world, just as our physical senses put us in touch with the material world.[26] The basic premise behind this concept is the maxim of empiricism, "There is nothing in the understanding which was not first perceived by some of the senses."[27] Since knowledge comes through the senses, spiritual senses are required for God to be known. This is what faith supplies to the seeking heart:

> But the wise and gracious Governor of the worlds, both visible and invisible, has prepared a remedy for this defect. He hath appointed faith to supply the defect of sense; to take us up where sense sets us down, and help us over the great gulf. Its office begins where that of sense ends. Sense is an evidence of things that are seen; of the visible,

---

[25] This is the only reason why Acts 10:35 is not referred to as an axiom in this study. In reality, this text highlights two maxims: (1) the universal fatherhood of God, and (2) the demand of inward holiness for final salvation. According to this text a person must believe in one God who rewards those who diligently seek to please him by righteous living (Heb 11:6).

[26] *On Living Without God* §§9-11; *On Eternity* §17.

[27] *On the Discoveries of Faith* (1788) §1; Maddox, *Responsible Grace*, 27.

the material world, and the several parts of it. Faith, on the other hand, is the 'evidence of things not seen', of the invisible world; of all those invisible things which are revealed in the oracles of God.[28]

Accordingly, faith as a spiritual sense begins with prevenient grace instilling the "first wish to please God." Wesley now believes the beginning point of the faith journey is no longer the faith of a child (new birth), as at Aldersgate, or even that of a servant, but takes place even earlier at the very dawn of awareness of God and his righteousness.[29]

To summarize, the first contribution Wesley's Gospel of Universal Holiness gave to his theology of perfection is to further delineate the faith journey within the pre-Christian states. Wesley's *ordo salutis* is now becoming more complete, and the life transformation process more empowered to meet the needs of a greater number of people in the world. Wesley's theology of perfection now encompasses all people, not just those in Christian nations, but even to the far recesses of the globe. Holiness as holy tempers is now the divine plan for *all* people.

Universal Holiness

The vision of God's universal fatherhood also carried with it eschatological expectations. Captivated by the post-millennial vision of "latter-day glory" when the knowledge of the one true God will fill the whole earth,[30] Wesley believed the evangelical revival signified the dawn of a new day when God's "general call" would go out to all the heathen.[31] As in Jesus' own day,

---

[28] *On the Discoveries of Faith* §4.
[29] *On Working Out Our Salvation* II.1.
[30] *The Signs of the Times* (1787) II.1. While JW long held to a post-millennial view (cf. *Scriptural Christianity*), in his later years his vision developed more fully than what he held before.
[31] *The Signs of the Times* II.10.

The Gospel of Universal Holiness

Wesley acknowledged that many in his day did not see the signs of the Kingdom's soon arrival. Yet, he was confident that the "loving knowledge of God, producing uniform uninterrupted holiness and happiness, shall cover the earth; fill every soul of man."[32] In spite of this vision of universal renewal, Wesley saw the world as it then was. New discoveries of nations in the South Seas brought to light just how many more cultures needed the gospel. Just as the heathen outnumber Christians, so the followers of Islam number "six to five" over the followers of Christ. And in Christian lands, it seemed the majority of Orthodox and Roman Catholic's lived at a lower moral standard than many Moslems and heathen.[33] This latter point was the "grand stumbling-block" for the gospel spreading to non-Christian lands,[34] and explains, once again, why Wesley believed so strongly in his holiness principles.

To counteract this obstacle was the Methodist revival. Looking back to Luther's comments that a revival never lasts longer than a generation, Wesley confidently boasted that the present revival had already surpassed this standard by lasting more than fifty years.[35] "As God is one," declares Wesley, "so the work of God is uniform in all ages."[36] And so he looked for his Gospel of Universal Holiness to spread through divinely appointed messengers until the grand Pentecost shall come, when the Spirit will be poured out on all people: Heathen, Moslem, Jew, Native American and African alike. What Wesley envisioned was a global revival producing a global faith! The one true God will then be the universal presence filling all things, with Christ his Son reigning as King from God's holy mountain:

> At that time will be accomplished all those glorious promises made to the Christian church, which will not then be

---

[32] *The General Spread of the Gospel* (1783) §8.
[33] *The General Spread of the Gospel* §§2-7.
[34] *The General Spread of the Gospel* §§17-18.
[35] *The General Spread of the Gospel* §16.
[36] *The General Spread of the Gospel* §10.

> confined to this or that nation, but will include all the inhabitants of the earth. 'They shall not hurt nor destroy in all my holy mountain' (Is 11:9) 'Violence shall no more be heard in thy land, wasting nor destruction within thy borders; but thou shalt call thy walls, Salvation, and thy gates, Praise' (Is 60:8). Thou shalt be encompassed on every side with salvation, and all that go through thy gates shall praise God. 'The sun shall be no more thy light by day; neither for brightness shall the moon give light unto thee; but the Lord shall be unto thee an everlasting light, and thy God thy glory' (Is 60:19). The light of the sun and moon shall be swallowed up in the light of his countenance shining upon thee.[37]

This is the end for which Christ came: to destroy the works of the devil. In *The End of Christ's Coming* (1781) Wesley catalogs how sin and evil originated with Lucifer, son of the morning, abusing his liberty and through self-temptation giving birth to the sinful tempers of pride and self-will. Drawing a third of the angels into his rebellion, he then enticed Adam and Eve to support the revolt. In this way man lost the moral image of God and fell under the sentence of death. Accordingly, Satan works through pride and idolatry to promote sin in the human race.

Into this bleak situation God sent his Son. Christ came, born of a virgin—fully God and fully man—and through his death "made a full, perfect, and sufficient sacrifice, oblation, and satisfaction for the sins of the whole world" (II.6). After ascending to heaven he poured out the Holy Spirit so he might indwell believers and thereby destroy the works of the devil.

How does Christ specifically do this? In response Wesley rehearses his standard two-works gospel: Prevenient grace enables the lost sinner to believe by enlightening their spiritual eyes to

---

[37] *The General Spread of the Gospel* §26. Some other promises JW quotes in support of his post-millennial vision are Rom 11:25; Dt 30:3; Jer 32:37; Eze 36:24.

see God in Christ reconciling the world to himself (2 Cor 5:17).[38] The stages of childhood (forgiveness), adolescence (full assurance) and adulthood (perfection) are next described. Rounding off this depiction is the candid admission the "Son of God does not destroy the whole work of the devil in man, as long as he remains in this life" (III.3). Human infirmity continues as long as the soul dwells in a "corruptible body."[39] Only in death is this cancer removed. Only in the resurrection will death, the "last enemy," be vanquished forever and our renewal in God's image complete.

In this sermon Wesley views Christian perfection as the "Son of God striking at the root of that grand work of the devil." The sinful tempers of pride, self-will, love of the world, and idolatry ("seeking, or expecting to find, happiness in any creature") are finally *destroyed*. Wesley then summarizes:

> Thus it is, by manifesting himself, he (Christ) destroys the works of the devil; restoring the guilty outcast from God, to his favour, to pardon and peace; the sinner in whom dwelleth no good thing, to love and holiness; the burdened, miserable sinner, to joy unspeakable, to real, substantial happiness.[40]

Wesley believed his fully developed two-works gospel of universal holiness would be God's means by which the latter-day glory of a thousand year reign of a global Christian faith would be ushered in. This will be the time when the true church (real Christians) flourishes through the defeat of heathenism, Islam and Roman Catholicism.[41] The world will then experience "new, full, and lasting immunity from all outward and inward evils."[42] Yet,

---

[38] *The End of Christ's Coming* III.1.
[39] In this sermon JW makes a clear distinction between sin and infirmities. The latter he explicitly denies calling sin.
[40] *The End of Christ's Coming* III.2.
[41] NT Notes (1756), Rev 19:19.
[42] NT Notes, Rev. 20:2.

John Wesley's Theology of Christian Perfection

Wesley's vision of renewal did not stop there. The perfecting of the cosmos entails much more: the full redemption of a new creation.

Universal Restoration

Throughout his life and career the meta-narrative of Wesley's gospel is humanity's full restoration and renewal in the image and likeness of God. In other words—what Adam lost, Christ regains; what the serpent stole, Christ restores. Yet, the elderly Wesley came to see Christ restoring much more than what Adam lost. This bold vision of a new creation finds its most cogent exposition in the twin sermons: *The General Deliverance* (1781) and *The New Creation* (1785).

In the first homily Wesley builds his eschatology on the maxim of God's universal fatherhood—his unfailing love for all his creatures, including the animal kingdom. Along with the human race, the animal kingdom once enjoyed an original state of perfection; meaning, in their creation they shared alongside humanity a capacity for self-motion, understanding, will (affections), and liberty of choice. Though animals possess these qualities to a lesser degree than their human counterparts, the most significant difference is man's capacity to know, love, and obey God. Wesley calls this distinction the "great gulf" which animals at present cannot "pass over."[43] As such, the animal kingdom shares in Adam's original perfection and blessing, with humanity serving as the conduit of divine favor to the rest of creation.

But Adam fell into sin and became subject to death. In a similar manner, "as man is deprived of *his* perfection, his loving obedience to God; so brutes are deprived of *their* perfection, their loving obedience to man."[44] In consequence, "irregular passion" and "unlovely tempers"[45] took possession of the animal world so

---

[43] *The General Deliverance* I.5.
[44] *The General Deliverance* II.2 (emphasis his).
[45] *The General Deliverance* II.5.

The Gospel of Universal Holiness

that one beast now kills another for survival, and all kinds of weaknesses and diseases plague them. As death reigns over the human race, so death rules over the animal kingdom. But then Wesley asks, "Will the brute creation always remain in this deplorable condition?" Drawing upon Romans 8:19-22, he sees a promise of universal restoration for all of God's creatures:

> The whole brute creation will, then, undoubtedly, be restored, not only to the vigour, strength, and swiftness which they had at their creation, but to a far higher degree of each than they ever enjoyed.[46]

What Wesley envisions is a full, complete renewal of their powers of understanding, will, liberty and motion far above their original perfection, as far as an "elephant is beyond that of a worm":

> What, if it should please him, when he makes us "equal to angels," to make them what we are now, —creatures capable of God; capable of knowing and loving and enjoying the Author of their being?

Such is the fullness of God's love for all his creation! Four years later he once again picks up the theme of universal restoration and this time envisions a completely restored physical creation. Building on the eschatological promise, "Behold, I make all things new," (Rev 21:5) Wesley sees no change transpiring in the heavenly realm where God dwells, but he does portend of no more comets or any other of "those horrid, eccentric orbs" of "half-formed planets, in a chaotic state."[47] All will be in "exact order and harmony." Chaos will be fully removed and universal harmony will reign in the heavens.

---

[46] *The General Deliverance* III.3.
[47] *The New Creation* §8.

Other renovations will fill the lower heavens and earth. The earth will no more be "torn by hurricanes," "furious storms" or "destructive tempests."[48] Even "pernicious" meteors will be no more. In their place all will be "light, fair, serene; a lively picture of the eternal day."[49] Even the elements of air, fire, and water will be transformed on that perfect day. Fire will lose its ability to consume; no longer will it burn or cause pain (except in hell!). The air will remain calm and placid; no more will rain fall upon the earth. Water will then be pure from "all unpleasing or unhealthy mixtures." Once again paradise will prevail upon the surface of the earth. No longer will heat and cold cover the surface, for the temperature will be "most conducive for fruitfulness. This means no more earthquakes, "horrid rocks, or frightful precipices; no wild deserts, or barren sands; no impassible morasses, or unfruitful bogs, to swallow up the unwary traveler."[50]

In this new world order both the animal and human realms will attain the heights of their potential perfection. Animal will no longer kill animal, as the human race finally attains the perfection of an "unmixed state of holiness and happiness, far superior to that which Adam enjoyed in Paradise."[51] But the crowning jewel of the new creation will be a "deep, an intimate, an uninterrupted union with God" that all creation will enjoy. In the end, all creation will bask in the beauty of the Three-in-One God, enjoying eternal fellowship with the Father, Son, and Holy Spirit. The universal fatherhood of God will fill the new creation with his bountiful love and universal presence.

Adding to this delineation of the faith journey beyond this life is the contribution his last written sermon offers to the believer's eschatological hope. Completed less than two months before his death, Wesley muses over what the intermediate state will be like between death and the resurrection. With faith in God's word as his spiritual sense, Wesley *sees* he will soon become a disembod-

---

[48] How could JW ever forget those storms at sea while on route to America!
[49] *The New Creation* §9.
[50] *The New Creation* §15.
[51] *The New Creation* §18.

ied spirit dwelling with all the righteous souls in the service of God. In this semi-glorified state, new senses of a different nature will open up in his soul. Travel will be at the speed of thought. Even more significant is how the human spirit will "swiftly increase in knowledge, in holiness, and in happiness."[52] Ever expanding in growth and in the "whole image of God" Wesley envisions himself employed alongside the angels in leading "many sons to glory," or by serving in whatever domain the Lord will appoint him.[53] Thus, Wesley's Gospel of Universal Holiness delineates more sharply the faith journey beyond death itself. While his two-works gospel came to hold that involuntary sin finally expires in the article of death, his universal-holiness gospel pierced beyond the veil to see further stages of development and growth, culminating in the new creation.

We would be amiss not to mention how this vision of the new creation contributed to Wesley's understanding of theodicy. As the Enlightenment challenged many of the presuppositions of the Christian faith, Wesley responds in his later sermons by arguing that since evil is only temporary, and that God's eternal purposes include a restored creation which surpasses what Adam lost, God had good reasons in allowing evil to manifest for a season. In other words, Wesley believed this present world is the best possible way to attain the best possible world.[54]

A final thought. Randy Maddox observes that the vision of universal restoration of the physical creation was quite unusual in Wesley's day.[55] He notes how Wesley over time shifted his hope from a "heaven above" to a concept of a fully restored physical creation. But should this change so surprise us? In chapter one,

---

[52] #132 *On Faith* (1791) §6.
[53] JW also sees evil disembodied humans involved in promoting evil in sinful people alongside the demons and fallen angels.
[54] This latter phrase comes from Norman Geisler. See JW's sermons: *God's Approbation of His Works* II.1-3; *On The Fall of Man* P.1; *God's Love to Fallen Man*; *The General Spread of the Gospel* §27; *On Divine Providence* §19. See also other sermons dealing with deism and atheism, like *On Faith* #106; *The Unity of the Divine Being*; and *What is Man?* #103.
[55] *Responsible Grace*, 253.

John Wesley's Theology of Christian Perfection

we learned that Wesley borrowed several sermons from other authors and preached them during his Oxford period. In one of them, *On the Resurrection of the Dead* (1732),[56] Wesley affirmed his belief that God is able to preserve the very elements of a decayed corpse for the future physical resurrection. As God formed Adam from the dust of the ground, so at the end-time resurrection God will re-form each individual body from the dust of their remains. Thus the soul will re-inhabit the same body, yet with the glory, power and immortality of resurrection grace. So, early Wesley did entertain some notions of a restored physical creation.

The Gospel of Universal Holiness

As Wesley approached the end of his life, his understanding of the faith journey continued to evolve and shift in subtle ways. The search for balance between his two early gospel systems (holiness and faith alone) led ultimately to an *ordo salutis* that held in tension several principles and practices.[57] The two core axioms underlying both gospel systems were the demand for inward holiness and salvation by faith alone. As his two-works gospel evolved into his universal-holiness gospel, a third maxim began to emerge: the universal fatherhood of God. These three foundational truths created a blend that still proclaimed a message of salvation by faith in Christ, yet allowed for a parallel message that God loves all his creation and will save pre-Christians who exercise saving faith too. Holding both proclamations together is the demand for holy tempers (inward holiness). Bottom line, God accepts everyone who fears him and works righteousness according to the moral light they possess (Acts 10:35). This is the faith that pleases him (Heb 11:6). This is the single intention that is the

---

[56] Works B 4:528; Works J 7:474.
[57] This includes: instant/process; faith/works (means of grace); voluntary sin/involuntary sin; justification/sanctification; church (Anglican)/society (Methodist).

The Gospel of Universal Holiness

foundation of true religion.[58] Universal holiness is the only sure way of attaining salvation in the end. Faith alone cannot give such assurance because it so easily slips to antinomianism. Wesley shuddered at the thought that such faith could be saving.

Coupled with these core principles was another that Wesley held throughout his life: God cares more about the tempers of the heart than he does about the opinions of the head. This truism theologically made salvific room for those who entertain confused notions about God, Christ, sin and salvation. This is why under the universal-holiness system holy tempers became the standard of salvation for *all* people—Christian and pre-Christian alike. Surely the former are privileged with more "light" than the latter, yet more is expected from them. Whatever level of faith one has, the bottom line is sincere reverence for God and a life of authentic holiness (Acts 10:35). Only this kind of faith is acceptable, no matter if it is the faith of a heathen, Moslem, Catholic or Protestant. It is not necessarily the correctness of the creed that separates a sheep from a goat, but whether one's faith issues in a life of reverence and inward holiness. Only universal holiness of heart and life prepares one for the eternal kingdom.

Essential to the universal-holiness gospel system was the enlarged role prevenient grace assumes. The faith journey now properly begins with the "first wish to please God," the "first dawn" of spiritual light. Preventing grace became the foundation for the universal phenomenon of human conscience as well as the spring for spiritual awakening. Even here Wesley acknowledges in this nascent awakening that "some degree of salvation" is at work.[59] After this *convincing* grace cultivates repentance which brings greater deliverance from the heart of stone, leading to *justifying* grace (servant state), then *converting* grace (new birth), and finally *sanctifying* grace (adolescence and adulthood). Since the Gospel of Universal Holiness incorporates the prior two-works system, the standard framework of moment-process-

---

[58] *On a Single Eye* (1789) II.2-3.
[59] *On Working Out Our Own Salvation* II.1.

moment-process continues to inform Wesley's interpretation of the faith journey from new birth to death. Yet, he now accedes that many Christians, including Methodists, settle for a lower path and do not press on to perfect love.[60]

Up to this point little has been said about involuntary sin in Wesley's later years. After the doctrine was formally incorporated into his two-works gospel system it became a basic staple in his thought and theology.[61] Human infirmity became an important qualifier in his doctrine of Christian perfection as a consequence of the revival wildfire and schism in the early sixties.[62] Of interest is how Wesley speaks of human infirmity in the sixties compared to the eighties. In *Thoughts on Christian Perfection* (1759) Wesley acknowledges that these weaknesses and mistakes incur guilt before God. As a result he openly calls them sin, even if he adds the qualifier "improperly so-called," and the appellation, "involuntary." Culpable mistakes need God's forgiveness, Wesley argues, and hence, are sinful in some sense.

By the eighties he more often refers to these human infirmities and weaknesses as "innumerable violations" of Adamic and angelic law, but resists calling them sin.[63] Sin is a term he reserves for "voluntary transgressions of a known law."[64] These inevitable imperfections of fallen human nature remain following perfect love since they are rooted in the fall of Adam.[65] One of Wesley's last written sermons is an exposition on the relationship between the treasure of God's inward kingdom and the earthen vessel of human weakness (2 Cor 4:7). False judgments, wrong inferences, mistakes in practice all stem from a disordered brain resulting from Adam's loss of the image of God. "Human nature

---

[60] *The More Excellent* Way (1787) §5.
[61] *The Fall of Man* II.2; *The End of Christ's Coming* III.3, 6; *On Perfection* I.3, II.8; *The Christian's Treasure* II.1.
[62] See PA Introduction; 19:7-25; chs 20-22.
[63] JW writes in *The End of Christ's Coming*, "We know, weakness of understanding, and a thousand infirmities, will remain, while this corruptible body remains; but sin need not remain" (III.5); see *On Perfection* (1784) I.1-3.
[64] *On Perfection* (1784) II.9.
[65] *The Fall of Man* (1782) II.2.

The Gospel of Universal Holiness

now is not only sensual," says Wesley, "but devilish."[66] God's primary purpose is to keep people humble, especially in their own eyes, so they will trust in God alone[67]:

> The heavenly treasure now we have
> In a vile house of clay!
> Yet He shall to the utmost save,
> And keep it to that day.[68]

Whereas Wesley's two-works gospel did not develop the faith journey much beyond death, his universal-holiness gospel penetrated beyond the veil to spell out further degrees of renewal in God's redemptive plan. Drawing once more on the maxim of the universal fatherhood of God, Wesley envisions *restoration* grace in which the basic elements of the present creation are lifted from their present bondage to decay and made completely new. The animal kingdom attains new heights of perfection as they become as we are now, and redeemed humanity becomes exalted to the level of angels. Together, all creation will praise and worship the one God who loves all his creatures unconditionally and to whom he gave his one and only Son to redeem back to himself. In the end God's love triumphs.

Such a vision of *total* renewal called for a robust doctrine of redemptive grace that encompasses all of life, starting with the first flicker of spiritual awareness, culminating in the new creation itself. Thus, the Gospel of Universal Holiness delineated, quantified, and, more importantly, embraced the *totality* of the life transformation process. The faith journey is now complete. Wesley's theology of perfection encompasses the totality of life. When Wesley began his societies he had only one requirement for those who wanted to join: a desire to flee the wrath to come.[69]

---

[66] *The Heavenly Treasure in Earthen Vessels* (1790) P.2.
[67] *The Heavenly Treasure in Earthen Vessels* II.5, 7.
[68] *The Heavenly Treasure in Earthen Vessels* II.7.
[69] *The Nature, Design, and General Rules of the United Societies* §4; Works B 9:70.

John Wesley's Theology of Christian Perfection

In the end John Wesley developed a gospel message that centered on that single requirement.

Full Circle

As Wesley approached the end of his life an interesting characteristic emerges in his theological orientation: a return to his earlier roots at Oxford. In chapter four we noted that by the early seventies Wesley began to look back to his Oxford period with fondness.[70] Since he now realized that the foundation of his faith journey was in 1725, a new appreciation for his early period began to surface. By the eighties many of his sermons focus on themes and motifs found in his Gospel of Holiness. Of course, this does not mean he abandoned his two-works scheme of spiritual development. To the contrary! To his grave John Wesley proclaimed a gospel containing two distinct moments of divine deliverance.[71] But the sharpness of his two-works message was softened by the process orientation of his holiness gospel principles. This explains the inclusivist leanings in his later thought that opened the door of salvation for those of other faiths who fear God and work righteousness.

What were the themes and motifs of his early period that began to reappear in his later writings? For starters, several of his sermon titles are explicit motifs of his holiness gospel. In 1782 Wesley penned the sermon, *On Redeeming the Time*, in which he emphasizes the importance of disciplining oneself in regard to sleep. A perusal of this homily reminds one of the strict disciplines the Holy Club practiced many decades earlier. The very next year he picked up the theme of family religion in which he exhorts his people to pattern their service to the Lord after the

---

[70] See ch 4 n 92. In the eighties JW referred positively to his early period several times: *The More Excellent Way* (1787) VI.4; *On Family Religion* (1783) P.3; *On a Single Eye* (1789) P.1; *On God's Vineyard* I.1-5.

[71] See note 1 above.

The Gospel of Universal Holiness

holy angels above.[72] As was noted in chapter one, the linking of perfection with angelic nature was a recurring motif in his early period.[73] Then there is the publishing in 1787 of his 1733 sermon, *The Duty of Constant Communion*. This homily emphasizes the necessity of communicating as often as possible. Wesley's thoughts on this matter not only remained the same over several decades, but reflect renewed interest in themes of his early period. Another discourse that picked up an early motif is *Human Life a Dream* (1789). In the 1720's Wesley was fond of comparing this earthly existence to the dream state.[74] Life here on earth is likened to living in a perpetual dream only to be awakened when ushered into eternity. Then, "all is *real* here! All is permanent; all eternal!"[75] The ungodly simply do not realize the true nature of existence. Though this life seems to be real and solid, in truth it is only temporary; and as such, this life can be likened to a dream.

But no sermon returns more to the themes and motifs of his holiness gospel than *On a Single Eye*. The single intention became the very heart and soul of his Gospel of Holiness. As he did decades earlier, Wesley reaffirms in the eighties that the decision of the single eye (intention) forms the beginning point of vital religion in the soul. In this discourse Wesley returns with praise to his early mentors—Bishop Taylor and William Law. Once again, he identifies vital religion with the single intention and the new birth:

---

[72] Besides JW's reference to angels as models of obedience in *On Family Religion* I.4, in his last written homily he expounds the idea that departed humans serve along with demons and angels depending on one's spiritual state in eternity (*On Faith* Heb 11:1, §§8-14).
[73] *The Promise of Understanding* III.3; *In Earth as in Heaven*. Compare JW's early sermon *On Guardian Angels* (1726) with his last one *On Faith* (1791) to see how he understood the ministry of angels, and how the redeemed saints in paradise participate in this ministry.
[74] E.g. *On Mourning the Dead* §3.
[75] *On Mourning the Dead* §7.

Considering these things, we may well cry out, "How great a thing is it to be a Christian; to be a real, inward, scriptural Christian, conformed in heart and life to the will of God! Who is sufficient of these things?" None, unless he be born of God... With how many instances of this melancholy truth, —that those whose eye is not single are totally ignorant of the nature of true religion, —are we surrounded on every side![76]

The reason, Wesley says, people fail spiritually is primarily due to not having a single eye to be holy before God. So important is the single intention to having the life of God within, that he cautions his readers to not let any profession, family member, or companion in life divert one's focus to seek God with a pure heart.[77]

Wesley has finally returned full circle to his early themes and motifs, but with a twist. For, while invigorating his foundational axiom on the necessity of inward holiness, he never abandons the maxim of salvation by faith alone in Christ alone. While he can cry out to the people that holiness is the only wedding garment that fits one for God's celestial presence,[78] he also reminds his readers it is only by "faith we are saved from sin, and made holy."[79] These two maxims remain the core of Wesley's theology of perfection.[80] Even though a third maxim was added to his gos-

---

[76] *On a Single Eye* P.3; II.2. The reader should note a subtle shift taking place here regarding the single intention. JW's GosH and GosFA placed the single intention at the beginning of the faith journey. In his GosTW the single intention was moved to a second moment following the new birth to make room for perfection as a second work of grace. In this discourse JW once again places the single intention at the beginning point of vital religion. This is a return to his pre-Aldersgate roots. Upon the whole, though, JW did maintain the single intention as a second moment since he continued to believe in perfection as a second work of grace (e.g. *On Perfection* I.10-11; *On Patience* §8).

[77] *On a Single Eye* III.8.

[78] *The Wedding Garment* §§10, 17.

[79] *The Wedding Garment* §18.

[80] *On God's Vineyard* II.1.

pel scheme (the universal fatherhood of God), this later core belief did not set aside the other two maxims, but provided a way to apply them to those who faith is pre-new birth and pre-Christian. Though he gravitated back to his theological roots, Wesley could never fully return to what he once was; simply because, he no longer was the same man, nor could he ever be. God's grace had brought him on a journey that zigzagged back and forth, but had finally led him to a place where he did find assurance, and thereby peace in the gracious love of God revealed in the cross of Christ. As Wesley was so fond of quoting, "We love because he first loved us."

The Faith Journey
John Wesley's Path of Spiritual Renewal

What follows is a summary description of the faith journey according to Wesley's Gospel of Universal Holiness:

Non-Faith: The lowest level of faith is that of a materialist (atheist), who believes only in the material universe. Wesley rightfully questions whether we should call this *faith* since by definition faith is an "evidence or conviction of God." Still, he affirms that even the materialist has a conscience springing from preventing grace. What is needed is for grace to stir an awareness of God within the human spirit.

Faith of Pre-Christian: Deism, Heathenism, Islam and Judaism all reflect the work of prevenient grace enlightening the heart and conscience with varying degrees to the reality of God and his righteousness. While deists believe in God but deny his supernatural revelation, the heathen hold to both, yet are often plagued by distorted notions concerning God's nature and his righteousness. Moslems and Jews reflect a higher stage on the faith journey path since both share with Christianity a strong belief in monotheism (belief in one God), and often teach principles of true religion (holy tempers). However, Moslems follow a different revelation that redefines Jesus and the way of salvation. Wesley saw Judaism in terms of Old Testament faith and the Mosaic Law. Though attaining a stage higher than Islam, Jews have a veil covering their hearts when the Hebrew Scriptures are read concerning the identity of the Messiah. All these faiths need further enlightenment to the truth of Jesus Christ as revealed in the Christian Scriptures (New Testament).

Faith of Nominal Christian: This stage includes everyone who has the outward form of the Christian religion but lacks its inward saving power. Often resting in a mental assent to official church doctrine and the Bible as God's word, the nominalist needs the deeper work of convincing grace to feel their need for repentance and personal salvation.

Faith of Servant: This is the lowest level of saving faith, but the highest level of prevenient grace. God accepts *everyone* who by faith sincerely reverence God and live an authentic life of inward holiness (Acts 10:35; Heb 11:6). Acceptance entails justification and forgiveness before God but not the assurance of adoption and the new birth. The servant needs to press on in the faithful practice of the means of grace (works of piety and mercy) until converting grace renews the heart and the next level of the faith journey is attained.

Faith of Childhood: Having been born again by the Spirit of Christ, the child of God enjoys the witness of adoption and power over outward sin. In this state of liberty the child can err by thinking all sin is gone. Soon doubts over one's salvation arise as fears to whether one will persevere shake one's confidence. This is the wilderness state. Old bosom sins arise to assault the believer's peace, thereby bringing many attacks in its wake:

> Will I be able to persevere? Or, will I falter?
> Was I deceived when I thought God had forgiven me?
> Am I really God's child?
> Is my heart really renewed in God's love?
> Did my emotions deceive me since sin still remains in my heart?

In this state the child of God is tempted to forestall the faithful practice of the means of grace; yet, through a persistent effort to practice works of piety and compassion God prepares the believer for the next stage of the faith journey.

Faith of Adolescence: The chief mark of this stage is full assurance over fear and doubt, establishing the Christian in God's word and in victory over the attacks of the enemy. The adolescent Christian has now attained stability. The adolescent is now ready to enter the next level of inward renewal. God works a second repentance by exposing the depths of pride, anger, self-will and unwholesome desires that remain in the heart. In this state the adolescent hungers after full deliverance from inward sin and to be filled with the divine presence of holy love. The believer is now ready for the next stage of life transformation: full renewal in God's image.

Faith of Adulthood: This is the crowning jewel of salvation in this life. As perfect love fills the heart, full salvation from inward sin becomes complete. The holy temper of "humble, gentle, patient love" now reigns uncontested in the heart of continual prayer, thanksgiving, and holy joy. Sinful tempers are rooted out and destroyed. The single intention rules as the believer's dispositional nature is transformed and renewed after the character (image) of Christ. Still, a second wilderness state often follows the grace of perfection, in which the believer struggles with spiritual darkness, clouding the mind to think perfection is something higher and greater than what they have experienced.

Moreover, human infirmities and weaknesses remain due to fallen Adamic nature. These imperfections inevitably lead adult Christians to commit culpable mistakes that still need the intercession of Christ's atoning sacrifice. This means that even the most perfect still have need to pray daily, "Father, forgive us our sins." Yet, as the adult believer grows in Christ-like wisdom they attain higher levels of maturity and discernment, thereby learning how to not commit these involuntary sins as frequently, or as seriously, as before.

Faith of Paradise: Between death and the resurrection the spirits of the righteous continue to experience further renewal in the image of God. With the casting off of the mortal body, involuntary sin is finally vanquished forever. New senses are now opened: an increase in knowledge seems unlimited; holy tempers are even more pervasive and dominant; travel is at the speed of thought; all leading to a degree of happiness not conceived before. Growth never ends. What purpose do these new senses serve? To the surprise of many, these new capacities are put to work by the departed to serve alongside angels in ministering to the salvation of people remaining on earth. Yet, for all these perfections full complete renewal in God's image remains incomplete as long as the righteous continue as disembodied spirits.

Faith of New Creation: In the eschatological resurrection all things in heaven and earth are restored to their pristine perfection, yet in greater glory than what Adam possessed

The Gospel of Universal Holiness

in the garden. The new creation encompasses the entire universe. No longer will the symptoms of chaos wreak havoc in the heavens or on earth. All will be calm, serene, and in absolute harmony. The animal world will be elevated in capacity to what man is now, with new senses to fellowship with God (and us). On the human plane the righteous will be lifted to the level of angels, but with glorified bodies patterned after their Lord's. In the end the redeemed will spend eternity in the presence of their Lord and Savior, growing in the love and knowledge of God throughout all ages. The faith journey has no end as all creation worships in the beatific vision of the face of him who sits on the throne. And the loving presence of Triune God shall fill the renewed earth as the waters cover the sea.

We conclude by returning to our charts in section one.[81] Only now we compare the subtle shifts that took place from Wesley's Gospel of Two Works to his Gospel of Universal Holiness. As the latter gospel continued to promulgate his two-works message, it continued to emphasize the core beliefs of that system. But as Wesley gravitated toward his Gospel of Holiness in the last two decades of his life, he began to stress even more certain aspects of that theological system. The following chart serves to highlight these nuances that shaped the development of his later theology of perfection:

Gospel of Two Works	Gospel of Universal Holiness
Axioms:	
Inward holiness	Inward holiness
Faith alone	Faith alone
	Fatherhood of God

---

[81] Cf. page 176.

John Wesley's Theology of Christian Perfection

Ground:
Justification begins
sanctification

Justification begins
sanctification

Object of faith:
Christ alone &
God's promises

Christ alone &
God's promises

Focus:
Present & future salvation

Present & future salvation

Salvation by:
Faith alone & ordinances

Faith alone & ordinances

Salvation is:
Gift and process

Gift and process

Salvation begins:
Faith of a child

Faith of a servant

Foundation of Assurance:
Witness of Spirit
& life transformation

Witness of Spirit
& life transformation

Holiness complete:
Adulthood

Adulthood & death

Faith complete:
Adulthood

Adulthood, death
& resurrection

Christian complete:
Adulthood

Adulthood, death
& resurrection

Section Three

Making Sense of John Wesley's Theology of Christian Perfection

This doctrine is the grand depositum which God has lodged with the people called Methodists; and for the sake of propagating this chiefly he appeared to have raised us up.

Letter to Robert Brackenbury
September 15, 1790

Eight
A Plain Account of Christian Perfection

We now turn our attention to clarifying various aspects of Wesley's theology of perfection and its development. Countless pages have been written on this subject seeking to make his views "plain" (even by Wesley himself). If his teachings were that straightforward then all this ink would not have been needed, and this book would never have been written. The truth is Wesley's theology of perfection is complex since it contains subtle nuances that affect its meaning and application. Moreover, as we have seen in prior chapters, his views on holiness did continue to evolve throughout his life, which in turn altered aspects of his theological system. Besides looking to secondary literature, which is always a step removed from Wesley's own thoughts and expressions, where can we turn in his entire corpus and find a comprehensive summary of his views on perfection? The only response is *A Plain Account of Christian Perfection*. The *Plain Account* is the most significant and enduring work Wesley ever penned on the subject, even with all its warts.[1] The work went through six editions during his lifetime and has been reprinted countless times since. We are safe to say the *Plain Account* has become a spiritual classic.

If becoming a spiritual classic isn't enough to warrant our diligent inquiry, there are other reasons to consider. Even Wesley realized the significance of this "tract" (as he often referred to it) for he repeatedly encouraged his followers to diligently peruse

---

[1] W. Stephen Gunter refers to the *Plain Account* as "piecemeal apologetics" that contributed, rather than calmed, the enthusiast excesses of the perfection revival (*Love Divine*, 211-12). While this author does not totally agree with Gunter's assessment, he is correct about the book's major weakness. JW needed to write a comprehensive systematic work. The *Plain Account* is surely not this kind of document.

A Plain Account Of Christian Perfection

the book while on their journey to become "all love."[2] Further, he includes the book in his published editions of his collected works, and in 1789, near the close of his life, incorporated it in *The Discipline of the Methodist Episcopal Church*, thus securing its legacy for future generations. To appreciate the *Plain Account's* wisdom in clarifying and thereby codifying Wesley's doctrine of perfect love, let us review briefly the context and reasons he wrote the book.[3]

The *Plain Account* was written at a critical time when Wesley's theological views and his two-works gospel were entering their mature articulation. As we covered earlier, during the late fifties and early sixties a powerful perfection revival swept in its wake hundreds professing the experience. But with blessing came excess and abuse. Wesley's "son in the gospel," Thomas Maxfield, and a spiritually young recruit, George Bell, initiated a schism that eventually split the societies, mostly around London. These enthusiasts experientially claimed much more than John Wesley ever intended: gifts of healing, miracles, deliverance from physical death, freedom from human err, and the impossibility to sin again. This "angelic perfection"[4] was carried to such a pitch that in December 1762 Bell prophesied the world would end on February 28. Wesley opposed the prophecy and schism ensued until Maxfield, Bell and a couple hundred of their supporters formally separated from Wesley and his societies.

---

[2] PA 15:14. For example, JWL 6/10/81 "As I apprehend your mind must be a little confused by reading those uncommon treatises, I wish you would give another deliberate reading to the 'Plain Account of Christian Perfection;' and you may be assured, there is no higher religion under heaven higher or deeper than that which is there described." Again, JWL 3/31/72; 5/13/72; 4/12/82.

[3] For a more thorough review see the *Plain Account*, Introduction: Why Wesley Wrote; also chs 20-22, 25:108-167 (The Seven Advices).

[4] PA 25:14; *On Perfection* I.1. An example is JW's early sermon fragment *In Earth as in Heaven* which does identify perfection with the angels (Works B 4:346). As JW's two-works gospel developed over time with more and more qualifiers the ideal of linking Christian perfection to the angels necessarily fell to the wayside.

John Wesley's Theology of Christian Perfection

The revival, with its excess and schism, led to much criticism of Wesley for espousing an attainable perfection in this life. The criticism came from two directions. First, the schismatics, who were members of Wesley's societies, accused him of changing his views over time. But from those outside the societies criticism mounted over the revival's excesses. Fear of perfection swept through many Methodist circles as the doctrine became associated with extremism. We further saw that even Charles began to pull back from supporting the doctrine.[5] This was the historical setting that compelled Wesley to pen the *Plain Account*, and explains why the material in the book is organized as it is.

Wesley's first objective was to answer his critics. To those who accused him of changing his views, he includes several excerpts from previously published works and placed them in their general chronological order to show that his views had not materially changed over time.[6] In response to those who feared the revival's excesses, Wesley documented in the *Plain Account* what he taught and when he taught it, thus showing he did not share the views of the enthusiasts. But he had a second reason for writing. Many sincere Christians had either professed perfect love or had been seeking the experience and they needed guidance. To both groups the doctrine needed to be *clarified* and thereby *codified* (using this latter term in a more general sense). So in 1765 Wesley compiled his material and wrote the *Plain Account*, publishing the work in early 1766.[7]

The Plain Account & Wesley's Doctrinal Evolution

In sections one and two we chronicled in detail the development of Wesley's perfection theology and how this evolution

---

[5] Cf. JWL 6/27/66; 7/9/66; 2/12/67; 5/14/68; 6/14/68.

[6] In response to Gunter (see n 1 above) I feel this move by JW to include prior works in order to show his views had not materially changed over time was a wise decision on his part, and not a "piecemeal" response as Gunter thinks.

[7] See his letter to John Newton; JWL T 2/28/66.

shaped his gospel system. Here we want to dig for clues in the *Plain Account* that can add understanding to this process; or, at least, confirm we are on the right track in our conclusions. Let's begin by looking at the book's general structure. The bulk of the *Plain Account* naturally coalesces into three main sections: chapters 2-10, 11-18, and 19-26.[8] What should stir our interest is when we put dates to these sections and compare them with the standard divisions for Wesley's ministry and the four-gospel scheme we are using in this study[9]:

The Four Gospels		The Plain Account	Ministry Periods
Gospel of Holiness	1725-38	Chapters 2-10 1725-39	Early 1725-38
Gospel of Faith Alone	1738-39		Middle 1738-1765
Gospel of Two Works	1740-68	Chapters 11-18 1740-49	
		Chapters 19-26 1759-65	Late 1765-1791
Gospel of U. Holiness	1768-91		

To start, note how section one of the *Plain Account* (chs 2-10) overlaps the transition between Wesley's early and middle periods, including his holiness and faith-alone gospels. These couple years (1738-39) cover Wesley's Aldersgate era, the beginning of field preaching and the start of his United Societies.[10] Historians and scholars correctly see Aldersgate as a major watershed in Wesley's ministry and theological development.[11] But as Wesley

---

[8] Chs 1, 27-28 are introduction and epilogues to main arguments found in chs 2-26.

[9] The date of 1768 was chosen to divide the GosTW from the GosUH, because in that year JW formally incorporates his servant state into his theological system. Otherwise, it is very hard to draw a firm date between the two. Remember, JW's universal-holiness gospel continued to teach and hold to the two-works structure. The difference is one of nuance. The universal-holiness gospel (1) broadened or expanded the two-works gospel description of the faith journey, and (2) began to move toward his earlier holiness gospel in a number of emphasizes.

[10] See ch 3 for a full description of this period of time.

[11] PA ch 7 end note.

looked back from the vantage point of several decades and then rehearsed how he saw his perfection doctrine develop through that period of time, he *passes over* Aldersgate and picks up the story when he was in Germany, in the summer of 1738.[12] Implicitly, Wesley acknowledges that Aldersgate did not play a significant role in the development of his perfection doctrine as he articulated it in the 1760's. Instead, he mentions his trip to Germany in the summer of 1738. This agrees with our study. For while Aldersgate did in large part introduce the principle of instantaneousness into his *ordo salutis*, his two-works gospel was more owing to the influence of the German Moravians. For it was in Germany he learned to distinguish two works of grace in this life (from Christian David and the other testimonies). Of course, this initial insight took Wesley a year or two to work out in forming his own theological system, the Gospel of Two Works. This confirms that our conclusions are on the right track. The roots to Wesley's two-works gospel are found more in Christian David and German Moravian influence, than they are to his Aldersgate conversion under the tutelage of the English Moravians.

We saw in chapter four how the *Plain Account* was Wesley's first post-Aldersgate published writing in which he speaks positively of his early faith journey. This leads to other relevant insights. To begin, in the *Plain Account* Wesley articulates his conversion to holiness in a manner similar to how he described his conversion at Aldersgate many years earlier. Both are described as instantaneous, evangelical conversions producing definite results. In the former, he refers to complete dedication to God; in the latter he speaks of full assurance and salvation from sin. In reality, both testimonies overlap in meaning and significance, since both involve a definite victory over sin and fresh awakening to God. The fact that in 1765 Wesley can describe his 1725 conversion in evangelical terms testifies to significant changes in his views regarding his early faith journey. In addition, as we saw in

---

[12] *Plain Account* chs 7 & 8. Ch 7 ends with JW returning from America and ch 8 opens with him in Germany.

A Plain Account Of Christian Perfection

chapter four, this change of mind over his prior faith journey is what opened the door for his servant theology to begin exerting influence on his theological system, culminating in his Gospel of Universal Holiness.[13]

Turning back to the above chart, the second significant date the matches up between the *Plain Account* and our study is 1740. In chapter eleven of the *Plain Account* Wesley admits twenty-five years later of the personal pain he felt from those who opposed his teaching of perfection. This chapter forms the dividing line between sections one and two in the book. After this point Wesley begins to delineate not only what perfection *is*, but also what perfection is *not*. Once again, we chronicled this process in chapter three of our study; thus confirming the conclusions we reached there. When we turn to the later chapters in the *Plain Account* we find the same theological developments coming to light as we found in our study. We begin by noting the formal shaping of his doctrine of sin as voluntary and involuntary.[14] During this same period Wesley embraced the idea that perfection can be lost. This led to considerable changes in how he counseled people who were seeking the blessing. His letters contain much encouragement to those who lost the gift to seek it again and again.[15] By placing limitations on the experience of perfect love, Wesley inadvertently heightened the instantaneous nature of the gift. All these modifications in his thinking contributed to the perfection revival since it opened the door wider for people to receive the gift soon after the new birth.[16] In small but important ways, the *Plain Account* confirms our study and alerts us to subtle shifts within Wesley's theological development.

---

[13] Cf. ch 7.
[14] Cf. ch 5.
[15] Cf. ch 6.
[16] Cf. ch 24 end note.

John Wesley's Theology of Christian Perfection

The Wisdom of the Plain Account

The major strength of the *Plain Account* is its comprehensiveness. As mentioned above, the revival and its excesses required the doctrine be clarified and codified if it was to serve future generations. Since Wesley was not fond of systematics, a work from his hand needed to be produced which would be comprehensive enough to clarify the variety of nuances inherent in the doctrine. All the key terms and concepts needed to be clarified, elaborated, and illustrated. While Wesley was slow at realizing this, one of his strengths was persistence. Even so, a variety of genres are found in the book: biography and narrative, homily, hymns, poetry, Q & A sessions, testimony, specific lists, devotional and theological tracts, and reflective questioning. Plus, the alert reader will notice that every page is saturated with scripture quotations and allusions.[17] In a day when there were no media opportunities as we know them, the *Plain Account* did appeal to a variety of tastes and offered something for everyone. And while it is true Wesley sometimes erred in the details of his chronology; yet, the overall flow of the book does tell his story: how he came to believe in holiness, what he believed at various times, and whether he had been consistent in his principles. Of course, the latter point was disputed and does require qualification. Yet, from 1740 on, a strong argument can be made that Wesley was more consistent with the doctrine than is often supposed, then or now.

But the real jewel is found in the book's repetitive diet of the doctrine's central themes and motifs. While various aspects of Wesley's holiness views are addressed throughout his sermons and writings, only here is found a large block of material incorporating a wide range of writings from an extended period of time. Stated another way, the span of time it covers, the breadth of material it encompasses, combined with its repetitive subject matter is what gives this little book its lasting value. The *Plain Account*

---

[17] There are approximately 500 scripture quotations or allusions in the PA. This is very significant since the book is so short.

A Plain Account Of Christian Perfection

has become Wesley's written legacy on the subject of full salvation, the definitive statement of his position. Since Wesley first selected, then edited the material found between its covers, and later republished the book several times during his lifetime, we can be sure that what is contained therein is his mature and settled thoughts on the subject. This calls us to carefully note the motifs that repeatedly appear in the book. By doing so we can have confidence that we grasp his maxims and core convictions, thereby helping us to understand what Wesley meant when he called people to love God perfectly and their neighbor compassionately. We can now turn to the *Plain Account* and see which themes were central to his perfection theology.[18]

The Single Intention:

> Instantly I resolved to dedicate all my life to God, all my thoughts, and words, and actions; being thoroughly convinced, there was no medium; but that every part of my life (not some only) must either be a sacrifice to God, or myself, that is, in effect, to the devil.
>
> Plain Account 2:2[19]

The early chapters of the *Plain Account* express the ideal of perfection in terms of complete and total devotion to God. From this perspective, Christian perfection is *purity* of *intention* (2:1), the dedication of *all* our *thoughts, words, and actions* to God (2:2). To be perfect means to center one's *affections* on God alone, with *one desire* reigning in the heart (3:3). Full salvation is simply to be *all devoted* to God (4:2). What is more, the demand for perfect devotion implies that one cannot be a *half Christian* (4:2) by seeking to serve both God and self, which is, in effect,

---

[18] In the following descriptions all the words in italics are quoted directly from the *Plain Account*. The references in parentheses are to the *Annotated Edition*.

[19] The reader should remember that the early chapters in the PA represent JW's early perfection views that are still sanctioned in 1765 (and thereafter). By comparing these chapters with ch 1 in our study further insights into JW's early views can possibly be detected.

serving the devil (2:2-3). This is the *single eye*, where *God reigns alone* (10:15) with *one desire and design ruling every temper!* (28:7).

As Wesley's doctrine of perfect love continued to evolve over time and became richer in nuance, this single, fundamental idea was never let go: Christian perfection begins with the single intention—complete devotion to God, out of gratitude to the Father for his love revealed in the cross of Christ (16:4).

The Fullness of Faith:

> Repose in the blood of Christ;
> a firm confidence in God, and persuasion
> of his favor; the highest tranquillity,
> serenity, and peace of mind, with a
> deliverance from every flesh desire,
> and a cessation of all, even inward sins.
>
> Plain Account 8:2

When Wesley came under the influence of Peter Böhler in the spring of 1738 his initial reaction was to affirm that saving faith is all or nothing. This was in sharp contrast to what he had believed up to that time. But as the emotional storms of fear and doubt engulfed him,[20] Wesley came to understand there are degrees of saving faith.[21] This laid the foundation for an understanding of perfection as the *fullness of faith*. As our faith grows, so does our experience of God's grace purifying the heart.

Wesley came to understand faith as an *assurance* or *firm confidence* in God, in his character, power, and promises, and in the power of Christ to redeem us through his death and resurrection. Regarding perfection, faith is the *conviction* or inner certainty[22]

---

[20] The storms JW faced which altered his theology were physical (at sea; 1735), emotional (fear and doubt; 1738), theological (stillness; 1740), schismatic (enthusiasts; 1763), and spiritual (personal disappointment, 1766). Each storm profoundly shaped his doctrine of perfection. Cf. ch 10.
[21] Cf. PA ch 7 end note.
[22] Heb 11:1. This is a favorite text of JW on the nature of saving faith.

we must have in God's promise that he will deliver us from inward sin and fill us with his love.[23] Hence, the words of Jesus: "According to your faith will it be done to you" (Matt 9:29). Faith is our *repose* in Christ, a *firm persuasion* that Jesus does now forgive and save from *all* sin—*even inward* sin (cf. Matt 1:21). Consequently, faith is the sole and immediate condition for salvation from sin.[24]

The Faith Journey:

> A man may be dying for some time; yet he does not, properly speaking, die, till the instant the soul is separated from the body; and in that instant he lives the life of eternity. In like manner, he may be dying to sin for some time; yet he is not dead to sin, till sin is separated from his soul; and in that instant he lives the full life of love.
>
> Plain Account 19:73

The unfolding of salvation does not happen only when God intersects our lives at specific moments. Rather, we must view Christian perfection as a journey involving the ongoing process of *dying to sin*, both voluntary and involuntary, and *growing* in the *grace* and *knowledge of Christ*. The spiritual life parallels the natural life so we can grasp the process side of Christian perfection. Perfection begins when one is an infant, a mere *babe in Christ* (12:9). The power of new life in Christ delivers from the power of *outward sin* (12:28). As we grow and die further to *inward sin* (17:5), we enter into spiritual adolescence—a *young man* (1 Jn 2:14). At this stage we overcome the lingering doubts and fears that have hampered us from waging spiritual warfare

---

[23] *The Scripture Way of Salvation* (1765) defines this faith to be four-fold: 1. belief that God has promised full salvation from sin. 2. Belief God is able to save from all sin. 3. Belief God is willing to save from all sin. 4. Belief God now saves from all sin. (III.14-17)

[24] The other conditions listed in the PA are: desire (19:81, 83), keeping God's ordinances (15:4-6), prayer (16:19-20; 19:79-80), universal obedience (15:4; 19:76-81).

with confidence (12:9 n; 13:25). As we continue to walk in the Spirit and practice the means of grace (19:76-81), we die to that nature within us, which is contrary to God's love reigning within. We then arrive at the threshold of *scripture perfection*, the state of spiritual *adulthood* (19:64; 12:29). The *moment* we believe in Christ as our sanctification (1 Cor 1:30) he touches our heart a second time (18:18) and removes those *sinful tempers* which have plagued our devotion to God. He fills us with his love (16:2), even his *perfect love*. From this point we continue to grow as we overcome our *involuntary sin* and attain further heights in the Spirit's fruit (25:88-100). Finally, our growth continues as we rely solely on Christ's intercession and indwelling presence (25:41). Thus, the adult believer—though sanctified entirely—remains imperfect in their humanity until the day they lay this body down and enter the realm of the angels.

The Witness and Fruit of the Spirit:

> We know it by the witness and by the fruit of the Spirit... As, when we were justified, the Spirit bore witness with our spirit, that our sins were forgiven; so, when we were sanctified, he bore witness, that they were taken away.
>
> Plain Account 25:50

Since perfect love is a gift of divine grace (18:18), the Holy Spirit testifies to this gift in the same manner as he does with the first gift—by his *witness* and his *fruit*.[25] The *witness*, in relation to sanctification, is the *direct testimony* of the Spirit to our spirit that our sins have been *taken away* and that we *know the things that are freely given to us* in Christ (25:50, 57). In this way every believer may know the state of their soul and have assurance of divine favor and inward cleansing. The *fruit* is that work of the Spirit *manifesting* in our *words and actions* that our *renewal* is complete. *Universal holiness* now characterizes the life of the perfect as *pride, anger, self-will,* and a *heart bent toward back-*

---

[25] These are known formally as the direct and indirect witness.

A Plain Account Of Christian Perfection

sliding are fully removed and purged (21:3; 25:74). The witness of the Spirit is the new covenant privilege for every believer in Christ.

Do you lack the Spirit's testimony? If so, come to the Savior and receive. For Jesus invites us: "If any man thirst, let him come unto me, and drink. He that believeth on me, as the scripture hath said, out of his belly shall flow rivers of living water" (Jn 7:37-38).

Perfect Love:

> 'Love is the fulfilling of the law, the end of the commandment.' It is not only 'the first and great' command, but all the commandments in one.
>
> Plain Account 6:3

Christian perfection is that *habitual disposition* of love to God and neighbor, reigning in our hearts through the removal of all other rival dispositions and attitudes (6:2). Love is the *one thing*, the *one happiness*, and the *one design* being sought after with all the heart, so that our lives are *continually offered up to God in flames of holy love* (6:6-7, 11). Love reigning within is to have the *mind which was in Christ*, motivating us to *fulfill the will of him* that sent his Son into the world (6:14). Love as a *habitual disposition* is to be *perfect as your Father in heaven is perfect* (6:2; cf. Matt 5:48). Love alone is the *heaven of heavens;* for there is *nothing higher in religion*, and, *in effect, there is nothing else* (25:131). Love is the *highest gift of God* (25:130). Thus, love is the one temper that comprises our perfection in this life. For when we love our Father with all our heart, *no wrong temper, none contrary to love, remains in the soul* (19:5).

At last, God's plan from the beginning of creation has now been revealed. Our heavenly Father desires to renew us after his own image and likeness: What Adam lost—Christ regains. What the serpent stole—Christ restores. God's redeeming love in Christ is the essence and heart of our perfection, the one jewel that makes up our crown. With it, we are rich; without it, we are "poor, blind and naked" (Rev 3:17). Our heavenly Father desires this one thing—that we be perfect in his love.

May the Father of heaven above open your eyes and heart to see the riches that are yours in Christ. Amen.

Full Salvation from Sin:

> Christians are saved in this world from all sin, from all unrighteousness; that they are now in such a sense perfect, as not to commit sin, and to be freed from evil thoughts and evil tempers.
>
> Plain Account 12:44

Christian perfection is truly a glorious freedom! It is none other than salvation from our *outward sins,* and from the *sins of our hearts* (12:36). To phrase it another way, Christian perfection is *inward* and *outward holiness* (12:42). This great privilege is not only for those who have attained spiritual *adulthood* (12:29), but begins the very moment we become a *babe in Christ* (12:9). The birthright of every child of God includes salvation "from the power of sin, as well as from the guilt of it" (*Salvation by Faith* II.5). But this is not all. Our very birthright in Christ promises us salvation from sinful *thoughts* and *tempers.* This is the grand privilege of the new covenant. This is full salvation from sin. God is now perfecting every believer by removing from their dispositional nature *pride, anger, self-will,* sinful *desire,* and all the other traits of the *carnal mind* (16:9). In Christ the adult believer can now exclaim, "*My evil nature, the body of sin, is destroyed*;" and *positively, "Christ lives in me"* (12:32, 34). Wesley uses this kind of language to emphasize that in Christ a real emancipation from sin is available to every believer. He often refers to this blessing as a deeper *cleansing* (6:2; 12:25-26, 38-44), or as a *dying* to sin (19:73). That the message of salvation in Christ includes freedom from *all* sin is one of the twin pillars Wesley builds his doctrine of perfection upon (26:6-7). The essence of which is that *all* believers share in the glorious privilege of God's salvation from sin, and are *perfect* to the degree of their spiritual growth (12:9).

The Transformation of Nature:

> Heavenly Adam, life divine,
> Change my nature into thine;
> More and spread throughout my soul,
> Actuate and fill the whole.
>
> Plain Account 9:5

The early poems in the *Plain Account* speak of the ideal of Christian perfection as a change deep down in one's nature. It is not merely a surface transformation, where the outer fringes of life are affected, but one where the *full stream of nature's tide* within us is altered to center on God, his glory, and his will (9:2). Our perfection involves the taking on of the nature of Christ, the *heavenly Adam* (9:4), so that our life's *sole business* is to bring God praise. Perfection is God swallowing up our soul so that it is *plunged in the Godhead's deepest sea, and lost in thine immensity*. Transformed and changed, Christ becomes our all, and is in all (Col 3:11).

The Limits of Perfection:

> Not only sin, properly so called – that is, a voluntary transgression of a known law – but sin, improperly so called – that is, an involuntary transgression of a divine law, known or unknown – needs the atoning blood.
>
> Plain Account 19:23

As great and glorious as Christian perfection is, it remains an experience with definite limitations. For starters, perfect love is limited to a freedom from *voluntary sin* (19:23). Everyone filled with perfect love still falls short of God's perfect law by their *omissions, shortcomings, mistakes in judgment and practice,* and *defects of various kinds* (19:20). In short, there is no *sinless perfection* in this life (19:25). All Christians continue to *transgress* God's absolute standard of holiness so that even the most perfect need to pray daily, *"forgive us our transgressions"* (19:12).

Moreover, perfection is limited by our continual dependence on Christ. At no time can anyone claim a perfection of our own. For the Christian, perfection is not like a *tree* that draws life on its own, but like a *branch, which united to the vine, bears fruit; but severed from it, is dried up and withered* (19:18). As a consequence, our perfection must be understood as the impartation of the mind of Christ in holy tempers, and in the intercession of Christ before our heavenly Father continually covering our *involuntary sin*.

Finally, perfection is limited by the total process. As an *instantaneous* experience it takes place in a *moment* (19:73), but this *instant* is both preceded and followed by a continual process of growth and maturation. Therefore, the initial experience (*instant*) of perfect love serves as a significant milestone in our spiritual journey ushering us into new realms of growth and development. An Old Testament example is Israel crossing the Jordan River. While crossing the river was a significant milestone for the nation, it was only one step in their development toward nationhood. Seen in this light, perfect love should never be understood as the end of life's race. Instead, just as a bicycle racer shifts into a higher gear, perfect love empowers us for more effective service to God and neighbor, thus preparing us for service in the eternal Kingdom.

To summarize, Christian perfection has definite limits and our complete renewal awaits us in the new creation. There is no eschatological perfection in this life. As long as this present age continues our redemption in Christ is never fully realized.

A Plain Account Of Christian Perfection

Process and Moment:

> Unfold the hidden mystery, the second gift impart;
> Reveal thy glorious self in me, in every waiting heart.
> Come in this accepted hour, bring thy heavenly kingdom in!
> Fill us with the glorious power, rooting out the seeds of sin.
> Plain Account 18:18, 20

Christian perfection is a state we grow towards, enter into instantaneously, and continue to grow in afterwards, even into all eternity. Therefore, just as justification and new birth are gifts from God, perfection is the *second gift* to be received *now* by faith.

Wesley integrates his gradual and instantaneous motifs by likening the sanctification process to physical death (19:73). Gradually, the physical life ebbs away until the very *moment* the soul separates from the body. In that *instant* the person begins to live the life of eternity. So it is with Christian perfection. When we believe in Christ the process of dying to sin and growing in love begins. This process continues through several stages until, by a second act of faith, we enter instantaneously into the grace of perfect love. From that point we continue to grow toward greater maturity as we continue to overcome the imperfections of our fallen humanity (19:20-25).

This entire process involves a soteriological tension in our lives. To his credit, Wesley was consistent when he taught we must hold together both the gradual and the instantaneous motifs of spiritual development, without diminishing the importance of either. He saw maintaining this tension as the only way to remain open to the work of God's grace within our hearts (21:4-5; 25:75-79). The apostle Paul speaks of this tension in several letters.[26] In these passages both the instantaneous and gradual motifs are dynamically intertwined and expounded upon in relation to spiritual

---

[26] Romans 6-8; 2 Corinthians 4:7-21; Galatians 5:16-6:8; and Philippians 3:7-16.

growth. In the end, our destiny as God's children is to be "conformed to the likeness of his Son" (Rom 8:29).

Perfection Distorted:

> Two or three began to take their own imaginations for impressions from God, and thence to suppose that they should never die; and these, laboring to bring others into the same opinion, occasioned much noise and confusion.
>
> Plain Account 20:3

As wonderful and sweet as full salvation is, Christian perfection can be, and often is abused and distorted by those who claim its fruit. While chapters 20-22 of the *Plain Account* do not offer explicit information on what the experience entails, they do instruct us against its perversion. Three specific abuses were noted by Wesley:

> *Enthusiasm.* Christians can be prone to overly rely on their imagination and impressions, as if they all come from God. Thomas Maxfield and George Bell came to believe they were above any correction from those deemed "less spiritual." They reasoned that they alone had the true experience, and consequently, they alone could judge its merits. Their "heat" had no "head" to keep them in balance. Akin to the above problem was their overemphasis on the charismata of the Spirit, equating it to being "spiritual." Paul's first letter to the Corinthians reminds every generation of the need to guard against this abuse (1 Cor 12-14).[27]

> *Doctrinal Error.* George Bell and others denied the continuing reality of the fall in the life of the perfect, believing they were as pure as Adam in his innocence. All of Wesley's qualifiers concerning perfection were ignored or rejected. They denied any present dependency upon Christ's interces-

---

[27] See also the Seven Advices 25:105-168.

sion; and, as a consequence, stopped partaking of the Lord's Table. This demonstrates how dangerous a concept can become when mixed with unrestrained emotion.

Millennial Expectations. George Bell's enthusiasm led him to connect their experience of "angelic" perfection to end-time events. How Bell came to all his conclusions we do not know, but an important lesson can be learned here. Wesley's rejection of Bell's prophecy stems from more than a lack of interest in the subject (cf. ch 22); instead, he found in his reading of scripture and the church fathers a universal call to the necessity of holiness in this life. He saw further that perfection is not an end-time experience for a select few, but a new covenant gift for every believer in Christ. Thus Bell's prophecy diluted the doctrine of perfect love of its power to shape each generation of Christians.

To conclude, the *Plain Account* gives us clear-cut boundaries to keep our spiritual experience in check. We would do well to heed its counsel.[28]

---

[28] Another way to do a thematic study of the PA is to reflect on the themes found in individual chapters: *single intention* (chs 2-4), *Christ-likeness* (chs 5, 15), *love* (chs 6-7), *faith* (ch 8), *the ten ingredients of holiness* (ch 10), *salvation from sin* (ch 12) *renewal in God's image* (ch 13), *Sabbath rest* (ch 14), *entire sanctification* (ch 15), *Christ's atonement* (ch 16), *Bible doctrine* (ch 17), *instantaneous motif* (ch 18), *limitations and qualifications* (ch 19), *abuse* (chs 20-22), *testimony* (ch 24), *theological foundation and assurance* (ch 25), *concise summary* (ch 26).

NINE
The Faith Journey

At the heart of Wesley's theology of perfection is the faith journey. Wesley correctly understood that the gospel's central theme is the restoration of the human race in the image and likeness of God.[1] He further discerned that for this goal to be fully realized sinful humanity needs more than forgiveness and a declaration of righteousness. Adam's children need to be inwardly transformed and changed in character and spirit. Wesley instinctively believed every aspect of salvation, including both process and instant, must pertain to the transformation of the tempers.[2] Now the tempers are those dispositions which are habitual, rule one's character, and orient the life.[3] For that reason Wesley's primary understanding of Christian perfection must be seen as the *transformation of the dispositional nature*. This is confirmed by the most significant definition he ever penned on inward holiness:

> In general we may observe it is that *habitual disposition* of soul which in the Sacred Writings is termed 'holiness',

---

[1] Gen 1:26-28; 5:1; Eph 4:23-24; Col 3:11. Of course, as we saw in chapter 7 (and below) JW did believe the new creation transcends what Adam enjoyed in the garden.

[2] This is my firm conviction about JW's doctrine of perfect love (PA 6:2; 9:2, 5; 10:3-5; 12:29-36, 44; 19:5, 32, 44).

[3] Randy Maddox explains, "These affections are not simply passive 'feelings' for Wesley, they are motivating dispositions of the person. In their ideal expression, they integrate the rational and the emotional dimensions of human life into a holistic inclination toward particular choices and actions. Thus, the primal example of affection for Wesley is love to God and neighbor. It is equally important to note that Wesley assumed that these motivating affections were not simply transitory, but can (and should) be habituated into enduring dispositions. To capture this potential Wesley traded on a slight - but significant - distinction between affections and tempers. He was using 'temper' in this connection in a characteristic eighteenth-century sense of an enduring or *habitual* disposition of a person" (*Responsible Grace,* 69; emphasis his).

and which directly implies the being cleansed from sin, 'from all filthiness both of flesh and spirit', and by consequence the being endued with those virtues which were also in Christ Jesus, the being so 'renewed in the image of our mind' as to be 'perfect, as our Father in heaven is perfect'.[4]

Since the faith journey's sole aim is to renovate the dispositional nature, Wesley interpreted the *ordo salutis* as a process of life transformation. But he did not stop there. Over the decades as his theology of perfection matured, he also worked out the particulars of the process. In so doing, Wesley combined both faith and the means of grace to form a unique blend of process and instant in a journey toward complete renewal. Speaking in general terms, the roles that faith and the means of grace play are straightforward. Faith serves as the human response to grace received, especially in the instant.[5] The means of grace serve as God's way of imparting grace over time, that is, through the process.[6] Since salvation, as dispositional transformation, involves both instant and process, then both faith and the means of grace play indispensable roles in the renewal process. In other words, spiritual development happens only as the believer learns to exercise faith in Christ and obedience through the consistent practice of the means of grace. For while God does work salvation in the instant, these God-moments are grounded on a lifelong process whereby holy tempers are infused in the character of the person. Contrary to what some might assume, Wesley did not see human response as initiating or controlling the reception of grace.[7]

---

[4] *The Circumcision of the Heart* (1733) I.1; emphasis mine. Though this definition has been quoted before, its significance merits another look.
[5] I am speaking in very general terms here. See JWL 9/1/71; 4/29/89.
[6] PA ch 17 end note, 1745 Q. 9; 19:76-81.
[7] JW favorite text "We love because he first loved us" (1 Jn 4:18) expresses this point succinctly. This is contrary to how some view the believer's role in salvation. This view sees the seeker or believer taking on a more active role by grounding the response to grace in the native free will of the person. JW's

John Wesley's Theology of Christian Perfection

In 1763 Wesley published his mature thoughts on how God works in the instant compared to the process:

> Q. 25. But is not this the case of all that are justified? Do they not gradually die to sin and grow in grace, till at, or perhaps a little before, death God perfects them in love?
>
> A. I believe this is the case of most, but not all. God usually gives a considerable time for men to receive light, to grow in grace, to do and suffer his will, before they are either justified or sanctified; but he does not invariably adhere to this; sometimes he *'cuts short his work:'* He does the work of many years in a few weeks; perhaps in a week, a day, an hour.[8]

God's *usual* way of working is through process, the faithful practice of the means of grace. But he is always free to "cut short" this work. In a moment, even in an instant, God can accomplish what normally takes "many years" to realize. Interestingly, the moment is here qualified further as a series of shorter processes—from an hour to several weeks! To repeat, Wesley never envisioned the believer as *initiating* or *controlling* the impartation of grace. In his letters he reminds his people that God is sovereign over the entire discipleship process and he knows which path is best for each of his children.[9] This is where the witness of the Spirit comes into play. For only the witness can confirm what divine grace is imparting. Only then can the Christian have the necessary confidence to cast off all the doubts and fears which

---

view on free will is much more nuanced: grace gifts the person with liberty of choice.

[8] *Plain Account* 25:75-76.

[9] "If anything medicinal profit you, probably it will be this. But perhaps God will not suffer you to be healed by outward medicines. It may be, he is determined to have all the glory of his own work. Meantime, he designs, by this weakness of body, to keep your soul low, as a weaned child. There is a wonderful mystery in the manner and circumstances of that mighty working, whereby he subdues all things to himself, and leaves nothing in the heart but his pure love alone" (JWL 3/6/59).

The Faith Journey

arise. With the perfection revival's excesses and schism, Wesley felt compelled to reemphasize the Spirit's fruits as the final arbiter of life change.[10] This gradually led to a reemphasis on works within his holiness *ordo salutis*.[11] Faith, then, to be saving must produce holiness of heart and life. Of course, the Calvinists distrusted such subtle distinctions. They suspected that Wesley was teaching, at least implicitly, a system of salvation by merit. Wesley, to be expected, strongly denounced such accusations.

Through the sixties and seventies the faith journey continued to take shape as his doctrine of involuntary sin began to reverberate through his theological system. Wesley could now explain with greater consistency how the adult believer is free from all sin, yet needs Christ's intercession for daily shortcomings and errors. Only when this mortal body is discarded, Wesley affirmed, will this kind of sin be fully vanquished.

Another corollary was the introduction of the servant state. This state differed from the other states in that it temporally severed justification from the new birth.[12] Yet, such a distinction became necessary for Wesley to explain his own faith journey in the twenties and thirties. It also made sense of what many converts experienced in their faith journey—spiritual renewal apart from the witness of the Spirit. These believers did love God and sincerely desired to serve him through the faithful practice of the means of grace, but they lacked the one sure evidence of the new birth—the direct testimony of the Spirit. As Wesley became more aware of other religious faiths, he came to see that the servant state could explain how the life of God could be given to devout believers of these other faiths. In this way the faith journey became more nuanced in the area of prevenient grace as salvation was now affirmed to begin with a faith that reverences God and practices good works (Acts 10:35).

---

[10] PA 25:70, 88-100. This is a very important passage in the *Plain Account*.
[11] Cf. ch 4.
[12] Even in his GosH the new birth and justification were linked in timing at the final judgment.

John Wesley's Theology of Christian Perfection

Toward the end of his life Wesley came to appreciate even more that the faith journey continues into the new creation. While he had always affirmed continued growth into all eternity, he now delineated this growth more specifically. Just as humanity will share in the glory of the angels, so the brute creation will one day rise to the level of reason and spiritual intuition that the human race now enjoy. Universal holiness will then characterize all creation. Wesley came to expect that upon death he would join the holy angels in serving the kingdom of God by ministering to the heirs of salvation remaining on earth. Only in the new creation will the faith journey be complete. For then all sin and evil will be vanquished and the believer's love attain a capacity possible only in the resurrection. In this way the Wesleyan understanding of the faith journey became complete and fully articulated.

To summarize, the faith journey (salvation) properly begins at the first dawn of spiritual awakening, to be fully realized in the new creation; yet, at each step faith is the essential human response.

Charting the Faith Journey

One way to capture significant nuances of the Wesleyan path of renewal is to chart these gradations of emphasis. In this way we can visually see Wesley's philosophy of disciple-making. We begin with *The Degrees of Faith Chart*. Wesley's concept of degrees was based firmly on the belief that God's eternal plan is to renew his creation in his own image and likeness. By disposition Wesley was an optimist. Being ever confident that what God began he would also finish, Wesley envisioned each stage of development as already perfect according to its degree:

> In what sense then are Christians perfect? This is what I shall endeavour...to show. But it should be premised that there are several stages in Christian life as well as in natu-

ral: some of the children of God being but new-born babes, others having attained to more maturity. And accordingly St. John, in his first Epistle, applies himself severally to those he terms little children, those he styles young men, and those whom he entitles fathers...It is of these chiefly I speak in the latter part of this discourse; for these only are perfect Christians. But even babes in Christ are in such a sense perfect...not to commit sin.[13]

The stages of the faith journey represent progressively higher degrees of perfection in the renewal process. With each degree serving as a definite stage, definitional markers serve to identify each stage. More important, these markers reveal the nature of renewal at each stage in the process. In this way the entire path becomes a continuous journey with marked transitions of inner transformation. Now let's turn to the chart itself (next page). On the left are listed the levels or stages of faith (perfection) beginning at the bottom and working up to the new creation at the top. At the lowest level is the materialist, which Wesley accurately defined as non-faith since God's existence is formally denied.[14] From this state of non-faith, prevenient grace leads upward to the stages found in a proper Christian faith. The reader will notice sandwiched between several states are two instantaneous moments and two sub-states. The God-moments of new birth and Christian perfection are what define Wesley's *ordo salutis* as a gospel of two works of grace. The two wilderness states follow upon the heels of these two God-moments as believers solidify their experience and become settled in their spiritual development.[15] Let's now look at the chart on the following page:

---

[13] *Christian Perfection* II.1, 2.
[14] Cf. *On Faith (Heb 11:6)* I.1. This sermon provides the states of prevenient grace in the Degrees Chart.
[15] See ch 6 for a discussion of a wilderness state following perfect love.

John Wesley's Theology of Christian Perfection

Degrees of Faith Chart[16]

Stages of
Faith/Perfection   Description

New Creation: Resurrection body; reception of rewards and grades of glory

Paradise: Body no longer a hindrance to holiness; all involuntary sin removed

~ ~ ~ Wilderness State II ~ ~ ~

Adulthood: Holy tempers replace sinful dispositions; love perfected with divine fullness; full, complete devotion to God; though involuntary sin continues

- - - - - - - - Christian Perfection - - - - - - - -

Adolescence: Full assurance; all fear and doubt vanquished; a conqueror in spiritual warfare; prepared to enter adulthood

~ ~ ~ Wilderness State I ~ ~ ~

Childhood: Justified and a child of God; but in a mixed state: outward sin defeated, yet inward sin remains; struggles with fear & doubt

- - - - - - - - - New Birth - - - - - - - - - -

Servant: Fears God, works righteousness, partially accepted – i.e. justified, but lacks the new birth/witness of adoption

Nominal: Has the form of religion, but lacks divine power to transform the life; faith as assent

Pre-Christian: Prevenient grace enlightens and empowers choice towards
*Jew   the true God and righteousness
*Moslem
*Heathen
 Deist
 Materialist (atheist)

(* These three levels can also be found in the servant state)

---

[16] The primary sources for The Degrees of Faith Chart are: JWS *Christian Perfection, The New Creation, On Faith (Heb 11:6), On Faith (Heb 11:1), On the Discoveries of Faith, The Scripture Way of Salvation*; *The Explanatory Notes on the New Testament* (Acts 10:35); *Plain Account* 19:23-25, 25:2-41; JWL 12/26/61, 10/13/64, 4/7/68.

The Faith Journey

The benefit of the *Degrees of Faith Chart* is that it clarifies the level of attainment at each stage in the total process. We can know our level of faith (perfection) by matching our experience to the definitions on the right. Moreover, the chart facilitates pastors and other church leaders in counseling their people toward full renewal by identifying the next level of spiritual growth. The strength of the Wesleyan path is that each stage is distinctively marked so the Christian can *know* where they stand in the renewal process. Of course, Wesley believed the testimony of the Spirit serves to confirm one's spiritual attainment at each level.[17] This testimony becomes even more necessary in an atmosphere of revival where emotions are heightened and people often presume more change has been internalized than has been done in reality.

Another way to view the Wesleyan path of renewal is to list across the page the major components of each stage in the faith journey. Here a component is just another word for a definitional marker used in the above chart. Then, like a checklist, we can check off the components received as the person rises higher in the renewal process. This allows each stage to be more clearly distinguished from the others. For example, Wesley understood the nominal Christian to mentally assent to the formal doctrines of the Christian faith, but without any experiential knowledge of them. Accordingly, this level of faith does not know by experience the new birth, the witness of the Spirit, or perfect love. These latter marks identify higher stages on the faith journey. As the believer grows and attains these higher stages more and more components are added to their experiential faith and mark their spiritual character. Accordingly, in the Wesleyan path the number of components one possesses does measure the level of their spiritual maturity:

---

[17] *Plain Account* 19:69; 25:51-56.

John Wesley's Theology of Christian Perfection

The Components Chart

Stages	Faith as Assent	Justification	New Birth/ Adoption	Full Assurance	Perfect Love	Adamic Perfection	Glorified Body
New Creation	"	"	"	"	"	"	"
Paradise	"	"	"	"	"	"	
Adult	"	"	"	"	"		
Adolescent	"	"	"	"			
Child	"	"	"				
Servant	"	"					
Nominal	"						

Of course, the above list of components could be divided into more detail and thereby enlarged, thus identifying smaller increments of renewal. What is shown are the key components of each major stage in Wesley's mature *ordo salutis*. The *Components Chart* points to the impartation of additional gifts within the believer's dispositional nature (tempers) as they grow in Christ-likeness. Since the coming of Christ's kingdom entails renewal in our Father's likeness, the gifts of his reign affect this renewal within the dispositional nature.

We can now progress to the next chart, which uses the idea of a stairway to illustrate a very important insight into Wesley's theology of perfection. Here we view the faith journey as part of the grand meta-narrative of redemption. The story of God is the redemption of his people from the curse of Adam's sin. This is the purpose of the faith journey: to renew us in our Father's likeness. But this renewal requires that many steps (stages) be taken if the goal is to be realized. Once again, from Wesley's perspective, underlying this entire process is the transformation of the tempers. As the Christian reaches for and attains one step after another their dispositional nature becomes more holy and Christ-like, and thereby more like their Father in heaven. *The Step Chart* exemplifies very well how Wesley envisioned the faith journey: a

The Faith Journey

series of stages leading upward to the character of Christ and of God. The reader will see under each step a one to two-word definition identifying the primary gift received at that stage in the process:

The Step Chart

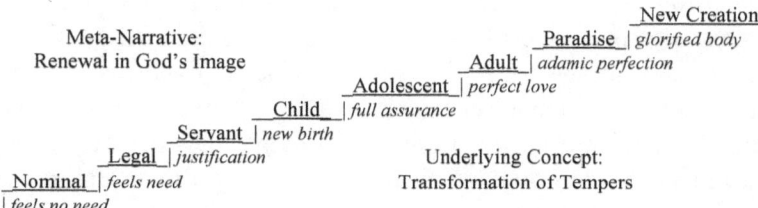

From chapter three we learned that beginning in 1739 Wesley began to teach two definitive God-moments in the faith journey. We called this message the Gospel of Two Works of Grace. Yet, as we view the above chart we see there are many potential God-moments within the renewal process. A close reading of Wesley's writings points to the same conclusion. For example, the servant and adolescent states are defined by the gifts of justification and full assurance. But a little reflection on the nature of these gifts leads logically to the conclusion that both are instantaneous in their reception. After all, one is either declared righteous before God or is not. The same holds true regarding full assurance. The believer has overcome all fear and doubt or they have not. Even though Wesley did not explicitly articulate these stages as definitive God-moments in his two-works gospel, as he did for the new birth and full salvation,[18] his teaching regarding both states necessarily leads to the conclusion that both are entered into instantaneously. Of course, the same could be said of paradise and the new creation. Both are entered in an instant; the for-

---

[18] The reader should be reminded that until the late sixties justification was identified with the new birth in relation to timing. Even late JW continued to connect the two in timing since most in his audience continued to receive forgiveness and regeneration in the same God-moment.

mer when the soul separates from the body and the latter when the disembodied spirit is reunited with their glorified body. The same could be said for the stages of prevenient grace. Therefore, the Wesleyan path recognizes a dynamic process punctuated with many divine moments, but with two as dominant: the new birth and perfect love. This is one of the unique features of Wesley's mature theological system and is illustrated by the above chart.

Wesley interpreted eschatological salvation in terms of renewal in God's image and likeness. The point to Jesus' birth, death, resurrection, ascension and return is to bring God's kingdom rule to sinful humanity. Inherent in every part of this work of salvation is the removal of sinful tempers by the infusion of holy dispositions. Wesley was consistent on this point: true religion consists in holy tempers.[19] To convey this truth, Wesley picked up and utilized the language and categories which Christian David had used: sin reigns, sin remains, and sin removed.[20] Over time Wesley worked out his own terminology. Salvation from sin was now threefold: from sin's *guilt* (justification), sin's *power* (outward sin), and sin's *being* (inward sin).[21] By the early seventies Wesley identified these three gifts with the servant, child and adult states of the faith journey.[22] By contrast, in his *Explanatory Notes Upon the New Testament* (1756) Wesley explains how one's love is purified from "slavish" fear as the person moves from awakening to child to adult:

---

[19] It is almost pointless to demonstrate this point since this idea pervades his corpus. But in *On Zeal* he once again says it with clarity, "We conclude from the whole...that true religion, in the very essence of it, is nothing short of holy tempers" (III.12). From this idea alone we must define perfection primarily in terms of dispositional transformation.

[20] *On Sin in Believers* III.8; IV.3, 12; V.2; the latter term is my paraphrase of JW's position.

[21] *On Sin in Believers* IV.4. Implicit to JW's doctrine of involuntary sin is the moment of deliverance from the *plague* of sin in the article of death and the resurrection.

[22] Cf. ch 4.

The Faith Journey

> A natural man has neither fear nor love; one that is awakened, fear without love; a babe in Christ, love and fear; a father in Christ, love without fear.[23]

As sin expires by degrees, from one stage to another, so one's love becomes perfect, from one stage to another. In a similar manner Wesley understands the witness of the Spirit to increase by degrees as one passes from one stage to another. In *Farther Thoughts on Christian Perfection* (1763), Wesley explains that the direct testimony is felt intermittently by the child, but becomes consistent in the adolescent and adult.[24] Hence, the "highest class of Christian" (i.e. adult) enjoys uninterrupted fellowship and communion with their heavenly Father.[25] By comparison, the "lowest" class (child) continues to wrestle with insecurity in their relationship with God due to remaining sinful tempers (inward sin), fear over their inconsistent devotion and obedience, and from the imperfection of their love. In other words, as a person grows from a child to an adolescent and then to an adult, their relationship with God moves from a mixed condition (fear and love) to a pure one (love, no fear), imparting greater security to the Christian. Pertinent at this point is to see that the process of renewal is realized only as holy tempers replace sinful ones. This alone makes one fit and ready to enjoy God's eternal glory.[26] Holy tempers are at the heart of Wesley's philosophy of discipleship, and in many ways govern his perfection theology. On the following page the *Tempers Chart* highlights the transition from sinful tempers ruling in the natural person to holy tempers reigning in the entirely sanctified believer. Above are listed sequentially the stages of the faith journey (from left to right) and at the bottom of the chart are listed references from Wesley's writings highlighting the transition:

---

[23] NT Notes 1 Jn 4:18.
[24] *Plain Account* 25:59-62.
[25] *Plain Account* 25:60, 66-67.
[26] Cf. PA 21:3 note on this point; *On the Wedding Garment* §10.

John Wesley's Theology of Christian Perfection

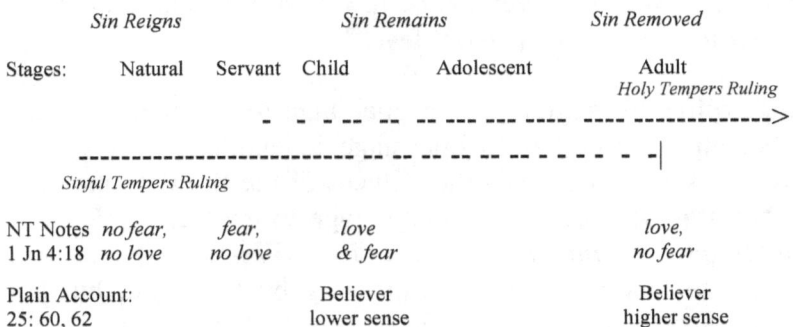

The above chart fixes in the mind that the heart of the faith journey is the replacement of sinful tempers with holy ones. Simply stated, holiness is pure dispositions and attitudes toward God and neighbor. As Wesley was fond of saying, holiness is having the mind that was in Christ, and to walk as Jesus did.[27] The purpose of identifying various stages is so the Christian (or seeker) can know what progress means, and to know if it is being attained. The grand vision of renewal in God's image only becomes tangible when specific signs or markers are identified at specific stages in the overall path. So while the faith journey concerns the meta-narrative of complete renewal, on a practical level it focuses directly on developing holy dispositions and attitudes (tempers) in the character. This sets the Wesleyan path apart from other evangelical counterparts. Wesley saw justification not as an end in itself, but as divine empowerment to love God so as to enjoy uninterrupted communion with him.[28]

In a similar manner, the gift of full assurance was never seen by Wesley as a doctrine merely to support one's theological system.[29] Instead, Wesley believed assurance to be essential for the believer to have confidence in their walk and relationship with

---

[27] This is another very common affirmation of perfection. See PA 5:2.

[28] This is the significance of JW's use of 1 Th 5:16-18 to define perfection.

[29] As JW believed Calvinism tended to do with its teaching on the perseverance of the saints and other related doctrines.

The Faith Journey

God. As we all know, relationships do not function well when the parties lack trust in each other. Connected to this is the reality check that relationships do not live on just a legal level. Instead, how both parties interact and relate determines how close and comfortable each party is with the other. The same principles hold true to our relationship with God. Wesley saw this and therefore believed assurance to involve much more than a proposition that our eternity is secure. To the contrary, he intuitively grasped that for two to walk together in love and sweet communion, there must be agreement of heart.[30] As a consequence, Wesley connected assurance to experiential realities, that is, with a change of heart toward God and his will. In this way, as the dispositions and attitudes conform more and more to the Father's will, the believer enjoys a stronger sense of confidence and assurance in their walk before God. Therefore, Wesley believed the witness of the Spirit to serve as confirmation of one's harmony with God and his perfect will.

This sets the context for the last chart. The *Image Renewal Chart* builds on the prior step chart but broadens it to include Adam's original perfection. Through his entire life Wesley held to Adam's perfection at the beginning:

> Now, he was created free from any defect, either in his understanding or his affections. His body was then no clog to the mind; it did not hinder his apprehending all things clearly, judging truly concerning them, and reasoning justly, if he reasoned at all. I say, *if he reasoned*; for possibly he did not. Perhaps he had no need of reasoning, till his corruptible body pressed down the mind, and impaired its native faculties. Perhaps, till then, the mind saw every truth that offered as directly as the eye now sees the light.[31]

---

[30] Amos 3:3 "Can two walk together, except they be agreed?"
[31] PA 25:5-6; emphasis his. See *Justification By Faith* I.1-3.

But the fall took him and his posterity down to the depths of the pit. According to Wesley three interlocking consequences followed. To begin, Adam's soul died and became separated from God. His body likewise became mortal and corrupt, sentenced to physical death. And if this was not enough, having been alienated from God and under the sentence of death, Adam now faced the prospect of eternal death, "the destruction both of body and soul, in the fire that is never to be quenched."[32] So Adam lost the image in which he was created by the finger of God.

His posterity, now in a state of nature, continues to live after sinful desires which control their dispositional nature; primarily, pride, anger, selfishness, idolatry and unbelief.[33] But even here the finger of God's grace is felt preveniently. Grace reveals the eternal Godhead through the creation (Rom 1:20), giving witness to God's goodness through his blessings of harvest and the meeting of other needs (Acts 14:17). God graciously instills the "first wish" to please him by awakening the conscious to his will.[34] Wesley, in the 1780's, referred to this as implying "some tendency to life; some degree of salvation."

From this angle of perspective the faith journey becomes the meta-narrative of redemption, the story of God restoring his people to what Adam lost and more. For the new creation rises higher than what Adam enjoyed in the beginning; higher than what the angels now enjoy. Our future is to share in the resurrection of Christ, with our bodies patterned after his glorified one. The chart below illustrates the grand theme of the Wesleyan path: our eschatological renewal in the plenitude of God's eternal fullness given to us in Christ:

---

[32] *Justification By Faith* I.5.
[33] JWL 9/15/62.
[34] *On Working Out Our Own Salvation* II.1.

The Faith Journey

The Image Renewal Chart

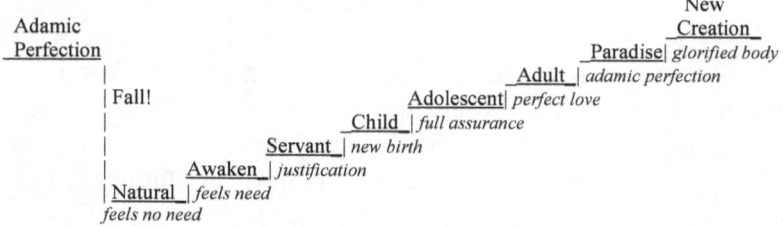

Wesley could say it no better than he does in *The Wedding Garment*:

> What then is that holiness which is the true wedding garment, the only qualification for glory? 'In Christ Jesus' (that is, according to the Christian institution, whatever be the case of the heathen world) 'neither circumcision availeth anything, nor uncircumcision, but a new creation,' the renewal of the soul 'in the image of God wherein it was created'…In a word, holiness is the having 'the mind that was in Christ', and the 'walking as Christ walked'. (§17)

The faith journey is now complete. The Wesleyan *ordo salutis* embraces the entire story of redemption from creation to consummation, from the breath of God in Adam to the breath of Christ in the new creation.

TEN
Evolving Contours

We now turn our attention to the evolution of John Wesley's perfection theology. Our present purpose is two-fold: to summarize the major contours of his theological journey and to identify those factors which shaped the development of his thought. This should help answer our original inquiry: over time was Wesley consistent in his perfection doctrine? Our study (Sections I & II) has confirmed that his theology of perfection did pass through several major phases, along with turbulent transition points. But it has also revealed a consistency in his principles and core convictions. To articulate these phases and transitions a four-gospel scheme was chosen.

But other schemes are equally valid for making sense of Wesley's theological journey. Most popular is the three-epoch scheme: early, middle, and late.[236] It was explained that the early era begins with Wesley's conversion to holiness in 1725, continues through his time at Oxford and America, and closes on February 1, 1738 when he steps foot on English soil once again. The middle period begins here and continues nearly thirty years into the mid-sixties. The transition from middle to late Wesley is often marked with the publication of *The Scripture Way of Salvation* (1765). This is the same year *A Plain Account of Christian Perfection* was written and soon after published.[2] Wesley's late period covers from the mid-sixties till his death in 1791. These three periods chronologically match up to our four-gospel approach as follows:

Three Periods　　　　　Four Gospels

Early 1725-1738　　　　Gospel of Holiness 1725-1738

---

[236] Cf. Maddox, Randy *Responsible Grace*, 20. Rack, Henry *Responsible Enthusiast*, xi. See also *Plain Account* 1:3 note.
[2] February 1766. This is from a letter to John Newton dated 2/28/66.

Evolving Contours

Middle 1738-1765   Gospel of Faith Alone 1738-1739
                               Gospel of Two Works 1739-1768
Late 1765-1791   Gospel of Universal Holiness 1768-1791

The two differences regarding dates point to the advantage the four-gospel approach has over the three-epoch scheme: It highlights the transitional time Aldersgate served in the development of Wesley's theology, and it dates the transition between his middle and late periods as finally culminating in early 1768, not 1765. In chapter four we learned Wesley experienced a spiritual crisis in the mid-sixties, leading to the formation of the servant state in his gospel system.[3] The servant state broadened Wesley's theological horizon by expanding his *ordo salutis* into the pre-Christian states. We labeled this the Gospel of Universal Holiness.[4] Since both transition periods reflect a time frame of a few years (1738-39 & 1765-68 respectively) these periods can be seen as short eras in their own right. This gives us *five* periods, not three, to organize his doctrinal development. The latter transition period has been somewhat enlarged to incorporate other relevant factors. So a five period approach looks as follows:

Early	1725-1738
Aldersgate I	1738-1739
Middle	1739-1759
Aldersgate II	1759-1768
Late	1768-1791

We will use this model to broad brush the contours of Wesley's theological development. To do this we will use a series of simple charts to visually enhance what Wesley's perfection theology looked like in each period. Then will follow a short synopsis of each period. After this we will look at those factors which shaped

---

[3] Cf. ch 4.
[4] Cf. ch 7.

the formation of Wesley's perfection theology throughout his career. So let us begin.

Early Period: 1725-1738
Perfection in the Article of Death[5]

Single Intention		Death... Glory
x		x
	Pursuing holiness...	CP
	NB begins......	J/NB

Chart key: CP = Christian Perfection; J = Justification; NB = New Birth

In 1725 Wesley experienced a profound spiritual awakening to the divine call for inward holiness.[6] His primary motivation was to prepare himself for death and a face-to-face encounter with God. So, for early Wesley, sanctification became the means to salvation, with justification serving as final acquittal before the divine tribunal. At the time perfection, new birth, and justification were intertwined and linked in his theology. To be justified was to be perfect and fully born again. As the above chart illustrates, a *real* Christian is one who has made the decision to seek holiness as the "one thing needful;" that is, to have a single intention to renew one's fallen nature.[7] This renewal process is attained through the faithful practice of the means of grace—works of piety and works of mercy. Wesley understood works of piety

---

[5] A short bibliography on this era: *Plain Account* ch 3 end note; 6:1 note; ch 7 end note; 23:8 note. Sermons: *The Image of God* (1730); *Circumcision of the Heart* (1733); *The Love of God* (1733); *One Thing Needful* (1734, Works); *Trouble and Rest of Good Men* (1735); *Single Intention* (1736); *Journal, Extract One*; *Preface to 'The Christians Pattern* (Works J 14:199-210).

[6] Cf. *Plain Account* ch 2.

[7] "Now this great work," writes JW, "this one thing needful, is the renewal of our fallen nature. In the image of God was man made...His nature was perfect, angelical, divine...But sin hath now effaced the image of God. He is no longer nearly allied to angels. He is sunk lower than the very beasts of the field...To recover our first estate, from which we have thus fallen, is the one thing now needful" (*One Thing Needful* I.2, 5).

to be those devotional habits that cultivate one's relationship with God, like prayer, scripture reading, church fellowship, fasting, and regular attendance at the Lord's Table. Works of mercy focused more on human relationships, good works, and the avoidance of evil behavior.

To be more specific, the aim of inward holiness is three-fold: justification before God, renewal in the image of God (regeneration), and victory over all sin (that is, inward corruption). All three are intertwined and correlated. Since we live in a mortal body, which is always tainted with Adam's sin, Wesley held such holiness is never fully attained in this life.[8] Only in death is there *rest* from all sin.[9] The major weakness in this system concerned the need for present assurance. While he did maintain assurance is available, grounded on (1) sincerity of devotion, (2) communicating regularly, and (3) the Spirit's fruit of transformed tempers, this foundation proved too weak when Wesley faced the possibility of sudden death and a face-to-face encounter with God.[10] As we saw in chapter two, this crisis led to a radical overall of his theological system.

Still, Wesley's early period proved to have a profound and lasting effect on his perfection theology. This is especially true in regard to what we might call its meta-narrative: our renewal in God's image. Adam's original perfection and righteousness is repeatedly affirmed in several early sermons. We can summarize this meta-narrative:

Adam created in the image of God
Adam lost the image of God
Christ, the Second Adam, restores the image of God

Creation, fall, and redemption in Christ are the primary motifs of this perfection theology. This basic paradigm never changes

---

[8] *On Love* §§ 8-6.
[9] *The Trouble and Rest of Good Men*, Preamble; II.4.
[10] I refer to JW's fear of death when confronted by the storms during his trip to and from America.

throughout Wesley's life, and serves as a constant in his gospel system. Early Wesley envisioned sanctification in terms of (1) the defeat of those passions and tempers which are contrary to love, (2) the vanquishing of fear (especially of death), and (3) the formation of a single intention centered solely on God. Sanctification is primarily understood to involve the transformation of the dispositional nature, from sinful tempers ruling to holy ones dominating.

What led early Wesley to evolve in his thinking over inward holiness? The answer is found in his trip to America. For in this endeavor to perfect his character by taking the gospel to the Native Americans, he was unexpectedly confronted by the heart-wrenching realization—his unwillingness to die. This realization compelled him to confess that his heart (tempers) was not as transformed as he before assumed. Combined with his exposure to a group of Moravian Christians who did have such confidence, this cast a long shadow over his early theological system from which it never recovered. Wesley now had unshakable doubt regarding his salvation. He was now ready for a radical change in his theology and life.

Aldersgate I Period: 1738-1739
Perfection in the Article of Conversion[11]

	Conversion		Glory
	X		X
Almost...	J/NB FA/CP	*Altogether...*	AP

Chart key: J = Justification; NB = New Birth; FA = Full Assurance; CP = Christian Perfection; AP = Absolute Perfection.

---

[11] A short bibliography: *Plain Account* ch 7 end n; chs 8-10. Sermons: *Salvation by Faith* (1738); *The Almost Christian* (174); *Journal Extracts 2 & 3*; Letters: *Brother Samuel; Oct. 1738*; Writings: *Preface to An Extract of the Life and Death of Mr. Thomas Halyburton* (Works J 14:211). See ch 2 for a thorough discussion of JW's Aldersgate theology.

Evolving Contours

Soon after Wesley returned to England he met Moravian missionary Peter Böhler. In contrast to Wesley's then held views, Böhler taught that justification, new birth, and victory over sin and doubt are experienced instantaneously *before* the article of death.[12] This compelled Wesley to seek after an instantaneous assurance of salvation until he finally broke through on May 24 at a Moravian society meeting on Aldersgate Street.

Aldersgate represents a transitional phase between the early and middle periods. Wesley understood Böhler to teach that perfection is attained in an instant. The components of this moment include justification (forgiveness), new birth, full assurance, victory over all sin (outward and inward), and Christian perfection.

To illustrate just how radical of a change Wesley made in his gospel system at this time, let us use an egg basket in which individual eggs represent the different components of Christian doctrine and experience. Early Wesley placed the egg basket, with all the eggs, at the article of death, for it was at death the Christian attains perfection in their tempers (new birth) and are fit to face God for justification. Aldersgate Wesley moved the egg basket, with the eggs, back in time to the point of conversion.

This was a bold move. As our chart above illustrates, justification, new birth, full assurance and perfection now characterize all genuine believers in Christ. To be a Christian is to be an *altogether* one. Those who fall short are at best only *almost* Christians. Hence, a person is complete and saved, or they are incomplete and lost. In this system the seeker passes from imperfection to perfection in an instant, in the moment of new birth. There is no place for degrees or shades of salvation. It is all or nothing. Wesley now had a theology fit for revival and immediate response.

---

[12] In his letter to Elizabeth Hardy JW acknowledged that before Aldersgate he did believe perfection was attained only in the article of death. But since then he was of another mind on the subject (JWL 4/5/58).

John Wesley's Theology of Christian Perfection

One other point bears comment. At this time Wesley did distinguish between Christian perfection and absolute perfection, though this was not his main emphasis.[13]

This triumphant gospel system proved to be short lived, though it did leave an indelible mark on the development of his perfection theology. First, justification would always mark the commencement of salvation and sanctification. Second, the concept of an instantaneous reception of grace was forever burned into Wesley's soul. Yet, following his conversion on May 24 doubts continued to persist. At the time these doubts were interpreted by many that Wesley's tempers were not fully renewed; thereby implying he was not saved (i.e. justified). Wesley finally came to understand that since inward sin remains in the heart, his renewal (new birth) in God's image was only partial.[14] The emotional storms of doubt taught him to see perfection attained in a second moment, following the gift of justification. While the path to this new insight was personally painful, Wesley was well on his way to settling into his middle period.

Middle Period: 1739-1759
Perfection in Maturity[15]

Child	Adolescent	Adult	Glory
x	x	x	x
J/NB	FA	CP	AP

Chart key: J/NB = Justification & New Birth; FA = Full Assurance; CP = Christian Perfection; AP = Absolute Perfection.

---

[13] Reference is to JW's Aldersgate manifesto, *Salvation By Faith*, which speaks of future growth in the perfect Christian (at the end of II.7).

[14] See his many journal confessions in the latter half of 1738.

[15] Short bibliography: *Plain Account* chs 11-18; Sermons: *Christian Perfection* (174), *First Fruits of the Spirit* (1745), *The Great Privilege of those that are Born of God* (1748), *The Spirit of Bondage and of Adoption* (1746); *Journal: Extract Three*; Writings: *The Conference Minutes, 1744-1747*. See ch 3 for a full discussion of this period.

Evolving Contours

By late 1739 "stillness" was stirring unrest within the societies. This led Wesley to eventually part paths with the Moravians the following summer. The controversy struck a nerve in Wesley because stillness advocates despised the means of grace.[16] When we place this controversy in parallel with Wesley's own faith journey we see that a definite path begins to emerge. While the pendulum had swung from an emphasis on process in Wesley's early period to an accent on instant in his Aldersgate era, the stillness debate swung the pendulum back toward an emphasis on process once again. Over the next several years Wesley would move both perfection (by late 1739) and full assurance (by 1747) to later points on the faith journey path; thus demarcating them as separate, distinct gifts from justification. Going back to our egg basket illustration, Wesley's renewed appreciation for the means of grace led him to remove individual eggs from the basket and place them at different locations on the faith journey path (compare the above two charts). Once again, the eggs represent individual components of the life transformation process. These components begin to take on a distinctively Wesleyan flavor in his middle period.

Middle Wesley now divides the faith journey into three basic stages patterned after natural development: child, adolescent, adult.[17] The child is defined by justification and new birth (low degree). These are the first gift and empower victory over outward sin and the suppression of inward sin.[18] Since the child continues to wrestle with fear and doubt, they only have a degree of faith and assurance. The struggles that follow compel the immature believer to seek relief found in full assurance. This is the stage of adolescence, when the believer's walk becomes settled and confirmed, when their confidence before God attains consis-

---

[16] Cf. ch 3 for the full story.
[17] *Plain Account* 12:9.
[18] "Q. 7 What are the fruits of justifying faith? A. Peace, joy, love, power over all outward sin, and power to keep down inward sin" (*Conference Minutes 1744*, Works J 8:276).

tency.[19] The adolescent is now prepared to enter adulthood. While the adolescent has attained consistency in their assurance, they still wrestle with inward sin. The indwelling Spirit draws the adolescent to hunger after a full removal of this malady:

> Then God is mindful of the desire of them that fear him, and gives them a single eye, and a pure heart; He stamps upon them his own image and superscription; He createth them anew in Christ Jesus; He cometh unto them with his Son and blessed Spirit, and, fixing his abode in their souls, bringeth them into the "rest which remaineth for the people of God."[20]

The believer has now attained spiritual adulthood. Yet, Wesley is careful to qualify the experience. Even the most perfect are never free from mistake, ignorance, human weakness, or temptation.[21] There is no absolute perfection in this life, and there is no state in which we arrive in a complete sense. Full renewal remains incomplete in terms of the total process. All Christians continue to depend on Christ, practice the means of grace, and grow in their likeness of Jesus. Though undeveloped, these ideas are the soil from which his doctrine of sin will evolve into its mature position in the Aldersgate II era (1760's). Wesley's basic paradigm of the faith journey is now in place. His *ordo salutis* includes two definitive God-moments (new birth and Christian perfection) within a larger continuum of growth and renewal in the image of God.

What distinguishes middle Wesley from Aldersgate II Wesley? The answer is two-fold. First, in 1758 Wesley changes his mind as to whether perfection can be lost.[22] This change implies that perfect love is more transitory and fluctuating than was previously considered. Believers move in and out of the experi-

---

[19] *Preface to Hymns and Sacred Poems II* §11, Works J 14:327; see also PA 13:26; *Christian Perfection* II.1.
[20] *Plain Account* 13:29-30.
[21] *Christian Perfection* I.1-8; PA 12:5-8.
[22] *Plain Account* 19:98-99; 25:64, 102-107.

ence. Retaining full salvation becomes a critical concern for Wesley. Second, as a corollary Wesley begins to emphasize the *instant* when perfection is received. This led to faith being accentuated over the means of grace in the reception of the gift. This offers insight into how Wesley's thought could polarize at different periods. Finally, there is the perfection revival and schism, which had a profound and lasting affect on Wesley personally, and on the development of his perfection theology.

Aldersgate II Period: 1759-1768
Perfection in a Second Moment[23]

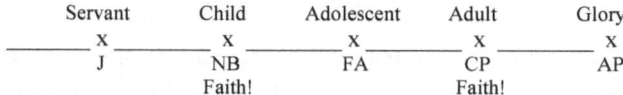

Servant	Child	Adolescent	Adult	Glory
x	x	x	x	x
J	NB	FA	CP	AP
	Faith!		Faith!	

Chart key: J = Justification; NB = New Birth; FA = Full Assurance; CP = Christian Perfection; AP = Absolute Perfection.

Just as Aldersgate I served as the transition period between early and middle Wesley, Aldersgate II serves as the transition period between middle and late Wesley. The major force in this era of nine years is the perfection revival and schism, leading Wesley to publish his most definitive statement on his perfection theology: *A Plain Account of Christian Perfection*. Yet unknown to Wesley at the time, the writing of the *Plain Account* would culminate in a spiritual crisis within his own life, producing an-

---

[23] Short bibliography: Plain Account chs 19-26; Sermons: *The New Birth* (1759), *On Sin in Believers* (1763), *The Scripture Way of Salvation* (1765), *The Repentance of Believers* (1767); Journal 5/14/65, 12/1/67; Letters: Charles Wesley 6/27/66, 7/9/66, 1/27/67, 2/12/67. I titled this era Aldersgate II after chapter 4 even though I realize this can be somewhat misleading regarding my overall thoughts on this era. I am simply seeking to keep continuity in the book. I formally referred to this era as the Plain Account Period.

other mega-shift in his theological system.[24] But first let us review what distinguishes this era from the previous one.

As the revival and schism spurred changes in Wesley's views, changes within his theology helped spearhead the revival and possibly contributed to the schism. By the late fifties Wesley changed his mind on whether perfection could be lost. This made the experience more volatile. In addition, in late 1759 Wesley published his *Thoughts on Christian Perfection* in which he formally presents his mature doctrine of involuntary sin.[25] As a consequence, perfection became by definition more limited in scope; or, in other words, the expectations were lowered, which made perfection even more accessible than before. This encouraged converts to seek perfection immediately following the gift of justification/new birth.

In the same year he wrote a significant homily on the new birth culminating his evolution on this vital truth.[26] Whereas perfect love had been understood as the highest degree of regeneration, Wesley now separates them into distinct works of grace. By so doing he stressed even stronger that perfect love is a second gift following justification. All combined, these changes made perfection more viable, more desirable, more attainable, yet more volatile. By lowering the expectations it can be argued that Wesley inadvertently encouraged the schismatics to revolt to the opposite extreme.[27] Either way, as the revival heated up the pendulum swung back to an emphasis on moment over process. This is evident in Wesley's journal, which records many testimonies of full salvation being received upon the heels of the new birth.[28]

Christian perfection is now viewed as an experience received by faith in a second moment, but a moment still connected to the

---

[24] Cf. ch 4.
[25] *Plain Account* ch 19.
[26] Cf. Appendix D.
[27] The schismatics—Maxfield, Bell, and their supporters—accused JW of changing his views, and used this to support their own version of perfection. One of the goals of the *Plain Account* is to refute this charge.
[28] *Plain Account* ch 24 end note. Cf. Appendix Three.

process.²⁹ The moment is conditioned upon faith, while the process is conditioned upon the faithful practice of the means of grace.³⁰ Wesley interprets the moment as God being sovereign and free to 'cut short' the process and do the work of months and years in a few weeks, days, or even hours.³¹ This is how Wesley integrates the gradual and instantaneous motifs in his perfection doctrine.

Critical to his position, at the time, was his definition of sin as voluntary and involuntary.³² Wesley now clarifies that only voluntary sin—i.e. inward and outward sin—can be removed in this life. Believers continue to sin involuntarily against God's perfect law until physical death.³³ All believers must depend on Christ's continual intercession in heaven to cover their involuntary sin. So, even the most perfect need to pray daily for forgiveness.³⁴ To summarize, *outward* sin is overcome in the new birth, but *inward* sin (sinful tempers) in the moment of perfect love. Believers are then said to be *full* of the *life of love*, and can testify, "I feel no sin, but all love."³⁵

Theologically, Wesley builds his doctrine of perfect love on the concept of Christ, the second Adam.³⁶ In the beginning Adam was perfect and could fulfill God's righteous law. But due to his fall into sin, Adam's posterity can no longer keep the law of Edenic righteousness. In its place God now requires the law of faith. God can soften the standard because Christ's death and resurrection steps in on behalf of sinful humanity. Christ in his death atones for sin, and in his resurrection he ever lives to intercede on the believer's behalf. So God now requires a lower standard of obedience than what was expected of Adam in the garden.³⁷

---

²⁹ *Plain Account* 19:68-75; 25:77-79.
³⁰ *Plain Account* 19:76-81.
³¹ *Plain Account* 21:4-5; 25:75-79.
³² *Plain Account* 19:21-25.
³³ *Plain Account* 19:7-10; 25:8-9.
³⁴ *Plain Account* 19:11-12; 21:5; 25:29.
³⁵ *Plain Account* 19:44, 73, 98.
³⁶ *Plain Account* 25:2-15; 1 Cor 15:45, 47.
³⁷ *Plain Account* 25:5-14, 29, 41 n.

John Wesley's Theology of Christian Perfection

By the spring of 1765 Wesley begins to turn back to his early period to explain how he came to believe in Christian perfection.[38] The realization that his own faith journey began in 1725, not 1738, started a process of personal reevaluation that finally culminates in December 1767 with the declaration that a vital Christian faith begins when one fears God and works righteousness (Acts 10:35).[39] Then in the following spring Wesley uses the term "servant" to describe this pre-new birth, post-justification state. Wesley is well on his way to forming a holistic message that integrates even more his theologies of the early and Aldersgate periods. In this way he was able to create a vision of the faith journey that begins with the first spark of divine awareness, but fully realized only in the new creation: perfection grounded on degrees of faith.

Late Period: 1768-1791
Perfection in Degrees of Faith[40]

/-------------------- The Renewal of All Creation to a New Heaven and Earth ---------------------\

Faith of:

Prev. Grace	Servant	Child	Adolescent	Adult	Paradise	New Creation
x	x	x	x	x	x	x
A	J	NB	FA	CP	AP	RP

Chart key: A = Awareness; J = Justification; NB = New Birth; FA = Full Assurance; CP = Christian Perfection; AP = Adamic Perfection; RP = Resurrection Perfection.

By the 1780's prevenient grace was coming to the forefront in Wesley's thought. With exposure to other religious faiths he became less confident in the idea of a Christian nation, since so many professing (nominal) Christians displayed little moral life

---

[38] Cf. his letter to John Newton, JWJ 5/14/65.
[39] JWJ 12/1/67.
[40] Short bibliography: *Plain Account* footnotes chs 13 and 17; Sermons: *On Patience* (1781), *The End of Christ's Coming* (1781), *The General Spread of the Gospel* (1783), *On Perfection* (1784), *On Working Out Our Own Salvation* (1785), *Discoveries of Faith* (1788), *On Faith Heb 11:6* (1788), *The Wedding Garment* (1790).

above that of a "heathen." This led Wesley to appreciate faith and righteousness wherever he saw it. The faith journey is now expanded to begin at the "first dawn of light" concerning God and his will, not necessarily when a person embraces Christ or a proper Christian faith.[41] By so doing, the older categories of *natural* and *legal* to describe the status of pre-Christians became, in some ways, obsolete.[42] Wesley now realizes that the realities of spiritual life are much more complex than what he thought in the 1740's. In many ways, this realization is the working out of his core principle that what matters before God is not religious opinion or ritual, but a pure heart of faith and righteousness (Acts 10:35).

Not surprisingly, Wesley returns to his early roots with renewed interest in the single intention as the foundation of vital religion, "It is certain there can be no medium between a single eye and an evil eye; for whenever we are not aiming at God, we are seeking happiness in some creature."[43] Just as early Wesley made the single intention the cornerstone of a vital faith, and middle Wesley moved it to a second moment (the instant of perfection), late Wesley once again picks up this early truth and reinstates it as a core principle for being a "real, inward, scriptural Christian."[44] To lack the single eye, Wesley now reaffirms, is to be "totally ignorant of the nature of true religion."[45]

The other end of Wesley's gospel system was also expanded. Perfection is now envisioned to include not only the renewal of humanity in the image of God, but also the transformation of all creation into a new heaven and earth. While this idea is certainly not new to Wesley in the 1780's, it was during this period that he devotes sermonic energy to the subject. Perfection is an unfolding cosmic reality, an eschatological vision of the future. In the final end, Wesley envisions a path of renewal that spans the entire

---

[41] *On Working Out Our Own Salvation* II.1. See ch 7.
[42] As used in *The Spirit of Bondage and Adoption* (1739, 1746).
[43] *On a Single Eye* II.1.
[44] Ibid. P.3.
[45] Ibid. II.2.

process of spiritual transformation, from the first spark of prevenient grace to the final step into glory with the risen Christ; all grounded on the processal development of holy dispositions and attitudes.

In so doing, the pendulum swings toward process over instant. While the God-moments are still affirmed, the enlarged vision of total renewal stresses the process side of Wesley's theology. A corollary is a change in the role faith plays within his overall *ordo salutis*. The soteriological nature of prevenient grace pointed to the reality that at each stage in the total renewal process faith is the key element. Critical to this insight is Wesley's use of Hebrews 11:1. Here faith is defined as a "'divine evidence and conviction of things not seen.'"[46] Wesley calls this the "most comprehensive definition of faith that ever was or can be given," which includes "every species of faith, from the lowest to the highest." As the above chart illustrates, late Wesley sees the faith journey as primarily a path to perfect one's *faith*. The gift of faith begins at the first dawn of spiritual light and grows by stages until consummated in the new creation. Each progressive stage represents higher levels of faith in God and in working righteousness within the heart (Acts 10:35), leading to greater and greater transformations of the dispositional nature. By so defining faith and conjoining it with perfection, Wesley is able to link the prevenient states with the proper Christian stages to form one continuous path of renewal in the divine image.

If we return to our illustration of the egg basket we can easily see how the basic contours of Wesley's perfection theology evolved over time. Early Wesley placed the basket, with all the eggs, in the article of death. Aldersgate Wesley moved the basket to the article of conversion. From this point forward Wesley's theology transitions by removing individual eggs from the basket and placing them at different points on the faith journey path. The egg basket represents his theological system (*ordo salutis*) and the eggs individual components of the faith journey. Over the

---

[46] *On Faith* (Heb 11:6) P.1.

next several decades as his theology evolved, one component after another was removed from the basket and placed at different points on the faith journey path, until in the 1780's when the overall system consists of a single path (process) dotted with multiple God-moments of instantaneous renewal. Though late Wesley continued to stress two primary God-moments (new birth and perfect love), his mature gospel system implicitly affirmed many potential God-moments on the faith journey path, including justification (servant state), full assurance (adolescence), and Adamic righteousness (death).

Evolving Contours

It is time we seek to answer several questions pertinent to our study. Such as, why did Wesley's theology develop as it did? Which factors shaped the contours of his thought? Are there patterns that repeat themselves? Which doctrines proved to mold his theology of perfection more than others? And how does our above survey help to identify these factors and doctrines? To make sense of Wesley's theology, his *ordo salutis*, and most importantly, his doctrine of Christian perfection, these questions now require our attention.

We begin by looking at the poles of ***process*** and ***instant***. The above summary makes it evident that Wesley's theology oscillated from one pole to the other as it moved from one period to another. By placing justification, new birth and perfection in the article of death, early Wesley necessarily gravitated toward process. Central to this system was the disciplined practice of the means of grace instilling holy tempers in the heart. As was pointed out in chapter one, early Wesley did affirm the idea of the instant/moment by identifying the decision of the single intention as the commencement of vital religion in the heart. Yet this emphasis was muted due to the overwhelming weight that process played in his gospel system.

John Wesley's Theology of Christian Perfection

All this changed when Wesley stepped foot once again on English soil in February 1738. With his failures in America and the exposure of his fear of death, Wesley became willing to hear a different message. Peter Böhler, the Moravian missionary, became Christ's ambassador to both Wesley brothers as they tutored him in the English language.[47] Böhler's gospel message emphasized the instant, even the radical instant. Within two months John Wesley was won over. As typified by his Aldersgate conversion on May 24, Wesley boldly proclaimed that God works salvation in the moment. However, it was only days later when he began to struggle with doubts again. Determined to know the truth, he set sail for Germany to learn from the Moravian mother church. To his amazement, he found the German Moravians countering what Böhler taught on assurance and justification. Over the next two years Wesley's thought shifts back toward the pole of process. This is most evident in the homily *Christian Perfection* where he uses maturational language to define spiritual development. While he would later argue that he had always believed perfection to be received in the moment, the emphasis clearly fell on the processal nature of perfecting grace.[48]

By the late fifties Wesley's theology of perfection began to shift back to the pole of instant once again. In the heat of revival the pressure for instantaneous deliverance tended to swallow up the significance of process. The enthusiasts ran with perfection until they believed they were like the angels of God. Though Wesley tried to correct such excesses, his own theological adjustments probably contributed to the problem. Finally, after much soul searching over perfection and his own faith journey, Wesley embraced a robust view of prevenient grace working salvation at much earlier stages than previously considered with any

---

[47] CW was hired as Böhler's tutor until he left for America in May 1738.

[48] For example, "Q. 1. When does inward sanctification begin? A. In the moment we are justified. The seed of every virtue is then sown in the soul. From that time the believer *gradually* dies to sin, and *grows* in grace" (*The Conference Minutes 1745,* Works J 8:285; emphasis mine).

seriousness. This meant that Wesley's theology in the seventies and eighties shifted back to an emphasis on process, while not abandoning the instantaneous motif.

Thus process and instant offer a lens through which to make sense of the contours by which Wesley's theology evolved. Let it be remembered, at each phase his theology included both process and instant. The point being made is one of emphasis. Also, in different periods the pole of instantaneousness fixed on different components. In early Wesley it was the single intention. Aldersgate Wesley focused on the instant of new birth and present assurance (the witness of the Spirit). Middle Wesley split the instant to form two moments, justification and perfect love. And late Wesley held to the idea of twin moments but implicitly opened the door to the possibility of multiple moments on the faith journey path. The strength of Wesley's system is its attempt to balance process and instant. Yet, as his posterity have found, this is a very difficult task. For the tides of revival stir up emotionalism, which places a premium on the instant, while the relative calm of gradualism make it very difficult to integrate both poles with proper symmetry and balance.

No less important is the idea of ***storm***. Physical storms can be very powerful. A single storm can change the landscape of an entire region and leave a lasting imprint on the human spirit. So it did with Wesley's theology. All the major shifts in his thought happen during a storm. First, there were the storms at sea which caused him to recognize his spiritual bankruptcy. So shaken by his fear of death Wesley could no longer rest in the path he was traveling. For a time he found solace in his Aldersgate conversion. But the storms of doubt soon began to trouble him. Simply stated, Wesley could not find rest in the message he received from Peter Böhler. At last, he found peace in a gospel embracing two works of grace. Though Wesley knew he had not attained the gift of perfect love, he was, nonetheless, assured of his salvation. Then the storm of stillness arose. We have already tracked how this controversy played a profound role in shaping his theological system.[49]

When we move a couple decades later another storm arises. This time it is schism. The perfection revival of the early sixties, along with the schism it birthed, profoundly shaped Wesley's perfection theology in two ways. First, the schism forced Wesley to clarify and thereby codify his doctrine of perfection to a degree he had not done so before. Second, in defending what he believed about perfection, and why he believed it, Wesley came to grips with the twists and turns of his own faith journey. In so doing, he once again came to appreciate his early faith journey.

Then there was the doctrinal storm over the 1770 Conference Minutes.[50] These conference minutes served to reinforce an emphasis on faith-generated works within Wesley's mature gospel system. Even though the Calvinists objected, Wesley persisted in maintaining that if time allows (and it usually does) saving faith will produce the fruit of holy, God-pleasing works of righteousness. Wesley's holiness DNA could allow no other position.

As the poles of process and instant, combined with the concept of storms, help to explain why Wesley's theology developed along the contours it did, there are doctrinal elements to consider.

We start with the ***single intention***. As we saw in chapter one, early Wesley defined vital Christianity in terms of seeking first the kingdom of God. In this system spiritual life begins in the decision of the single intention. This alignment between total devotion and spiritual life also carried over into the Aldersgate era as Wesley conjoined into one instant justification, sanctification, new birth and assurance. Implicit was the inclusion of the single intention, since to be saved from all sin is to be delivered from its "whole being"[51] and this includes a pure heart. As we chronicled in chapter three, one significant factor that made room for a second work of grace in Wesley's thought was moving the single

---

[49] Cf. ch 3.
[50] Cf. ch 4.
[51] *Salvation by Faith* II.7, original text.

intention to a second moment.[52] The single eye continued to be identified with perfection over the next several decades. But as his theology matured, he gravitated back to his early roots. The single intention was once again asserted as a core principle of spiritual life. In this way, undivided devotion conceptually played a significant role in the evolution of his perfection theology.

Another factor was his understanding of *faith*. Historians and scholars are quick to point out Wesley's early understanding of faith as assent, not trust.[53] However, we showed that in many of the early sermons he implicitly calls for faith as trust. So it is fair to say early Wesley, in a measure, grasped the volitional aspect of faith. Yet, what was implicit became explicit at Aldersgate. Faith is now defined according to the Anglican Homilies, "a sure trust and confidence which a man hath in God, that through the merits of Christ his sins are forgiven, and he reconciled to the favour of God."[54] Very significant to this new understanding was a change in the *object* of faith. Prior to this he placed his trust in God and his promises of holiness. Wesley now placed his faith in *Christ alone* for salvation. Then in the early forties he began to delineate faith in terms of Hebrews 11:1, "Now faith is the substance of things hoped for, the evidence of things not seen."[55] As his theology transitioned during the 1760's into its mature articulation, Wesley found this latter definition decisive for the development of the servant state in his gospel system, which opened up the possibility through prevenient grace for eternal life to be given to those who do not personally know Christ:

> But what is the faith which is properly saving; which brings eternal salvation to all those that keep it to the end? It is such a divine conviction of God, and the things of

---

[52] *Preface to Sacred Hymns and Poems II*, Works J 14: 322.
[53] For example, see Kenneth Collins *John Wesley – A Theological Journey*, 36-38.
[54] JWJ 4/22/38.
[55] Heitzenrater, Richard *Great Expectations* in Randy Maddox, Ed. *Aldersgate Reconsidered*, 88

God, as, even in its infant state, enables every one that possesses it to "fear God and work righteousness." And whosoever, in every nation, believes thus far, the Apostle declares, is "accepted of him." He actually is, at that very moment, in a state of acceptance.[56]

Not only were changes in Wesley's definition of faith critical to explaining why his theology evolved as it did, his views on faith were grounded on the interplay between the twin doctrines of *justification* and *sanctification*. Once again, let us retrace how Wesley understood these two doctrines at different periods of his career.

Prior to Aldersgate Wesley held firmly that justification is granted when perfect righteousness is attained. Though forgiveness is given at the Lord's Table, he never equates the gift of present forgiveness with justification. The latter is consistently identified with the infusion of inward holiness. This means, of course, that sanctification is the ground for justification and acceptance before God.[57]

All this changed at Aldersgate. Peter Böhler was successful in convincing Wesley that justification is a gift granted in the moment of conversion, not in the article of death. Moreover, not only did the timing of justification move to an earlier point on the faith journey path, justification itself was redefined at this time. Justification is now the gift of present forgiveness. Justification replaces sanctification as the foundation for salvation and spiritual life. This radical readjustment of justification in relation to sanctification means that Wesley's gospel message took on completely new contours fit for revival and mass appeal. But important to our study, justification was still conjoined with sanctification, for both blessings are experientially appropriated in the same existential moment, the new birth. It would take Wesley nearly one and a half years to formally separate the two into dis-

---

[56] *On Faith* (Heb 11:6) I.10.
[57] See ch 1 for a full discussion.

tinct gifts of divine grace. This change also empowered him to formulate two distinct works of grace within his theological system. For the rest of his life justification would serve as the foundation for spiritual life in his gospel system. So even in Wesley's mature period, while the servant enjoys acceptance (justification) before God only the child tastes the new birth, witnessed by God's Spirit.

This brings up another factor which shaped Wesley's perfection theology: the **new birth**. Early Wesley identified regeneration with the attainment of perfection, signifying that a process view was inherent in his thought. As we learned above, Wesley incorporated new birth terminology in his description of the single intention. Through the thirties we can note a progressive interest by both Wesley brothers in the new birth culminating in 1738, the year of Aldersgate. As Wesley's theology moved from the pole of process toward that of instant, so his new birth doctrine crystallized into the instantaneous reception of perfecting grace. Now regeneration is completed in the gift of perfection received in an instant by faith alone in Christ alone.

As his doubts and fears persisted over questions of assurance, Wesley once again was confronted with the reality that regeneration must be realized by degrees. So in early 1739 we find him speaking of lower and higher degrees of regeneration.[58] The splitting of regeneration into two levels or stages also fed the development of two distinct works of grace. This continued to be Wesley's position on the new birth until the latter part of the 1750's.[59] In the groundbreaking sermon, *The New Birth*, Wesley finally broke free from identifying the new birth with full salvation.[60] With the new birth as its own distinct gift from God, per-

---

[58] JWJ 1/25/39.
[59] I say "full" because JW is notorious for his situational communication in which he does not express his full, complete position on a subject or topic. Such is the case with regeneration. One can find quotes referring to only the lower degree of regeneration as if that is the only meaning he worked with. Yet, other writings point to a more nuanced and fuller meaning.
[60] Cf. Appendix D.

fection also came into greater focus as its own unique gift. Throughout the early sixties the new birth and perfection were the two divine gifts he sought to lead his people to receive.

With the formation of the servant state the final chapter in the evolution of the new birth took place. From his early period vital Christianity was inextricably bound to regeneration. Now, with salvific grace being preveniently given, even to those who do not yet know Christ, the new birth no longer could serve as the ground for vital religion. A more elementary standard took its place, specifically, fearing God and working righteousness (Acts 10:35). Yet, the need to be born again by faith in Christ continued to be stressed and proclaimed as the foundation for a proper Christian faith. Wesley's theology of perfection finally rests on the conviction that being born again is vital for the faith journey toward full renewal in God's image.

Last, the Wesleyan path of renewal was profoundly shaped by his conception of *sin*. While we covered this subject in detail in chapter five, here we want to outline how his views transitioned along with his theological journey. When we turn to Wesley's early sermons, what stands out regarding his doctrine of sin is its holistic perspective. In other words, Wesley sees sin in terms of the loss of the divine image. Since the fall deprived humanity of its original perfection, sin became identified with that corruption of nature consequent upon Adam's transgression. Early Wesley does not focus so much on the specifics of sin. But as he moved into his Aldersgate era we see his doctrine of sin becoming more sharply nuanced.

When he stood before his university peers following his heart-warming conversion, Wesley divides his doctrine of sin into two main categories, guilt and power. And then he subdivides the latter into habit, willful, desire and infirmity.[61] These four subcategories would prove to be the main contours by which he develops his doctrine of full salvation. Habit signifies sin

---

[61] *Salvation By Faith* II.6. Though infirmity was treated as separate from the other three, in this sermon JW did place it in the same general category (power of sin) as the other three.

reigning, pointing to the unregenerate condition. By 1740 Wesley took the next two subcategories (willful and desire) to delineate sin as outward and inward. Outward (willful) sin refers to the actual commission of disobedience. Inward sin demarcates those sinful tempers which feed outward sin; specifically pride, anger, self-will and unwholesome desire.[62] The distinction between inward and outward sin plays a significant role in the development of Wesley's doctrine of two works of grace.

By the late fifties and early sixties Wesley's doctrine of sin reaches maturity through two more changes: (1) the formalization of his doctrine of involuntary sin; and (2) the delineation of sin as power and being. Let's start with the latter. Whereas in *Salvation By Faith* sin's power and being were treated as synonymous, by 1763 sin's power and being are clearly distinguished.[63] Sin's power is now identified solely with outward sin, the reign of sin; while sin's being points to inward sin, the remains of sin polluting the believer's devotion and inward holiness. So Wesley's mature articulation on sin speaks of guilt, power and being, with a divine answer for each: forgiveness (justification), new birth, and full salvation. Only involuntary sin remains until death. So Wesley's doctrine of involuntary sin means that even the "most perfect" continue to transgress God's perfect law and need daily forgiveness. Wesley's four categories of sin (guilt, power, being, involuntary) define four of the major stages on the faith journey path toward full renewal: servant, child, adult, and paradise (death/intermediate state).

Finally, three more thoughts deserve our brief attention. Wesley saw sin bringing spiritual and moral darkness due to alienation. As he grew in awareness of other religions he came to appreciate the benefits that prevenient grace bring by awakening the heart to divine light and truth.[64] Another factor is fear caused by sin's guilt before God. The answer to such fear is found in the

---

[62] *Christian Perfection* II.26; PA 12:34-36.
[63] Compare *Salvation by Faith* II.6, 7 with *On Sin in Believers*. In *What is Man?* §14 the categories are guilt, power and root.
[64] *On Working Out Our Salvation*.

John Wesley's Theology of Christian Perfection

gift of the Spirit's testimony, which by the mid-forties was identified with the adolescent state.[65] And last, Wesley sees sin as the curse continuing to plague all creation. Only in the new creation will this aspect of sin be removed and purged.[66] So when we stand at a distance and look at Wesley's mature description of the faith journey, we see that at each major stage of spiritual development a greater level of freedom from sin is enjoyed. We can now chart how Wesley's theology of perfection integrates the different stages of the faith journey with his doctrine of sin and God's remedy in the gospel:

Faith Journey Stages	Nature of Sin	God's Remedy
Prevenient	Darkness	Awakening
Servant	Guilt	Forgiveness
Child	Power	New Birth
Adolescent	Fear	Full Assurance
Adult	Being	Perfection
Paradise	Involuntary	Intermediate state
Glory	Curse	Resurrection

---

[65] *On The Discoveries of Faith* §15.
[66] Cf. JWS: *The New Creation*; *The General Spread of the Gospel*; *The General Deliverance*.

Eleven
The Achilles Heel

Most of us are probably familiar enough with the story of Achilles, Paris and the Trojan War to know that the great warrior Achilles had only one vulnerable spot—his heel. In this final chapter we want to examine what this author considers to be the one weak spot in Wesley's theological system that could undermine his doctrine of Christian perfection. We have already noted its strengths. Yet, his mature views on involuntary sin conclude that we all continue to err in this life. Our finitude alone guarantees that none of us understand all aspects of life and reality, including the realm of the divine. In addition, the plague of sin remains so that we continue to live in houses made of clay. As the Apostle Paul reminds us, we now "see through a glass darkly" for we only "know in part."[1] Only in the new creation will we see "face to face" and know even as we are known. This means, of course, that every theology is incomplete and imperfect. Very early in his career Wesley recognized this truth:

> One great reason why God suffers this cloud to rest upon us, why he cuts our knowledge so short on every side, and shows so small a part of his ways, is that ignorance may teach us the usefullest knowledge, may lead us to *humility*.[2]

---

[1] 1 Cor 13:12.
[2] *The Promise of Understanding* III.1 (emphasis mine). In 1784 JW expressed the same sentiments, "How astonishingly little do we know of God! How small a part of his nature do we know! Of his essential attributes! What conception can we form of his omnipresence? Who is able to comprehend how God is in this and every place? How he fills the immensity of space?" (*The Imperfection of Human Knowledge* I.1).

John Wesley's Theology of Christian Perfection

Humility served as one of the cardinal virtues in Wesley's holiness gospel, since it roots out pride and a spirit of self-sufficiency in one's "opinions."[3] In an age that prided itself for its ability to reason, Wesley intuitively saw that such a path would only lead to "practical atheism."[4] In response he promoted a concept of faith as spiritual sense, when awakened by grace enables the believer to see the divine realities of the eternal Godhead and divine holiness. Yet, such knowledge remains partial and incomplete throughout this life. Human imperfection also pertains to our understanding of the world; and, more importantly, to the human spirit. So our theology is always at best "seeing through a glass darkly" and "knowing in part."

Then what could be the Achilles heel in Wesley's perfection doctrine? What potentially is that one vulnerable spot in his theological armor? Let us first dispel with what others have considered.

One possibility is the *process of development* Wesley's perfection theology went through over time.[5] After all, this was a chief complaint of his critics: Wesley simply contradicted himself from one writing to the next. There is some truth in this claim. Our study has chronicled in detail how his perfection theology did change and shift through the decades. Yet, we also found that apart from large epochal changes, like Aldersgate, Wesley's pri-

---

[3] *The Circumcision of the Heart* I.2.

[4] The term is JW's but note D. Stephen Long's analysis regarding the relationship between ethics and theism, and how JW foresaw the fruit of a humanistic approach, "This immanent, humanist ethic is coming to its end, and we can see what Wesley only dimly saw: the rise and fall of humanism where God would be policed out of human affairs in the name of morality" (*John Wesley's Moral Theology*, 13-14).

[5] For example, W. Stephen Gunter makes several remarks concerning JW's inconsistency. Regarding the preface in the 1740 hymnal Gunter remarks, "The destructive result of these kinds of perfectionistic phrases was a confusion which Wesley dealt with throughout his life." He then adds later, "When we observe how Wesley himself was not consistently clear in his explication of perfect love, we are not, or should not be, surprised that there was continual disagreement and confusion among his followers" (*The Limits of Love Divine*, 209, 212). Cf. John Peters *Christian Perfection & American Methodism*, 63.

mary writings on perfection reveal much continuity in regard to his principles and core convictions. Simply stated, Wesley's spiritual DNA meant that his theology did not materially change over time.[6] This becomes especially true following the formulation of his two-works gospel. From 1740 on Wesley never wavers from the core principles of his two-works system. Furthermore, and contrary to what others might expect, to require that his thought not change at all over a very long career (65+ years) is unrealistic to say the least.

Another possibility is the term *perfection*. This argument says that if the word "perfection" had been dropped from his vocabulary Wesley would have been more consistent in his views. To counter, Wesley was correct when he reminds his critics that perfection is a Bible term, and it is only incumbent upon the preacher to rightly define it.[7] But Wesley should have pressed this point more forcefully. Yet some scholars disagree. Ronald Stone feels Wesley would have been "well advised to drop the term."[8] Stone believes such terminology implicitly mixes together certain aspects of Enlightenment ideology, which Wesley did not support, with his own explication of the gospel. He also feels the term opened Wesley to more attacks than he otherwise would have received.[9] This last point is certainly correct. John Peters speaks of Wesley's doctrine as affirming an "imperfect perfection."[10] Again, such language only opens the door for endless wrangling.

---

[6] Albert Outler commented on this question, "There are important developments in nuances and emphasis, but the main outlines of the doctrine remain constant" (Works B 3:70).
[7] See *A Plain Account* 11:4; 26:1 notes.
[8] *John Wesley's Life and Ethics*, 148.
[9] Ibid. 149.
[10] *Christian Perfection & American Methodism*, 72. Peters is here quoting John Fletcher (who is quoting an Anglican archbishop). He then adds, "In developing his doctrine Wesley's choice and use of terms was unfortunate. 'Perfection,' for instance, inevitably suggests some sort of absolute status—no matter how much the relative character of a particular usage may be insisted

John Wesley's Theology of Christian Perfection

Yes, Wesley agrees perfection is relative in nature. This is why he often prefixed it with the term "Christian" to point out its limited nature. And yes, perfection is a term that must be carefully nuanced in its use. Still, Wesley's use of perfection terminology is not the Achilles heel we are looking for. Instead, we must examine his substantive theological and experiential claims. For the critics can cry out continually, "There is no perfection in this life!" and still Wesley (and those who support his perspective) can respond by pointing to both Old and New Testament texts which describe the people of God in such terms.[11] If the Scriptures use such terminology, and the preacher correctly interprets the specific passages correctly, one only beats against the air in assailing the use of the term and its cognates.[12] While the terminology of perfection did create hurdles for Wesley to overcome, such language is hardly the Achilles heel that can topple the entire edifice of his sanctification doctrine.[13] To find the Achilles heel, if one exists, we need to look in a different direction.

We turn next to Reformed theologian Anthony Hoekema's criticism of Wesley's holiness doctrine. Hoekema offers several reasons for rejecting the doctrine of Christian perfection, or as he defines it, to "live without sin during this present life." Hoekema argues that advocates of perfection (1) weaken the definition of sin, (2) lower the standard of perfection, (3) teach sanctification as a second work of grace, and (4) believe the Bible supports their position. While each criticism deserves a response, it is his

---

upon. It was against this inescapable connotation that opposition always arose" (63).

[11] In the KJV the following texts use the term "perfect" to describe the people of God: Gen 6:9; 1 Kgs 8:61; 15:14; Job 1:1; Eph 4:12; Php 3:15; Heb 6:1.

[12] We will return to this question in volume 5 of the series, *John Wesley's Preaching of Christian Perfection*. In light of contemporary translations we cannot use the same argument as JW did since the language of perfection has been mostly excised out of our modern bibles.

[13] Pentecostal theologian J. Rodman Williams, while arguing against the Wesleyan doctrine of perfection, still maintains that scripture speaks of a relative perfection (*Renewal Theology II*, 90-92).

first objection that points in the direction of a possible Achilles heel. For when we isolate the four objections, they all rest on the validity of the first one.

To be succinct, Hoekema believes Wesley weakens the definition of sin by "limiting it only to deliberate sin."[14] Like the children's game, pin-the-tail-on-the-donkey, Hoekema's criticism points us in the right direction and yet misses the mark. Wesley was consistent when he argued perfection regards only the removal of voluntary sin, and therefore is relative in nature. In light of this response Hoekema's argument fails to probe where the real Achilles heel possibly lies. But his argument does point us in the right direction. If we are going to find an Achilles heel it will be found in Wesley's doctrine of sin compared to what he claims for the experience. Hoekema would had been more effective if his criticism would have proceeded to show, not that perfection lowers the standard of sin, but that Wesley was inconsistent in his claim that all sin is removed in the gift of perfect love while affirming at the same time that involuntary sin remains. In other words, a possible Achilles heel is to be found in Wesley's definition of perfection as the removal of *all* sin. Let's examine this in more detail.

As we saw in chapter five, Wesley categorizes sin as voluntary and involuntary. Voluntary sin is "sin, proper so called." Involuntary sin is "sin, improperly so called." The problem does not lie with the former but with the latter category. Since Wesley firmly states that involuntary sin exposes one to God's judgment, such transgressions require Christ's atonement and intercession.[15] As a consequence Wesley affirms that all believers, even the

---

[14] *Five Views On Sanctification*, 83.
[15] JW is very clear on the subject, "(1) Everyone may mistake as long as he lives. (2) A mistake in opinion may occasion a mistake in practice. (3) Every such mistake is a transgression of the perfect law. Therefore, (4) Every such mistake, were it not for the blood of atonement, would expose to eternal damnation. (5) It follows, that the most perfect have continual need of the merits of Christ, even for their actual transgressions, and may say for themselves, as well as for their brethren, '*Forgive us our trespasses*'" (*Plain Account* 19:11-12; emphasis his).

most perfect, need daily forgiveness. Yet, to our surprise, he turns an about face and then denies that these involuntary transgressions are sin at all![16] Here, Wesley affirms, are transgressions of God's law, which bring divine disapproval and need Christ's atoning work. But then he adds that they are not sin according to Holy Scripture. This is simply incongruous. As was shown in chapter five, inherent in Wesley's doctrine of sin is the idea of two divine standards, leading to two different kinds of perfection: Christian and Adamic. The first is attainable in this life, the latter is not. All together, Wesley leaves an unresolved tension in his doctrine of sin, and consequently, in his doctrine of perfection, for he repeatedly claims that in the gift of Christian perfection *all* sin is removed. This can be easily shown from his most definitive work on the subject, *A Plain Account of Christian Perfection*.

The *Plain Account* contains numerous statements which speak of sin's complete removal and destruction. A few examples should suffice. In chapter six the perfect believer is cleansed from "all filthiness both of flesh and spirit."[17] The word *all* defines the degree of deliverance expected: from "all sin" and "all unrighteousness;"[18] the soul then becomes "all love" (15:14); Wesley prays, "Redeem from all iniquity;"[19] and again affirms that in perfection the "evil nature, the body of sin, is destroyed."[20] Other examples could be listed. Those who taste full salvation experience a "total death to sin" and an "entire renewal" in God's image. Therefore, their sanctification is "entire," for they "feel all love and no sin."[21]

These examples illustrate that Wesley did look for a complete and finished sanctification in this life in regard to sin.[22] If we take

---

[16] Again, JW is unmistakably clear, "Now, mistakes, and whatever infirmities necessarily flow from the corruptible state of the body, are no way contrary to love; nor therefore, in the Scripture sense, sin" (*Plain Account* 19:22).
[17] PA 6:2. Quoted from *The Circumcision of the Heart* (1733).
[18] PA 12:44. Quoted from *Christian Perfection* (1741).
[19] PA 16:3. Quoted from *Hymns and Sacred Poems III* (1742).
[20] PA 12:32. Again from *Christian Perfection*.
[21] PA 19:68-69. Quoted from *Thoughts on Christian Perfection* (1759).
[22] PA 26:6-7, 15 notes.

these claims at face value, in the experience of perfection *all* sin is removed and the believer becomes *all* love.[23] Yet, at the same time Wesley insists that the cleansing from sin is never fully complete in this life.[24] Even when perfected in love the believer continues to sin daily against God's absolute standard and consequently needs Christ's intercession for divine forgiveness.[25] It is at this point that a real Achilles heel surfaces. We just need to ask a couple questions:

> If some kind of sin remains in this life (call it what one chooses), can we ever say a person is free from *all* sin?
>
> If we assume Wesley's definition of perfection—the removal of *all* sin—and agree with Wesley that some kind of sin must remain, even in the "best of men,"[26] can we ever say one is therefore perfect?

According to Wesley's principles an honest answer demands a straightforward "No" to both questions. This exposes a real Achilles heel in his perfection doctrine. Remember, Wesley's full orbed doctrine of sin says that both deliberate acts and inadvertent errs are culpable before God. But his definition of perfection claims that *all* sin is removed in the blessing. So a negative answer to either question undermines the claim Wesley attempts to build and defend. In the end, his doctrine of sin denies that any perfection from *all* sin is attainable in this life because sin is never fully removed. This does not deny a possible perfection in regard to devotion, love, or even from voluntary sin (as we will soon see). But to claim perfection entails a deliverance from *all* sin, while at the same time affirming involuntary sin persists till death is to undermine the attainability of that claim. This is a real Achilles heel since it collapses his doctrine of Christian perfec-

---

[23] PA 15:14; 26:15.
[24] PA 19:7-12, 20-21; 25:39-40.
[25] Note 15 above.
[26] PA 25:29. A synonym for perfect love.

tion into a denial of the very perfection he seeks to support. In other words, Wesley's doctrine of involuntary sin denies an attainable perfection from all sin in this life. Therefore, only in the article of death is sin fully removed and vanquished (as his holiness gospel affirmed). Until that day we depend on Christ's intercession and atonement for *daily* forgiveness and mercy. Let us ask, how is this position that different in substance from a balanced Calvinist one? (Just a thought![27]).

Two alternatives were available for Wesley to make his system internally and logically consistent, and defendable. First, he could have affirmed a complete and total deliverance from all sin by *redefining sin as only voluntary in nature*. This would have entailed a denial of his doctrine of involuntary sin and a readjustment in his reading of Scripture.[28] But Wesley would have been consistent in his claim that in perfection *all* sin is removed. In relation to sin's full removal he could have then taught that a full, complete renewal in the image of God is possible in this life.[29]

Second, Wesley could have chosen to maintain his dual definition of sin (voluntary and involuntary) but *deny that all sin is removed in this life*. At first glance, this option appears to deny the attainability of perfection in this life. But does it? All that is being denied is the claim that *all* sin is removed in the gift of perfection. This position does not deny the attainability of perfect devotion or love. This position does not even deny the attainability of a deliverance from sin per see; only that some sin must remain. If Wesley had chosen this position then logically he would have needed to *adjust his claims* to fit his theology. His theology

---

[27] This is one of John Maxwell's favorite rhetorical quips.

[28] This is basically what Charles Finney did. Many in the Holiness Movement have appeared to follow Finney's lead by stressing only one definition for sin, the voluntary one.

[29] The question becomes a scripture one: Does God's word teach that sin is only voluntary in nature? In response, JW believed that scripture points to a more corrosive and pervasive effect of sin on human nature than is supported only by a limited definition. Cf. *On Sin in Believers*.

could then claim a *relative* perfection that includes a *partial* deliverance from sin; specifically, voluntary sin.[30] In reality, his language supports the assertion of the first alternative while his theology of sin undermines its basis. At the same time, his theology of sin affirms the second alternative while his language overreaches by claiming that which is explicitly denied by his theology.

Wesley never chose either of these options. To his grave he continued to maintain (1) perfection involves the removal of all sin, and (2) the continuing reality of involuntary sin, even in those who are perfect. This is confirmed by one of his best summary homilies on the subject (and written late in his career).

In the sermon, *On Perfection,* Wesley attempts to once more answer the qualms of his critics by placing his beloved doctrine on solid footing. He begins by defining what perfection is not. Full salvation lays no claim to angelic or Adamic perfection. Once more, Wesley explains that Adam in his original state was absolutely perfect in his understanding and affections so that he always judged, spoke and acted right (I.2).[31] But upon his lapse into sin Adam could "no longer avoid wrong affections; neither can he always think, speak, and act right" (I.2). As a consequence, the "highest perfection which man can attain while the soul dwells in the body does not exclude ignorance, error, and a thousand other infirmities" (I.3). In this way Wesley affirms his doctrine of involuntary sin, but refuses to call these "innumerable violations" of the Adamic law, sin.

After explaining what perfection is not, he proceeds to assert what he means by full salvation, which "man is capable while he dwells in a corruptible body" (I.4). Using his standard list of descriptive markers, Wesley defines perfection in terms of perfect love, the mind of Christ, the fruit of the Spirit, renewal in God's image, universal holiness and full devotion (single intention). In general, all these marks are internally consistent with his doctrine

---

[30] Logically, this is JW's mature position, though his language states the opposite.
[31] For a fuller explanation see *Plain Account* ch 25.

of involuntary sin as enunciated above. But when we turn to his *specific claims* found in these marks the Achilles heel resurfaces.

Wesley continually makes claims that are absolute in nature. Again, the word "all" and other related terms become the key. Perfection entails the "*whole* disposition" of Christ, possessing "*all* his affections, *all* his tempers, both toward God and man" (I.5).[32] In regard to the fruit of the Spirit, perfection is to have "*all* these things to be knit together" in the "soul of the believer" (I.6). As complete devotion perfection means we "offer up to him *all* (our) thoughts, and words, and actions" (I.11). Then to cap his position, Wesley claims a sanctification that is complete and entire:

> Thus you experience that he whose name is called Jesus does not bear that name in vain; that he does in fact 'save his people from their sins', the *root* as well as the *branches*. And this 'salvation from sin', from *all* sin, is another description of perfection, though indeed it expresses only the least, the lowest branch of it, only the negative part of the great salvation.[33]

Wesley might say salvation from *all* sin is the "lowest branch" of perfection, yet he is making a mighty strong claim. Moreover, it is a claim which his doctrine of involuntary sin explicitly denies. That he is aware of the inconsistency is confirmed in the next section of the sermon.

Wesley addresses several of the common criticisms hurled at his perfection doctrine. Of interest to us is the objection that perfection from all sin is impossible while we remain in this "sinful body."[34] Wesley admits "there is a great deal of force in this ob-

---

[32] Emphasis is added in the following quotes to make the point even more clear to the reader.

[33] I.12; emphasis mine.

[34] II.8. JW objects to the language, but is this really substantively different than his own terminology of "corruptible body"? Both terms communicate the

jection." He agrees with his critics that we can never be free from culpable mistakes and practices, but he disagrees this is "no way inconsistent" with the perfection he believes and teaches. But the objector counters that Wesley's claim for salvation from all sin is inconsistent with our present fallen condition. Wesley's response is classic, yet sheds light on the core problem:

> I answer, It will perfectly well consist with salvation from sin, according to that definition of sin (which I apprehend to be the scriptural definition of it): 'a voluntary transgression of a known law'.[35]

Notice how Wesley *limits* or *narrows* his definition of sin to *support* his claim. Then, while affirming our continual need for the merits of Christ's atonement, even after we attain perfection, he denies these involuntary transgressions are sin:

> "Nay, (says the objector), but all transgressions of the law of God, whether voluntary or involuntary, are sin. For St. John says, 'All sin is a transgression of the law.'" True, but he does not say, 'All transgression of the law is sin.' This I deny: let him prove it that can.
> To say the truth, this is a mere strife of words. You say none is saved from sin in your sense of the word; but I do not admit of that sense, because the word is never so taken in Scripture. And you cannot deny the possibility of being saved from sin in my sense of the word. And this is the sense wherein the word 'sin' is over and over taken in Scripture.[36]

Wesley might say this is a "mere strife of words," but if scripture teaches sin to be only voluntary in nature then why does he con-

---

same idea—our mortal, fallen condition persists until death and to some degree the new creation.
[35] II.9.
[36] II.9.

tinue to maintain that these involuntary transgressions, if not atoned for, expose to eternal damnation?[37] Also, if Wesley is correct then why do Christians need forgiveness for transgressions that are not sin?

We must conclude that Wesley's response to the above objection does not solve the dilemma his dual definition of sin creates for his perfection claims. He simply chooses to conveniently limit his definition of sin to make room for his claim that in perfection all sin is removed, while continuing to affirm these involuntary transgressions expose to God's justice and require daily confession and forgiveness. *This is a real Achilles heel since both claims cannot be consistently maintained at the same time.* Either sin is limited to deliberate choice and all sin can be removed, or sin encompasses deliberate and inadvertent failures and is never fully removed in this life. Wesley's perfection doctrine claims the first while his full orbed doctrine of sin affirms the latter. And if the latter is true, there is no salvation from *all* sin in this life and his doctrine of Christian perfection evaporates into thin air.[38]

Obviously, Wesley did not see the internal contradiction this produced within his theology of perfection. Nor that his doctrine of involuntary sin implies there is no perfection from all sin in this life. Why he never resolved the dilemma is probably due to the depth of conviction he felt over the necessity of inward holiness for salvation. After all, the depth of Wesley's belief in a full

---

[37] Cf. note 15 above.

[38] Critical in this assertion is JW's definition of perfection as the removal of *all* sin. If he had defined it as the removal of only voluntary sin then he would had remained consistent. But he did not. Therefore, JW's view of perfection is not attainable since some kind of sin always remains until death. Let's say it in a different way. The believer can be said to be perfect in the sense of being "fully committed" (1 Kgs 15:14), "blameless" (Gen 6:9; Job 1:1), obeying the Great Commandment (2 Kgs 23:25), "living sacrifice" (Rom 12:1), and being mature (Eph 4:13; Php 3:15). In this limited sense a Christian can be said to be perfect ("complete" according to the Hebrew and Greek terms). But the believer can never be said to be free from all sin so as to never need to pray daily the Lord's prayer, "Forgive us our trespasses" (Matt 6:12). Is this a freedom from *all* sin? Let the reader decide.

deliverance from all sin formed the core of his spiritual DNA early in his career.[39] In the end, John Wesley could not deny this hope no matter what his later beliefs about sin implied. The roots of his character had drunk too deep in the holiness tradition to consider any alternative.

Turning toward the future, what Wesley bequeathed to his posterity is a theology of perfection bound with unresolved tensions. The generations that followed him have tended to gravitate toward one alternative or the other. The Holiness Movement, in particular, has traditionally favored the first option by limiting sin to voluntary choice.[40] Others within Methodism have leaned toward the second alternative; at times seeming to deny any attainable perfection in this life.[41] So the dialog continues and will inevitably shape how his descendants understand and pass on the doctrine of Christian perfection to future generations.[42]

---

[39] *Plain Account* chs 2-5.
[40] Wesley Tracy writes, "Millions of Wesley's ecclesiastical descendants had used his words about gradual sanctification as the bridge on which they marched away from the demands and distinctives of his teaching on instantaneous sanctification. Therefore, when the Holiness Movement got going, it made sure that no one could use that bridge again. They blew it up. They almost never spoke of gradual sanctification—but only of growth in grace" (*Uniting Worship, Preaching, and Theology*, WTS Journal Vol. 33:1, 45).
[41] Methodist historian Thomas Langford summarizes, "Methodist Episcopal interpreters, on the whole, stressed growth in grace and tended to doubt the validity of two distinct events in Christian experience...Perhaps most critically, they challenged the idea of instantaneously experienced holiness" (*Practical Divinity Vol. I*, 117).
[42] In this series volumes 4 and 5 will attempt to work through the central issue raised in this chapter, first, by systematizing JW's doctrine (vol. 4), and then by addressing the question of proclamation and explication (vol. 5).

APPENDICES

Timeline on Wesley's Doctrinal Development
John Wesley's Confessions
Early Testimonies of Perfect Love
The Evolution of the New Birth
The Roots of Wesley's Servant Theology
Clement of Alexandria: A Second Century Wesleyan?
Doctrinal Resource Lists

APPENDIX A
Timeline on Wesley's Doctrinal Development

June 22, 1703	John Wesley born
December 18, 1707	Charles Wesley born
1713	JW loses his baptismal washing of grace (JWJ 5/24/38)
Early Period	
Feb/Mar 1725	JW begins reading Jeremy Taylor and Thomas Kempis. He experiences spiritual awakening of a single intention
4/5/25	JW begins keeping a spiritual diary tracking his spiritual progress
9/25/25	JW ordained deacon in the Anglican Church
10/3/25	JW's first sermon: *Death and Deliverance*. He highlights that perfect salvation from inward sin is found only in the article of death
11/21/25	JW's second sermon: *Seek First the Kingdom*. The Christian's goal is the eternal kingdom attained through the single-minded pursuit of inward holiness. Both sermons delineate the broad contours of JW's Gospel of Holiness
9/22/28	JW ordained priest in the Anglican Church
11/15/29	JW returns to Oxford, soon takes charge of Holy Club (begun by CW the prior summer)
Winter/29-30	JW becomes a person of one book, the Holy Bible

Timeline on Doctrinal Development

1730	JW begins reading William Law
8/24/30	JW and Holy Club begin ministering to the prisoners
11/15/30	JW preaches his first university sermon, *The Image of God*. JW outlines his meta-narrative of Adam created in God's image, losing that image, and Christ, the second Adam, restoring the original image in believers
9/19/31	JW's writes *The Wisdom of Winning Souls*. He lays out an agenda for winning converts via the Gospel of Holiness
1732-34	JW studies church fathers, mystics, and keeps an exacter diary
10/28/32	JW transcribes the sermon *On Grieving the Holy Spirit*. He begins to emphasize the work of the Spirit in his theological system
1/1/33	JW preaches *The Circumcision of the Heart* before the University defending his holiness gospel. Perfection is defined as a fully transformed (holy) dispositional nature through the acquisition of holy tempers (humility, faith, hope and love) by the Holy Spirit's work
4/34	JW writes *One Thing Needful*. He proclaims the "great work" as the "renewal of our fallen nature" in God's love. He begins to emphasize the necessity of making a decision to have a single intention
9/21/35	JW writes and publishes *The Trouble and Rest of Good Men* – perfection from inward sin is fully attained only in the article of death
10/15/35	JW departs to America as a missionary to the Georgian Indians

John Wesley's Theology of Christian Perfection

11/35-1/36	Storms at sea arouses conviction of deeper need
2/4/36	JW's sermon *Single Intention* clearly identifies conversion (using new birth terminology) with the decision of a single intention, thus explicitly linking the new birth to perfection in his gospel of holiness
6/36	JW witnesses Henry Lascelles testimony to Christian perfection in the article of death (JWJ)
1/38	Upon his return to England JW makes a series of confessions acknowledging his spiritual need
2/1/38	JW sets foot on English soil

Middle Period

2/7/38	JW meets Peter Böhler
3/6/38	JW convinced salvation is by faith alone. He begins preaching his "new" gospel
3/23/38	JW is convinced that holiness and happiness with God are attained by faith alone
4/23/38	JW embraces instantaneous conversion, the witness of the Spirit, and concludes he is not a Christian (i.e. saved)
5/21/38	CW experiences conversion by faith alone
5/24/38	JW's Aldersgate "heart-warming" conversion ratifies his new gospel. He believes he is saved from all sin
6/11/38	JW preaches *Salvation By Faith* before the university. His faith-alone gospel proclaims perfection in the new birth. Sin is categorized in terms of guilt and power

Timeline on Doctrinal Development

8/38	JW at Hernhutt. He records the preaching of Christian David and testimonies of perfection. He learns there are degrees to faith a second post-regeneration experience in holiness
9/28/38	JW distinguishes between saving faith and a full assurance of faith (JWL); he begins accepting degrees of faith
1/25/39	JW formally accepts degrees to faith and the new birth (JWJ)
2/9/39	JW writes preface for the *Life of Mr. Halyburton*. Perfection is identified with not committing sin and JW appears to embrace an intermittent view of holiness (Works J 14: 211)
4/2/39	JW begins field preaching. The world becomes his parish. He begins teaching perfection as a post-regeneration experience (JWJ)
4/29/39	JW preaches and later publishes the sermon *Free Grace*, a polemic against Calvinism (JWJ)
9/13/39	JW separates justification from sanctification (JWJ)
11/1/39	The stillness controversy begins (JWJ)
11/17/39	JW teaches on the nature and extant of perfection at Bristol (JWJ)
Spring/40	JW publishes a second volume of hymns containing a preface teaching perfection as second work of grace (Works J 14:322)
7/20/40	JW formally separates from the Moravians over stillness, degrees of faith and the means of grace. JW affirms the latter two

John Wesley's Theology of Christian Perfection

early/41	JW publishes *Christian Perfection*, delineating in what sense Christians can and cannot be perfect in this life. He distinguishes between outward sin (committing sin) and inward sin, and identifies three levels of believers: child, adolescent, adult, with perfection associated with the latter group
Spring/41	JW formally separates with the Calvinists (JWJ 4/28/41)
1742	JW publishes *The Character of a Methodist*. Perfection is presented in ideal terms
1744-1747	*The Conference Minutes* addresses several doctrines and issues related to perfection
7/31/47	JW officially separates justifying faith from assurance (JWL)
1756	*N.T. Notes* are published. Cornelius is called a servant of God, and defined as accepted by God before receiving the Pentecostal Spirit (Acts 10:35). JW's servant theology begins moving in new directions
1758	JW starts teaching perfection can be lost. He begins to emphasize more strongly that perfection is received by faith alone in an instant.
1759-1763	The great revival of perfection within Methodist societies. Multitudes profess perfection received by faith in an instant
10/16/59	JW finishes *Thoughts on Christian Perfection*. He clarifies his doctrine of sin with the twin categories of voluntary and involuntary. Perfection is limited to freedom from voluntary sin (PA 19:6-25)
1760	JW publishes *The New Birth*. He formally separates regeneration from perfection and sanctification in his theological system.

Timeline on Doctrinal Development

1762-63	Perfection schism by Maxfield and Bell (PA chs 20-22)
12/62	Bell predicts the world will end on Feb. 28, 1763. The prophecy proves false. Maxfield and Bell separate from JW in early 1763. The schism brings disrepute on Christian perfection
3/28/63	JW writes *On Sin in Believers*. Sin is defined in three categories: guilt, power and being
Spring/63	JW publishes *Farther Thoughts on Christian Perfection*. He seeks to bring balance to the perfection revival by giving a theological basis for the doctrine and offering correction to excesses. The fruits of Spirit are presented as final evidence for attainment (PA ch 25)
1764	Wesley reevaluates his perfection doctrine and writes out an eleven point summary of his beliefs (PA ch 26)

Mature Period

1765	JW writes *The Scripture Way of Salvation*. His mature position on perfection is clarified: perfection as a second work, by faith alone, instantly given, witnessed by the Holy Spirit
Spring-Fall/65	JW writes *A Plain Account of Christian Perfection* defending his perfection views for the past 40 years. It becomes the official statement on JW's doctrine of Christian perfection and is his first publication following Aldersgate that is positive toward his pre-Aldersgate faith journey
6/27/66	JW writes to CW despairing over his post-Aldersgate Christian experience. He defines his present spiritual experience in pre-new birth terms

	and believes he is just a servant of God, yet saved (JWL T)
1/22/67	JW writes to Charles (and others) defining perfection as humble, gentle, patient love; received by faith alone, often given in the article of death (JWL T)
12/1/67	JW affirms believing in justification by faith alone is not necessary for salvation; what is required is the faith of a servant (Acts 10:35)
4/7/68	The first time JW uses the term "servant" for the pre-new birth stage in which the person is already justified.
8/2/70	The *1770 Conference Minutes* reasserts works into JW's gospel system as a vital condition for final salvation. JW also reaffirms the servant status for those who have never heard of Christ.
1774-75	JW adds qualifying notes to his 1738 journal re-evaluating his pre-Aldersgate spiritual condition. He affirms he was a servant (justified), though not a son (born again). Justification is now formally separated from the new birth in point of time (JWJ footnotes 2/1/38; 4/25/38; 5/24/38; 7/12/38)
1781-85	JW solidifies his eschatological vision with the sermons *The End of Christ's Coming* (1781), *The General Deliverance* (1781), *The General Spread of the Gospel* (1783), and *The New Creation* (1785).
10/85	The sermon *On Working Out Our Salvation* clarifies the role that works plays in the salvation process. But most significantly JW presents salvation beginning with preventing grace instilling holy tempers toward God.

Timeline on Doctrinal Development

1788-1790	Several in JW's last group of sermons open up the gospel for pre-Christians[1] attaining final salvation based on Acts 10:35 and Heb 11:6.
3/26/90	*The Wedding Garment* sums up JW's mature faith in holy tempers as the best ground for assurance of final salvation.
1/17/91	JW's last written homily explores the blessings of paradise between death and the resurrection. The immortal spirit of the righteous grows in knowledge and holiness, enjoying ever-increasing happiness in the service of God.
March 2, 1791	John Wesley dies.

---

[1] Cf. chapter 7 for an explanation of a pre-Christian.

APPENDIX B
John Wesley's Confessions

Anyone who has read Wesley's journals is probably aware of the deep despair he passed through upon his return to England in early 1738. During these days Wesley penned several confessions outlining his inner struggles. Three of the confessions were included in his first journal extract (published May 1740). A fourth confession was written on January 25, 1738. While this last confession did not find a place in his published journal, it is included in the footnotes of the Bicentennial Edition of the Works of John Wesley (18:212-213). A comparative study of these confessions reveals a surprising conclusion: Wesley did *not* write the postscript of his first journal extract on February 1, but *after* he embraced his new faith-alone gospel. This new gospel he learned from Peter Böhler in March/April of that year. Many, if not most, have read this postscript confession as an accurate portrayal of Wesley's thoughts and feelings on February 1, 1738. This assumption must now be rejected. Instead, the postscript reflects Wesley's point of view *after* he embraced his new gospel and therefore expresses a *later* perspective. The three January confessions, which are dated by Wesley, theologically agree with his Gospel of Holiness, while the post-script (not dated) is a faithful expression of his faith-alone gospel. Thus, the post-script was not written at the same time as the other three confessions, or by the same John Wesley. What follows is each confession with annotations explaining their theological orientation. At the end we will conclude by highlighting the significance this insight plays in understanding the evolution of Wesley's perfection theology in 1738.

John Wesley's Confessions

Confession One: The Feeling of Emptiness
January 8, 1738

Introductory Note: In the days leading up to this confession Wesley pessimistically records the good attendance of the people on board ship to the worship services, and even their attentiveness to his preaching. Yet he doubts that much good will come from it just as in Frederica, Georgia. On the next day he acknowledges how his depth of sorrow and heaviness is affecting his ability to minister to people. Just a couple days before he penned this confession, Wesley finished reading an extract of the life of Mr. De Ranty, in whom he felt a kindred spirit. Such a life, Wesley must have felt, was in sharp contrast to his own. In response he penned the following words while under the shadow of that great man's life:

In the fullness of my heart I wrote the following words:

By the most infallible of proofs, inward feeling,[I.1] I am convinced:

1. Of unbelief, having no such faith in Christ as will prevent my heart from being troubled; which it could not be if I believed in God, and rightly believed also in him [i.e., Christ].
2. Of pride, throughout my life past, inasmuch as I thought I had what I find I have not.

[I.1] The reason why JW here considers inward feelings as "infallible" is that he is examining the degree of transformation within his character. Remember, according to JW's GosH assurance is grounded upon three realities (1) The indwelling presence of the Holy Spirit, witnessed by life transformation, (2) the benefit of the Lord's Table, as long as one communicates in a worthy manner, and (3) the sincerity of one's single intention. Underlying all three is the reality of the life transformation process. The central purpose of JW's Oxford program was to prepare one for eternity through the infusion of holy tempers. JW's brush with death exposed his unwillingness to die, which in turn exposed his lack of inward transformation. This lack, so deeply *felt*, was infallible proof that (1) his life was less transformed than what he had thought (hence, his pride; see paragraph #2), and (2) sin still had a grip on his heart.

3. Of gross irrecollection, inasmuch as in a storm I cry to God every moment, in a calm, not.
4. Of levity and luxuriancy of spirit, recurring whenever the pressure is taken off, and appearing by my speaking words not tending to edify; but most, by my manner of speaking of my enemies.[I.2]

'Lord save, or I perish!' Save me,[I.3]

1. By such a faith as implies peace in life and in death.[I.4]

[I.2] The sins confessed here all relate to the storms at sea and his failure in America. His *unbelief* was exposed because his heart became deeply troubled when death knocked at his door. This was in sharp contrast to the Moravians who continued to worship and praise God, revealing they had a faith JW knew nothing about experientially. JW felt his heart must be deceitful and full of *pride* for thinking he was much more spiritual than he really was. Such self-deception is irreconcilable with a profession of sincerity. At this time he sees himself as being very negligent in his devotion to God.

Gross irrecollection, as defined above by JW, was surely seen by himself as the opposite of a single intention to please God. His last criticism of himself was first mentioned about six months earlier. In a letter to a friend on July 23, 1737, JW acknowledged the awkward dilemma he found himself in America—"ease, and honour, and abundance." This is what he least desired or expected when he made the decision to become a missionary to Georgia.

[I.3] Everything JW desires here fits perfectly with his holiness gospel. In this confession there is not the slightest hint that salvation is by faith alone; nor is saving faith wrought instantaneously in the heart as a gift from God, bringing peace (present justification), holiness of heart, and joy of the divine fullness (happiness). When JW cries out for God to save him, he is thinking in terms of (gradual) life transformation. While early JW did believe in present conversion, in the sense of the decision of a single intention, it was the infusion of inward virtues, like the ones listed here, that impart God's life to the soul. These characteristics clearly mark this confession theologically as belonging to his early period and reveal his theological orientation at the time.

[I.4] In the sermon *On Love* (1737) JW tells his American audience that the gospel (of holiness) brings peace and comfort in death. In his journal (6/6/36) and in the homily's conclusion (III.8) JW shares how Mr. Lascelles died with great peace and comfort because his heart was pure. At the time JW understood faith

John Wesley's Confessions

2. By such humility as may fill my heart from this hour for ever with a piercing, uninterrupted sense, *Nihil est quod hactenus feci* (I have done nothing hitherto), having evidently built without foundation.[1.5]

3. By such a recollection as may cry to thee every moment, especially when all is calm, Give me faith or I die; give me a lowly spirit; otherwise *Mihi non sit suave vivere* (Let life be a burden to me).[1.6]

4. By steadiness, seriousness, *semnotes* (i.e. honesty), sobriety of spirit, avoiding as fire every word that tendeth not to edifying, and never speaking of any who oppose me, or sin against God, without all my own sins set in array before my face.[1.7]

---

mostly in terms of sanctification. What he desires in this confession is a faith that will prepare him for death and eternity.

[1.5] Humility was the foundational virtue in JW's early soteriology. It heads the list of stages in the sermon *The Circumcision of the Heart* and in his *Preface to the Christian's Pattern*. His early letters abound with strong remarks on the importance and necessity of humility for salvation. Since pride is one of the primary expressions of Adamic sin, humility became the foundation in one's progress to perfection and eternal salvation.

[1.6] This request implies one of the deep-seated beliefs JW had about perfection: a pure heart will be full of God's presence; and, moreover, such a heart will experience continual communion with their heavenly Father. What separates one from God? Sin! So if all sin is removed then perpetual communion can be enjoyed. But such communion implies a change in the person's conscious awareness of God in everyday life. To be holy is to be full of God. To be full of God is to have a constant awareness of him. To have constant awareness is to be fully devoted. Note, once again, JW's concern is to be fit and ready to face death with confidence. This agrees exactly with his GosH.

[1.7] This confession plays a big role in starting the process that finally leads JW to repudiate many of his holiness gospel principles. He realizes that after transversing the ocean twice, and experiencing mixed results in America, he must somehow be on the wrong path. After all, he knows he is not prepared to face death. Compare this paragraph with his letter to John Burton, in which JW explains why he went to America. Obviously, one reason was to find a solution to his lack of self-control concerning his tongue:

> Further, a sin which easily besets me is unfaithfulness to God in the use of speech. I know that this is a talent entrusted to me by my Lord,

John Wesley's Theology of Christian Perfection

Confession Two: The Failed Mission
January 24, 1738

My mind was now full of thought, part of which I writ down as follows:

I went to America to convert the Indians; but Oh! who shall convert me?[II.1] Who, what is he that will deliver me

---

> to be used as all other, only for his glory...Yet I am almost continually betrayed into it by the example of others, striking in with my own bad heart. But I hope, from the moment I leave the English shore under the acknowledged character of a teacher sent from God, there shall no word be heard from my lips but what properly flows from that character. As my tongue is a devoted thing, I hope from the first hour of this new era to use it only as such, that all who hear me may know of a truth the words I speak are not mine, but his that sent me. (JWL 10/10/35)

From this confession on January 8 we can conclude JW felt he had failed miserably to achieve this goal. This was an important lesson. The problem was not England, nor English society; it was JW who needed to change. He was beginning to see this basic truth, but with the spectacles of his GosH system. He longs for a holy heart, and still conceives of salvation through his present holiness framework. There is not the slightest hint in this confession that salvation is by faith alone, in Christ alone, received in an instant, witnessed by the Holy Spirit. JW is still on the treadmill of works (PA ch 7 end note).

[II.1] While JW uses the word "convert" twice in this sentence, he does so in two somewhat different, yet related, senses. As the word is applied to the Native Americans it means to become an adherent of a particular religion or philosophy. For example, JW records in his journal of meeting his "first convert" to Deism in America (5/18/37). The man had been a zealous Christian, but through "indulging" a wrong crowd he lost his zeal and then lost his faith. To *convert* the Native Americans meant to win them over as followers of Jesus Christ. But this is not his meaning in the second use. JW was already a follower of Jesus Christ. We learned in chapter one that early JW stressed a progressive view of the life transformation process, which he often referred to as "conversion." In this latter sense to be converted was to attain Christian perfection. The remainder of the confession's content makes this meaning clear.

John Wesley's Confessions

from this evil heart of unbelief? I have a fair summer religion. I can talk well; nay, and believe myself, while no danger is near: but let death look me in the face, and my spirit is troubled.^{II.2} Nor can I say, 'To die is gain!'

> I have a sin of fear, that when I've spun
> My last thread, I shall perish on the shore!

I think verily, if the gospel be true, I am safe.^{II.3} For I not only have given, and do give, all my goods to feed the poor; I not only give my body to be burned, drowned, or whatever God shall appoint for me, but I follow after charity (though not as I ought, yet as I can) if haply I may attain it. I now believe the gospel is true. 'I show my faith by my works,' by staking my all upon it. I would do so again and again a thousand times, if the choice were still to make. Whoever sees me sees I would be a Christian.^{II.4}

JW had gone to America, officially to convert the Native Americans, unofficially to convert or to save his own soul. He failed at both tasks. His religion is only a *fair summer* one. He realizes he still is unfit to face death; hence, his heart is unsanctified.

^{II.2} His remarks about death clarify what exactly caused his despondency—his close encounter with death. JW did not suffer continual bouts of uncertainty throughout his early period. Contrary to other opinions, JW did not decide to go to America because he lacked certainty over his eternal salvation, as if he believed he was presently on the path to hell (contrary to Heitzenrater, Gunter, and others). How do we know this is true? In confession four JW openly declares that what he *least expected* when he decided to go to America was to learn he was unconverted at the time. Obviously, JW did have confidence in his spiritual state upon his leaving for America.

^{II.3} What JW describes in the next several paragraphs refers to his faithful practice of the means of grace. JW believed these means were the normal channels God uses to infuse holy dispositions within the heart, leading the believer to higher levels of perfection and salvation. JW was confident he had been faithful in keeping these disciplines. But he wrestles with a lack of faith.

^{II.4} *I would be a Christian.* That is, a Christian in the full sense of the word, a perfect Christian. Under the GosH this level of Christian development was in reality unattainable till the article of death. While he was in America, JW for the first time met believers whom he believed had attained a high degree of

Therefore 'are my ways not like other men's ways'. Therefore I have been, I am, I am content to be, 'a byword, a proverb of reproach'. But in a storm I think, 'What if the gospel be not true?' Then thou art of all men most foolish. For what hast thou given thy goods, thy ease, thy friends, thy reputation, thy country, thy life? For what art thou wandering over the face of the earth? A dream, 'a cunningly devised fable'?[II.5] O who will deliver me from this fear of death! What shall I do? Where shall I fly from it? Should I fight against it by thinking, or by not thinking of it? A wise man advised me some time since, 'Be still and go on.' Perhaps this is best, to look upon it as my cross; when it comes, to let it humble me, and quicken all my good resolutions, especially that of praying without ceasing; and at other times to take no thought about it, but quietly to go on 'in the work of the Lord'.[II.6]

---

perfection. First, there were the Moravian believers aboard ship who did not fear death. In JW's holiness system this was a sure mark of attaining a high degree of perfection in one's devotion to God. Second, there was the testimony of Mr. Lascelles, who attained complete peace soon before his departure from this life (JWJ 6/6/36; sermon *On Love* III.8).

[II.5] *A cunningly devised fable*. His struggle involves more than just the lack of holy tempers. JW lacks faith in the gospel's veracity. In the sermon *On Mourning for the Dead* JW likens this present life to a dream state, emphasizing the shortness of life. Here, he wonders if the good news of Christ is only a dream, a made-up story. Since these doubts are located in a confession acknowledging his unwillingness to die, they must have been fed by the struggles to face death with confidence. It is a rule of life: one doubt feeds other doubts. This confession is an honest admission that his GosH failed to give him the peace he longed for, and explains why upon his return to England he searched for another gospel message to fill the void he felt within.

[II.6] JW attempts to calm his troubled heart by interpreting his present uncertainty in light of his belief that salvation is attained through progressive stages. From this perspective what he needs to do is to keep pressing on in his present path by taking up the cross, practicing the means of grace (especially continual prayer), and letting the present crisis work humility in his heart. Maybe, just maybe, this crisis will pass and his spirit will calm down. The reader must note how these remarks by JW "fit like a glove" with his GosH system. Again, note there is not even a hint in this confession of salvation received in a moment by

John Wesley's Confessions

Confession Three: Tossed About
January 25, 1738

Introductory Note: The following memorandum offers important insights into Wesley's theological understanding upon his return to England. Written only six days before he set foot on English soil, it clarifies his present understanding of salvation at the time, and how he viewed his past thirteen years as a seeker of inward holiness. Moreover, Wesley's definition of salvation in paragraph one offers a concise summary of his early soteriology. A thoughtful reading of this confession reveals that its soteriology is in direct opposition to that of the fourth confession. Hence, both statements could not have been written only a few days apart.

Me` Kludonizomenoi Panti Avemo Tes Didaches[III]
('not tossed to and fro by every wind of doctrine', cf. Eph. 4:14)

Second Paper.

Different views of Christianity are given, (1) by the Scripture, (2) the Papists, (3) the Lutherans and Calvinists, (4) the English Divines, (5) the Essentialist Nonjurors, (6) the Mystics.

Jan. 25, 1738

1. For many years have I been tossed about by various winds of doctrine. I asked long ago, What must I do to be saved? The Scripture answered, 'Keep the commandments. Believe, hope, love; follow after these tempers till thou hast fully attained, that is, till death, by all those

---

faith alone. Instead, this confession reveals JW's frame of mind is definitely pre-Aldersgate (pre-GosFA), showing this statement was written in January 1738.

[III] This is a transliteration of the Greek text in JW's Journal.

outward works and means which God hath appointed, by walking as Christ walked.'[III.1]

2. I was early warned against laying, as the Papists do, too much stress either on outward works or on a faith without works, which, as it does not include, so it will never lead to, true hope or charity. Nor am I sensible that to this hour I have laid too much stress on either, having from the very beginning valued both faith, the means of grace, and good works, not on their own account, but as believing God, who had appointed them, would by them bring me in due time to the mind that was in Christ.[III.2]

[III.1] This definition of salvation highlights the primary emphasis in JW's GosH: personal obedience, dispositional transformation, redemption from sin in the article of death, grace infused by the means of grace, and the equation of salvation with inward holiness (Christian perfection). The reader should note how faith is defined in this paragraph: a temper of the heart instead as a condition for instantaneous salvation. This paragraph highlights that while JW did believe in the new birth prior to 1738 (as the single intention and full salvation); still, the progressive element to salvation dominates his thinking. The importance this paragraph plays in our understanding of JW's theological development should be clear. If this confession reveals what JW understood of salvation in January 1738, then the next confession could not have been written at the same time.

[III.2] JW confesses to being warned "early" in life against the perceived errors of both Catholic and Reformed traditions. The former stressed outward works in attaining salvation (strong sacramental theology), and the latter emphasized *sola fide*, salvation by faith alone. JW is here opting for the *via media* (middle way) of Anglicanism. W. Stephen Gunter explains that "Anglican theological identity was forged between the opposing sides of traditional Roman Catholicism and Puritanism or Reformed Protestantism" (Gunter, W. Stephen...[et al.] *Wesley and the Quadrilateral*, 18). JW believes he has remained balanced (the middle way) in his spiritual pursuit of the "mind that was in Christ"—that is, inward holiness. JW is furthermore confident he has maintained a genuine faith in God to save him through the appointed means of salvation. The reader should note (1) that his object of faith is not Christ and his cross, but God and his promises to sanctify the believer. This single fact distinguishes JW's two gospels as separate systems (see JWJ 5/24/38 §11). (2) In paragraphs one and two JW rejects any notion of salvation by faith alone, which becomes the foundation of his GosFA (JWJ 3/6/38).

3. But before God's time was come I fell among some Lutheran and Calvinist authors, whose confused and indigested accounts magnified faith to such an amazing size that it quite hid all the rest of the commandments. I did not then see that this was the natural effect of their overgrown fear of popery, being so terrified with the cry of 'merit and good works' that they plunged at once into the other extreme. In this labyrinth I was utterly lost, not being able to find out what the error was, nor yet to reconcile this uncouth hypothesis either with Scripture or common sense.[III.3]

4. The English writers, such as Bishop Beveridge, Bishop Taylor, and Mr. Nelson, a little relieved me from these well-meaning, wrong-headed Germans. Their accounts of Christianity I could easily see to be, in the main, consistent both with reason and Scripture. Only when they interpreted Scripture in different ways I was often much at a loss. And again there was one thing much insisted on in Scripture—the unity of the Church—which none of them I thought clearly explained, or strongly inculcated.[III.4]

[III.3] *Before God's time.* A probable reference to his spiritual awakening in the winter/spring of 1725. We have learned that JW's early faith journey embraced the middle way of Anglicanism, but at some point in this journey he began reading Lutheran and Calvinist authors whose magnification of faith violated the *via media* of his Anglicanism. At the time he rejected their version of *sola fide*. All these issues will come to play a significant role as JW embraces the Lutheran gospel of the Moravians in the spring of 1738, only to later part paths with them over the question of the means of grace in 1740. This paragraph reveals JW's strong commitment to the Anglican principle of the middle way in attaining salvation.

[III.4] Let's look at each author in chronological order as JW introduces them. From late winter to early spring in 1725 JW began reading Anglican bishop Jeremy Taylor's *Rules and Exercises of Holy Living and Dying* (PA 2:1). Taylor's impact upon JW led him to begin a spiritual diary on April 5 of that year. Taylor stressed making resolutions and setting practical rules to govern one's spiritual pursuit. But what JW later remembers as most memorable was his emphasis on purity of intention (PA 2:2; JWJ 5/14/65). This latter point ig-

5. But it was not long before Providence brought me to those who showed me a sure rule for interpreting Scripture, viz., *Consensus veterum*—'*Quod ab omnibus, quod ubique, quod semper creditum.*'[III.5] At the same time they sufficiently insisted upon a due regard to the One Church at all times and in all places. Nor was it long before I bent the bow too far the other way: (1) by making antiquity a co-ordinate (rather than subordinate) rule with Scripture; (2) by admitting several doubtful writings as undoubted evidences of antiquity; (3) by extending antiquity too far, even to the middle or end of the fourth century; (4) by believing more practices to have been universal in the ancient Church than ever were so; (5) by not considering that the decrees of one provincial synod could bind only that province, and the decrees of a general synod only those provinces whose representatives met therein; (6) by

---

nited a fire in his heart that he came to see as a spiritual awakening. At this time he became a "servant" of God. Steven Harper comments that JW read Taylor often in this early period (*The Devotional Life of John Wesley, 1725-1738*, 87-88, 102, 110, 283).

JW read several of Non-juror John Nelson's writings on primitive Christianity and the Anglican Church. These include *True Devotion, Companion for Festivals and Fasts of the Church of England*, and most importantly, *The Great Duty of Frequenting the Christian Sacrifice* (Harper, *Devotional Life*, 113, 124, 140, 153). The latter one JW edited and transcribed in 1732 as a sermon to encourage the frequent practice of communicating at the Lord's Table. It appears Nelson inspired JW in 1730 to begin collecting prayers which later became JW's first published work in 1733.

Last, JW began reading William Beveridge's *Private Thoughts* in late 1731. Beveridge emphasized Scripture above all other means and standards, and referred to God's word as "the star by which I am to be guided" (Harper, *Devotional Life*, 144). JW's diaries record that he spent the first several months of 1732 in systematic reading of Scripture. While in America JW began to read Beveridge's *Codex Canonum Ecclesiae Primitive Vindicatus ac Illustratus* (JWJ 9/13/36 & 9/20/36 [see also the MS Journals]). This book convinced JW that he had relied too heavily upon traditions passed on from the early church as being apostolic (cf. par. 5).

[III.5] Translation: "The consensus of antiquity: 'What is believed by everyone, everywhere, and always.'" (Heitzenrater, *The Elusive Mr. Wesley, Vol. I*, 95).

not considering that most of those decrees were adapted to particular times and occasions, and consequently when those occasions ceased, must cease to bind even those provinces.[III.6]

6. These considerations insensibly stole upon me as I grew acquainted with the mystic writers, whose noble descriptions of union with God and internal religion made everything else appear mean, flat, and insipid. But in truth they made good works appear so too; yea, and faith itself, and what not? These gave me an entire new view of religion, nothing like any I had had before. But alas! It was nothing like that religion which Christ and his apostles lived and taught. I had a plenary dispensation from all the commands of God. The form ran thus: 'Love is all; all the commands beside are only means of love; you must choose those which you feel are means to you, and use them as long as they are so.' Thus were all the bands burst at once. And though I could never fully come into this, nor contentedly omit what God enjoined, yet, I know not how, I fluctuated between obedience and disobedience: I had no heart, no vigour, no zeal in obeying; continually doubting whether I was right or wrong, and never out of perplexities and entanglements. Nor can I at this hour give a distinct account how or when I came a little back toward the right way. Only my present sense is this: all the other enemies of Christianity are triflers; the mystics are the most dangerous of all its enemies. They stab it in the vitals, and its most serious professors are most likely to fall by them. May I praise him who hath snatched me out of

---

[III.6] This paragraph describes the changes in JW's perspective while in America (see III.5 n). He came to realize that he had placed too much trust in those writings purporting to have come, or to have passed traditions from the apostolic era (JWJ 9/13/36 & 9/20/36). JW's interest in primitive Christianity increased measurably in 1732 with his acquaintance of John Clayton (Heitzenrater, *Wesley and the People Called Methodists*, 44).

John Wesley's Theology of Christian Perfection

this fire likewise, by warning all others that it is set on fire of hell.[III.7]

[III.7] Harper records that JW's devotional interest in Christian mysticism was a lifelong interest. In defining mysticism Harper is careful to delineate between a "broad" and "narrow" sense. Broadly speaking, mysticism refers to (1) the capacity of the soul to see and perceive spiritual things, (2) in order to know God the believer must become a partaker of the divine nature (2 Pet 1:4), and (3) that holiness is required for salvation (Heb 12:14). Narrowly speaking, mysticism stresses extremes in both ascetic practices and seeking visionary experiences of the divine (*Devotional Life*, 41). Heitzenrater informs us that JW's interest in mysticism increased after his personal meeting with William Law in 1732. Law encouraged JW to read the medieval treatise *Theologia Germanica*. Soon after, JW began to read other mystic authors (*Wesley and People*, 52). One of the most influential mystic books JW read was *The Life of Monsieur de Renty, A Late Nobleman of France*. Harper states that this was "one of the most significant devotional works" that JW ever read (*Devotional Life*, 102). JW's diary records his reading this book in May 1729, showing his early interest in the mystics.

In the paragraph above, what bothered JW the most about the mystics was their neglect of the means of grace and the Anglican middle way. He admits of being drawn to their vision of union with God and the heart filled with divine love, but *how* they attempted to attain such perfection was contrary to JW's instinctive conviction that the means of grace are essential to having holy dispositions infused within the heart.

By the fall of 1736 JW was becoming disenchanted with the mystic path toward inward holiness and salvation. In a letter to his older brother, JW asks Samuel for his opinion of mystic writings and their theology. JW complains of their demotion of the means of grace, spiritual disciplines, and their rejection of human reason in the pursuit of working out our salvation (JWL 11/23/36). By the time JW wrote this memorandum on January 25, 1738, his animosity toward the mystic way of attaining inward holiness had become complete. He uses strong language to denounce their theology. This reflects JW's own spiritual state at the time. He is deeply frustrated with himself and in his lack of progress in attaining holiness. In 1739 he takes another stab at the mystics in his preface to the first volume of hymns by attacking their principle of solitary religion (Works J 14:319).

Confession Three Summary

JW offers in this memorandum a brief sketch of his faith journey up till January 1738. The structure of the confession is as follows:

John Wesley's Confessions

Confession Four: A New Gospel Needed
February 1, 1738

Introductory Note: We now arrive at the confession located at the end of his first journal extract (2/1/38). This postscript reflects his views at a later time, after he embraced his faith-alone gospel. The contrast between this confession and the other three is very stark. The footnotes will alert the reader to these contrasts.

It is now two years and almost four months since I left my native country in order to teach the Georgian Indians the nature of Christianity. But what have I learned myself in the meantime? Why (what I the least of all suspected), that I who went to America to convert others, was never myself converted to God.[IV.1] 'I am not mad', though I

Par. 1: JW's present understanding of salvation and how it is attained—*via media*.
Par. 2-3: Wesley's faith journey prior to 1725.
Par. 4: Wesley's journey from 1725 to early 30's.
Par. 5-6: Wesley's journey from 1732-present.

The confession ends on a negative note because JW is at a low point in life. As Confessions 1 & 2 reveal, JW has now lost confidence because of his unwillingness to die when faced with the storms at sea; combined with his failures in America. This explains his despair and confusion at the time. But certain convictions have set in. JW no longer trusts in early councils and traditions to guide him spiritually, and he has firmly come to the conviction that the mystic path is dangerous. He began this confession affirming his early affirmation in the middle way of attaining salvation (faith and works), and closes by reaffirming this same basic conviction. Hence, in a sense JW has come full circle. Salvation is still defined as the infusion of holy dispositions within the heart, fully attained in the article of death. This is simply a succinct summary of the heart of JW's GosH. By comparing this memorandum with the one that follows, and his Aldersgate memorandum recorded on May 24, 1738 we see a sharp contrast in the way JW understands salvation from January to May.

[IV.1] Compare the use of the word *convert* in this confession to its use in confession two. In both confessions he says he went to "convert" the Native Ameri-

thus speak, but 'I speak the words of truth and soberness'; if haply some of those who still dream may awake, and see that as I am, so are they.[IV.2]

Are they read in philosophy? So was I. In ancient or modern tongues?[IV.3] So was I also. Are they versed in the science of divinity? I too have studied it many years. Can they talk fluently upon spiritual things? The very same could I do. Are they plenteous in alms? Behold, I gave all my goods to feed the poor. Do they give of their labour as well as of their substance? I have laboured more abundantly than they all. Are they willing to suffer for their brethren? I have thrown up my friends, reputation, ease,

---

cans, yet in the process he came to realize that he himself needed a conversion. But there is a twist. A close reading of both confessions reveal he is referring to related, yet, different kinds or aspects of conversion in each confession. In confession two JW's concern is overcoming his fair weather religion: his fear of death and the doubts he feels over the gospel's veracity. But he still believes this is his cross to bear. He resolves that the solution is to renew his resolutions to keep the means of grace. The latter confession contains a much sharper self-criticism. JW now declares his *whole heart is altogether corrupt* and he is *alienated* from the *life of God*. He confesses, *I am a child of wrath, an heir of hell*. JW adds to this that the faith he presently possesses is similar to that of a devil. This is a far cry from confession two; suppose to have been written only a few days before this one. Conversion here refers to a more drastic, life altering change. No resolution will solve this wound. JW needs a different kind of faith altogether (compare with JWL 5/24/38). Did he really change his theology that much in just a few short days?

Moreover, the reader should note JW states this realization was what he *least expected* when he went to America. This acknowledgment clarifies that JW did not go to America because he lacked assurance regarding his eternal salvation (in an evangelical sense).

[IV.2] This is the language of apology. JW is not speaking to himself, but to those who are critical of his new GosFA theology. They thought him to be *mad* because of his new gospel message. This includes both friends and family (JWJ 4/25/38; JWL 5/1/38). Heitzenrater adds, "To many who had known Wesley during the previous decade of his ministry, this assumption (JW was saved at Aldersgate) seemed utter nonsense" (*The Elusive Mr. Wesley* 2:65).

[IV.3] All the disciplines described in this paragraph were practiced by JW and the Holy Club (Hattersley, *Life of John Wesley*, 76; Heitzenrater, *Wesley and People*, 39-41; Rack, *Reasonable Enthusiast*, 84-100).

country; I have put my life in my hand, wandering into strange lands; I have given my body to be devoured by the deep, parched up with heat, consumed by toil and weariness, or whatsoever God should please to bring upon me. But does all this (be it more or less, it matters not) make me acceptable to God? Do all I ever did or can know, say, give, do, or suffer, justify me in his sight? Yea, or 'the constant use of all the means of grace'?—which nevertheless is meet, right, and our bounden duty. Or that 'I know nothing of myself,' that I am, as touching outward, moral righteousness, blameless? Or (to come closer yet) the having a rational conviction of all the truths of Christianity? Does all this give me a claim to the holy, heavenly, divine character of a Christian? By no means. If the oracles of God are true, if we are still to abide by 'the law and the testimony', all these things, though when ennobled by faith in Christ they are holy, and just, and good, yet without it are 'dung and dross', meet only to be purged away by 'the fire that never shall be quenched'.[IV.4]

This then have I learned in the ends of the earth, that I am 'fallen short of the glory of God'; that my whole heart is 'altogether corrupt and abominable', and consequently my whole life (seeing it cannot be that 'an evil tree' should 'bring forth good fruit'); that 'alienated' as I am 'from the life of God', I am 'a child of wrath', an heir of hell; that my own works, my own sufferings, my own righteousness, are so far from reconciling me to an offended God, so far from making any atonement for the least of those sins, which 'are more in number than the

---

[IV.4] The point of this paragraph is that his holiness program at Oxford, including the faithful use of the means of grace, failed to justify JW before God. He even denies these means will bring a *holy, heavenly, divine character*. This is only another way of saying that his holiness program was a dismal failure; it cannot attain Christian perfection. This repudiation of his GosH is contrary to what he affirms in the first three confessions.

hairs of my head', that the most specious of them need an atonement themselves or they cannot abide his righteous judgment; that 'having the sentence of death' in my heart, and having nothing in or of myself to plead, I have no hope, but that of being justified freely 'through the redemption that is in Jesus'; I have no hope, but that if I seek I shall find Christ and 'be found in him, not having my own righteousness, but that which is through the faith of Christ, the righteousness which is of God by faith.'[IV.5]

If it be said that I have faith (for many such things have I heard, from many miserable comforters), I answer, So have the devils—a sort of faith; but still they are strangers to the covenant of promise. So the apostles had even at Cana in Galilee, when Jesus first 'manifested forth his glory'; even then they, in a sort, 'believed on him'; but they had not then 'the faith that overcometh the world'.[IV.6] The faith I want is, 'a sure trust and confidence in God, that through the merits of Christ my sins are forgiven, and I reconciled to the favour of God'.[IV.7] I want

---

[IV.5] Compare this acknowledgement of personal sinfulness to similar confessions in JW's Aldersgate statements (JWL 5/24/38; 10/30/38; JWJ 5/24/38 §§ 9-10; *The Almost Christian* I.13). We note there is no comparable confession of utter sinfulness in any of JW's writings from his early period. In fact, this confession of deep sinfulness is incompatible with JW's theology of assurance in his GosH (see ch 1). In addition, it is hard to reconcile this confession of total sinfulness with the prior one made only a few days before which denied any lack of balance in his spiritual journey (Confession Three §2).

[IV.6] Compare with JW's Aldersgate manifesto *Salvation By Faith* I. 2-3, where he describes defective faith in terms of a *devil* and the pre-Calvary *disciples* (compare also with *The Almost Christian* II.4). Thus, the perspective of this paragraph better fits the time when Wesley wrote *Salvation By Faith* (June 1738) than January 1738.

[IV.7] JW here quotes from the *Homilies, 'Of Salvation',* Part III. He later quotes this definition in his journal on April 22, 1738. JW states it was in the following November he began to "inquire what the doctrine of the Church of England is concerning the much controversial point of justification by faith" (JWJ 11/12/38). Harper says JW read the Homilies during the month of April leading up to his discussion with Böhler on April 23 when he finally accepted the

that faith which St. Paul recommends to all the world, especially in his Epistle to the Romans; that faith which enables everyone that hath it to cry out, 'I live not, but Christ liveth in me; and the life which I now live, I live by faith in the Son of God, who loved me and gave himself for me.'[IV.8] I want that faith which none can have without knowing that he hath it (though many imagine they have it who have it not). For whosoever hath it is 'freed from sin'; 'the whole body of sin is destroyed' in him.[IV.9] He is freed from fear, 'having peace with God through Christ, and rejoicing in hope of the glory of God'. And he is freed from doubt, 'having the love of God shed abroad in his heart through the Holy Ghost which is given unto him';[IV.10] which 'Spirit itself beareth witness with his spirit, that he is a child of God'.[IV.11]

---

premise that saving faith converts instantaneously (JW: "convinced faith converts at once" [JWD 4/23/38]). Harper adds the Homilies appealed to JW because of their reliance on Scripture, the Primitive Church, and Anglican tradition (*Devotional Life*, 252). From the above evidence we must conclude JW was not aware of the Homilies position regarding salvation by faith until months after February 1st.

[IV.8] Compare with JW's Aldersgate testimony on May 24 (§14). The language, references and wording are nearly identical.

[IV.9] This parallels the original language of *Salvation By Faith* II.7 (The text reads "whole being of sin" until 1771 when JW changed it to "power of sin;" Works B 1:124, n 64). This is Christian perfection attained in the instant of faith.

[IV.10] JW testifies to struggling with fear and doubt in the earlier confessions. On March 6 he told Peter Böhler that "he sometimes felt certain of his salvation, but sometimes he had many doubts." And then adds, "If what stands in the Bible be true, then I am saved" (Works B 18:228, n 49). This was suppose to been said two months *after* he made the above confession. The best solution to this inconsistency is to recognize that the above confession post-dates his discussion with Böhler on March 6. JW confesses to receiving assurance—freedom from doubt and fear—in his Aldersgate "heart warming" conversion (JWJ 5/24/38 §14).

[IV.11] JW was taught by Böhler the Holy Spirit bears witness to salvation (JWJ 4/22/38). Thus, this desire for the Spirit to witness to the reality of his faith points to a later date for this confession to be written than January 1738. JW's

John Wesley's Theology of Christian Perfection

Concluding Thoughts

Three conclusions can be drawn from this small study. First, Wesley did not write confession four on February 1, 1738. If we summarize the lines of argument, they rest on two facts: (1) Wesley could not have interpreted the Homilies as regarding salvation by faith alone since he did not read them until the following April at the very earliest.[1] More likely, as Wesley records in his journal, it was not until the following fall when he began to seriously read the Homilies regarding the question of justification by faith alone.[2] (2) The theology of the last confession is incongruent with Wesley's beliefs at the time. The confession's theology reflects Peter Böhler's influence: salvation is by faith alone; there are no degrees of saving faith; peace with God is a mark of salvation by faith alone; instantaneous conversion characterizes the moment of salvation; and the Holy Spirit testifies to the reality of one's salvation and faith. All these points are incorporated in this confession. This incongruency is further confirmed when this confession is read alongside the other three (which we know were written in January 1738). The first three confessions are

---

prior understanding of the Spirit's testimony was markedly different by being connected to the life transformation process of infused holy dispositions (*The Circumcision of the Heart* II.4-5). The witness of the Holy Spirit to one's present justification became a staple of JW's gospel beginning with Aldersgate.

---

[1] This is Steven Harper's position (*The Devotional Life of John Wesley, 1703-38* PhD Thesis: Duke University, 1981; 252). Since Harper gives no footnote explaining his position I assume he drew this conclusion because JW includes in his journal (4/22/38) a quotation from the Homilies. I agree with Heitzenrater and others that JW more likely began reading the Homilies several months later as he records in his journal (JWJ 11/12/38). It is possible CW introduced JW to the Homilies on the question of salvation by faith. CW first records of reading the Homilies four days before his evangelical conversion (CWJ 5/17/38; see also 6/10/38; 8/10/38; 8/16/38; 8/29/38). So it is possible that JW did read the Homilies before going to Germany in June 1738 (see n 8 below).
[2] JWJ 11/12/38.

theologically very different in tone and content from the last one. The differences between the last confession and the first three are the same differences that distinguish Wesley's Gospel of Holiness from his Gospel of Faith Alone.

Second, what this entails for the student and historian of John Wesley is the realization that we cannot use confession four as a window into Wesley's state of mind upon his return to America. Wesley was despondent, as the first three confessions make clear; but, at the time, he did not see himself as unconverted or facing eternal punishment. Instead, he sought to renew his resolutions and to see the ordeal as his cross to bear.[3] As late as March 6 Böhler records that Wesley still believed he was saved "if what stands in the Bible be true."[4] Wesley changed his mind concerning his spiritual condition *after* he embraced his new gospel, which he learned from Böhler. At the time he correctly concluded that if saving faith has no degrees, and he lacks this faith, then he must be in an unsaved condition.[5] This heightened his inner anguish that drove him to seek relief through the supernatural witness of experiential assurance. This is what Wesley professed to have received on May 24. The central point of the argument is that the last confession reveals a later perspective than what he had on February 1—that is, *after* he embraced his new gospel. Therefore Wesley could not have written this post-script on February 1.

Third, these conclusions offer important insights into why Wesley published his first journal extract for the general public, and why he openly shared his inner struggles for all to see. Simply put, Wesley used the opportunity afforded by Captain William's affidavit to explain why he changed his theology so drastically after his return to England. From this perspective the post-script serves as a powerful *apologia* for his new message. By sharing his own journey to salvation by faith alone, Wesley promoted his new gospel and helped confirm his revival converts in

---

[3] See confession two.
[4] Works B 18:228, n 49.
[5] JWJ 4/23-25/38.

their new-found faith. This same lesson must be remembered about Wesley's next two journal extracts in which he shares his continuing struggles following Aldersgate. His purpose was theological and apologetic, not therapeutic. Wesley uses his own faith journey to answer the arguments of the English Moravian's and their stillness doctrine. The all-or-nothing approach which the English Moravian's took regarding faith and salvation is challenged by Wesley's own faith journey following his conversion on May 24.[6]

Since it has been shown this last confession was not written on February 1, can we discern when Wesley possibly wrote it? While any time between May 1738 and May 1740[7] is possible, there are hints which lead us to the spring 1738. Numerous verbal and theological links to *Salvation By Faith*, the Aldersgate memorandum, and the theology which Peter Böhler passed on to Wesley can be found in the confession. If this author had to choose a time of original composition then sometime around May to June 1738 appears to fit best. This would place the post-script close to the purported time in the published journal, yet explains all its distinctive aspects. Most likely, the postscript was first composed upon the heels of Wesley's Aldersgate conversion and was later polished up for final publication in the journal.[8] Either

---

[6] See chapter three.

[7] May 1740 was when JW wrote the preface to his first journal extract and soon after published it.

[8] One of the arguments that the post-script was written later is the inclusion of a quotation from the Anglican Homilies on salvation by faith. It is certain JW could not have believed and espoused this view of faith before meeting Peter Böhler. Nor could he have understood the Homilies to teach Böhler's message. One possibility is that JW was introduced to the Homilies by his brother CW since CW does mention reading the Homilies four days before his conversion. This would mean that JW was introduced to them in May, or probably later in September after he returned from Germany. What all this means is that JW did not compose the postscript in February 1738. He probably wrote it in May/June of that year, or possibly in the coming fall. This preserves the obvious links between the postscript and JW's writings in the spring of 1738.

Let me add one more thought. Regarding CW's awareness of the Homilies, we noted that in his journal he mentions reading them four days before his

way, the last confession reveals how John Wesley *interpreted* his pre-Aldersgate spiritual state from the vantage point of his new gospel experience.

---

conversion (May 17). But it was during the summer months when John was in Germany that CW began using the homilies to defend the revival and their GosFA. By December 1738 CW was incorporating the Homilies in his written sermons. Since JW admits of perusing the Homilies in the fall, it is possible that CW reintroduced them to JW upon his return from Germany in September.

APPENDIX C
Early Testimonies of Christian Perfection

In *A Plain Account of Christian Perfection* Wesley chose to include the testimony of Jane Cooper to illustrate his doctrine of Christian perfection (PA ch 24). Testimonies are powerful. Today advertisers rely upon them to sell their products, even though the consumer knows the actors are paid. In volume one of this series, in an end note following Jane's testimony several other testimonies are included to illustrate Wesley's message of full salvation. We now include several early testimonies from John and Charles' journals. Brief introductory notes introduce the reader to the historical context of each testimony. The testimonies are grouped according to the three gospel scheme used in this study.

The Gospel of Holiness

The following two testimonies were retold by Wesley at Savannah Georgia on February 20, 1737, in the sermon On Love *(Works B 4:378). The text is 1 Corinthians 13, which also was the scripture reading for that Sunday.*

The first testimony is that of his father Samuel toward the end of his last illness in April 1735. John also speaks of his father's experience in a letter to John Smith (JWL 3/28/48) and in the later sermon On Temptation *(III.5).*

The second testimony is of Henry Lascelles who passed away on June 20, 1736. During the prior month Wesley had time to converse with Henry and to listen to his testimony of complete acquiescence to God (JWJ 5/31-6/7/36). These testimonies illustrate Wesley's early understanding of perfection. Perfect love prepares one to enter God's holy presence. In this way the believer has confidence when facing death. The comments in the parentheses are for clarification.

Early Testimonies of Christian Perfection

To show this (perfect love makes death comfortable), I can't indeed appeal to your own experience; but I may to what we have seen of the experience of others. And two I have myself seen going out of life in what I call a comfortable manner, though not with equal comfort. One had evidently more comfort than the other, because he had more charity (love).

I attended the first during a great part of his last trial, as well as when he yielded up his soul to God. He cried out: 'God doth chasten me with strong pain; but I thank him for all, I bless him for all, I love him for all!' When asked, not long before his release, 'Are the consolations of God small with thee?' he replied aloud, 'No, no, no!' Calling all that were near him by our names, he broke out: 'Think of heaven, talk of heaven! All the time is lost when we are not thinking of heaven!' Now, this was the voice of charity; and so far as that prevailed, all was comfort and peace and joy. But as his love was not perfect so neither was his comfort. He had intervals of anger or fretfulness, and therein of misery, giving by both an incontestable proof that as love can sweeten both life and death, so when that is either absent from, or obscured in, the soul, there is no peace or comfort there.

It was in this place that I saw the other good soldier of Christ grappling with his last enemy, death. And it was indeed a spectacle worthy to be seen, of God and men and angels. Some of his last breath was spent in a psalm of praise to him who was then giving him the victory; in assurance whereof be began the triumph even in the heat of the battle. When asked, 'Hast thou love?' he lifted up his eyes and hands, and answered, 'Yes, yes!' with the whole strength he had left. To one that inquired if he was afraid of the devil, whom he had just mentioned as making his last attack upon him, he replied: 'No, no: our loving Saviour hath conquered every enemy. He is with me. I fear nothing.' Soon after he said, 'The way to our loving Saviour is sharp—but it is short.' Nor was it long before he fell into a sort of slumber, wherein his soul sweetly returned to God that gave it. Here, we may observe, was no mixture of any passion or temper contrary to charity. Therefore was there no misery, perfect love casting out whatever might have occasioned torment. And whosoever thou art who hast the like measure of love, thy last end shall be like his!

The Gospel of Faith Alone

Testimony of Arvid Gradin

Wesley includes a portion of Gradin's testimony in the Plain Account *(ch 8), which he says was the "first account (he) had ever heard from a living man" testifying to perfection before the article of death (PA 8:3). During his stay with the German Moravians in August 1738 Wesley recorded several other testimonies of a similar nature. Gradin's profession is just more explicit on deliverance from inward sin than most of them. Below is Arvid's larger testimony as recorded by Wesley in his Journal (Source: Works B 18:290-91).*

Arvid Gradin, a Swede, born in Dalecarlia, spoke to this purpose:

On the 22nd of May last (1738) I could think of nothing but, 'He that believeth hath everlasting life.' But I was afraid of deceiving myself, and continually prayed I might not build without a foundation. Yet I had a sweet, settled peace, and for five days this Scripture was always in my thoughts. On the 28th those words of our Lord were as strongly impressed upon me, 'If ye, being evil, know how to give good gifts to your children, how much more shall your heavenly Father give the Holy Ghost to them that ask him.' At the same time I was incessantly carried out to ask that he would give me the witness of his Spirit. On the 29th I had what I asked of him, viz., the *full assurance of faith* which is:

'*Requies in sanguine Christi. Firma fiducia in Deum et persuasio de gratia divina; tranquillitas mentis summa, atque serenitas et pax; cum absentia omnis desiderii carnalis, et cessatione peccatorum etiam internorum. Verbo,*

Early Testimonies of Christian Perfection

cor quod antea instar maris turbulenti agitabatur, in summa fuit requie, instar maris sereni et tranquilli.'

(Wesley's translation) 'Repose in the blood of Christ. A firm confidence in God, and persuasion of his favour; serene peace and steadfast tranquillity of mind, with a deliverance from every fleshly desire, and from every outward and inward sin. In a word, my heart, which before was tossed like a troubled sea, was still and quiet, and in a sweet calm.'

Testimonies of William Fish and William Delamotte (?)

The following two testimonies come from Wesley's Journal in early December 1738. During the months leading up to December Wesley had been going through internal struggles over his faith. He wrote to the society in London wanting to learn how things were going and received back several responses (including these two). The first testimony comes from William Fish. While the authorship of the second testimony is conjecture, Curnock believed it was from William Delamotte (see Ward's comments Works B 19:26 n 11). These testimonies express Wesley's faith-alone gospel which collapses entire sanctification into justification and the article of conversion.

My Dear Friend, whom I love in the truth,

    I know my Saviour's voice, and my heart burns with love and desire to follow him in the regeneration. I have no confidence in the flesh. I loathe myself and love him only. My dear brother, my spirit even at this moment rejoices in God my Saviour, and the love which is shed abroad in my heart by the Holy Ghost, destroys all self-love, so that I could lay down my life for my brethren. I know that my Redeemer liveth, and have confidence towards God that through his blood my sins are forgiven. He hath begotten me of his own will and saves me from sin, so that it has no dominion over me. His Spirit bears witness with my spirit, that I am his child by adoption and grace. And this is not for works of righteousness which I have done. For I am his workmanship, created in Christ Jesus unto good works: so that all boasting is excluded. It is now about eighteen years since Jesus took possession of my heart. He then opened my eyes and said unto me, Be of good cheer, thy sins are forgiven thee. My dear friend, bear with my relating after what manner I was born of God. It was an instantaneous act. My whole heart was filled with a divine power, drawing all the faculties of my soul after Christ, which continued three or four nights and days. It was as a mighty rushing wind coming into the soul, enabling me from that moment to be more than conqueror over those corruptions which before I was always a slave to. Since that time the whole bent of my will hath been towards him day and night, even in my dreams. I know that I dwell in Christ, and Christ in me; I am bone of his bone, and flesh of his flesh. That you, and all who wait for his appearing, may find the consolation of Israel, is the earnest prayer of

Your affectionate brother in Christ,
William Fish

My most Dear and Honoured Father in Christ,

In the twentieth year of my age, 1737, God was pleased to open my eyes and to let me see that I did not live as became a child of God. I found my sins were great (though I was what they call a sober person) and that God kept an account of them all. However, I thought if I repented and led a good life, God would accept me. And so I went on for about half a year and had sometimes great joy. But last winter I began to find that whatever I did was nothing. My very tears I found were sin, and the enemy of souls laid so many things to my charge that sometimes I despaired of heaven. I continued in great doubts and fears till April 9, when I went out of town. Here for a time I was greatly transported, in meditating and seeing the glorious works of God, but in about three weeks I was violently assaulted again. God then offered a Saviour to me, but my self-righteousness kept me from laying hold on him.

On Whitsunday I went to receive the blessed sacrament, but with a heart as hard as a stone. Heavy laden I was indeed, when God was pleased to let me see a crucified Saviour. I saw there was a fountain opened in his side for me to wash in and to be clean. But alas! I was afraid to venture, fearing I should be too presumptuous. And I know, and am sure, I at that time refused the atonement which I might then have had. Yet I received great comfort. But in about nine days time my joy went out, as a lamp does for want of oil, and I fell into my old state, into a state of damnation. Yet I was not without hope, for ever after that time I could not despair of salvation: I had so clear a sight of the fountain opened in the side of our Lord. But still when I thought of death, or the day of judgment, it was a great terror to me. And yet I was afraid to venture to lay all my sins upon Christ.

This was not all. But whenever I retired to prayer I had a violent pain in my head. This only seized me when I began to pray earnestly, or to cry out aloud to Christ. But when I cried to him against this also, he gave me ease. Well, I found God did love me and did draw me to Christ. I hungered and thirsted after him and had an earnest desire to be clothed with his righteousness. But I was still afraid to go boldly to Christ and to claim him as my Saviour.

July 3. My dear sister came down to see me. She had received the atonement on St. Peter's Day. I told her I thought Christ died for me, but as to the assurance she mentioned I could say nothing. July 5. She went. That night I went into the garden, and considering what she had told me, I saw him by faith, whose eyes are as a flame of fire, him who justifieth the ungodly. I told him I was ungodly, and it was for me that he died. His blood did I plead with great faith, to blot out the handwriting that was against me. I told my Saviour that he had promised to give rest to all that were heavy laden. This promise I claimed, and I saw him by faith stand condemned before God in my stead. I saw the fountain opened in his side. I found, as I hungered, he fed me: as my soul thirsted, he gave me out of that fountain to drink. And so strong was my faith that if I had had all the sins of the whole world laid upon me, I knew and was sure one drop of his blood was sufficient to atone for all. Well, I clave unto him, and he did wash me in his blood. He hath clothed me with his righteousness and has presented me to his Father and my Father, to his God and my God, a pure, spotless virgin, as if I had never committed any sin. It is on Jesus I stand, the Saviour of sinners. It is he that hath loved me and given himself for me. I cleave unto him as my surety, and he is bound to pay God the debt. While I stand on this rock I am sure the gates of hell cannot prevail against me. It is by faith that I am justified and have peace with God through him. His blood has made reconciliation to God for me. It is by faith I have received the atonement. It is by faith that I have the Son of God and the Spirit of Christ dwelling in me. And what then shall separate me from the love of God which is in Christ Jesus my Lord?

You must think what a transport of joy I was then in, when I that was lost and undone, dropping into hell, felt a Redeemer come, who is 'mighty to save',99'to save unto the uttermost'. Yet I did not receive the witness of the Spirit at that time. But in about half an hour the devil came with great power to tempt me. However, I minded him not, but went in and lay down pretty much composed in my mind. Now St. Paul says, 'After ye believed, ye were sealed with the Spirit of promise.' So it was with me. After I had believed on him that 'justifieth the ungodly', I received that seal of the Spirit which is the 'earnest of our inheritance'. But at that time I did not know anything of this. My sins were forgiven, but I knew I was not yet born of God.

July 6. In the morning, being by myself, I found the work of the Spirit was very powerful upon me (although you know God does not deal with every soul in the same way). As my mother bore me with great pain, so did I feel great pain in my soul in being born of God. Indeed I thought the pains of death were upon me, and that my soul was then taking leave of the body. I thought I was going to him whom I saw with strong faith standing ready to receive me. In this violent agony I continued about four hours, and then I began to feel 'the Spirit of God bearing witness with my spirit, that I was born of God'. 'Because I was a child of God he sent forth the Spirit of his Son into me, crying, Abba, Father.' For that is the cry of every newborn soul. O mighty, powerful, happy change! I who had nothing but devils ready to drag me to hell, now found I had angels to guard me to my reconciled Father and my Judge, who just before stood ready to condemn me, was now become my righteousness. But I cannot express what God hath done for my soul. No; this is to be my everlasting employment, when I have put off this frail, sinful body, this corrupt, hellish nature of mine; when I join with that great multitude which no man can number, in singing praises to the Lamb that loved us and gave himself for us! O how powerful are the workings of the Almighty in a newborn soul! The love of God was shed abroad in my heart, and a flame kindled there, with pains so violent, yet so very ravishing, that my body was almost torn asunder. I loved. The Spirit cried strong in my heart. I sweated. I trembled. I fainted. I sung. I joined my voice with those that excel in strength. My soul was got up into the holy mount. I had no thoughts of coming down again into the body. I who not long before had called to the rocks to fall on me, and the mountains to cover me, could now call for nothing else but, 'Come, Lord Jesus, come quickly.' Then I could cry out with great boldness, There, O God, is my surety! There, O death, is thy plague! There, O grave, is thy destruction! There, O serpent, is the seed that shall forever bruise thy head. O, I thought my head was a fountain of water! I was dissolved in love. 'My Beloved is mine, and I am his.' He has all charms. He has ravished my heart. He is my Comforter, my Friend, my All. He is now in his garden, feeding among the lilies. O, 'I am sick of love.' He is altogether lovely, 'the chiefest among ten thousand'. O how Jesus fills, Jesus extends, Jesus overwhelms the soul in which he dwells!

John Wesley's Theology of Christian Perfection

The Gospel of Two Works of Grace

Testimony of Averel Spenser

Charles records that Averel came to faith on October 5, 1739 (CWJ 1:186). The following testimony is from John's journal one week later on October 12. Characteristic of this time were the physical manifestations that many converts experienced and were interwoven in their testimonies. Leading up to Averel's testimony were several days of spiritual renewal sweeping through the society.

Soon after I was sent for to one of these, who was so strangely torn by the devil that I almost wondered her relations did not say, 'Much religion hath made thee mad.' We prayed God to bruise Satan under her feet. Immediately we had the petition we asked of him. She cried out vehemently, 'He is gone, he is gone!' And was filled with the spirit of love and of a sound mind. I have seen her many times since, strong in the Lord. When I asked abruptly, What do you desire now?' she answered, 'Heaven.' I asked, 'What is in your heart?' She replied, 'God.' I asked, 'But how is your heart when anything provokes you?' She said, 'By the grace of God I am not provoked at anything. All the things of this world pass by me as shadows.' 'Ye have seen the end of the Lord.' Is he not very pitiful and of tender mercy?

Testimony of Nancy Morris

In spring 1741 Wesley was a frequent visitor in the Morris home. The following excerpt is from John's May 1741 Journal. There are some common themes in this testimony with those of his father and of Henry Lascelles. Included is Wesley's record of his conversation with Peter Böhler the next day.

Thur. 14. Hearing that one was in a high fever of whom I had for some time stood in doubt, I went to her, and asked how she did. She replied, 'I am very ill—but I am very well. Oh, I am happy, happy, happy, for my spirit continually rejoices in God my Saviour. All the angels in heaven rejoice in my Saviour. And I rejoice with them, for I am united to Jesus.'

She added, 'How the angels rejoice over an heir of salvation! How they now rejoice over me! And I am partaker of their joy. O my Saviour, how happy am I in thee!'

Fri. 15. I called again. She was saying as I came in, 'My Beloved is mine. And he hath cleansed me from all sin. O how far is the heaven above the earth! So far hath he set my sins from me. O how did he rejoice when he "was heard in that he feared". He was heard, and he gained a possibility of salvation for me and all mankind. It is finished. His grace is free for all. I am a witness. I was the chief of sinners, a backsliding sinner, a sinner against light and love. But I am washed. I am cleansed.'

I asked, 'Do you expect to die now?' She said, 'It is not shown me that I shall. But life or death is all one to me. I shall not change my company. Yet I shall more abundantly rejoice when we stand before the Lord; you and I, and all the other children which he hath given you.'

In the evening I called upon her again, and found her weaker and her speech much altered. I asked her, 'Do you now believe? Do not you find your soul in temptation?' She answered, smiling and looking up, 'There is the Lamb. And where he is, what is temptation? I have no darkness, no cloud. The enemy may come. But he hath no part in me.' I said, 'But does not your sickness hinder you?' She replied, 'Nothing hinders me. It is the Spirit of my Father that worketh in me. And nothing hinders that Spirit. My body indeed is weak and in pain. But my soul is all joy and praise.'

Sat. 16. I mentioned this to Peter Böhler. But he told me, 'There is no such state on earth. Sin will and must always remain in the soul. The old man will remain till death. The old nature is like an old tooth. You may break off one bit, and another, and another. But you can never get it all away. The stump of it will stay as long as you live, and sometimes will ache too.'

John Wesley's Theology of Christian Perfection

From Charles Wesley's Journal

Testimony of Grace Murray

Grace's testimony is dated May 2, 1740. We see the imprint of Wesley's two-works gospel with a wilderness state sandwiched in between both gifts of grace. The reader should compare this testimony to Wesley's description of the faith journey in his Preface to Sacred Hymns and Poems II (Works J 14:322; PA 13:20-30).

My Rev. Father in Christ, - My heart being now open before God, I write as in his presence.

The first gift I received after I had seen myself a lost sinner, bound with a thousand chains, and dropping into hell. Then I heard his voice, 'Be of good cheer, thy sins are forgiven thee;' and could say, 'The Son of God loved me, and gave himself for me.' I thought I saw him at the right hand of his Father, making intercession for me. I went on in great joy for four months. Then pride crept in, and I thought the work was finished, when it was but just begun. There I rested, and in a little time fell into doubts and fears, whether my sins were really forgiven me, till I plunged myself into the depth of misery. I could not pray; neither had I any desire to do it, or to read, or to hear the word. My soul was like a troubled sea. Then did I see my own evil heart, my cursed, devilish nature, and feel my helplessness, that I could not so much as think a good thought. My love was turned into hatred, passion, envy; and

> 'I felt a thousand hells my due,'

And cried out in bitter anguish of spirit, 'Save, Lord, or I perish.' In my last extremity, I saw my Savior full of grace and truth for me; and heard his voice again whispering, 'Peace, be still.' My peace returned, and greater sweetness of love than I ever knew before.

Early Testimonies of Christian Perfection

Now my joy is calm and solid; my heart drawn out to the Lord continually. I know my Redeemer liveth for me. He is my strength and my rock, and will carry on his work in my soul, to the day of redemption.

Testimony of Sister Hooper
May 6, 1741

I found our sister Hooper just at the haven. She expressed, while able to speak, her fullness of confidence and love; her desire to be with Christ; her grief at their preaching the other Gospel (i.e. Predestination)...At my next visit, I saw her in her latest conflict. The angel of death was come, and but a few moments between her and a blessed eternity. We poured out our souls to God for her, her children, ourselves, the Church and Ministers, and all mankind. I had some perception of her joy. My soul was tenderly affected for her sufferings, yet the joy swallowed up the sorrow. How much more then did *her* consolations abound! The servants of Christ suffer nothing. I asked her whether she was not in great pain. "Yes," she answered, "but in greater joy. I would not be without either." "But do you not prefer life or death?" She replied, "All is alike to me; let Christ choose; I have no will of my own." This is that holiness, or absolute resignation, or Christian perfection.

Testimony of Hannah C. and Another Sister
May 7, 1741

I visited Hannah C., full of love to her Savior, crying out, "Liberty, liberty! This is the glorious liberty of God's children. O, who can name the name of Jesus and not depart from iniquity? God loves me. God loves every man. Jesus Christ is the Savior of the whole world."

John Wesley's Theology of Christian Perfection

May 16, 1741

I visited another of our sisters, who was triumphing over death. I asked her, "Do you know Christ died for you?" "Yes," she answered joyfully, "for me, and for the whole world. He has begun, and he will finish, his work in my soul." "But will he save you," I said, "from *all* sin?" She replied, "I know he will. There shall no sin remain in me."

Reflection and Evaluation

When we compare these early testimonies to those two decades later we see both similarity and difference (cf. *Plain Account* ch 24 end note). Similarity is mostly found in the nature of the experience itself. These early professions of perfect love include an exhilarating release of emotion. The holy tempers of love, joy, peace, and divine fullness so flooded the heart that contrary affections—like pride, anger, unwholesome desire and unbelief—felt extinguished so that inward sin had been destroyed. Though Wesley never meant to ground the experience in emotion he did give much weight to their validity. In *Thoughts on Christian Perfection* (1759) he states unequivocally:

> 1. I have abundant reason to believe, this person will not lie;
> 2. He testifies before God, "I feel no sin, but all love; I pray, rejoice, and give thanks without ceasing; and I have as clear an inward witness, that I am fully renewed, as that I am justified." Now, if I have nothing to oppose to this plain testimony, I ought in reason to believe it. (19:44)

Emotion did play a significant role in the early experiences of confessors of perfect love, both as validation and as essential component. This only makes sense. If Christian perfection is nothing less than a deeper transformation of the dispositional nature so that one's tempers are all love toward God and neighbor, then it is reasonable to expect the emotions will be powerfully moved.

The similarity of experience points strongly to continuity in Wesley's beliefs and teachings on the subject. That these early confessors received the experience instantaneously, just as their brothers and sisters did in the 1760's, confirms this very point. This bolsters Wesley's argument in the *Plain Account* that his views did not materially change over time. Of course, Wesley's gospel system went through a huge mutation in 1738. Even he conceded this on many occasions. Before 1738 perfection was to be found in the article of death. Aldersgate changed all that. After this Wesley consistently looked for a perfection located in this life. The above testimonies reflect this radical alteration within his gospel system.

As we saw in chapter two, the above testimonies from 1738 characterize Wesley's own theological position at the time. Perfection, justification, new birth and adoption were encapsulated into one divine moment. William Fish's testimony is a strong witness to perfection attained in the article of conversion. Fish shares, "The bent of my will hath been towards him day and night, even in my dreams." So full was his heart that even his dream life was powerfully affected.

The most significant difference between these early testimonies and those in the 1760's is the theology informing them. Those from the early forties are less structured in their description; while the later testimonies are much savvier in their theology. The later testimonies delineate with greater clarity two distinct works of grace, and they are more clear in their description of the path leading to perfect love. Wesley devotes an entire chapter to the testimony of Jane Cooper in the *Plain Account*. In this spiritual affidavit her description "fits like a glove" Wesley's portrayal of the faith journey to perfect love (compare PA 19:68-69 to ch 24). One possible explanation for this greater clarity is that Wesley reworked these testimonies before incorporating

John Wesley's Theology of Christian Perfection

them into his published Journal to better fit his theology and message. Yet, he did not do this to the early testimonies when he included them in his Journal. This author is more inclined to think the later professors were better *taught* in understanding and articulating the experience. This makes sense in light of Wesley's own theological journey and the history of his published writings. For by the 1760's he had four volumes of sermons plus many more articles and tracts available for his people to read and study.

Our understanding of Wesley's theology of perfection must remain cognizant of what his people actually experienced, and why they articulated their experience as they did. Their words were simply seeking to convey what they felt.

APPENDIX D
The Evolution of the New Birth

One of the interesting twists in the development of Wesley's perfection theology is the interplay between his doctrines of regeneration and perfection. Several times our study has touched on this relationship. This appendix will explore further how Wesley's views on the new birth evolved in relation to his perfection doctrine.

In his early period we see unmistakable signs that he associated the new birth with perfection. For example, we saw in chapter one that Wesley used new birth language to describe the single intention. When he arrived in America in early 1736 he exhorted his listeners to "give (God) your hearts; love him with all your souls; serve him with all your strength...Behold, all things about you are become new! Be ye likewise new creatures!"[1] Now the Gospel of Holiness grounded vital religion on the single intention. For that reason the Christian was called to pursue inward holiness with certain hope that he or she would attain perfection in the article of death. This gospel proclaimed that only in death is the corruption of nature fully removed and the believer made perfect. Sin is then exhausted and the process of renewal is made complete. The Christian is fully renewed in pristine holiness and takes on the nature of angels. For the "great work," even the "one thing needful," declared Wesley, is the "renewal of our fallen nature."[2] Hence, early Wesley identified the work of regeneration with the single intention and perfection.

Since early Wesley linked the new birth to the single intention, regeneration became logically connected to the commencement of vital religion in the heart. But since regeneration was also associated with the attainment of perfection, a process view of

---

[1] *Single Intention* II.9.
[2] *One Thing Needful* I.2.

John Wesley's Theology of Christian Perfection

the new birth necessarily followed.[3] So, early Wesley maintained a dualism in his doctrine of the new birth, which begins in the single intention but is fully realized in the attainment of perfection.

When we move to Aldersgate we do not see any material change in Wesley's views. In fact, the connection between regeneration and perfection is only tightened since Wesley's faith-alone gospel collapsed the new birth and perfection into a single God-moment. Along with justification and adoption, both blessings are received in a single act of saving faith:

> This then is the salvation which is through faith, even in the present world: a salvation from sin and the consequences of sin, both often expressed in the word 'justification', which, taken in the largest sense, implies a deliverance from guilt and punishment, by the atonement of Christ actually applied to the soul of the sinner now believing on him, and a deliverance from the whole body of sin, through Christ 'formed in his heart'. So that he who is thus justified or saved by faith is indeed 'born again'. He is 'born again of the Spirit' unto a new 'life which is hid with Christ in God'.[4]

What Wesley sought he apparently received about a quarter to nine on May 24, 1738 when he testified to being saved "from the law of sin and death." Thus the new birth became a synonym for perfection. To be born again is to be saved from sin, even the "whole body of sin": habitual, willful and dispositional (desire).[5]

---

[3] The reader should remember JW's baptismal regeneration views (JWJ 5/24/38 §1). Regeneration began initially in the baptismal font, but was later lost or retarded due to voluntary sin. This provided the theological ground for a new spiritual birth grounded on the single intention that was completed in the full renewal of the believer in the image of God (perfection).
[4] *Salvation By Faith* II.7.
[5] *Salvation By Faith* I.3-6.

The Evolution of the New Birth

As fear and doubt continued to plague Wesley following his Aldersgate conversion, he learned from the Moravian mother church that justifying faith and full assurance do not always coexist in the believing heart. In relation to timing, the witness of assurance can often lag far behind one's justification before God.

By late January 1739 Wesley appears to have finally resolved in his own mind there are degrees to perfection and the new birth. Embracing principle of degrees was a return to his holiness gospel. As his journal records, the majority of those he had recently baptized were born again only in a low sense (i.e. justification).[6] As his two-works gospel developed over the next year and a half, the idea that regeneration embraces the entire renewal process became characteristic of the period. We see this in July 1739 when Wesley defines the new birth as a "thorough change," from the old man to the new man.[7] Two months later the identification of the new birth to perfection was made even more explicit. In response to a fellow clergyman, Wesley explains that the new birth is an "entire change" from the image of the devil to that of God. No stronger identification could be made. The new birth comprehends the entire renewal process and makes one perfect before God.

What can we say about Wesley's comments which delineated degrees within regeneration? The 1744 Conference Minutes unravel for us how Wesley nuanced his new birth doctrine in relation to perfection:

Q.3. Is not every believer a new creature?
A. Not in the sense of St. Paul, 2 Cor 5:17, "All old things are passed away in him who is so a new creature and all things become new."

Q.4. But has every believer a new heart?

---

[6] JWJ 1/25/39.
[7] JWJ 7/31/39.

John Wesley's Theology of Christian Perfection

A. A great change is wrought in the heart or affections of every one as soon as he believes; yet he is still full of sin, so that he has not then a new heart in the full sense.

Q.5. Is not every believer born of God, a temple of the Holy Ghost?
A. In a low sense he is. But he that is in the proper sense born of God cannot commit sin.

Q.6. What is implied in being made perfect in love?
A. The loving the Lord our God with all our mind and soul and strength.

Q.7. Does this imply that he who is thus made perfect cannot commit sin?
A. St. John affirms it expressly. He cannot commit sin because he is born of God (1 Jn 3:9). And, indeed, how should he, seeing there is now none occasion of stumbling in him? (1 Jn 2:10)

Q.8. Does it imply that all inward sin is taken away?
A. Without doubt, or how should he be said to be saved from all his uncleannesses? (1 Jn 2:29; Eze 36:29).[8]

Three points follow. First, a clear nexus between the new birth and perfection is visible in the above minutes. The new birth, in its "proper sense," is that inner transformation by which "all things become new" so that the Christian "cannot commit sin." This is a restatement of Wesley's doctrine of perfection. By collapsing sanctification into justification, the Gospel of Faith Alone identified the new birth with entire sanctification. But the linking of regeneration to perfection persisted for many years, as the above minutes confirm.

---

[8] Outler, *John Wesley*, 140-41.

The Evolution of the New Birth

Second, Wesley read standard biblical texts on regeneration—like 2 Corinthians 5:17 and 1 John 3:9—as affirmations of perfection. At the time he often defined perfection in terms of becoming a new creation and not committing sin. Again, this shows a strong connection between the new birth and perfection in his thought.

Third, the above minutes recognize degrees within the new birth. Those born again in a "low sense" are not regenerate in its "proper sense;" yet, they are still born again and saved. Wesley realized from his own post-Aldersgate struggles that Christians normally experience deliverance from sin by degrees. Even though a "great change" has taken place in the initial moment when spiritual life is received, the immature believer remains "full of sin." Consequently, the partially renewed believer lacks consistency when it comes to obedience (i.e. not committing sin).[9] Altogether, these three points demonstrate a linkage between regeneration and perfection in Wesley's perfection theology.

Throughout the 1740's Wesley continued to hold to a dualism in his new birth doctrine. This produced confusion for his readers (then and now) since he often failed to clarify which meaning he was referring to when addressing the subject.[10] This vagueness, or lack of discrimination, is seen in two classic sermons on the new birth in the late forties.

The Marks of the New Birth draws from Wesley's early manifesto on inward holiness to define the new birth. In *The Circumcision of the Heart* (1733) four qualities make up the perfect Christian: humility, faith, hope and love. In *Marks* Wesley utilizes the latter three qualities to draw a picture of the born again Christian, thus hinting that both sermons are describing the same individual.[11] Moreover, the *Marks* homily links regeneration to perfection by emphatically declaring that in the new birth God

---

[9] This possibly explains JW's despairing confession on January 4, 1739 (JWJ).
[10] For example, see *The Almost Christian* and JWL 9/28/45.
[11] In JW's second volume of sermons *The Marks of the New Birth* directly follows *The Circumcision of the Heart*.

gives "power over sin: power over outward sin of every kind...and over inward sin; for it 'purifieth the heart' from every unholy desire and temper."[12] Then a few paragraphs later Wesley utilizes his favorite perfection text of the period (1 John 3:9) to separate the wheat from the chaff: the new birth is defined as freedom from committing sin (I.6). What makes the *Marks* sermon vague is that it can be read from two fundamentally different perspectives. First, it can be read according to Wesley's later perspective when he no longer links the new birth with perfection (more below). Or, it can be read from his earlier standpoint when he did conjoin the two. As written, the sermon fits *both* theologies and can be read accordingly.

The second sermon is even vaguer when carefully studied. *The Great Privilege of Those that are Born of God* follows on the heels of the *Marks* sermon. Its message is the grand truth that salvation entails freedom from sin. Once again, Wesley draws upon his favorite perfection verse (at the time) as the homily's text (1 John 3:9). But a casual reading leads most to conclude that Wesley was not referring to perfection when he describes the liberty that the Christian enjoys. Yet, when we look at the sermon in light of Wesley's then present new birth theology (that identified regeneration to perfection) such a reading must be held in suspect. Let's explain.

In *Great Privilege* Wesley likens the new birth to its physical counterpart. He then proceeds to qualify the commission of sin to outward sin: an "actual, voluntary 'transgression of the law'; of the revealed, written law of God" (II.2). Now we learned earlier that by 1741 Wesley was already distinguishing between outward and inward sin within his perfection doctrine.[13] But as we have amply seen he also consistently read and used 1 John 3:9 as a key text supporting his perfection doctrine (full salvation is to cease from committing sin).[14] If the sermon is read from this perspec-

---

[12] *The Marks of the New Birth* I.4.
[13] Cf. *Christian Perfection*.
[14] Besides the examples given in this appendix see his letter to Anne Dutton (JWL B 6/25/40).

The Evolution of the New Birth

tive, it becomes apparent that Wesley implicitly connects the new birth to perfection in this homily. Since, at the time, perfection was defined by Wesley as not committing sin (1 John 3:9), and he saw this verse as explicitly referring to regeneration, then logically to be born again (in full sense) is to attain perfection.

We can confirm this conclusion by looking fifty years later at another sermon, *On Perfection*. In this later homily Wesley uses the same definition for sin (voluntary transgression of a known law of God) to set the standard for his mature perfection doctrine. So we conclude that the *Marks* and *Great Privilege* sermons do convey vagueness in Wesley's new birth doctrine. Does the new birth refer to the initial impartation of the Spirit of adoption and new life? Or, does it pertain to the completeness of the renewal process? Wesley embraces both definitions and he often carelessly neglects to inform his audience which definition he is using at the time. Simply stated, in the 1740's Wesley held to a dualism in his new birth doctrine.

When we move to the mid-fifties this same vagueness persists. In *Explanatory Notes Upon the New Testament* we find some comments identifying the new birth with perfection and other notes distinguishing them. When we turn to Wesley's comments on 2 Corinthians 5:17, we find that the phrase—"all things are become new"—is interpreted to mean the true believer in Christ has "new life, new senses, new faculties, new affections, new appetites, new ideas and conceptions. His whole tenor of action and conversation is new, and he lives, as it were, in a new world." This language does not necessarily link regeneration with perfection (though it can). Yet when we turn to Titus 3:5 Wesley does identify the "renewal of the Holy Ghost" with that inner cleansing which renews the soul in the "whole image of God." This comment does appear to imply that the new birth is connected to perfection. When we turn to 1 John 3:9 we find Wesley's comments very interesting. It would be good to quote them in full:

John Wesley's Theology of Christian Perfection

> *Whosoever is born of God*—By living faith, whereby God is continually breathing spiritual life into his soul, and his soul is continually breathing out love and prayer to God, *doth not commit sin. For* the divine *seed* of loving faith *abideth in him; and,* so long as it doth, *he cannot sin, because he is born of God*—Is inwardly and universally changed.

This comment is so nuanced that it can refer to either meaning Wesley gave to the new birth. We first note that the definition of faith fits both levels of regeneration (low or full sense). Yet, the explanation of inward and universal transformation appropriately applies only to those born again in the full sense (perfect love). This same dualism is found in his notes on John 3:3, 7. Here salvation comes by receiving Christ by faith, yet to be born of the Spirit refers to an "entire change of heart," even an "inward change from all sinfulness to all holiness." Since Wesley used the same language in 1739 to identify the new birth with full salvation,[15] it appears that in the mid-fifties Wesley continues to be vague concerning the new birth doctrine by using the exact same language.[16]

But by 1757-59 his views had definitely changed. In the late fifties Wesley preached on John 3:7 twenty-seven times,[17] thus reflecting a renewed interest in the subject. The distillation of this oral preaching is summarized in the homily *The New Birth*. In this sermon Wesley formally presents his mature doctrine of re-

---

[15] JWJ 9/13/39.

[16] In 1741 JW referred to adult believers as the only ones who were "properly" Christians (*Christian Perfection* II.2). He changed "properly" to "perfect" in 1771, thus giving us another clue that his new birth doctrine had underwent transition during this time.

[17] Outler lists 14 times in 1758 and 13 times in 1759 (Works B 2:186). This was JW's favorite text on the new birth during this period. In 1757 JW distinguished the new birth from sanctification in his major work on original sin (Works J 9:310) but more clearly enunciated his new position in the *New Birth*.

generation to the public, but this time a significant change appears: the new birth is distinguished from perfection.

Wesley opens with a description of humanity's creation in the three-fold image of God (natural, political and moral) and quickly digresses to describing our sinful condition as children of Adam. This sets his new birth doctrine within the broader context of his *imago Dei* meta-narrative. Regeneration is next described in classic Wesleyan terms as renewed spiritual senses. Spiritual birth is similar to physical birth in that the person becomes alive to the world of God, just as a new born becomes alive to the physical world. While Wesley continues to speak of regeneration as a "great change which God works in the soul," this time he *explicitly distinguishes* the new birth from sanctification. In response to those who believe regeneration involves a slow work of renewal within the heart, Wesley declares regeneration to be only a "part of sanctification, not the whole; it is the gate to it, the entrance into it" (IV.3):

> A child is born of a woman in a moment, or at least in a very short time. Afterward he gradually and slowly grows till he attains the stature of a man. In like manner a child is born of God in a short time, if not in a moment. But it is by slow degrees that he afterward grows up to the measure of the full stature of Christ. (IV.3)

Regeneration is now formally distinguished from sanctification. The new birth brings the impartation of life, not its fullness. It begins the process of renewal, not perfects it. After this homily was written other subtle changes in Wesley's perfection theology can be detected.

Whereas before, in the years following Aldersgate, Wesley spoke of higher and lower degrees of the new birth, in *Farther Thoughts on Christian Perfection* (1763) he now uses such language to reference differing classes of "Christians" (PA 25:59-60). Several years later he acknowledged, "I have frequently observed that there are two very different ranks of Christians, both

John Wesley's Theology of Christian Perfection

of whom may be in the favour of God, —a higher and a lower rank."[18] No longer is there higher and lower degrees of regeneration, such language is now reserved for the category of "Christian." The new birth stands as its own complete work.

We find this trait in other sermons from the early to mid sixties. In the same year he published *The New Birth*, Wesley followed up with another sermon, *The Wilderness State*, wherein he describes the struggles and wanderings that a vast majority of converts face between the twin gifts of new birth and perfection.[19] Implicit in this sermon is a clear distinction between the new birth and perfect love. Again, in 1765 the new birth was clearly distinguished from sanctification and perfection in the landmark sermon *The Scripture Way of Salvation*. Justification is defined as a *relative* change, while the new birth is a *real* one. New converts, Wesley acknowledges, often feel so elated in their newfound liberty they imagine all sin is gone and "utterly rooted out of their heart" (I.4). But it isn't long before sin revives and the realization that sin was only suspended sets in. Two contrary principles—the Spirit and the flesh—battle for dominance in the heart. Therefore, a second definitive work of grace is needed if the believer is to love God with all the heart. Once again, implicit in such reasoning is a clear distinction between the twin gifts of new birth and perfection.

To conclude, we see that Wesley's doctrine of regeneration did evolve along parallel paths with his doctrine of perfection and full salvation. As his Gospel of Two Works matured so did his understanding and articulation of the new birth. While at first Wesley linked the new birth with perfection so that the two were seen as nearly synonymous, he later came to distinguish regeneration from justification and perfection. In this way he could communicate more effectively how God's grace works at each milestone on the faith journey path from servant to child to adolescent to adult.

---

[18] JWL T 1/1/70; Works J 12:250.
[19] *The Wilderness State* P.1.

APPENDIX E
The Roots of Wesley's Servant Theology

Though Wesley's servant theology took formal shape in the mid to late sixties, the roots of this theology reach back into his early post-Aldersgate era. To uncover what these roots were we need to do more than look at explicit statements that refer to the servant. We must peruse his use of Acts 10:35 and his references to Cornelius, and the nexus this biblical passage has with his later servant theology. In chapter four we generalized that the spiritual state of the servant is pre-new birth, yet post-justification. In other words, the servant lacks the direct witness of adoption by which birth in the Spirit is identified; nevertheless, the servant stands accepted and forgiven by God. Wesley was consistent on this point. The servant lacks a "proper Christian faith."[1] Since Wesley grounds the new birth and the Spirit's witness in God's pardoning love, those in the servant state serve God out of reverential fear, not filial love. Yet, as Wesley also affirmed, the servant is accepted (in "some degree")[2] by God because their faith is evidenced by sincerity and the presence of holy tempers. It is not our purpose to trace out every detail of Wesley's servant theology in his earlier writings. We only want to show that his later theology is the logical outworking of inherent principles within his theological system after Aldersgate.

Early References to the Servant

Albert Outler, in his footnotes on *The Spirit of Bondage and Adoption* (1746), states that this homily contains the earliest men-

---

[1] JWJ 5/24/38 (1774 footnote); Works J 1:97.
[2] NT Notes on Acts 10:35 have "in some measure." The 1745 Minutes has "some degree" (but see note 5 below).

tion of the servant state in Wesley's published sermons.[3] In this homily humanity is classified according to three groups—natural, legal and evangelical—with the servant state squarely placed in the middle group. The servant is one who (1) lacks the Spirit of adoption, (2) remains under sin's guilt and power, and (3) falls short of God's kingdom (III.4). They serve God out of "slavish fear," not from divine love living in the heart through the new birth. At best, Wesley concludes, the servant is one who has reached the highest level of the legal state. Having been awakened to their spiritual poverty, the servant fears God and future judgment, yet sincerely seeks to please him. But this attempt fails because of enslavement to sin. Put in simple terms, Wesley sees the servant as "carnal, sold under sin" (Rom 7:14). So the servant lives in Romans chapter seven. Longing for spiritual freedom and God's love, the servant continues under sin's reign. Wesley further categorizes the servant (and the legal state) under the Jewish dispensation of the Old Testament (III.8). This possibly explains why the servant is defined as lacking a "proper Christian faith."

We now turn to the 1746 Conference Minutes. On May 13 John and his brother Charles, along with five others, sat down to discuss several questions confronting the societies and revival. Three questions pertain directly to the status of the servant:

> Q. 9. By what faith were the Apostles clean before Christ died?
> A. By such a faith as this; by a Jewish faith: For "the Holy Ghost was not then given."
>
> Q. 10. Of whom then do you understand those words "Who is among you that feareth the Lord, that obeyeth the voice of his servant, that walketh in darkness, and hath no light?" (Isaiah 50:10.)

---

[3] Works B 1:250 §4.

The Roots of Wesley's Servant Theology

A. Of a believer under the Jewish dispensation; one in whose heart God hath not yet shined, to give him the light of the glorious love of God in the face of Jesus Christ.

Q. 11. Who is a Jew, inwardly?
A. A servant of God: One who sincerely obeys him out of fear. Whereas a Christian, inwardly, is a child of God: One who sincerely obeys him out of love.[4]

It appears clear enough how Wesley understands the servant in the above minutes. The servant is not born again, and therefore lacks those motives that arise from God's gracious love. Instead, reverent fear serves as the source for the servant's desire to please God. Moreover, in looking for the roots of Wesley's servant theology we notice allusions in the above minutes to a couple earlier sermons: *Salvation By Faith* (1738) and *The Almost Christian* (1741). Let's look at each in turn.

Just as question nine in the above minutes addresses the spiritual state of the pre-Calvary disciples; Wesley had previously discussed this same question in 1738. In *Salvation By Faith* the disciples are defined as having a deficient faith because they did not yet know Christ as crucified and risen, living and reigning in the heart. In 1738 Wesley believed faith in Christ alone was essential for saving faith. Yet in *Salvation By Faith* Wesley was unclear regarding the exact spiritual condition of the pre-Calvary disciples. Were they justified or not? Did he believe they were saved, or unsaved? This is where his 1746 Conference Minutes shine. These Minutes confirm the disciples did lack a proper Christian faith; however, Wesley acknowledges that Jesus did declare the disciples "clean" before God. This implies, in Wesley view, they were already justified and therefore acceptable to God.[5]

---

[4] Outler, *John Wesley*, 157.

[5] In June 1740 JW had appealed to Jn 15:3 to show that a weak faith is acceptable to God, and therefore justified. This is true even though they had not yet experienced a "clean heart" in the sense of entire sanctification (JWJ 6/22/40).

John Wesley's Theology of Christian Perfection

When we turn to *The Almost Christian* other parallels appear. Wesley describes the almost Christian under the three headings of heathen honesty, nominal Christian belief, and devout sincerity. While these three qualities comprise the character of the almost Christian, more important for our study is to recognize an ascending gradation from heathen honesty to devout sincerity. Just as the servant serves as the highest level of the legal state (in *The Spirit of Bondage and Adoption*), so devout sincerity defines the highest level in *The Almost Christian*. Therefore, both devout sincerity and the servant point to the same pre-Christian state. Two corollaries follow.

Though the servant/almost Christian lacks the Spirit of adoption, a "real, inward principle of religion" does live in the servant's heart.[6] Such a person has a "real design to serve God" and a "hearty desire to do his will."[7] Thus the servant works righteousness by pursuing the good and avoiding the evil. To press this point even more, these two post-Aldersgate sermons understand the servant as already *partially alive to God*. Since the servant has not yet experienced the Spirit of adoption (new birth), they lack the assurance springing from God's pardoning love. This explains why the servant cannot reciprocate out of filial love. But this does not mean the servant is totally void of spiritual life. The fact they have a "hearty desire" to please God reveals that some degree of spiritual life subsists within the servant's heart.

Following Aldersgate Wesley openly identified his pre-Aldersgate faith journey with the servant/almost Christian state.[8] At the time he believed this level of faith fell short of full gospel justification.[9] But in 1766, when John opened his heart to Charles, he surprisingly defined his present spiritual condition in the same terms as the servant/almost Christian: an honest heathen who fears God. Yet, he also confessed of not feeling any con-

---

[6] *The Almost Christian* II.9.
[7] *The Almost Christian* II.10.
[8] *The Almost Christian* II.13.
[9] JWJ 1/8/38; 2/1/38 (Ext. One); 4/23-25/38; 5/24/38.

demnation for being in this state. This led Wesley to begin qualifying the servant/almost Christian as the bottom line standard for acceptance before God.[10] When we remember that one year prior (1765) he had come to believe his conversion to vital religion took place in 1725, not 1738, this conclusion makes even more sense. Wesley finally arrived at the position that "real, inward religion" begins in the *faith of a servant*. The scripture passage that most shaped his thought on this point was the story of Cornelius in Acts 10.

Cornelius and Acts 10:35

In the Wesley corpus the one scripture text that most defines his servant theology is Acts 10:35. This single verse is part of a larger story dealing with a Roman centurion named Cornelius. The Apostle Peter, records Luke, acknowledged before everyone present that "God is not a respecter of persons: But in every nation he that feareth him, and worketh righteousness, is accepted by him."[11] Wesley's comment on this verse is instructive, "Through Christ, though he knows him not. The assertion is express, and admits of no exception. He is in the favour of God…in some measure, accepted." Several verses earlier Wesley acknowledged that in a "Christian sense, Cornelius was then an unbeliever" because "he had not then faith in Christ."[12] So here we have Cornelius, an unbeliever according to the Christian faith, nevertheless accepted by God because of his sincere reverence (fear) and practice of the means of grace.[13]

But this was not the first time Wesley drew upon Cornelius or Acts 10 to formulate his position. One of the central questions to the stillness controversy in 1740 concerned the validity of the

---

[10] JWJ 12/1/67. See chapter four for a fuller discussion of this point.
[11] Quoted from NT Notes.
[12] NT Notes, Acts 10:4 note.
[13] The text specifically mentions prayer and acts of charity (alms), both means of grace in JW's theology.

means of grace as tools for conversion. This became the first setting in which Wesley looked to Cornelius and Acts 10 for support. He saw that Cornelius' prayers and offerings were acceptable to God even though he was an unbeliever in the Christian sense.[14] This cut through the Moravian argument that stated any use of the means of grace prior to justifying faith was "full of sin." But this same argument also cut through Wesley's own position that no good works could be done prior to regeneration, which in 1740 was temporally linked to justification.[15] As long as Wesley maintained that justification, regeneration, adoption (Spirit's witness) and saving faith were received in the same God-moment then no good work could be done prior to justification and the new birth. But by the mid-forties his perspective was beginning to change. Wesley started to see the Spirit's witness does not always coincide with the moment of justification or the new birth. This acknowledgment opened the door for some works to be considered good by God even though the person lacked the new birth and the Spirit's witness.

Five years later the question of Cornelius' pre-Christian spiritual standing came up again at the annual conference. Still seeking to find greater consistency in his doctrine of justification, the question was asked if Cornelius was already in God's favor before he believed in Christ. Wesley's response was simply, "It does seem that he was."[16] When asked if Cornelius' pre-Christian prayers and offerings were at best "splendid sins," Wesley again answers with a straightforward "No." He must have been musing over this passage, for he adds that these good deeds of Cornelius, though an unbeliever, were done by the "grace of Christ"! This is a remarkable change from just four years prior when Wesley declared to his university audience that before 1738 he was only an

---

[14] JWJ 6/25/40.

[15] "I believe no good work can be previous to justification, nor consequently, a condition of it; but that we are justified by faith alone, faith without works, faith including no good work" (JWJ 9/13/39); see Outler, *John Wesley*, 132 §§ 9-11.

[16] Outler, *John Wesley*, 149.

almost Christian, whose faith was merely that of a devil.[17] Already shifts in Wesley theology can be seen that will eventually lead to the formulation of his later servant theology.

Four years later Acts 10:35 began to serve as a kind of shorthand for vital religion. In a letter to the Rev. Vincent Perronet, Wesley shared the story how the Methodist societies originally started with seekers coming to him for spiritual counsel. Out of this was birthed the United Societies, which had only one requirement for admission: a "desire to flee from the wrath to come, and to be saved from their sins."[18] Wesley then identified these seekers as those who "fear God and work righteousness." A little later in the same letter Wesley proceeded to share how he began to issue tickets to weed out the wayward from his societies. The tickets represented his strong approval that the bearer was a genuine seeker of salvation, a person who "fears God and works righteousness." To these believers he gave the right hand of fellowship.[19]

That same year Wesley reiterated the same point in the sermon *Catholic Spirit*. Fearing God and working righteousness was again affirmed as the ground for Christian fellowship and unity (III.5). So by the end of the 1740's, the language of Acts 10:35 was becoming shorthand for vital religion and the benchmark for Christian fellowship. It would take only a small step for him to state in 1755 that Cornelius was already accepted, enjoying the favor of God, even though he was officially an unbeliever.[20]

---

[17] *Almost Christian* II.4; compare with I.13.
[18] *A Plain Account of the People Called Methodists* I.8.
[19] *A Plain Account of the People Called Methodists* IV.2, 3.
[20] NT Notes. Cf. Outler, *John Wesley*, 177 for another implied reference to Acts 10:35. In the early sixties JW continued to use Acts 10:35 as a benchmark for vital religion (JWJ 7/19/61; 8/19/63). In a letter to Rev. Horn JW clarified himself on the spiritual state of the servant. While agreeing with Horn that those who fear God and work righteousness are accepted by God, JW disagreed this implies our works play a role in our justification; for "none can either fear God or work righteousness till he believes, according to the dispensation he is under" (Works B 11:452). Thus the servant is accepted by faith,

John Wesley's Theology of Christian Perfection

Acceptance & Holy Tempers

In several ways Wesley's servant theology was a return to his earlier roots in the 1730's.[21] In chapter two we saw that in 1738 he did radical surgery on his gospel system. Having embraced salvation by faith alone in Christ alone by the Spirit alone meant rejecting his prior view that assurance is grounded on sincerity and the Spirit's transformation of the dispositional nature. By 1765 Wesley's views were changing once more in powerful ways. He now affirmed that his conversion to vital religion took place in 1725, not 1738. This momentous paradigm shift led to greater appreciation of the themes and motifs of his early period and theology. In chapter one, we learned the Gospel of Holiness centered on the demand for inward holiness as the foundation for acceptance before God. The heart of Wesley's quest was to attain inward holiness. While the mature Wesley maintained a proper emphasis on present justification by faith alone, by the later sixties the tendency to couple holy tempers with justification becomes visible again. The servant, Wesley maintains, is accepted because they "fear God and work righteousness." Though he clarified this to mean their salvation was by faith according to their level of moral and spiritual light (dispensation),[22] this explanation avoided the implication of his servant theology: people find acceptance before God, not by faith in Christ alone, but by a sincere faith in the one God that produces good works (holy tempers). The key word here is *sincere*.

Wesley himself could not escape the implications of his servant theology. As he grew older he became more and more open to the idea that people of other religious faiths could be saved on the ground they are sincere in their faith of the one true God, and

---

not works; nevertheless, it is a lower faith than that of a child of God. JW is well on his way to embracing the servant theology of his later period.

[21] JWL T 12/15/72; cf. ch 7.

[22] See note 20.

The Roots of Wesley's Servant Theology

show their sincerity by pursuing good works and righteousness.[23] This meant that God's preventing grace works life transformation *prior* to the new birth. As Randy Maddox explains:

> Wesley's eventual judgment that God's pardoning grace is effectual in our lives from the most nascent degree of our responsiveness, even the mere inclination to fear God and work righteousness (i.e., the faith of a servant).[24]

Since the servant has been awakened to God, by having the principle of inward religion implanted in the heart,[25] their spiritual senses must have been awakened too. In *The Great Privilege of Those that are Born of God* Wesley explains the new birth by its counterpart, physical birth. As the newborn's lungs take in air for the first time, their eyes come alive to physical objects and their sense of hearing and touch come alive to a new environment. So those born of God are awakened to divine realities. Faith becomes the ground for spiritual life.[26] Faith sees, tastes, touches and feels God. While the servant cannot taste God's pardoning love, since they lack the Spirit of adoption, they still can know God in "some measure" (to use Wesley's favorite qualifier when speaking of the servant's acceptance before God). As the author of Hebrews acknowledges, the servant believes that God exists and he rewards those who diligently seek him (11:6).

Hence, the servant pleases their heavenly Father, and, consequently, is accepted by him. Simply put, Wesley no longer believed the new birth to be the bottom-line foundation for holy tempers or vital religion. As we saw in chapter seven, his robust doctrine of prevenient grace proved to be sufficient in infusing holy tempers, even if in a low degree. What the new birth does

---

[23] 1770 Minutes; *On Charity* (1784) III.6, 7, 12, 13; *On Faith* I.11, II.3; *On Living Without God* §§14-15.
[24] *Responsible Grace*, 173.
[25] See *The Almost Christian* I.9.
[26] JW's favorite text on this point is Heb. 11:1.

introduce is greater transformative power through the impartation of divine love within the heart.

Consistent with this emphasis was another long cherished conviction that Wesley held: true religion does not consist of correct opinions, even of a doctrinal nature. In 1742 Wesley published the tract *The Character of a Methodist* in which he acknowledges that though Methodists differ from Jews, Moslems, Catholics, Socinians and Arians over many doctrines, "all opinions which do not strike at the root of Christianity, we think and let think."[27] Three years later he reiterated that Methodists "profess to pursue holiness of heart and life" with "universal love filling the heart and governing the life."[28] Consequently, Wesleyan Methodism did not stress correct opinion or specific modes of worship (on non-essential matters). In these matters Wesley was flexible. After all, as his doctrine of involuntary sin affirmed, even the most perfect err in many things unrelated to salvation.[29] This acknowledgment opened the door for Wesley to later consider that those who err in their understanding of God, like Jews and Moslems, can find acceptance before God if they fear him and work righteousness.[30]

In the end Wesley's servant theology led his theological system to swing full circle by reaffirming the core axiom of his holiness gospel: the demand of inward holiness for final salvation. This, Wesley declared in 1733, is the "distinguishing mark of a true follower of Christ" and of "one who is in a state of accep-

---

[27] Works J 8:340 §1.
[28] *Advice to the People Called Methodists,* Works B 9:123-24. JW's later servant theology even softened this standard by not requiring people of other faiths to necessarily affirm the tenets of Christianity (see ch 7).
[29] *A Plain Account* 12:5-8; 15:7-8.
[30] The aged JW wrote, "I believe the merciful God regards the lives and tempers of men more than their ideas. I believe he respects the goodness of the heart, rather than the clearness of the head; and that if the heart of a man be filled with humble, gentle, patient love of God and man, God will not cast him into everlasting fire, prepared for the devil and his angels, because his ideas are not clear or because his conceptions are confused" (1790, *On Living Without God* §15).

tance with God."³¹ They seek to have that "habitual disposition of soul which in the Sacred Writings is termed 'holiness'" and look forward to the day when the "great Master" says to them, "Well done, good and faithful servant!"³²

Concluding Thoughts

That the servant is acceptable to God, because their faith moves them to fear him and to work righteousness, is the natural evolution of a perfection theology that grounds vital religion in holy tempers. As Wesley came to see the utter bankruptcy of nominal Christianity, he came to realize that such mental assent would never save anyone, no matter what church or creed they affirmed. If salvation is to have meaning, its power must begin to transform now, in this present life. Whereas his early theology implicitly affirmed this truth, it was his Gospel of Faith Alone that put this truth on the front burner. Wesley wanted a faith that saved now, in the present. As he studied the workings of divine grace in the lives of his converts, he came to appreciate more and more how the faith journey starts even before one is born again. This led to a fresh evaluation of his faith journey in the mid sixties. Wesley's own struggles became the fulcrum for change within his theological system. Existing beliefs and concepts were funneled through the turbulent waters of deep personal questioning and heart-searching struggles to forge a new theological system; a system rooted in the one God, his holy nature, and in the cross of Christ. These three axioms became the bedrock for his Gospel of Universal Holiness.

To conclude, Wesley's servant theology offers important insights into the evolution of his perfection theology, which continually seeks to "present everyone perfect in Christ."³³

---

[31] *The Circumcision of the Heart* P.3.
[32] *The Circumcision of the Heart* P.3; I.1.
[33] Colossians 1:27 NIV.

John Wesley's Theology of Christian Perfection

A Response to Kenneth Collins. Collins has been a persistent opponent of the interpretation presented in chapter 4 and in this appendix. While his scholarship on JW is much appreciated and respected, the arguments he offers to show the servant is not justified in Wesley's mature gospel system does not make sense to this author. For JW appears to be very clear on the subject. In his book *The Scripture Way of Salvation* Collins offers three basic arguments to show the servant is not justified (p 104).

His first argument is that justification and new birth are repeatedly linked in JW's writings. His err is that he quotes from writings that pre-date JW's spiritual crisis in the mid-sixties to substantiate his point. As we learned in chapter 4, this crisis was the catalyst which finally moved JW to formally affirm the servant state. It is true, as we saw above in this appendix, JW did interpret the servant as justified as early as 1745, but this was only in context of those who had never heard of Christ or the Gospel. What we see following 1766 is that JW begins to see Christian believers, those who lack the witness of adoption, and its concomitant the new birth, as justified (JWJ 12/1/67). Of course, JW continued to link justification with the new birth for those under gospel preaching, since such preaching normally leads the believer to experience both justification and new birth in the same moment. But our study has confirmed that JW did not always link justification to the new birth in his writings. And later in life he opened the door wider for sincere followers of other faiths to be saved on the final day (ch 7).

Collins second argument is that according to JW acceptance does not mean justification. This has been shown to be wrong. As early as 1733 and as late as 1765 JW defined justification as acceptance before God (cf. *The Circumcision of the Heart* P.3; *Justification by Faith* II.5; *The Scripture Way of Salvation* I.3). Acceptance does serve as a synonym in JW's writings for justification. Logically the two terms must mean the same thing. Since the servant is saved from eternal punishment this necessarily implies they must also be pardoned or justified before God. To speak of salvation from eternal damnation while simultaneously lacking justification before God is a contradiction of terms, and of the meaning of salvation itself.

His third argument is that to separate justification from the new birth leads to antinomianism (which JW opposed). This argument fails to take notice that according to JW the servant is *not* void of vital religion in the heart, for the servant sincerely fears God and works righteousness (*The Almost Christian* I.9). It is important to stress: *God's grace is at work in the servant*. The servant is responding to God according to the light that one has. Since the servant is actively serving God, holy tempers have already begun to work in the heart. Thus grace is at work and the process of salvation already begun.

APPENDIX F
Clement of Alexandria:
A Second Century Wesleyan?[1]

When Wesley entered his "new period" of field preaching in the spring of 1739,[2] a public outcry began to arise against this new sect called "Methodist."[3] Wesley records in his journal of the criticisms he faced that summer and fall both in person and in print.[4] In defending the revival he also began to define what a Methodist is, which culminated in the tract *The Character of a Methodist*, which was published in 1742.[5] Rupert Davies informs us that though Wesley was inspired by Clement of Alexandria's *Stromata*, he sought in his tract to define the ideal Christian in more scriptural terms.[6] This linkage to Clement offers us an opportunity to see how Wesley was influenced by this early church father in shaping his message of full salvation.

Titus Flavius Clemens is believed to have been born around 150 in Athens, Greece, and to have died in 215 or shortly before. His parents were pagan. Nothing is known of his conversion, but

---

[1] Bibliography: *The Ante-Nicene Fathers, Vol. 2*. Grand Rapids: Eerdmans. Reprint, 1983. Questen, Johannes, *Patrology Vol. II: The Ante-Nicene Literature After Irenaeus*. Westminster: Christian Classics, Inc. Sixth printing, 1992.
[2] *Journal* 3/28/39, Works J 1:177.
[3] *The Character of a Methodist* P.1.
[4] Cf. *Journal* 7/31/39; 9/16/39; 10/16/39.
[5] Cf. *Plain Account* 10:1 and notes. It is this author's opinion the roots of the tract go back to the summer of 1739 when JW was busy defending the new movement. Though JW is wrong in the *Plain Account* concerning when he published the tract, it appears he could have written a first draft in that year and later rewrote and published it in 1742. The following clues stands out: 1. The tract lacks any appearance of the conflict which transpired in 1740 over his perfection doctrine between the revival parties. 2. The tone of the subject matter fits very well with what JW records in his 1739 journal. 3. While JW could easily err over the date when he published the tract, it is less likely he would err over which tract was his first to be written on a particular subject.
[6] Works B 9:31.

we do know he later traveled to Italy, Syria, Palestine, and finally to Alexandria where he remained for some time. He began to study under Pantaenus, who was the first instructor of the Christian school in Alexandria, and later became his assistant. Around 200 Clement succeeded his instructor as the head of the school. Soon thereafter persecution broke out and Clement had to flee Alexandria to find safe refuge in Cappadocia, never to return again. His surviving writings include *Exhortation To The Heathen*, *The Instructor*, *The Stromata*, *Who Is The Rich Man That Shall Be Saved?*, and some fragments. Our attention with be on the second and third works which show much affinity to Wesley's doctrine of Christian perfection. What follows is a skeleton description of each book with some concluding remarks.[7]

The Instructor

The Instructor (Gk. *Paedagogue*) consists of three books. In simple terms it is a second century discipleship manual. Book I lays out Clement's philosophy of discipleship, while Books II and III include practical advice for the disciple/pupil. Clement stresses Jesus Christ as the believer's instructor in the things of God. A very strong emphasis is placed on Christ's divine nature. As we read through Clement's writings we can sense the inspiration Wesley must have felt in Clement's definition of the ideal Christian. He was probably impressed with Clement's method of forming small groups for the purpose of providing practical guidance in the attainment of inward holiness. Clement discusses in Book II such matters as eating, drinking, feasting, laughter, speech, ointments, sleep, clothing, and jewelry. Book III discusses true beauty, the body, public baths, frugality, and other

---

[7] Clement's writings will be referenced according to book and chapter. All references to the *Plain Account* (P.A.) are to the Annotated Edition.

Clement of Alexandria: A Second Century Wesleyan?

issues of concern in second century Roman society. Parallels between *The Instructor* and Wesley's perfection theology are:

1. Clement sees discipleship as the formation of right (holy) habits, actions and passions.[8] This parallels Wesley's emphasis on developing holy tempers and the instructional goals within his classes.[9]

2. Clement defines sin as a disease and Christ the physician.[10] Wesley, too, spoke of sin as our disease and Christ our physician.[11]

While defining his terms somewhat differently than Wesley does, Clement speaks of voluntary and involuntary sin; and also of sin that is habitual. He states emphatically that only God never "sins at all in any way," and yet he maintains the "Word, the Instructor, has taken charge of us, in order to the prevention of sin."[12] Clement expounds on God's love for mankind and our response to such love:

---

[8] Bk 1, ch 1.

[9] PA 6:2; 19:5. D. Michael Hendricks lists eight major concepts behind JW's discipleship philosophy: "1. Human nature is perfectible by God's grace. 2. Learning comes by doing the will of God. 3. Mankind's nature is perfected by participation in groups, not by acting as isolated individuals. 4. The spirit and practice of primitive Christianity can and must be captured. 5. Human progress will occur if people will participate in 'the means of grace.' 6. The gospel must be presented to the poor. 7. Social evil is not to be 'resisted,' but overcome with good. 8. The primary function of spiritual/educational leadership is to equip others to lead and minister, not to perform the ministry personally" (*John Wesley's Class Meeting*, 128-29).

[10] Bk 1, ch 1.

[11] See PA 16:2-3. In *The Repentance of Believers* JW admonishes, "Though we watch and pray ever so much, we cannot wholly cleanse either our hearts or hands. Most sure we cannot, till it shall please our Lord to speak to our hearts again, to speak the second time, 'Be clean.' And then only the leprosy is cleansed. Then only the evil root, the carnal mind, is destroyed; and inbred sin subsists no more" (I.20).

[12] Bk 1, ch 2.

But what is lovable, and is not also loved by Him? And man has been proved to be lovable; consequently man is loved by God. For how shall he not be loved for whose sake the only-begotten Son is sent from the Father's bosom, the Word of faith, the faith which is superabundant; the Lord Himself distinctly confessing and saying, "For the Father Himself loveth you, because ye have loved Me;" and again, "And hast loved them as Thou hast loved Me?"... Now, it is incumbent on us to return His love, who lovingly guides us to that life which is best; and to live in accordance with the injunctions of His will, not only fulfilling what is commanded, or guarding against what is forbidden, but turning away from some examples, and imitating others as much as we can, and thus to perform the works of the Master according to His similitude, and so fulfill what Scripture says as to our being made in His image and likeness.[13]

Later Clement quips, "Now we call that perfect which wants nothing,"[14] and then he asks, "For what is yet wanting to him who knows God." In this context Clement argues in a manner similar to Wesley that all Christians are perfect because in comparison to the non-Christian they are the ones who are "complete," having been reunited with their heavenly Father. Clement can be even more explicit, "Straightway, on our regeneration, we attained that perfection after which we aspired."[15] From statements like this we can understand why Wesley linked the new birth to perfection. Yet, like Wesley, Clement distinguished between infants and adults in the faith.[16] And, like Wesley, Clement believed the goal of redemption to be renewal in the image of God:

---

[13] Bk 1, ch 3.
[14] Bk 1, ch 6.
[15] Bk 1, ch 6.
[16] PA 12:9, 29. JW often distinguishes between the first and second gifts with maturational language.

Clement of Alexandria: A Second Century Wesleyan?

> The view I take is, that He Himself formed man of the dust, and regenerated him by water; and made him grow by his Spirit; and trained him by His word to adoption and salvation, directing him by sacred precepts; in order that, transforming earth-born man into a holy and heavenly being by His advent, He might fulfill to the utmost that divine utterance, "Let Us make man in Our own image and likeness."[17]

Wesley could hardly have said it any better. We close this section on *The Instructor* with three quotes from chapter thirteen. Those who have read Wesley's *Plain Account,* and some of his other writings, will note several parallels to Clement's writings. Here is another sample of what Clement wrote on the subject of holiness:

> Everything that is contrary to right reason is sin. Accordingly, therefore, the philosophers think fit to define the most generic passions thus: lust, as desire disobedient to reason; fear, as weakness disobedient to reason; pleasure, as an elation of the spirit disobedient to reason. If, then, disobedience in reference to reason is the generating cause of sin, how shall we escape the conclusion, that obedience to reason—the Word—which we call faith, will of necessity be the efficacious cause of duty? For virtue itself is a state of the soul rendered harmonious by reason in respect to the whole life.

> The end of piety is eternal rest in God.

> Virtue is a will in conformity to God and Christ in life, rightly adjusted to life everlasting. For the life of Christians, in which we are now trained, is a system of reasonable actions—that is, of those things taught by the Word—an unfailing energy which we have called faith.

---

[17] Bk 1, ch 12.

> The system is the commandments of the Lord, which, being divine statues and spiritual counsels, have been written for ourselves, being adapted for ourselves and our neighbors.

The Stromata

The *Stromata* consists of several books that cover a variety of subjects. Yet it is in Book VII that Clement describes the ideal or perfect Christian. Because there is so much material in Book VII on the subject of perfection, only the most significant themes can be noted here. Clement refers to the perfect Christian as the true Gnostic.[18] Clement then identifies the Christian Gnostic as the true worshipper of God. A Gnostic for Clement is one who studies God in "ceaseless love."[19] The first step to knowing God is to have faith in Christ, who is the image of the invisible God (Col 1:15). Clement stresses Christ's closeness to the Father and in this way demonstrates that only the Christian can ever attain to the level of the true Gnostic. In the following quote Clement's views resonate with Wesley's belief in holiness as salvation from inward sin:

> For "to bring themselves into captivity," and to slay themselves, putting to death "the old man, who is through lusts corrupt," and raising the new man from death, "from the old conversation," by abandoning the passions, and becoming free of sin, both the Gospel and the apostle enjoin.[20]

Clement returns to the theme of renewal in God's image and likeness:

---

[18] Gnosis means knowledge in Greek.
[19] Bk 7, ch 1.
[20] Bk 7, ch 3; compare with PA 12:44.

Clement of Alexandria: A Second Century Wesleyan?

> The Gnostic, then, is pious, who cares first for himself, then for his neighbors, that they may become very good. For the son gratifies a good father, by showing himself good and like his father; and in like manner the subject, the governor. For believing and obeying are in our own power.[21]

This quote parallels Wesley's emphasis on the means of grace and good works.[22] Here is another quote of Clement's description of a perfect Christian:

> For pre-eminently a divine image, resembling God, is the soul of a righteous man...This is the true athlete—he who in the great stadium, the fair world, is crowned for the true victory over all the passions. For He who prescribes the contest is the Almighty God, and He who awards the prize is the only-begotten: Son of God. Angels and gods are spectators; and the contest, embracing all the varied exercises, is "not against flesh and blood," but against the spiritual powers of inordinate passions that work through the flesh. He who obtains the mastery in these struggles, and overthrows the tempter, menacing, as it were, with certain contests, wins immortality.[23]

These quotes reflect a vision of the Christian life very similar to Wesley's. The goal is renewal in the divine image. The great enemy is unholy tempers (dispositions). The conflict is spiritual and full sanctification is necessary to prepare one for heaven. These are all core motifs in Wesley's perfection theology.

Clement also defines perfection as continual communion with God. The perfect believer is one who "prays throughout his whole life, endeavoring by prayer to have fellowship with God." Wesley, too, defined perfection as continual communion with

---

[21] Bk 7, ch 3.
[22] PA 25:203-217.
[23] Bk 7, ch 3.

God, "For indeed he *'prays without ceasing;'* at all times the language of his heart is this, *'Unto thee is my mouth, though without a voice; and my silence speaketh unto thee.'* His heart is lifted up to God at all times, and in all places. In this he is never hindered, much less interrupted, by any person or thing. In retirement or company, in leisure, business, or conversation, his heart is ever with the Lord."[24]

Another corollary between Clement and Wesley is that both espoused two God-moments on the faith journey path. Clement writes in chapter ten, "In my view, the first saving change is that from heathenism to faith...the second, that from faith to knowledge. And the latter terminating in love." Clement teaches there are several stages to the believer's journey. The first stage is faith, then knowledge, after this love and finally, inheritance. This fourfold description of the journey parallels Wesley's child – adolescent – adult delineation, with two definitive moments in the process.[25] It is important to note that for Clement the kind of knowledge God imparts in sanctification is salvific: Christ, the Word, imparts life through knowledge of himself.

Clement begins an extended discussion in chapter eleven on the character of the perfect Christian. The emphasis now falls on possessing Christ-like character and disposition. Clement teaches victory over anger, the transformation of the dispositions, that suffering perfects, and that self-control and courage imbue one's character so their "whole life is prayer and converse with God."[26] There is much in these chapters that parallel Wesley's theology of perfection. It can be stated that for Clement the perfect believer is established in holiness and godliness: the heart is pure, sinful passions are vanquished, and universal obedience in all areas of life is enjoyed. The perfect Christian is blameless. They forgive those who sin against them, and are full of good works and acts of mercy. Inward and outward holiness characterize the

---

[24] PA 10:9.
[25] See ch 9. Also see PA ch 3 end note; 6:1 note for summary on JW's concept of degrees.
[26] Bk 10, ch 12.

Clement of Alexandria: A Second Century Wesleyan?

life. "The Gnostic is consequently divine, and already holy, God-bearing, and God-borne."[28]

One more striking parallel to Wesley's perfection theology needs to be mentioned. In the *Plain Account* 19:73-75 Wesley likens the attainment of perfection to physical death. Clement utilizes the same analogy:

> Do you not see how wax is softened and copper purified, in order to receive the stamp applied to it? Just as death is the separation of the soul from the body, so is knowledge as it were the rational death urging the spirit away, and separating it from the passions, and leading it on to the life of well-doing, that it may then say with confidence to God, "I live as Thou wishest."[29]

Closing Thoughts

Though this appendix only touches upon specific themes of Clement's writings and theology, it demonstrates how much Wesley's theology of perfection was influenced by early Christianity, the church fathers, and Clement himself. All of Wesley's basic themes and motifs that nuance his doctrine of Christian perfection are found here. Thus showing that in 1739 when Wesley was working through his perfection beliefs,[30] he once again looked to this early church father for inspiration and guidance.

What can we conclude from this short survey? I propose that Clement was a second century Wesleyan. Or, should we say, Wesley was an eighteenth century Clementian. Either way, the message of perfect love is an old one, grounded in Holy Scripture, and witnessed through the centuries.

---

[28] Bk 10, ch 13.
[29] Bk 10, ch 12.
[30] See chapter 3 above.

APPENDIX G
Doctrinal Resource Lists

What follows are resource lists to empower the reader's own study of Wesley's theology of perfection and its evolution. While many know where to find this information, others do not; or, at least, they can have this information already packaged in chronological order for easy use. The subsections are:

Early Period: 1725-1738
Aldersgate I: 1738-1740
Aldersgate II
Cornelius and Acts 10:35
Wesley's Doctrine of Sin: 1738-1784

Early Period
1725-1738
Chapter One

The following is a list in chronological order of the letters, sermons, and writings by Wesley that touch upon his theology of perfection in his early period. All references are to the Bicentennial Edition of Wesley's Works (Works B) unless otherwise noted.

1725
June-August: Letters to Susanna Wesley 25:162-170, 172-173, 175, 178-179
September: Sermon #133 *Death and Deliverance*
November: Sermon #134 *Seek First the Kingdom*
November 10: Letter from Susanna Wesley 25:183

1726
September: Sermon #135 *Guardian Angels*

Doctrinal Resource Lists: Early Period

1727
January 11: Sermon #136 *Mourning for the Dead*

1728
January 17: Sermon #137 *On Dissimulation*

1730
February 28: Letter to Susanna Wesley 25:244
July: Sermon #139 *On the Sabbath*
October 13: Sermon #140 *The Promise of Understanding*
November: Sermon #141 *Image of God*
December 12: Letter to Mary Granville 25:259

1731
February 11: Letter to Mary Pendarves 25:270
April 14: Letter to Mary Pendarves 25:276
June 11: Letter to Susanna Wesley 25:282
June 18: Letter to Ann Granville 25:285
June 19: Letter to Mary Pendarves 25:287
July 12: Sermon #142 *The Wisdom of Winning Souls*
July 19: Letter to Mary Pendarves 25:293
October 3: Letter to Ann Granville 25:317

1732
February 19: Transcribed *The Duty of Receiving the Lord's Supper*
  (Note: Later abridged and re-titled *The Duty of Constant Communion* #101)
February 28: Letter to Susanna Wesley 25:327
June 7: Transcribed *On the Resurrection of the Dead* Works J 7:474
Late Fall: *Preface to Collection of Prayers* Works J 14:270
October 19: Letter to Richard Morgan 25:335
October 28: Transcribed *On Grieving the Holy Spirit* Works J 7:485

1733
January 1: Sermon #17 *The Circumcision of the Heart*
February 15: Letter to Susanna Wesley 25:347
June 13: Letter to Samuel Wesley, Sen. 25:350
September 15: Sermon #144 *Love of God*

1734
January 1: Letter from Susanna Wesley 25:362

John Wesley's Theology of Christian Perfection

January 15: Letter to Richard Morgan 25:367
January 28: Letter to Susanna 25:371
March 15: Letter to Richard Morgan 25:379
May: Sermon #146 *One Thing Needful*
December 10: Letter to Samuel, Sen. 25:397

1735
January 13: Letter to Susanna Wesley 25:411
February 14: Letter to Susanna Wesley 25:418
Spring/Summer: Preface to *Christian Pattern* Works 14:202
September: Sermon #109 *The Trouble and rest of Good Men*
October 10: Letter to John Burton 25:439
October 15: Letter to Samuel, Jr. 25:444

1736
February: Sermon #148 *Single Intention*
September 10: Letter to George Whitefield 25:471
November 23: Letter to Samuel, Jr. 25:487

1737
February 16: Letter to Richard Morgan 25:491
February: Sermon #149 *On Love*
March 28: Letter to William Wogan 25:499
March 29: Letter to Mary Chapman 25:502
June 16: Letter to James Hutton 25:510
July 22: David Humphreys 25:514

1738
January 2: Letter from Charles Wesley 25:524

Aldersgate I Period
1738-1740
Chapter Three

This is another list in chronological order of Wesley's writings showing the development of his theology of perfection beginning with his Aldersgate conversion (5/24/38) till the writing of his preface for Journal Extract #2 (9/29/40). The symbols are as follows: JWJ – Journal; JWL – Letters (Bicentennial Edition); JWD – Diaries (Bicentennial Edition); Wk J – Works, Jackson Edition; Wk B – Works, Bicentennial Edition.

JWJ 5/24/38	JW experiences new birth and assurance of acceptance with God; believes he is saved from the law of sin and death, thereby attaining inward holiness and perfection.
JWJ 5/27-28/38	JW struggles with doubts and over his lack of joy.
JWJ 5/29/38	JW doubts his acceptance because his faith is weak in comparison with another believer.
JWJ 6/6/38	JW experiences doubt and fear over his state. He questions whether he has saving faith. He equates faith with perfection.
Wk B 6/11/38	JW preaches *Salvation by Faith*. He asserts that saving faith delivers from all sin: again, saving faith = perfection (1:117).
JWL 6/28/38	How the Moravian Church distinguishes between different kinds of faith, assurance and the new birth.
JWJ 7/6/38	Power of faith: salvation from inward and outward sin by love of God poured out into the heart; from all fear and doubt by the abiding witness of the Holy Spirit.
JWL 7/7/38	Faith brings peace, freedom from sin and a new creature in Christ.
JWL 7/7/38	Testifies of Moravian Church's perfection in relation to other Christians; highlights perfection as salvation from sinful tempers.

John Wesley's Theology of Christian Perfection

JWJ 7/9/38	Compares and contrasts Count Zinzendorf's doctrines of salvation with Peter Böhler's.
JWL 8/4/38	Believers at home (England) not yet perfect.
JWL 8/4/38	Gifts of holiness and happiness, freedom from sin, joy in Holy Spirit.
JWJ 8/10/38	Christian David's four sermons distinguishing those who are weak in faith from those who are perfect.
JWJ 8/10/38	A dozen testimonies affirming degrees of faith, deliverance from sin, and levels of assurance.
JWL 9/28/38	Distinguishes assurance from faith, and between the assurance of faith from that of salvation (perseverance).
JWJ 10/14/38	Examines himself and concludes he is in a mixed state.
JWL 10/30/38	Christian is saved from sin's dominion; JW in mixed state; not a Christian before 5/24; lacks assurance.
JWJ 11/12/38	Examines Church Homilies on justification and publishes an extract for the societies (Outler, *John Wesley*, 123).
JWL 11/16/38	Denies one must have full assurance to have justification, saving faith or the new birth.
JWL 11/22/38	Confesses to having peace but lacking the love and joy of the Spirit.
JWJ 12/3/38	Two testimonies identifying perfection with the new birth.
JWJ 12/16/38	JW confesses to being in a mixed state.
JWJ 1/4/39	JW confesses he is not a Christian, meaning a perfect one.
JWJ 1/25/39	Baptizes 5 people; acknowledges degrees of new birth – Lower (remission of sins) and fuller sense (thorough, inward change).

Doctrinal Resource Lists: Aldersgate I

Wk J 2/9/39	Preface to Life of Halyburton; proclaims freedom from sin; distinguishes committing sin from sins of infirmities (14:211).
JWL 3/20/39	The cause of salvation is Christ; the condition is faith alone; the branch is freedom from sin's dominion or committing sin.
JWJ 4/1/39	Begins field preaching – JW realizes his true calling. He teaches on the Sermon on the Mount and its themes of salvation and holiness (see 7/21, 9/17, 10/15).
JWJ 4/10/39	JW preaches on 1 Cor 1:30 and its theme of Christ providing full salvation: wisdom, justification, sanctification and redemption. This is a constant theme over the next several months, highlighting his emphasis on holiness in his message and thought.
JWJ 6/15/39	JW talks to a Quaker about perfection.
JWJ 7/23/39	JW seeks to guard young converts against the notion they have already attained, or are already perfect.
JWL 7/25/39	JW defends his doctrine of new birth as inward change; living faith as saving trust in Christ's merits; Holy Spirit working in the heart.
JWJ 8/10/39	Meets Quaker and Anabaptist with "large measure of love of God."
JWJ 8/29/39	Faith is the root, holiness the tree, and good works the fruit.
JWJ 9/13/39	Justification is distinguished from sanctification and precedes it; justification grounded on Christ alone by faith alone; sanctification defined as inward transformation of tempers; new birth as inward change.
JWJ 10/3/39	JW preaches on true and false holiness and answers the question, "How to be saved?"
JWJ 10/6-7/39	JW preaches on justification and on bondage and adoption (see sermons #5 and #9; also JWJ 10/18/39; 10/23-24/39).

John Wesley's Theology of Christian Perfection

	These sermons distinguish between Christ *for* and *in* us, and the three states: natural, legal, gospel.
JWJ 10/9/39	Inward and outward holiness distinguished, the latter required for initial salvation.
JWJ 11/1/39	Letter speaks of inward/outward holiness (Extract 3).
JWJ 11/1/39	Stillness teaching: no degrees to saving faith; the means of grace do not lead to faith.
JWD 11/7/39	JW "writ [Law's] *Christian Perfection*." Thus showing he was working on the subject.
JWJ 11/17/39	JW proclaims for the first time the "nature and extant" of Christian perfection. This is the same content as his sermon *Christian Perfection* (1741) addresses.
JWJ 12/13/39	JW defines justification and faith alone in contrast to Anglican clerics.
JWJ 12/31/39	Discussion with Molther over stillness; JW asserts degrees of faith, assurance, inward transformation, and the continued use and value of the means of grace.
JWJ 1/25/40	Salvation by faith means deliverance from inward and outward sin.
JWJ 3/5/40	Full renewal in God's image linked to taking the axe to the root of the tree.
JWL 3/26/40	From G. Whitefield: responds to JW that sin has no dominion over him but denies freedom from indwelling sin.
JWJ 3/28/40	JW teaches on the "wilderness state": doubts and fears many experience after receiving remission of sins.
Wk J Spring/40	*Preface to Hymns and Sacred Poems II*. JW clearly asserts two works of grace, delineates the journey to the second work, and defines perfection in terms of liberty (14:322).

Doctrinal Resource Lists: Aldersgate I

JWJ 4/25/40	JW confronts Molther and his "stillness" errs; refers to stillness as a "new gospel;" defends use of means; asserts degrees.
JWJ 5/4/40	JW recognizes two states: forgiveness and a clean heart.
JWJ 6/1/40	Perfection as "rest" (see JWJ 8/1/40).
JWJ 6/22-7/20	JW confronts stillness at society and is removed from the pulpit. JW defines weak faith and asserts degrees of faith, sin remains in convert but does not reign, means have value, perfection a later attainment, stillness is a new gospel.
JWL 6/25/40	JW defines perfection as crucifixion of flesh's affections and desires, freedom from doubt, fear and the first stirrings of anger, and as fulfilling the law of love toward God and neighbor. He affirms the new convert has sin still *in* them, but they do not *commit* sin.
JWL 8/8/40	JW writes to Zinzendorf arguing his side of the debate over stillness. JW argues for salvation from all sin, degrees of faith and for the means of grace.
JWJ 8/10/40	Perfection defined as clean heart, thorough renewal in God's image, righteousness and true holiness.
JWL 9/25/40	From G. Whitefield. He argues for no freedom from indwelling sin in this life, believes JW holds to "sinless perfection."
JWJ 9/29/40	JW writes preface to journal extract #2; asserts mixed state following forgiveness, degrees of faith, perfection as second work, and the continued use of the means of grace.

Additional Notes:

1741   Sermon *Christian Perfection* highlights two works of grace distinguished as child and father. The child is freed from outward (committing) sin, while the father is freed from inward (sinful thoughts and tempers) sin.

1742   *The Character of a Methodist* published. This work was inspired by the church father Clement of Alexandria (d. 223). JW explains in *The*

John Wesley's Theology of Christian Perfection

Plain Account that he wrote this tract in 1739, though the earliest published copy is 1742. We do know JW was studying Clement's writings in 1739. For in that year JW published a poem on Clement's vision of the perfect Christian in his first volume of hymns. Ted Campbell informs us that this poem "describes the distance between the state of a human being in pilgrimage and the state of a perfect Christian then, the power of God to bring human beings to the perfect state" (*JW and Christian Antiquity*, 42). JW's journal reveals in the summer of 1739 he was busy defending and defining what a Methodist is, which is the central purpose of the tract.

Aldersgate II
Chapter Four

Listed below are the primary documents that point to a spiritual crisis in the mid-sixties, producing further evolution within Wesley's gospel system. Below, our focus is on how Wesley understood his own faith journey and when he believed he received justification.

Converted (saved) in 1738:

Letter to Samuel (10/38)
 JW was not regenerated until May 24, 1738

Journal Extract I & II (1740)
 JW declares he was an unbeliever before 1738

The Almost Christian (1741)
 JW says he was only an almost Christian before 1738

A Plain Account of the Methodists (1749)
 JW begins the revival's history in 1739, thus neglecting his early period

Letter to Lavington (1751)
 JW says he was an unbeliever before May 24, 1738

Letter (4/58)
 JW says he was a non-believer before 1738

Converted (saved) in 1725:

1759-1763 Revival
 Hundreds profess perfection; schism transpires along with separation – Wesley is deeply affected and moved to examine what he believes

Summary of Perfection Views (1764)
 An 11 point summary of his perfection beliefs

Letter to John Newton (5/65)
 JW begins his faith journey in 1725, not 1738

John Wesley's Theology of Christian Perfection

A Short History of Methodism (1765)
    JW begins the revival's history in 1729, not 1739 (as above). This reflects a new appreciation for his early period

A Plain Account of Christian Perfection (2/66)
    JW says he was converted in 1725

Letter to Charles Wesley (6/27/66)
    JW lacks the witness of the Holy Spirit (new birth); confesses he is only a God-fearer; implies he is in a pre-new birth / post-justification state

Letter (4/20/67)
    A Christian (lower sense) is one who fears God and works righteousness

Journal (12/1/67)
    The bottom line of salvation is (1) not right opinion, but (2) to fear God and work righteousness (Acts 10:35)

Letters (3/28/68; 4/7/68)
    JW says the servant is accepted (justified)

Letter (12/15/72)
    JW longs for his Oxford days (early period)

1738 Journal Footnotes (1774-75)
    JW declares he was a *servant* before 1738 and that he became a *son* at Aldersgate

On Faith (4/88)
    JW says 50 yrs ago Methodists were mistaken that those who lacked the witness of adoption were not saved. JW now knows they are saved as God's servants

Cornelius & Acts 10:35
Chapter Four

Critical to any evaluation of when Wesley considered himself converted is based on his understanding of Cornelius' spiritual state and his use of Acts 10:35. The following chronological references summarize his comments on Cornelius and Acts 10:35.

JWJ 6/25/40
    JW views Cornelius as not saved before Peter came to preach.

Conference Minutes 8/2/45
    JW admits Cornelius was in the favor of God, in "some degree," even though he was not a Christian. JW concludes Cornelius' good works were by the "grace of Christ" and not sinful.

JWL 7/31/47
    Acts 10:35 is used as an argument against the necessity of conscious assurance for justification before God.

Catholic Spirit III.5 (1749)
    Acts 10:35 is cited as illustrating true religion and a catholic spirit.

A Plain Account of the People Called Methodist IV.2 (1749)
    JW commends those in the societies whose character demonstrates Acts 10:35.

NT Notes: Acts 10:4, 35; 11:14 (1756)
    Though not a Christian, Cornelius is already accepted and justified before God.

JWJ 7/19/61
    JW preaches to thousands whom Acts 10:35 describes.

JWL 1762 *Mr. Horn* II.1
    People can be saved if they believe according to the dispensation they are in.

John Wesley's Theology of Christian Perfection

JWJ 8/19/63
    JW visits Howell Harris' society and notes Acts 10:35 describe his people.

JWL 4/20/67
    Acts 10:35 defines the Christian in a lower sense.

JWJ 12/1/67
    Acts 10:35 is the bottom line standard for salvation.

JWL 3/28/68
    A Christian is defined according to Acts 10:35.

Minutes 1770
    Acts 10:35 is the standard of salvation for those who are ignorant of Christ.

"Imposture Detected" An Answer to Mr. Rowland Hill 1/28/77
    Acts 10:35 requires evangelically a "living faith" to be fulfilled.

Short History of Methodism §10 (1781)
    JW remembers the Moravians as an example of vital religion with Acts 10:35 as the standard.

On Charity I.3 (1784)
    Acts 10:35 is applied to pre-Christians (e.g. heathen) concerning their final salvation.

On Divine Providence §18, 26 (1786)
    Acts 10:35 describes "real Christians."

The Signs of the Times II.9 (1786)
    Acts 10:35 equals an "entire change" from profligate sinners to practicing real religion (Christianity).

On Faith (#106) I.11 (1788)
    Acts 10:35 is the faith of a servant and this level of faith is acceptable to God.

Doctrinal Resource Lists: Cornelius & Acts 10:35

On the Discoveries of Faith §13 (1788)
   Acts 10:35 is the faith of a servant and this level of faith is, "in a degree," acceptable to God.

Thoughts Upon A Late Phenomenon §3 (7/13/88) Works J 13:265
   In every nation there are a few that fear God and work righteousness.

The Ministerial Office §9, 21 (5/4/89)
   Acts 10:35 has been the standard for membership in the societies and for the right hand of fellowship.

JWJ 8/26/89
   The standard for membership in Methodism is not specific religious opinions or modes of worship, but Acts 10:35.

Wesley's Doctrine of Sin
1738-1784
Chapter Five

A chronological study of Wesley's sermons and other chief writings reveal how his doctrine of sin developed and took shape just as his doctrine of perfection matured through the decades. The following list serves as a good starting place for a thorough study of sin in Wesley's theology of perfection.

Salvation By Faith (1738)
    Sin is defined as:
        Guilt
        Power:
            Habitual (slave)
            Willful (outward acts)
            Desire (inward, carnal nature)
            Infirmity - not properly sin - no concurrence of the will

Conference Minutes (1744-47)
    Sin is:
        Outward
        Inward

The First Fruits of Spirit (1746)
    Sin is defined as:
        Past (guilt)
        Present
        Inward
        Sin cleaving (perfect law violated)
        Infirmities

The Marks of New Birth (1748)
    Sin is:
        Outward
        Inward
        Habitual (not a Christian)

Doctrinal Resource Lists: Wesley's Doctrine of Sin

The Great Privilege of Those that are Born of God (1748)
    Sin is:
        Outward: voluntary transgression of known law of God
        Inward: 1. negative: omitting duty (omission)
                2. positive: actual desire for sin (commission)

Thoughts on Christian Perfection (1759)
    Sin is categorized as:
        Voluntary: sin properly so-called; voluntary transgression of a known law
        Involuntary: involuntary transgression of a divine law, known or unknown.

Farther Thoughts on Christian Perfection (1763)
    Sin is qualified by:
        Adamic law: law of works – impeccable performance
        Law of Christ: law of faith – faith and love

On Sin in Believers (1763)
    Sin is:
        Outward (committing sin)
        Inward (sinful tempers)
    Sin further categorized as:
        Guilt
        Power
        Being

The Scripture Way of Salvation (1765)
    Sin is qualified as:
        Suspended, but not destroyed – lists outward sins
        Remains, but does not reign
        Cleaves until removed
        Salvation from all sin = inward sin

The Repentance of Believers (1767)
    Sin is categorized as:
        Sins of omission
        Inward defects
        Outward sin

John Wesley's Theology of Christian Perfection

Inward sin: power broken in conversion – no need to follow
inward sin remains and cleaves until perfection

On Perfection (1784)
   Sin is defined as:
      Voluntary transgression of a known law. This is the only kind of sin removed in this life.

Here is an outline of Wesley's mature doctrine of sin:

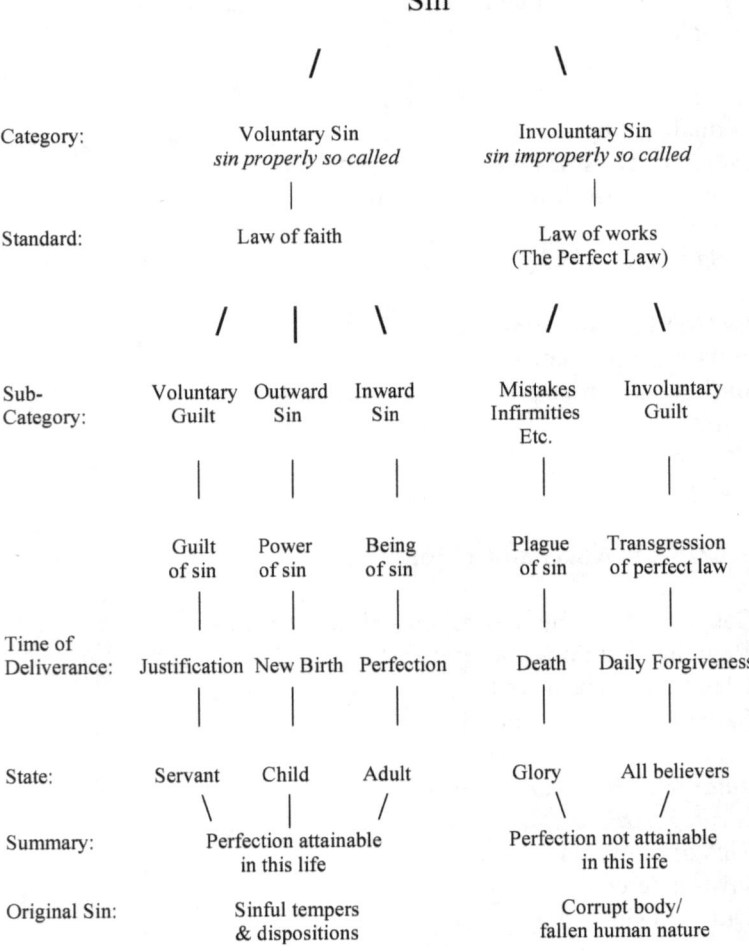

Bibliography

The John Wesley Christian Perfection Library
Mark K. Olson; Fenwick: Alethea in Heart

Vol. I: *John Wesley's 'A Plain Account of Christian Perfection*:
The Annotated Edition, 2005.

Vol. II: *John Wesley's Theology of Christian Perfection*:
Developments in Doctrine & Theological System, 2007, Revised 2009.

Vol. III: *The John Wesley Reader on Christian Perfection: 1725-1791*, 2008.

Primary Sources

John Wesley:

Works of John Wesley 14 volumes, 1872 Edition. Editor: Thomas Jackson. Grand Rapids: Baker Book House. 1984, Reprint.

Works of John Wesley: The Bicentennial edition, 34 projected volumes. Nashville: Abingdon Press. 1984-Present.

Explanatory Notes On The New Testament, 2 volumes Reprint. Grand Rapids: Baker Book House. 1983.

Internet and Software Sources:

Wesley Center for Applied Theology: www.wesley.nnu.edu

Heitzenrater, Richard Ed. *The Works of John Wesley: The Bicentennial Edition.* Nashville: Abingdon Press. 2005.

Master Christian Library: Version 8. Rio: Ages Software, Inc. 2000.

John Wesley's Theology of Christian Perfection

Other editions of John Wesley's writings:

Curnock, Nehemiah *The Journal of the Rev. John Wesley A.M., 8 vols*. London: Epworth Press. 1909-1916.

Kinghorn, Kenneth Cain *John Wesley on Christian Beliefs: The Standard Sermons in Modern English, Vol. 1, 1-20*. Nashville: Abingdon Press. 2002.

_____ *John Wesley on the Sermon of the Mount: A Modern Reading of the Standard Sermons, Vol. 2, 21-33*. Nashville: Abingdon Press. 2002.

Outler, Albert C. *John Wesley*, New York: Oxford University Press. 1964.

Sugden, Edward H. *Wesley's Standard Sermons, 2 vols*. Fourth Edition. Grand Rapids: The Zondervan Corporation and Francis Asbury Press. 1955.

Telford, John *The Letters of the Rev. John Wesley, 8 vols*. London: Epworth Press. 1931.

Charles Wesley:

Jackson, Thomas *The Journal of Charles Wesley,* 2 vols. Reprint. Grand Rapids: Baker Book House. 1980.

Beckerlegge, Kimbrough Editor: *The Unpublished Poetry of Charles Wesley,* 3 vols. Nashville: Abingdon Press. 1989, 1990, 1998.

Newport, Kenneth G. C. Editor: *The Sermons of Charles Wesley: A Critical Edition with Introduction and Notes*. Oxford: Oxford University Press. 2001.

Bibliography

Tyson, John R. *Charles Wesley: A Reader.* Oxford: Oxford Press. 1989.

Secondary Sources

Banks, John *'Nancy Nancy'*, Penwork (Leeds) Ltd.; 1984.

Borgen, Ole E. *John Wesley on The Sacraments: A Definitive Study of John Wesley's Theology Of Worship.* Grand Rapids: Francis Asbury Press. 1972.

Collins, Kenneth J. *The Scripture Way of Salvation: The Heart of John Wesley's Theology.* Nashville: Abingdon Press. 1997.

_____ *John Wesley's Critical Appropriation of Early German Pietism.* Wesleyan Theological Journal Vol.27. Marion: Wesleyan Theological Society.1992.

_____ *John Wesley: A Theological Journey.* Nashville: Abingdon Press. 2003.

_____ and John H. Tyson Ed. *Conversion in the Wesleyan Tradition.* Nashville: Abingdon. 2001.

Coppedge, Allen *John Wesley in Theological Debate.* Wilmore: Wesley Heritage Press. 1987.

Cox, Leo George *John Wesley's Concept of Perfection.* Salem: Schmul Publishing. 1999.

Cubie, David L. *Perfection in Wesley and Fletcher: Inaugural or Teleological?* Wesleyan Theological Journal Vol.11. Marion: Wesleyan Theological Society. 1976.

_____ *Placing Aldersgate in John Wesley's Order of Salvation.* Wesleyan Theological Journal Vol.24. Marion: Wesleyan Theological Society. 1989.

John Wesley's Theology of Christian Perfection

Gunter, W. Stephen *The Limits of Love Divine: John Wesley's Response to Antinomianism and Enthusiasm.* Nashville: Abingdon Press. 1989.

Harper, Steven J. *John Wesley's Message for Today.* Grand Rapids: Zondervan Corporation. 1983.

_____ , Scott J. Jones, Ted A. Campbell, Rebekah L. Miles and Randy L. Maddox *Wesley and the Quadrilateral – Renewing the Conversation.* Nashville: Abingdon. 1997.

_____ *The Devotional Life of John Wesley, 1703-1738.* Duke University PH.D. Dissertation: Duke University. 1981.

Heitzenrater, Richard P. *The Elusive Mr. Wesley, Vol. 1 John Wesley His Own Biographer.* Nashville: Abingdon Press. 1984.

_____ *The Elusive Mr. Wesley, Vol. 2 John Wesley As Seen By Contemporaries And Biographers.* Nashville: Abingdon Press. 1984.

Henderson, D. Michael *John Wesley's Class Meeting: A Model for Making Disciples.* Nappanee: Evangel Publishing House. 1997.

Jones, Scott J. *John Wesley's Conception and Use of Scripture.* Nashville: Abingdon Press. 1995.

Lindstrom, Harold *Wesley & Sanctification.* Nappanee: Francis Asbury Press. 1980.

Maddox, Randy L. *Responsible Grace: John Wesley's Practical Theology.* Nashville: Abingdon Press. 1994.

_____ Ed., *Rethinking Wesley's Theology For Contemporary Methodism.* Nashville: Abingdon Press. 1998.

Moore, D. Marselle *Development in Wesley's Thought on Sanctification and Perfection.* Wesleyan Theological Journal Vol. 20, Num. 2. Marion: Wesleyan Theological Society. 1985.

Bibliography

Oden, Thomas C. *John Wesley's Scriptural Christianity.* Grand Rapids: Zondervan Publishing House. 1994.

_____ and Leicester R. Longden Editors, *The Wesleyan Theological Heritage: Essays of Albert C. Outler.* Grand Rapids: Zondervan Publishing House. 1991.

Outler, Albert C. *The Wesleyan Quadrilateral in Wesley.* Wesleyan Theological Journal Vol. 20, Num.1. Marion: Wesleyan Theological Society. 1985.

Runyon, Theodore *The New Creation: John Wesley's Theology Today.* Nashville: Abingdon Press. 1998.

Smith, Robert Doyle *John Wesley and Jonathan Edwards on Religious Experience: A Comparative Analysis.* Wesleyan Theological Journal Vol. 25 Num. 1. Marion: Wesleyan Theological Society. 1990.

Spaulding II, Henry W. *A Reconstruction of the Wesleyan Understanding of Christian Perfection.* Wesleyan Theological Journal Vol. 33 Num. 2. Marion: Wesleyan Theological Society. 1998.

Stone, Ronald H. *John Wesley's Life & Ethics.* Nashville: Abingdon Press. 2001.

Taylor, Richard S. *The Question of "Sins of Ignorance" in relation to Wesley's Definition.* Wesleyan Theological Journal Vol. 22 Num. 1. Marion: Wesleyan Theological Society. 1987.

Tracy, Wesley D. *Uniting Worship, Preaching, And Theology.* Wesleyan Theological Journal Vol. 33 Num. 1. Marion: Wesleyan Theological Society. 1998.

Turner, George Allen *The Vision Which Transforms: Is Christian Perfection Scriptural?* Kansas City: Beacon Hill Press. 1964.

Wood, Laurence W. *Pentecostal Sanctification in John Wesley and Early Methodism.* Wesleyan Theological Journal Vol. 34, Num.1. Marion: Wesleyan Theological Society. 1999.

John Wesley's Theology of Christian Perfection

_____ and Randy L. Maddox *Wesley's Understanding Of Christian Perfection: In What Sense Pentecostal?*. Wesleyan Theological Journal Vol. 34, Num. 2. Marion: Wesleyan Theological Society. 1999.

Charles Wesley's Perfection Theology:

Tyson, John R. *Charles Wesley On Sanctification: A Biographical and Theological Study.* Grand Rapids: Zondervan Publishing House. 1986.

_____ *Charles Wesley Poet And Theologian.* Nashville: Abingdon Press. 1991.

Historical Studies

Barr, Josiah Henry *Early Methodists Under Persecution.* Salem: Schmul Publishers. 1978.

Benham, Daniel *Memoirs of James Hutton: Comprising the Annals of His Life and Connection with the United Brethren.* London: Hamilton, Adams, & Co., 1856.

Collins, Kenneth J. *A Real Christian: The Life of John Wesley.* Nashville: Abingdon Press. 1999.

_____ *20th Century Interpretations of John Wesley's Aldersgate Experience: Coherence or Confusion?* Wesleyan Theological Journal Vol. 24. Marion: Wesleyan Theological Society. 1989.

Dallimore, Arnold A. *George Whitefield: The Life and Times of the Great Evangelist of the 18th Century Revival* 2 Vols. Westchester: Cornerstone Books. 1970, 1980.

Goodwin, Charles H. *Methodist Pentecost: The Wesleyan/Holiness Revival Of 1758-1763.* Wesleyan Theological Journal Vol. 33, Num. 1. Marion: Wesleyan Theological Society. 1998.

Bibliography

Hattersley, Roy *The Life of John Wesley—A Brand from the Burning.* New York: Doubleday. 2003.

Heitzenrater, Richard P. *Wesley and the People called Methodists.* Nashville: Abingdon Press. 1995.

Lockmore, John P. *Memorials of the Life of Peter Bohler, Bishop of the Church of the United Brethren.* London: Wesleyan Conference Office, 1868.

Mitchell, T. Crichton *Charles Wesley: Man with the Dancing Heart.* Kansas City: Beacon Hill Press. 1994.

Peters, John L. *Christian Perfection and American Methodism.* Grand Rapids: Zondervan Publishing House. 1985.

Podmore, Colin *The Moravian Church in England, 1728-1760.* Oxford: Clarendon Press. 1998.

Rack, Henry D. *Reasonable Enthusiast: John Wesley and the Rise of Methodism* Nashville: Abingdon Press. 1992.

Smith, Timothy L. *A Chronological List of Wesley's Sermons and Doctrinal Essays.* Wesleyan Theological Journal Vol. 17 Num. 2. Marion: Wesleyan Theological Society. 1982.

_____ *John Wesley and the Second Blessing.* Wesleyan Theological Journal Vol. 21 Num.1 & 2. Marion: Wesleyan Theological Society. 1986.

Sweet, William Warren. *Methodism In American History.* New York: Methodist Book Concern. 1933.

Tyerman, Luke *The Life and Times of the Rev. John Wesley, 3 vols.* 6th Edition, Stoke-on-Trent, Staffs, UK: Tentmaker Publications, 2003.

Tyson, John R. *John Wesley and William Law: A Reappraisal.* Wesleyan Theological Journal Vol. 17 Num. 2. Marion: Wesleyan Theological Society. 1982.

Van Den Berg, Johannes and W. Stephen Gunter. *John Wesley and the Netherlands.* Nashville: Abingdon Press. 2002.

Holiness and Wesleyan Literature

Carter, Charles W. *A Contemporary Wesleyan Theology: Biblical, Systematic, and Practical 2 vols.* Grand Rapids: Zondervan Corporation. 1983.

Dunning, H. Ray *Grace, Faith, and Holiness: A Wesleyan Systematic Theology* Kansas City: Beacon Hill Press. 1988.

_____ Editor, *The Second Coming: A Wesleyan Approach to the Doctrine of Last Things* Kansas City: Beacon Hill Press. 1995.

_____ *Reflecting The Divine Image: Christian Ethics in Wesleyan Perspective.* Downers Grove: InterVarsity Press. 1998.

Exploring Christian Holiness, 3 vols. Kansas City: Beacon Hill Press. 1983, 1985:
- I   *The Biblical Foundations.* Purkiser, W. T.
- II *The Historical Development.* Bassett, Paul M. and William M. Greathouse.
- III *The Theological Formulation.* Taylor, Richard S.

Great Holiness Classics, 6 vols. Kansas City: Beacon Hill Press. 1984-1998:
- I.   *Holiness Teaching: New Testament Times to Wesley* Ed. Paul Basset
- II. *The Wesley Century* Ed. T. Crichton Mitchell
- III. *Leading Wesleyan Thinkers* Ed. Richard Taylor
- IV. *The 19th-Century Holiness Movement* Ed. Melvin Dieter
- V.   *Holiness Preachers and Preaching* Ed. William E. McCumber
- VI. *Holiness Teaching Today* Ed. Albert F. Harper

Greathouse, William M. *Wholeness In Christ: Toward a Biblical Theology of Holiness* Kansas City: Beacon Hill Press. 1998.

Bibliography

Grider, Kenneth J. *A Wesleyan-Holiness Theology.* Kansas City: Beacon Hill Press. 1994.

Gunter, W. Stephen Gunter and Scott J. Jones, Ted A. Campbell, Rebekah L. Miles, and Randy L. Maddox. *Wesley and the Quadrilateral: Renewing The Conversation.* Nashville: Abingdon. 1997.

Knight, John A. *All Loves Excelling: Proclaiming Our Wesleyan Message.* Kansas City: Beacon Hill Press. 1995.

Langford, Thomas A. *Practical Divinity: Theology in the Wesleyan Tradition, Vol. 1* Revised. Nashville: Abingdon Press. 1998.

_____ *Practical Divinity: Readings in Wesleyan Theology Vol.2* Revised, Nashville: Abingdon Press. 1999.

Maddox, Randy *Reconnecting The Means To The End: A Wesleyan Prescription For The Holiness Movement.* Wesleyan Theological Journal Vol. 33, Num. 2. Marion: Wesleyan Theological Society. 1998.

Miley, John. *Systematic Theology, 2 Vols.* Reprint. Peabody: Hendrickson. 1989.

Murphree, Jon Tal *The Love Motive: A Practical Psychology of Sanctification.* Camp Hill: Christian Publications. 1990.

Purkiser, W. T. and Richard S. Taylor, Willard H. Taylor. *God, Man, & Salvation: A Biblical Salvation.* Kansas City: Beacon Hill Press. 1977.

Seamands, Stephen A. *Holiness of Heart and Life.* Nashville: Abingdon Press. 1990.

Smith, Timothy L. Editor: *The Promise of the Spirit: Charles G. Finney on Christian Holiness.* Minneapolis: Bethany House Publishers. 1980.

John Wesley's Theology of Christian Perfection

Staples, Rob L. *Outward Sign And Inward Grace: The Place of Sacraments in Wesleyan Spirituality.* Kansas City: Beacon Hill Press. 1991.

Wiley, H. Orton *Christian Theology, 3 Volumes.* Kansas City: Beacon Hill Press. 1940, 1943, 1952.

Wood, Laurence W. *Pentecostal Grace.* Grand Rapids: Zondervan Publishing House. 1980.

Wynnkoop, Mildred Bangs *A Theology Of Love: The Dynamic of Wesleyanism.* Kansas City: Beacon Hill Press. 1972.

Differing Perspectives on Christian Perfection
The following list is for those who are interested in how other traditions interact with the Wesleyan position on sanctification and holiness.

Christian Spirituality: Five views of Sanctification Editor: Donald L. Alexander. Downers Grove: Inter Varsity Press. 1988.
Note: Lutheran, Reformed, Wesleyan, Pentecostal, and Contemplative views presented.

Five Views on Sanctification Melvin E. Dieter, Anthony A. Hoekema, Stanley M. Horton, J. Robertson McQuilkin, John F. Walvoord. Grand Rapids: Zondervan Corporation. 1987.
Note: Wesleyan, Reformed, Pentecostal, Keswickian, and Augustinian-Dispensational views are presented.

Anderson, Neil T. and Robert L. Saucy *The Common Made Holy: Being Conformed To The Image Of God.* Eugene: Harvest House Publishers. 1997.

Choy, Leona Frances *Powerlines: What Great Evangelicals Believed About The Holy Spirit 1850-1930.* Camp Hill: Christian Publications. 1990.

Finney, Charles G. *Lectures on Systematic Theology.* (2 volumes) Fenwick, MI: Alethea In Heart. 2005 (and XulonPress, 2003).

Bibliography

Gresham Jr., John L. *Charles G. Finney's Doctrine of the Baptism of the Holy Spirit.* Peabody: Hendrickson Publishers. 1987.

Hodge, Charles *Systematic Theology, 3 volumes.* Grand Rapids: Eerdmans Publishing Company. 1982.

Peterson, David *Possessed By God: A New Testament Theology of Sanctification and Holiness.* Grand Rapids: Eerdmans Publishing Company. 1995.

Tozer, A. W. *The Tozer Pulpit Vol. 1.* Camp Hill: Christian Publications. 1994.

Williams, J. Rodman *Renewal Theology: Systematic Theology from a Charismatic Perspective, Three volumes in One* Grand Rapids: Zondervan Corporation. 1996.

Standard References

Ante-Nicene Fathers, The 10 vols. Editors, Alexander Roberts and James Donaldson, Grand Rapids: Eerdmans Publishing Company.

Latourette, Kenneth Scott. *A History of Christianity, Vol. 2: Reformation To The Present. Revised Edition.* Reprint. Peabody: Prince Press. 1997.

Olson, Roger E. *The Story of Christian Theology: Twenty Centuries of Tradition & Reform.* Downers Grove: InterVarsity Press. 1999.

INDEX A
John Wesley's Writings

Included below are those writings that are quoted in the main text of the book (footnotes are not included).

Sermons
Early:
Death and Deliverance (1725) 16, 22, 32, 40, 217
Seek First the Kingdom (1725) 22, 49, 50, 66
On Guardian Angels (1726) 19
On Corrupting the Word of God (1727) 53
On Mourning for the Dead (1727) 23, 40, 299
On Dissimulation (1728) 68
The Promise of Understanding (1730) 33, 367
The Image of God (1730) 19, 28, 32
On the Sabbath (1730) 57, 58
On The Resurrection of the Dead (1732) 25, 36
On Grieving the Holy Spirit (1732) 13, 26, 64
The Circumcision of the Heart (1733) 13, 14, 22, 28, 33, 40, 45, 46, 47, 48, 63, 67, 69, 217, 259, 327, 367, 447
The One Thing Needful (1734) 11, 12, 16, 17, 19, 20, 22, 32, 70, 427
The Trouble and Rest of Good Men (1735) 32, 41, 64, 218, 237
A Single Intention (1736) 11, 35, 36, 70, 427
In Earth as in Heaven (1737) 19
On Love (1737) 28, 29, 34, 35, 37, 39
The Love of God (1737) 15, 18, 23, 33

Middle:
Salvation By Faith (1738) 100ff., 360, 428
Christian Perfection (1741) 163ff., 331
The Almost Christian (1741) 76, 105ff., 193, 440
Justification By Faith (1746) 138, 153
The First Fruits of the Spirit (1746) 221, 220, 229, 230
The Great Privilege of Those who are Born of God (1748) 221
The Marks of the New Birth (1748) 432

Index A: John Wesley's Writings

The New Birth (1760) 434
On Sin in Believers (1763) 138, 228, 239
The Scripture Way of Salvation (1765) 149, 178ff., 223

Late:
On the Trinity (1775) 279
The End of Christ's Coming (1781) 289
The General Deliverance (1781) 290, 291
On the Fall of Man (1782) 241
The General Spread of the Gospel (1783) 287
On Perfection (1784) 296, 375ff.
On Charity (1784) 278
The New Creation (1785) 291, 292
On Working Out Our Own Salvation (1785) 340
The Signs of the Times (1787) 286
On the Discoveries of Faith (1788) 285, 287
On Faith, Heb 11:1 (1788) 206, 284
On Faith, Heb 11:6 (1788) 293, 356, 362
On a Single Eye (1789) 300, 355
The Unity of the Divine Being (1789) 280
Heavenly Treasure in Earthen Vessels (1790) 296
On Living Without God (1790) 283, 285
On Wedding Garment (1790) 281, 300, 341

Journal
10/20/35	54
10/25/35	84
11/23/35	7, 84
1/17/36	7, 8, 85
1/25/36	86
2/7/36	86
1/8/38	85
1/24/38	8, 187
2/1/38	97ff.
2/19/38	88
3/5/38	88
3/23/38	88

4/22/38	361
4/23/38	89, 90
5/24/38	5, 91, 122, 437
6/6/38	123
6/7/38	123
7/6/38	129
7/12/38	130
8/10/38	132-33
8/12/38	134
11/23/38	124
12/16/38	125
1/4/39	108ff.
1/25/39	143
6/11/39	110
6/15/39	147
7/23/39	148
7/31/39	429
8/27/39	61, 87, 193
9/13/39	151, 169
11/3/39	154
11/17/39	154
12/31/39	154
1/2/40	156
3/28/40	157
4/3/40	157
4/25/40	156, 157
6/22/40	156
6/25/40	442
10/28/62	188
12/1/67	200

The Plain Account of Christian Perfection:
The Annotated Edition

2:1-3	192
2:2	9, 315
3:2	9
4:2	9
5:1	30

Index A: John Wesley's Writings

5:4	30
6:3	319
6:3-5	28
8:2	316
9:2, 5	238
9:5	238, 321
12:1-3	163
12:32	238
12:44	320
13:29-30	350
15:14	309
18:6-7	239
18:18, 20	321
19:8	240
19:23	321
19:23-25	31
19:68, 71	239
19:73	317
19:83	239
20:3	324
25:4, 5, 7	221
25:5-6	339
25:9	241
25:11	227
25:14	227, 309
25:41	227
25:50	318
25:60, 66	337
25:75-76	328

Explanatory Notes on the New Testament
John 3:3, 7   434
Acts 10:35   441
Titus 3:5   434
1 John 3:9   434
Revelation 20:2   289

John Wesley's Theology of Christian Perfection

Writings
Advice to the People Called Methodists (1745) 446
The Aldersgate Memorandum (1738) 98, 193
The Character of a Methodist (1742) 227, 449
A Plain Account of the People Called Methodists (1749) 443
Preface to the Christian's Pattern (1735) 29, 30, 45, 47, 54, 55, 70
Preface to a Collection of Prayers (1733) 45ff.
Preface to An Extract to the Life and Death of Mr. Thomas Halyburton (1739, 1741) 144ff., 160, 219
Preface to Hymns and Sacred Poems I (1739) 56
Preface to Hymns and Sacred Poems II (1740) 159ff.
A Treatise on Baptism (1759) 43
1744 Minutes 220, 429
1770 Minutes 207ff.

Letters
6/18/25   52, 64
7/29/25   66
2/28/30   65, 67, 72
12/12/30   28, 52
6/19/31   34
7/19/31   21, 34
8/12/31   55
10/3/31   25, 31, 67, 217
2/28/32   23
6/13/33   21
1/15/34   20
1/28/34   21
12/10/34   27, 57
1/13/35   30
2/14/35   31
5/8/35   75
10/1/35   61
10/15/35   20
11/23/36   57
3/29/37   34, 54
7/22/37   60
7/7/38   129

Index A: John Wesley's Writings

9/28/38	142
10/30/38	143
12/31/38	126
12/26/56	255
6/18/57	246
11/22/57	257
2/9/58	254
4/5/58	260
3/6/59	259
6/27/60	246
8/23/63	262, 265
9/15/62	233, 341
12/15/63	247
5/25/64	189
10/13/64	248, 261
10/13/65	264
2/8/66	189
2/28/66	189
3/29/66	253
6/27/66	194ff.
7/9/66	190
1/27/67	139, 260, 273
2/12/67	190
3/5/67	186
11/20/67	254
3/14/68	264
3/28/68	203
4/7/68	203, 251
5/14/68	190
1/1/70	247, 435
3/15/70	265
4/12/70	263
6/13/70	262
6/27/70	262
7/6/70	259, 269
8/11/70	260
8/12/70	204
10/5/70	264
3/17/71	253

4/14/71	263, 267
5/2/71	257
5/31/71	268
6/19/71	270
7/10/71	210
8/31/71	261
9/1/71	254
10/1/71	252
4/6/72	253
6/16/72	264
8/31/72	271
11/4/72	272
12/5/72	252
12/15/72	214
6/30/73	256
12/19/73	253
3/1/74	271
6/3/74	247, 262, 266
6/17/74	250
5/3/76	246
6/2/76	270
9/27/77	252
10/6/78	266
6/10/81	268
8/15/81	268
12/15/81	268
3/9/82	249
9/24/85	255
12/14/85	249
10/25/86	250
3/31/87	265
9/7/87	249
9/15/90	252

INDEX B
Scripture References

Psalm
   8:5   20

Matthew
   5:1-8   131
   5:48   58
   6:22-23   35
   6:33   22
   18:22   26

Luke
   9:23   30

John
   7:37-38   321
   15:3   131

Acts
   10:35   201, 203, 207, 284
   16:31   93
   26:25   97

Romans
   6:5   30
   7-8   131
   8:21   168

1 Corinthians
   1:30   146
   13:12   368

2 Corinthians
   5:17   142

Galatians
  5:6   20

Ephesians
  2:8   159
  5:14   11

Philippians
  2:5   20
  2:12   26
  2:12-13   249

Colossians
  1:27   451

1 Thessalonians
  5:16-18   258

Hebrews
  1:3   30
  11:1   170, 285
  11:6   285
  12:14   272

James
  1:4   259

2 Peter
  1:4   13

1 John
  2:12-14   233
  2:16   34
  3:9   145, 159
  4:19   51
  5:18   145

Index B: Scripture References

Revelation
- 3:17   320
- 21:5   291

INDEX C
Subject

A
Absolute Perfection   147
Adam   16, 17, 18, 20, 21, 28, 32, 51, 183, 217, 219, 226, 290, 292, 321, 334, 345, 353, 434
Adamic/Christian perfection   233
Aldersgate   50, 95, 111, 118, 143, 186, 195, 254, 311, 347, 437
Almost/Altogether Christian   70, 104, 106ff., 110, 112, 113, 260, 284, 349
Angel(s)   18, 19, 151, 288, 297, 299, 331, 428
Antinomianism   281
Art of dying   2, 22, 36, 39, 75, 83, 260, 344, 427
Assurance   8, 13, 46, 61ff., 81, 88, 95, 99, 109, 115, 119, 125, 129, 134, 141, 198, 201, 203, 248, 265, 277, 300, 316, 329, 333, 339, 345

B
Bands   255
Baptism   43, 143, 170
Believer's struggles   248, 251

C
Calvinism   41, 208, 271, 276, 329
Chaos   292
Charles & John's differences   189ff., 253, 310
Childhood, Adolescence, Adulthood   31, 123, 162, 165, 172, 184, 185, 220, 228, 234, 267, 275, 289, 302, 318, 333ff., 336, 349, 436
Christ-likeness   30
Christ's atoning death   19, 371, 373
Christ 2nd Adam   21, 42, 226, 353
Comets, meteors   291
Conversion   9, 15, 88, 93, 99, 104, 113, 193, 212, 329, 346, 352, 427
Covenant   67, 224, 226, 241

D
Degrees of perfection   270

Index C: Subject

Deliverance from sin at death   40

E
Entire sanctification   179
Eschatological perfection   188
Evil reasoning   262, 266

F
Faith   49, 88, 90, 93, 95, 98, 99ff., 180, 204, 210, 254, 271, 279, 281, 316, 348, 354, 389, 437, 443
Fall (Adamic)   18, 32, 41, 42, 217, 226, 228, 241, 290, 338
Final goal of holiness   21, 23, 36, 38
First & second repentance   181
Fruit of Holy Spirit   189, 265, 328

G
Global revival   287
Great perfection revival   187ff., 309

H
Happiness   32, 34, 38, 88, 289, 353
Heathen outnumber Christians   287
Holiness as means and goal   21, 28, 220, 281, 283, 342
Holy Club   5, 98, 298, 403
Holy Spirit   12ff., 35, 63, 149, 246, 251, 265, 269, 288, 318, 347, 440

I
Imago Dei   16ff., 26, 27, 32, 71, 151, 169, 171, 217, 226, 261, 290, 319, 333, 336, 343, 432, 453
Intermediate state following death   293
Intermittent perfection   145, 162, 166, 236, 248, 265, 348, 350
Involuntary sin   144, 164ff., 183, 188, 217, 222, 225, 229, 234, 237, 240, 259, 263, 279, 295, 318, 319, 348, 369ff.

J
Justification   159, 198, 200, 204, 211, 247, 275, 329, 345, 360, 433, 438
Justification & sanctification   11, 24, 112, 131, 136, 144, 146, 150, 155, 209, 295, 342, 359, 426

K
Kingdom of God/Heaven 22, 161, 285, 287, 334

L
Liberty 30, 217
Limited atonement 134
Lord's Table 299
Love 51, 70
Lucifer 33

M
Means of grace 42, 51ff., 75, 93, 114, 121, 126, 132, 155, 181, 207, 209, 255, 276, 282, 318, 327, 342, 439
Millennium 289
Moravians 41, 346, 442
Mortification 50

N
New birth 12, 15, 46, 103, 107, 119, 138, 143, 145, 149, 159, 167, 179, 197, 200, 218, 246, 275, 329, 345, 360, 425ff.
Newborn in perfection 269

O
Object of faith 87, 89, 111, 149, 180, 279
One thing needful 21, 95, 114, 261, 342
One true religion 280
Ordo Salutis 17, 118, 156, 170, 200, 205, 212, 231, 246, 267, 275, 282, 286, 294, 301ff., 323, 329, 331, 348, 353
Outward/inward sin 220, 222, 231, 316, 320, 350, 370

P
Perfect love 27ff., 47, 107, 268, 318, 319, 335
Perfection, change of nature 238, 321, 326
Perfection, 11 Pt. Summary 184
Perfection lost & regained 236, 349
Perfection & Parousia 254
Persecution 58
Power & Being of sin 105, 112, 133, 138, 144, 218, 222, 228, 231, 335

Index C: Subject

Prayer 53
Present perfection 103, 159
Prevenient grace 132, 171, 215, 271ff., 285, 288, 295, 352

R
Relative/Real change 179
Repentance & Means of Grace 181
Resurrection of the dead 24, 294, 304
Revival excesses 147, 309, 324, 328

S
Satan 266, 288, 289
Servant 110, 196, 202ff., 212, 232, 272, 276, 286, 302, 329, 351, 360, 434, 435
Sin 32ff., 149, 166, 218, 362ff.
Sin, suppression/destruction 220, 222, 370
Sincerity 66, 210, 343, 435, 442
Sinful nature 33
Single intention 15, 42, 44, 118, 119, 264, 299, 315, 319, 343, 425
Spiritual senses 285, 443
Stillness 120ff., 126, 132, 153ff., 209, 346

T
Tempers 27, 42, 115, 151, 167, 210, 238, 257, 259, 269, 278, 282, 318, 320, 325, 336, 343, 435, 442, 453
Theodicy 293, 365
Trinity of evil tempers 260
True Religion 21, 209

U
Unconditional election 134

V
Vital religion 209, 212, 221, 225, 284, 294, 299, 342, 353, 361, 425, 438, 440
Voluntary sin 183, 218, 220, 228, 296, 320, 350, 372ff.

W
Weak faith 123, 131, 134, 158

Wesley's DNA   42, 151, 187, 190, 253, 271, 282, 298, 345, 367
Wesley's early evangelicalism   10ff.
Wesley's early views on salvation   1
Wesley's pride   85, 389
Wesley, systematic theologian   245, 314
Wilderness state   131, 156ff., 172, 248, 261, 268, 303, 433
Willful sin   31, 43, 103, 427

www.ingramcontent.com/pod-product-compliance
Lightning Source LLC
Chambersburg PA
CBHW031957220426
43664CB00005B/54